ECOLOGICAL IMPERIALISM

STUDIES IN ENVIRONMENT AND HISTORY

EDITORS
Donald Worster   *Brandeis University*
Alfred Crosby   *University of Texas at Austin*

ADVISORY BOARD
Reid Bryson   *Institute for Environmental Studies,
University of Wisconsin*
Raymond Dasmann   *College Eight,
University of California, Santa Cruz*
E. Le Roy Ladurie   *Collège de France*
William McNeill   *Department of History, University of Chicago*
Carolyn Merchant   *College of Natural Resources,
University of California, Berkeley*
Thad Tate   *Institute of Early American History and Culture,
College of William and Mary*

OTHER BOOKS IN THE SERIES
Donald Worster   *Nature's Economy: A History of Ecological Ideas*
Kenneth F. Kiple   *The Caribbean Slave: A Biological History*

Ecological Imperialism

The Biological Expansion of Europe,
900-1900

ALFRED W. CROSBY

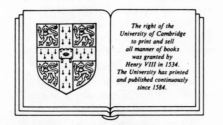

The right of the
University of Cambridge
to print and sell
all manner of books
was granted by
Henry VIII in 1534.
The University has printed
and published continuously
since 1584.

CAMBRIDGE UNIVERSITY PRESS

Cambridge
New York   New Rochelle
Melbourne   Sydney

Published by the Press Syndicate of the University of Cambridge
The Pitt Building, Trumpington Street, Cambridge CB2 IRP
32 East 57th Street, New York, NY 10022, USA
10 Stamford Road, Oakleigh, Melbourne 3166, Australia

First published 1986
Reprinted 1986, 1987 (twice), 1988

Printed in the United States of America

Library of Congress Cataloging-in-Publication Data
Crosby, Alfred W.
Ecological imperialism.
(Studies in environment and history)
Bibliography: p.
Includes Index.
1. Human ecology.   2. Europeans – Migrations.
3. Anthropo-geography.   4. Geographical distribution
of plants and animals.   I. Title.   II. Series.
GF50.76   1986   304.2   86-6106

British Library Cataloguing in Publication Data
Crosby, Alfred W.
Ecological imperialism: the biological
expansion of Europe, 900-1900. – (Studies
in environment and history.)
1. Animal migration – Europe – History
2. Plants – Europe – Migration – History
I. Title.   II. Series.
574.5'2'094   QL754

ISBN 0-521-32009-7 hard covers
ISBN 0-521-33613-9 paperback

To

JULIA AND JAMES TRAUE
AND THE STAFF OF THE
ALEXANDER TURNBULL LIBRARY,
WELLINGTON, NEW ZEALAND

THE DISCOVERY OF AMERICA, and that of a passage to the East Indies by the Cape of Good Hope, are the two greatest and most important events recorded in the history of mankind.
—Adam Smith, *Wealth of Nations* (1776)

YET, IF WE WIELD THE SWORD of extermination as we advance, we have no reason to repine the havoc committed.
—Charles Lyell, *Principles of Geology* (1832)

WHEREVER THE EUROPEAN HAD TROD, death seems to pursue the aboriginal. We may look to the wide extent of the Americas, Polynesia, the Cape of Good Hope, and Australia, and we find the same result.
—Charles Darwin, *The Voyage of the Beagle* (1839)

THE DISCOVERY OF AMERICA, the rounding of the Cape opened up fresh ground for the rising bourgeoisie. The East Indian and Chinese markets, the colonization of America, trade with the colonies, the increase in the means of exchange and in commodities generally, gave to commerce, to navigation, to industry an impulse never before known, and thereby, to the revolutionary element in the tottering feudal society, a rapid development.
—Karl Marx and Friedrich Engels, *Manifesto of the Communist Party* (1848)

Contents

CONTENTS

Illustrations

Acknowledgments

IT IS IMPOSSIBLE to give credit to all the people whose help in writing this book was indispensable: the legions of librarians, especially those who labored obscurely at the business of interlibrary loans, the colleagues who offered careful criticisms, and – more important and more difficult to remember – those who looked over my shoulder and made offhand remarks that set me on paths that otherwise I would never have found. I want particularly to thank the University of Texas Library for amassing such a magnificent collection of sources and the University of Texas for being generous in granting me time and funds for my research. A Fulbright fellowship at the Alexander Turnbull Library in New Zealand and a year and a half in New Haven, Connecticut, at the National Humanities Institute and as William B. Cardozo Lecturer at Yale University were also vital to my work. I also thank *The Environmental*

Review and *The Texas Quarterly* for permission to republish the parts of *Ecological Imperialism* that first appeared in their pages.

Most strongly I want to thank the individuals who directly encouraged and even rescued me when my energy waned, including, of course, Frank Smith, my editor. Further back there was Wilbury A. Crockett, the world's greatest English teacher, who first informed me that a life of the mind was respectable; Jerry Gough, who reaffirmed that point some decades later; Edmund Morgan and Howard Lamar, whose attentions suggested to me that I should keep on keeping on; and Donald Worster and William McNeill, who paid me the great compliment of taking for granted that I was doing so. I am especially grateful to Daniel H. Norris and Lynette M. McManemin, who read chapters of this book for me, and to William McNeill, who read the whole thing in first draft, splinters and bark and all.

I want last to express my gratitude for specific acts of assistance by the computer wizards at the University of Texas at Austin: Morgan Watkins, who prepared the final tape; Clive Dawson, who recaptured Chapter 10 late one Saturday night when it strayed beyond delete and even expunge; and Frances Karttunen, who started me off with "Al, this is a computer terminal. Now, don't be scared," and who provided me with many a bit and byte of advice in English and Spanish.

1

Prologue

GIVE ME A CONDOR'S QUILL! Give me Vesuvius' crater for an
ink stand! Friends, hold my arms!
—Herman Melville, *Moby Dick*

EUROPEAN EMIGRANTS and their descendants are all over the place, which requires explanation.

It is more difficult to account for the distribution of this subdivision of the human species than that of any other. The locations of the others make an obvious kind of sense. All but a relatively few of the members of the many varieties of Asians live in Asia. Black Africans live on three continents, but most of them are concentrated in their original latitudes, the tropics, facing each other across one ocean. Amerindians, with few exceptions, live in the Americas, and nearly every last Australian Aborigine dwells in Australia. Eskimos live in the circumpolar lands, and Melanesians, Polynesians, and Micronesians are scattered through the islands of only one ocean, albeit a large one. All these peoples have expanded geographically – have committed acts of imperialism, if you will – but they have expanded into lands adjacent to or at least near to those in which they had already been living, or, in the case of the Pacific peoples, to the next island and then to the next after that, however many kilometers of water might lie between. Europeans, in contrast, seem to have leapfrogged around the globe.

Europeans, a division of Caucasians distinctive in their politics and technologies, rather than in their physiques, live in large numbers and nearly solid blocks in northern Eurasia, from the Atlantic to the Pacific. They occupy much more territory there than they did a thousand or even five hundred years ago, but that is the part of the world in which they have lived throughout recorded history, and there they have expanded in the traditional way, into contiguous areas. They also compose the great majority in the populations of what I shall call the Neo-Europes, lands thousands of kilometers from Europe and from each other. Australia's population is almost all European in origin, and that of New Zealand is about nine-tenths European. In the Americas north of Mexico there are considerable minorities of Afro-Americans and *mestizos* (a convenient Spanish-American term I shall use to designate Amerindian and white mixtures), but over 80 percent of the inhabitants of this area are of European descent. In the Americas south of the Tropic of Capricorn the population is also dominantly white. The inhabitants of the "Deep South" in Brazil (Paraná, Santa Catarina, and Rio Grande do Sul) range between 85 and 95 percent European, and Uruguay, next door, is also approximately nine-tenths white. Some estimations put Argentina at about 90 percent and others at close to one 100 percent European. In contrast, Chile's people are only about one-third European; almost all the rest are *mestizo*. But if we consider all the peoples of that vast wedge of the continent poleward of the Tropic of Capricorn, we see that the great majority are European. Even if we accept the highest estimations of *mestizo*, Afro-American, and Amerindian populations, more than three of every four Americans in the southern temperate zone are entirely of European ancestry.[1] Europeans, to borrow a term from apiculture, have swarmed again and again and have selected their new homes as if each swarm were physically repulsed by the others.

The Neo-Europes are intriguing for reasons other than the disharmony between their locations and the racial and cultural identity of most of their people. These lands attract the attention – the unblinking envious gaze – of most of humanity because of their food surpluses. They compose the majority of those very few nations on this earth that consistently, decade after decade, export very large quantities of food. In 1982, the total value of all agricultural exports in the world, of all agricultural products that crossed national borders, was $210 billion. Of this, Canada, the United States, Argentina, Uruguay, Australia, and New Zealand accounted for $64 billion, or a little over 30 percent, a total and a percentage that would be even higher if the exports of southern Brazil were added. The Neo-

European share of exports of wheat, the most important crop in international commerce, was even greater. In 1982, $18 billion worth of wheat passed over national boundaries, of which the Neo-Europes exported about $13 billion. In the same year, world exports of protein-rich soybeans, the most important new entry in international trade in foodstuffs since World War II, amounted to $7 billion. The United States and Canada accounted for $6.3 billion of this. In exports of fresh, chilled, and frozen beef and mutton, the Neo-Europes also lead the world, as well as in a number of other foodstuffs. Their share of the international trade in the world's most vitally important foods is much greater than the Middle East's share of petroleum exports.[2]

The dominant role of the Neo-Europes in international trade in foodstuffs is not simply a matter of brute productivity. The Union of Soviet Socialist Republics usually leads the world in the production of wheat, oats, barley, rye, potatoes, milk, mutton, sugar, and several other food items. China outproduces every other nation in rice and millet, and it has the most pigs. In terms of productivity per unit of land, a number of nations outdo the Neo-Europes, whose farmers, small in number but great in technology, specialize in extensive rather than intensive cultivation. Per farmer, their productivity is awesome, but per hectare it is not so impressive. These regions lead the world in production of food *relative to the amount locally consumed,* or, to put it another way, in the production of surpluses for export. To cite an extreme example, in 1982 the United States produced only a minuscule percentage of the world's rice, but it accounted for one-fifth of all exports of that grain, more than any other nation.[3]

We shall discuss Neo-European productivity again in the final chapter, but now let us turn to the subject of the Europeans' proclivity for migrating overseas, one of their most distinctive characteristics, and one that has had much to do with Neo-European agricultural productivity. Europeans were understandably slow to leave the security of their homelands. The populations of the Neo-Europes did not become as white as they are today until long after Cabot, Magellan, and other European navigators first came upon the new lands, nor until many years after the first white settlers made their homes there. In 1800, North America,[4] after almost two centuries of successful European colonization, and though in many ways the most attractive of the Neo-Europes to Old World migrants, had a population of fewer than 5 million whites, plus about 1 million blacks. Southern South America, after more than two hundred years of European occupation, was an even worse laggard, having less than half a million whites. Australia had only 10,000, and New Zealand was still Maori country.[5]

Then came the deluge. Between 1820 and 1930, well over 50 million Europeans migrated to the Neo-European lands overseas. That number amounts to approximately one-fifth of the entire population of Europe at the beginning of that period.[6] Why such an enormous movement of peoples across such vast distances? Conditions in Europe provided a considerable push – population explosion and a resulting shortage of cultivable land, national rivalries, persecution of minorities – and the application of steam power to ocean and land travel certainly facilitated long distance migration. But what was the nature of the Neo-European pull? The attractions were many, of course, and they varied from place to place in these new-found lands. But underlying them all, and coloring and shaping them in ways such that a reasonable man might be persuaded to invest capital and even the lives of his family in Neo-European adventures, were factors perhaps best described as biogeographical.

Let us begin by applying to the problem what I call the Dupin technique, after Edgar Allan Poe's detective, C. Auguste Dupin, who found the invaluable "Purloined Letter" not hidden in a bookbinding or a gimlet hole in a chair leg but out where everyone could see it in a letter rack. A description of the technique, a sort of corollary to Ockham's razor, goes like this: Ask simple questions, because the answers to complicated questions probably will be too complicated to test and, even worse, too fascinating to give up.

Where are the Neo-Europes? Geographically they are scattered, but they are in similar latitudes. They are all completely or at least two-thirds in the temperate zones, north and south, which is to say that they have roughly similar climates. The plants on which Europeans historically have depended for food and fiber, and the animals on which they have depended for food, fiber, power, leather, bone, and manure, tend to prosper in warm-to-cool climates with an annual precipitation of 50 to 150 centimeters. These conditions are characteristic of all the Neo-Europes, or at least of their fertile parts in which Europeans have settled densely. One would expect an Englishman, Spaniard, or German to be attracted chiefly to places where wheat and cattle would do well, and that has indeed proved to be the case.

The Neo-Europes all lie primarily in temperate zones, but their native biotas are clearly different from one another and from that of northern Eurasia. The contrast becomes dramatically apparent if we look at some of their chief grazers and browsers of, say, a thousand years ago. European cattle, North American buffalos,[7] South American guanacos, Australian kangaroos, and New Zealand's three-meter high moa birds (now, sadly, extinct) were not brethren under the pelt. The most closely related, the cattle and buffalos, were no better than very distant cousins; even the buffalo and its closest Old World counterpart, the rare European bison, are different species. European colonists sometimes found Neo-European flora and fauna exasperatingly bizarre. Mr. J. Martin in Australia in the 1830s complained that the trees retained their leaves and shed their bark instead, the swans were black, the eagles white, the bees were stingless, some mammals had pockets, others laid eggs, it was warmest on the hills and coolest in the valleys, [and] even the blackberries were red.[8]

There is a striking paradox here. The parts of the world that today in terms of population and culture are most like Europe are far away from Europe – indeed, they are across major oceans – and although they are similar in climate to Europe, they have indigenous floras and faunas different from those of Europe. The regions that today export more foodstuffs of European provenance – grains and meats – than any other lands on earth had no wheat, barley, rye, cattle, pigs, sheep, or goats whatsoever five hundred years ago.

The resolution of the paradox is simple to state, though difficult to explain. North America, southern South America, Australia, and New Zealand are far from Europe in distance but have climates similar to hers, and European flora and fauna, including human beings, can thrive in these regions if the competition is not too fierce. In general, the competition has been mild. On the pampa, Iberian horses and cattle have driven back the guanaco and rhea; in North America, speakers of Indo-European languages have overwhelmed speakers of Algonkin and Muskhogean and other Amerindian languages; in the antipodes, the dandelions and house cats of the Old World have marched forward, and kangaroo grass and kiwis have retreated. Why? Perhaps European humans have triumphed because of their superiority in arms, organization, and fanaticism, but what in heaven's name is the reason that the sun never sets on the empire of the dandelion? Perhaps the success of European imperialism has a biological, an ecological, component.

2

Pangaea revisited, the Neolithic reconsidered

GOD SAID, 'Let the waters under heaven be gathered into one place, so that dry land may appear'; and so it was. God called the dry land earth, and the gathering of the waters he called seas; and God saw that it was good.
—Genesis 1:9–10

THREE SLENDER THINGS THAT BEST SUPPORT THE WORLD: the slender stream of milk from the cow's dug into the pail; the slender blade of green corn upon the ground; the slender thread over the hand of a skilled woman.
—*The Triads of Ireland* (ninth century)

IT IS NECESSARY TO BEGIN at the beginning in considering the Neo-Europes, and that means not in 1492 or 1788 but about 200 million years ago, when a series of geological events began that brought these lands to their present locations. Two hundred million years ago, when dinosaurs were still lolling about, all the continents were jammed together in one great supercontinent that the geologists call Pangaea.[1] It stretched over scores of degrees of latitude, and so we can assume that it had some variations in climate; but with only one land mass, there would not have been much variety among its life forms. One continent meant one arena for competition, and so only one set of winners in the Darwinian struggle for survival and reproduction. Reptiles, including all the dinosaurs, were the dominant kinds of land animals in Pangaea – and, therefore, the world – for three times as long as mammals have held that position since, and yet reptiles diversified into only two-thirds as many orders.

About 180 million years ago Pangaea began to break up like some immense tabular iceberg rotting in the heat of the Gulf Stream. First it split into two supercontinents, and then into smaller units that became, in time, the continents we know. The process was more complicated than we can describe here (indeed, more complicated than geologists completely understand as yet), but, in broad terms, Pangaea broke up along lines of intense seismic activity that later became undersea ridges. The most thoroughly examined of these is the Mid-Atlantic Ridge that boils and bubbles from the Greenland Sea to Spiess Seamount, twenty degrees of latitude and twenty of longitude southwest of Cape Town, South Africa. From this and other ancient drowned cordillera, lava poured (and in many cases still pours), generating new ocean floor and carrying continents on either side of a given ridge farther and farther from each other. Where these floors, moving away from the ridges that spawned them, back into each other, they curl

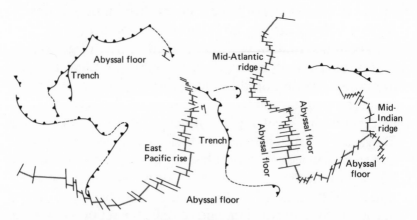

Figure 1. The seams of Pangaea. Reproduced by permission from
W. Kenneth Hamblin, *The Earth's Dynamic Systems* (Minneapolis:
Burgess Publishing Co., 1982), 23.

downward into the earth's mantle, grinding and grating,
sometimes scuffing continental mountain ranges up to the
skies, sometimes creating underwater trenches, the deepest
features on the surface of the planet. Geologists, who
sometimes have a stony insensitivity to nuances, call this
awesomely vast and eon-consuming activity "continental
drift."[2]

When mammals succeeded dinosaurs as the globe's
dominant land animals and began to diversify into their
myriad orders over the past few score million years, the
separations of the continents seem to have been at their
extremes, certainly more so than today, and there were
large inland seas partitioning South America and Eurasia
into two subcontinents each. On these fragments of
Pangaea, life forms developed independently, and in many
cases uniquely. This helps to account for the remarkable
degrees to which mammals diversified and the speed at
which they did so.[3]

Continental drift largely accounts for the differences,
often extreme, between the flora and fauna of Europe and

those of the Neo-Europes. A European traveler sailing to any of the Neo-Europes must cross one or more of these undersea ridges and trenches. Europe and the Neo-Europes have not been part of the same continental mass for many millions of years (except for ephemeral Arctic connnections between North America and Eurasia), years during which the ancestors of American buffalos, Eurasian cattle, and Australian kangaroos shambled and hopped down diverging paths of evolution. To cross these undersea seams is to step from one of those paths to another, almost to step into another world.[4] (There are seams that are not under water and do not separate continents, but let us ignore them for brevity's sake.)

When Pangaea first split into northern and southern supercontinents, only North America of all the Neo-Europes was in the same supercontinent with Europe, and so the two have shared the same latitude and have had anciently similar histories. The floral and faunal differences between Europe and North America are less striking than the differences between either of them and the other Neo-Europes. Even so, their differences were enough to take the breath away from the Finnish naturalist, Peter Kalm, in Philadelphia and fresh off the boat from Europe in 1748:

I found that I was now come into a new world. Whenever I looked to the ground I found everywhere such plants as I had never seen before. When I saw a tree, I was forced to stop and ask those who accompanied me, how it was called . . . I was seized with terror at the thought of ranging to many new and unknown parts of natural history.[5]

Biogeographers have properly designated North America and Eurasia, including Europe, as different biological provinces or subregions. After all, Nero threw Christians to the lions, not to the cougars.[6] As for the other Neo-Europes, there is no doubt about their deserving biogeographical

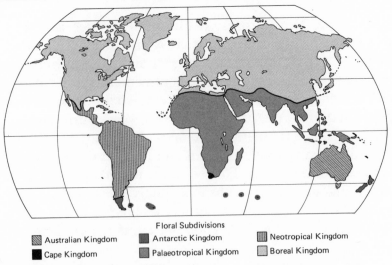

Floral Subdivisions

▨ Australian Kingdom   ▨ Antarctic Kingdom   ▥ Neotropical Kingdom

■ Cape Kingdom   ▨ Palaeotropical Kingdom   ▢ Boreal Kingdom

Figure 2. Floral regions of the world.

categories separate from that of Europe. All three, for instance, have large – some of them man-sized – flightless birds.

The breakup of Pangaea and the decentralization of the
processes of evolution began 180 or 200 million years ago.
For almost all the time since, except for a few instances
counter to the dominant trend (e.g., the periodic rejoining
of North America and Eurasia by reappearances of the
Bering land connection, and consequent intermixing of
biota), centrifugal forces have prevailed in the evolution of
life forms. This trend, prevalent since some of our distant
mammalian ancestors made a living by stealing dinosaur
eggs, halted about half a millennium ago (a tiny fraction of
a single tick on the geological clock), and centripetal forces
have dominated since. The breakup of Pangaea was a
matter of geology and the stately tempo of continental drift.
Our current reconstitution of Pangaea by means of ships
and aircraft is a matter of human culture and the careening,
accelerating, breakneck beat of technology. To tell that
tale, we have to go back not 200 million years, fortunately,
by only a million or three.

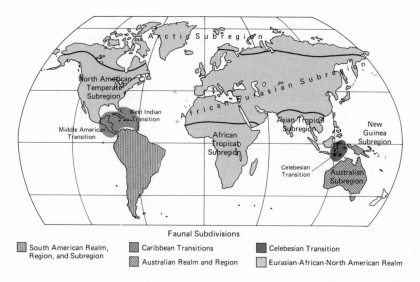

Faunal Subdivisions

South American Realm, Region, and Subregion

Caribbean Transitions

Celebesian Transition

Australian Realm and Region

Eurasian-African-North American Realm

Figure 3. Faunal regions of the world. Figures 2 and 3 reproduced by permission from Wilfred T. Neill, *The Geography of Life* (New York: Columbia University Press, 1970), 98, 99.

The most adaptable and therefore most widely distributed of today's large land animals are human beings, and this has been true of the members of the species *Homo sapiens* and their hominid predecessors for a very long time – long from their point of view. Other creatures had to wait for specific genetic changes to enable them to migrate into areas radically different from those of their ancestors – had to wait for incisors to lengthen into daggers before they could compete successfully with hyenas on the veldt, or had to wait for hair to thicken into fur before they could live in the north – but not humans nor hominids. They made not a specific but rather a generalized genetic change: They developed bigger and better brains wired for the use of language and for manipulation of tools.

That growth of nerve tissue crammed into the treasure box of the skull began several million years ago, and as it did, the hominid became increasingly capable of "culture."

Culture is a system of storing and altering patterns of behavior not in the molecules of the genetic code but in the cells of the brain. That change made the members of the genus *Homo* nature's foremost specialists in adaptability. It was as if the fisherman in the fairy tale to whom the princely flounder granted three wishes had asked first of all for all the wishes he would ever want.[7]

These plump-brained apes made use of their new skills of adaptability to migrate out of their ancestral home (probably Africa) and across dry Pangaean seams into Eurasia. Ever since, hominids and humans have migrated; they seemingly have tried to occupy every crack, cranny, and niche above the low-tide line. Our ancestors (*Homo erectus*), with brains, on average, hundreds of cubic centimeters smaller than ours, increased in numbers, migrated throughout the Old World tropics, and, by 750,000 years ago, moved into the northern temperate zone, taking up residence in Europe and China.[8] By about 100,000 years ago, the human brain was as large as it is today, which is probably as large as it ever will be.[9] We may or may not have folded in a few convolutions since, but there is no doubt that the actual physical development of the brain in our species was completed by 40,000 years ago, when *Homo sapiens* (the wise man!) appeared, face daubed with whatever raw pigments nature provided in the neighborhood, and a sharpened or stone-tipped stick clenched in his fist.

Humans were in occupation of the Old World from Europe and Siberia to the southern tip of Africa and the islands of the East Indies. Yet there were whole continents and myriads of islands we had not explored or settled. We had not yet passed over one of the expanding, deep-water seams of Pangaea.[10]

These early humans were about to do something of the same magnitude as moving from earth to another planet. They were about to leave a world – the riven core of Pangaea, Eurasia plus Africa – of life forms with which their ancestors had lived for millions of years and go to worlds where neither humans nor hominids nor apes of any kind had ever existed, worlds dominated by plants, animals, and microlife whose forms had often diverged sharply from the patterns of life in the Old World.

The new worlds were North and South America and Australia. (To get to New Zealand, a land mammal had to be a bat or an excellent sailor, and *Homo sapiens* arrived there tardily.) Members of the genus *Homo* had been in the East Indies for most of the time that the genus had existed; the waters between those islands were warm and the straits narrow, and the shallow strait between New Guinea and Australia becomes dry land during an ice age. Members of our species turned south and walked into Australia some 40,000 years ago, giving that continent its first large placental mammal. The second, the dog called the dingo, arrived some 8,000 years ago or even more recently. (These dates and others cited in this chapter are matters of controversy in which we need not involve ourselves. We are interested in sequences, not absolute dates.)

There is evidence that a number of species and even genera of Australian marsupials and reptiles, creatures considerably larger than those of historical times, disappeared at roughly the same time that humans spread through that continent. The temptation is to promote chronological coincidence to the level of proof and to blame those extinctions on the invaders, though it strains credulity to claim that Stone Age human hunters alone killed off Australia's giants. They may have had assistance from diseases that came south with them from the East Indies. They did have fire, which Aborigines in historical times have used to burn over vast areas of the continent annually, and in ancient times this practice conceivably could have altered the habitats of the giants sufficiently to make life and reproduction impossible.[11]

Getting from the East Indies to Australia was a matter of

crossing a few warm, narrow straits; getting to the Americas was something more difficult. The problem was not the cold, foggy, dangerous waters of the Bering Strait; indeed, that strait has been a broad highway of tundra for much of the time since the arrival of members of the genus *Homo* in Siberia. The problem was the hostility of the climate in the high latitudes. There were few human beings in Siberia to follow the herds of caribou and such across Beringia to Alaska, and once in Alaska the early migrant human fetched up against a continental ice cap that occupied much of America north of Mexico. There were warm periods that opened a corridor south from Alaska to Alberta and beyond, but all in all the pedestrian's passage from Asia to the lush grasslands and forests of North America was a miserably difficult one.

Humans probably did not arrive south of the North American ice cap until long after they set foot in Australia, but in the New World, as in Australia, there seems to have been a coincidence between the arrival of human big-game hunters and the extinction of many species of large mammals: mammoths, mastodons, giant ground sloths, giant buffalos, and horses, for example. Some individuals of these giant species were incontestably killed by humans – we have found stone spear points between the ribs of fossil mammoths – but most experts are reluctant to attribute the extinction of whole species to these human hunters. Again, humans may have been only part of a wave of invading species, including parasites and pathogens, that attacked the native fauna. But why would the latter concentrate on the larger mammals? Why and how would anything but humans kill mostly those animals representing the largest meals?[12] *Homo sapiens* found a hunter's paradise in Australia and the Americas. All three continents were chock-full of toothsome herbivores utterly inexperienced in defending themselves against human aggressors, providing the newcomers with seemingly inexhaustible quantities of protein, fat, hide, and bone. Expansion of *Homo sapiens* into Australia and the Americas must have led to a very large increase in the total number of humans on the earth. The Americas and Australia were Edens to which God added Adam and Eve very tardily. "There can be no repetition of this," wrote François Bordes in *The Old Stone Age,* "until man lands on a hospitable planet belonging to another star."[13]

Some 10,000 years ago all the larger ice caps melted, excepting those in Antarctica and Greenland, and the oceans rose to approximately their present levels, inundating the plains that had connected Australia with New Guinea, and Alaska with Siberia, and isolating the avant-garde of humanity in their new homelands. From that time until the Europeans made a common practice of sailing across the seams of Pangaea, these peoples lived and developed in complete or nearly complete isolation. One of the momentary respites from divergent evolution since the breakup of Pangaea had come to an end, and for the next few millennia genetic drift and, for the first time, cultural drift were in perfect consonance with continental drift.

Then humanity made its next giant lunge, not a matter of geographical migration but of cultural mutation: the Neolithic Revolution or, more accurately, Revolutions. According to classic definition, the Neolithic Revolution began when humans started to grind and polish rather than chip their stone tools into final form, and it ended as they learned to smelt metal in quantity and work it into tools that stayed sharp longer and were more durable than their stone equivalents. In between, the story goes, humans invented agriculture, domesticated all the animals of our barnyard and meadow, learned to write, built cities, and created civilization. The complete story would be a great deal more complicated, but this definition will serve for our purposes.[14]

The *technological* avant-garde of humanity, the peoples of the crossroads of the Old World, the Middle East, moved down the road toward becoming what we are today more rapidly than any others. The *geographical* avant-garde of humanity, the pioneers isolated in Australia and the Americas, had different histories. The Australian Aborigines[15] kept to their Paleolithic ways; they did not smelt metals or build cities. When Captain Cook and the Australians of Botany Bay looked at each other in the eighteenth century, they did so from opposite sides of the Neolithic Revolution.

The peoples of the New World had their own Neolithic Revolution or Revolutions, most spectacularly in Meso-America and Andean America, but theirs, relative to that in the Old World, began slowly, accelerated tardily, and spread as though the Western Hemisphere were somehow less hospitable to the techniques and arts of civilization than the Eastern. When the *conquistadores* arrived with iron and steel, the peoples of the high Amerindian cultures were still in the early stages of metallurgy. They used metals for ornaments and idols, not for tools.

Why was the New World so tardily civilized? Perhaps because the long axis of the Americas runs north and south, and so the Amerindian food plants on which all New World civilizations depended had to spread through sharply differing climates, unlike the staple crops of the Old World, which by and large spread east and west through regions of roughly similar climates. Perhaps because American farmers required a very long time to transform their most important staple, maize, from what was at first a niggardly sort of plant into the richly productive food source that Europeans first encountered in the 1490s. In contrast, wheat, initially the most important Old World cultivar, was already highly productive when it was first exploited. The first maize could not support large urban populations; the first wheat could, and so Old World civilization bounded a thousand years ahead of that in the New World.

This kind of speculation, even if correct, does not explain why the American Neolithic Revolution was so inferior to that in the Old World in the matter of domesticating animals. Amerindians were better at this than Aborigines, who domesticated only the dog, but they were amateurs compared with peoples of the Eastern Hemisphere. Compare the American assemblage of livestock (dogs, llamas, guinea pigs, and some fowl) with that in the Old World: dogs, cats, cattle, horses, pigs, sheep, goats, reindeer, water buffalo, chickens, geese, ducks, honeybees, and more. Why such a contrast? It is not likely that the Eastern Hemisphere's wild animals were intrinsically more tamable than those in the Western Hemisphere. Indeed, the ancestor of our cattle, the Old World aurochs, seems to have been as unlikely a candidate for domestication as the North American buffalo.[16] Some scholars believe that Amerindians placed a prohibitively high valuation on animals, considering them fellow creatures equal to or even superior to humans, not as potential servants. New World gods, in contrast to Old World gods (at least, one of the more widely publicized of them), did not give humans "dominion over the fish of the sea and over the fowl of the air, and over every living thing that moveth upon the earth."[17]

Or perhaps the contrast between the Old World and New World Neolithic Revolutions was simply a matter of timing. Mark Nathan Cohen, in his book *The Food Crisis in Prehistory, Overpopulation and the Origins of Agriculture,* posits population pressure as the true driving force behind the migration of Paleolithic humanity out of Africa and to the rest of the habitable continents. He also credits the pressure of numbers for the beginnings of agriculture. His thesis, brutally abbreviated and simplified, is this: When the Australian and American pioneers reached their final frontiers and looked out on waters that led only to Antarctica, the world behind them was filling up with hunters and gatherers. There was nowhere else for the surplus population to go, and there were about as many people on the earth as could be supported by means of Paleolithic technology. *Homo sapiens* needed, not for the only time in the history of the species, to become either celibate or clever. Predictably, the species chose the latter course.

All over the globe, east and west, people began to shift from dependence on the herds of large animals (many of which were in sharp decline) to exploitation of smaller animals and of plants. Gatherers became more important and hunters less so, and of necessity humanity produced its greatest practical botanists and zoologists of all time. Where conditions were particularly suitable – where, for instance, wild wheat grew in solid stands and included strains with ears that did not shatter and scatter wastefully when harvested with flint sickles – the jigsaw pieces of domestication came together, and gatherers became farmers. It would seem probable that the sense of population pressure, the *primum mobile,* was greater in the more ancient centers of human occupation (i.e., those of the Old World) than on the frontiers and that this may account for the faster acceleration of the Neolithic Revolution in the Old World relative to the New World.[18]

But enough time spent on footless or, at least, unconfirmable speculation. The Amerindians and Aborigines came late to the full Neolithic Revolution, for whatever reasons, and suffered for it. Traditionally, the keepers of domesticated fowl have taught their birds to hurry when called by using a stick to hit the last to arrive. History has similarly chastised latecomers to the Old World's style of Neolithic Revolution.

The triumph of the European invaders in the Americas and Australasia, we shall see, owed as much, or more, to the Old World Neolithic Revolution as to the developments in Europe between the age when Abraham tended his sheep in the Fertile Crescent and when Columbus, Magellan, and Cook crossed the seams of Pangaea. Therefore, if we seek the roots of the success of European imperialism, we must be off to the Middle East, to Abraham, to Gilgamesh and the cultural ancestors of all of us who eat wheaten bread, smelt iron, or record our thoughts alphabetically.

The Old World Neolithic Revolution, for all its dazzling advances in metallurgy, the arts, writing, politics, and city life, was at its base a matter of the direct control and exploitation of many species for the sake of one: *Homo sapiens*. The opposable thumb had enabled hominids to grasp and manipulate tools; in the Neolithic, these humans would reach out to grasp and manipulate whole divisions of the biota around them. Old World peoples conscripted wheat, barley, peas, lentils, donkeys, sheep, pigs, and goats about 9,000 years ago. (The dog was domesticated much earlier; in fact, it was the only Paleolithic domestication.)[19] Cattle maintained their independence for a few more millennia, and camels and horses for even longer, but by 4,000 or 5,000 years ago the humans of southwestern Asia and environs had completed the domestication of all but a few of the crop plants and livestock most crucially important to Old World civilization, then and now.[20]

Sumeria, humanity's first real civilization, appeared about 5,000 years ago in southern Mesopotamia in the flat lands around the lower reaches of the Tigris and Euphrates rivers. There the written chronicle of humanity begins, a manifestation first on clay and later on papyrus, vellum, cloth, and paper of the awesome continuity of Old World civilization. We – you who read and I who write this sentence – are part of that continuity; these words are in an alphabetical form of writing, a very clever Middle Eastern invention produced by peoples even more directly influenced by the Sumerian example than we are. The Sumerians and the inventors of the alphabet, and you and I, no matter what our genetic heritage, are in one category: heirs of post-Neolithic Old World cultures. All Stone Age peoples, including the few still living, and all pre-Columbian

Amerindians, however sophisticated, are in another. The indigenous populations of the Neo-Europes were in the second category until Europeans arrived from beyond the seams of Pangaea. The transition from one category to another was a harrowing one, and many individuals and even peoples faltered and failed.

If we, whoever we are, compare the Sumerians with the hunters and gatherers that preceded them or have lived since, we see that the contrast between these dawn people of civilization and any Stone Age people is greater than the contrast between the Sumerians and ourselves. In examining hunters and gatherers we are looking at people who are profoundly "other." In looking at Sumerians and other early civilized peoples of the Middle East (Akkadians, Egyptians, Israelites, Babylonians, etc.) we are looking into a very old, very dusty mirror. Let us begin by seeking there knowledge of who Columbus was and who we are.

The Sumerians were great and powerful, and they knew wherein lay their greatness and power: in their crops of barley, peas, and lentils, and in their herds of cattle, sheep, pigs, and goats. The Sumerians, more humbly conscious of the importance of their servant species than we tend to be, did not have the gall to take credit for their existence themselves. They thanked the gods and demigods for them: to Ehlis, Enki, Lahar, Ashnan, and their peers went all praise for bringing abundance to the houses of humans, who previously had lived "hugging the dust."[21] When these gods bestowed their blessings on the Middle Easterners, hunters and gatherers everywhere became obsolete, and the agriculturalists of the New World became obsolescent.

In sum – all articles added together – the Sumerians had food, fiber, leather, bone, fertilizer, and draft animals in greater and more dependable quantity than any other people in the world. Hunters and gatherers often had more nourishing food in greater variety than the farmers of the

Middle East, but their supplies were less abundant, except for the lucky few living in such paradises as the Pacific Northwest of North America. Surpluses that exceeded the immediate requirements of the hunters and gatherers and their families were often difficult to come by and very difficult to preserve. The farmers of the New World had crops as dependable and nourishing as those of Sumeria, crops such as maize and potatoes, but they were far inferior in terms of the quality and quantity of their livestock.

The most important contrast between the Sumerians and their heirs, on the one hand, and the rest of humanity, on the other, involves the matter of livestock. There was, for instance, nothing in the Neo-Europes (or, for that matter, in tropical America or Africa south of the Sudan) that could so enhance the mobility, power, military might, and general majesty of humans as did the horse. The poet or poets who wrote the book of Job were very impressed with the horse:

Trembling with eagerness, he devours the ground; And cannot be held in when he hears the horn; At the blast of the horn he cries 'Aha!' And from afar he scents the battle.

Jehovah claimed full credit for the horse for himself, asking poor Job, "Did you give the horse his strength? Did you clothe his neck with a mane?" Job did not answer, knowing a rhetorical question when he heard one, but he might have offered the thought that humanity had done something that, practically speaking, was almost as impressive as creating the horse. Humanity had tamed it. A millennium later, Sophocles, who did not have to live with a single omnipotent god and was freer in his praise of humanity, did declare that one of man's greatest accomplishments was the taming of "the wild horse windy-maned."[22]

Domestication of horses, oxen, and other Old World livestock gave the Sumerians and their heirs from Europe to

China an immense advantage over the peoples who had little more than the strength of their own bodies to draw on. Job, for instance, was a billionaire by the standards of the New World Neolithic revolutionaries. Before misery descended on him, swept away his worldly possessions, and blistered his poor hide, he owned 7,000 sheep, 3,000 camels, 500 yoke of oxen, and 500 asses. In comparison, Moctezuma, for all his legions, was in poverty in terms of protein, fat, fiber, leather, and especially power and mobility; and the indigenes of the Neo-Europes were all still "hugging the dust."[23]

The true strength of a society, however, lies not in its billionaires but in its common folk and their strength; and here again the heirs of Sumeria had the edge over the heirs of other cultures. They had as allies their livestock, which, somewhat like benign cousins in an extended family, provided the means for staying alive when the labor and luck of the nuclear family did not suffice. And by and large, these cousins – pigs and lambs and cows – provided for themselves while waiting to be called on to provide for their masters. Modern livestock may stand by the feeding trough and starve if it is not filled, but for most of the thousands of years since their ancestors were first domesticated, livestock scavenged for food, huddled together for shelter, and much of the time depended on their own tusks, horns, and speed for defense, with no more than skimpy guidance from their owners.

The examples of the importance of domesticated animals to the heirs of Sumeria that we could cite are thousands in number, ranging from the cozy to the bizarre. How many youngsters, meek and mild, driven from the breast by newborn siblings, survived on goat's milk or cow's milk until they could manage on a solid diet? (The name of the dreaded nutritional disease kwashiorkor, literally meaning "the sickness of the deposed baby when the next one is born," comes from the Ga language of Ghana, where the tsetse fly and trypanosomiasis exclude dairy animals.)[24] How many Mongol horsemen, fierce and terrible, persevered through the hungriest times of the great khan's campaigns by drinking measured amounts of their horses' blood, enough to keep themselves alive and yet not so much as to enfeeble their mounts?[25]

The farmers of western Europe north of the Pyrenees and Alps have often been praised for their skill in maintaining, even enhancing, the fertility of their land. At their most admirable, they actually create loam by carefully rotating crops, by cultivating and plowing under compost and plants especially rich in soil nutriments ("green manure"), and, above all, by folding into the soil the excrement of their animals. The livestock that provide these farmers with meat, milk, leather, and power also provide them with the means to raise grains and vegetables and fiber in plenty on the same plots of ground that their fathers' fathers' fathers cultivated. The farmers of western Europe are the priests, and their animals the acolytes, in the ancient rituals of sowing, harvesting, and replenishing.[26]

The successful farmer of Sumerian or European or any other society has usually had a spouse – nearly always if he or she has been able to sustain success. He has depended on her, she on him, and both on the servant organisms around them. If this extended family of species lost a major member – the sow, an oat crop, or the patriarch himself – the survival of the other family members was in jeopardy. In the preindustrial world, in which muscle was often more important than mind, a widow needed more than her traditional pittance. If she had dependent children she needed a good deal more than a pittance, even if it included a bit of land, unless, of course, the lamented husband had left her animals. Land she might or might not be able to work herself, but livestock, her cousins in the extended family mentioned earlier, could manage largely on their own on the commons and wastes.

The husband of the widow in Geoffrey Chaucer's "The Nun's Priest's Tale" died and left his poor wife but a patch of land, a meager income, and two daughters – surely a recipe for misery, even tragedy. But the three women did well enough, having also inherited a rooster ("His voys was murrier than the murie organ. . . ."), some hens, three sows, three cows, and a sheep named Molly. The animals provided the humans with a diet not likely to produce a Chaucerian friar's jowls, but one nourishing and sufficient in quantity. What the mother and daughters needed in addition, they could obtain by bartering the extra food and wool. They had no wine, of course, "neither whit ne reed," but did well on bread, bacon, sometimes an egg or two, and plenty of milk. These, along with easily acquired grains and vegetables, made up a diet containing all the essential nutrients, a luxury often beyond the means of people who perforce are vegetarians.[27]

The ability of domesticated animals, a renewable resource, to create foods for humans out of what humans cannot eat has served Europeans in sectors of the globe of which neither Sumerians nor Chaucer ever dreamed. In 1771, a survivor of Captain Cook's first voyage to the Pacific offered up thanks to a milch goat who had served Europeans well for three years in the West Indies, had traveled round the world once on H.M.S. *Dolphin* with Captain John Byron and again on the *Endeavour* with Cook, "and never went dry the whole time." Those whom she benefited (and the benefit may have been life itself, because malnutrition killed many on such voyages) pledged "to reward her services in a good English pasture for life."[28]

The metaphor of humans and domesticated animals as members of the same extended family is especially appropriate for northwest Europeans. The three women of "The Nun's Priest's Tale" and the Britons who crewed the *Dolphin* and *Endeavour* were among that minority of the human species and of the class Mammalia in general who maintain through maturity the infantile ability to digest quantities of milk. Few adult black Africans or East Asians, and fewer yet of the adult indigenes of Australasia or the Americas, can tolerate milk in any but small amounts after infancy. In fact, it makes them quite sick, and they must go to the trouble of changing it into cheese or yogurt before they can digest it. This must have discouraged at least some of them from taking up the pastoral life.[29] The advantage of being able to digest milk may seem slight today, but it may have been considerable in the past, when so many peoples so often skirted the edge of starvation. Domesticated milk producers can be especially valuable in a land before it is tamed by cultivators. For instance, when Julius Caesar invaded England, he found the interior inhabited by people – perhaps ancestors of Chaucer's characters and the sailors on the *Dolphin* and *Endeavour* – who did not hunt or farm, but depended on their herds, "flesh and milk forming the principal diet. . . ."[30]

Of all the admirable characteristics of the widow in "The Nun's Priest's Tale," none is more important than her fecundity and her knack for bringing children to maturity. Rearing two healthy daughters in Chaucer's time, the age of the Black Death, was an accomplishment worth praising. Success at procreation has been particularly characteristic of most of the heirs of Sumeria. God promised Abraham, one of the prominent figures among the early heirs, to "abundantly and greatly multiply your descendants until they are as numerous as the stars in the sky and the grains of sand on the sea-shore. Your descendants shall possess the cities of their enemies." Abraham, as a herdsman, had access to all the amino acids essential to make a strong beginning on such a future. Job, one of his descendants, had, prior to his troubles, not only his herds as evidence of his prosperity but also his children: seven sons and three daughters.[31]

The peoples who inherited the crop plants and domesticated animals of the advanced cultures of southwestern Asia (the Europeans, the Indians, the Chinese, etc.) prospered and multiplied, but they did so *despite* as well as because of the organisms, institutions, and ways of civilization. Farmers and pastoralists found that their new way of exploiting nature was a sword that cut both ways. They, though not necessarily the first on earth to cultivate plants, were the first to practice *extensive* agriculture. Tapping the strength of their animals by such means as the plow, they probably raised more food per human laborer (not per unit of land) than other early farmers. They cultivated the small grains, which are best raised in solid stands, not intermixed with other plants, as maize, beans, and squash were and are so often in Amerindian America. This Middle Eastern technique produced a great deal of barley and wheat, but it laid the earth bare twice a year, once before planting and once after harvesting, because all the seeds were sown at once and came to maturity at once.[32] Any system of cultivation, but particularly this one, produces inadvertently domesticated plants: weeds, as much the farmer's creation as his crop plants.

"Weeds" is not a scientific word. It refers not to plants of any specific species or genus or any category recognized by scientific taxonomy, but to whatever plants spring up where humans do not want them. More often than not they are plants that evolved originally to fill the minor role of colonizing bare ground after fires, landslides, floods, and such and that found themselves wonderfully preadapted to spread across the expanses stripped clean by the Neolithic farmer's plow or sickle. Already tolerant of direct sunlight and disturbed soil, they added tolerance of sandal, boot, and hoof. Always ready to spring up fast in the wake of disasters, they easily evolved to survive and sprout again in the wake of the tug, tear, and chomp of grazing livestock. The farmer calls them the bane of his life, and they are, but they also provide livestock with feed and help combat erosion.

The Neolithic farmer simplified his ecosystem to produce quantities of plants that would grow rapidly on bare ground and would survive grazing animals, and he got exactly what he tried for, but some of them he cursed: tufted vetch, ryegrass, cleavers, thistles, coriander, and others.[33] The book of Proverbs in the Old Testament describes his problems, telling us about "the field of an idle man":

It was overgrown with thistles
and covered with weeds,
and the stones of its walls had been torn down.
I saw and I took good note,
I considered and learnt the lesson:
a little sleep, a little slumber,
a little folding of the hands in rest,
and poverty will come upon you like a robber, want like a
    ruffian.[34]

The Middle East's farmers and village dwellers also unintentionally cultivated villains of the animal world, creatures who utilized human garbage and trash for food and shelter and entered into direct competition with humans for the food that humans raised and stored. Hunters and gatherers had their personal vermin – lice, fleas, and internal parasites – but few of the nomad humans remained long enough in one spot in sufficient numbers to accumulate filth enough to enable mice, rats, roaches, houseflies, and worms to multiply into armies. The farmers, however, did just that, and in doing so invented the animal equivalents of weeds: varmints. The Sumerians, trying to adjust to the new world they were willy-nilly creating, prayed to Ninkilim, goddess of field rodents and varmints in general, for the safety of their sprouting grain.[35]

The vermin were more than just burglars; they carried diseases. For example, we know today that rats are carriers of plague, typhus, relapsing fever, and other infections, and we can be sure that they, and the other varmints as well, played similar roles in the past. The first book of Samuel in the Old Testament tells us of an epidemic associated with swarms of mice or rats that swept the Philistines and the Hebrews, a disease that caused "tumors," or so say the scholars of ancient Semitic tongues. Today's epidemiologists might suggest "buboes," the swollen lymph nodes of bubonic plague, as a better translation.[36]

The vermin of civilization were not all visible; in fact, the worst were invisible. The Middle Eastern farmers and herdsmen were the first to raise large numbers of plants and animals of a very few species. They were experts at producing solid stands of plants and animals, and because they were able to create surpluses of food, they were able to raise solid stands of their own species. Along with these concentrations they produced large populations of predators, some visible, like worms and mosquitoes, and many micropredators: fungi, bacteria, and viruses. Farmers and herdsmen were able to drive off wolves and pull up weeds, but nearly helpless to stop infections raging through the packed crowds of their fields, flocks, and cities.

There are some human infections that are specifically called crowd diseases. For instance, maladies like smallpox and measles that either kill or produce lasting immunity and have no carriers except humans cannot exist for long among small groups of people for the same reason that forest fires cannot last long in scattered copses of trees. Both use all the available fuel quickly and gutter out. As for diseases of filth, like typhoid, hunters and gatherers usually moved too often to seriously foul their own homes, and therefore were seldom troubled with such.[37] The first really large accumulations of humans and of human garbage were in the Middle East, where archeologists dig our first cities out of hills that were the middens of scores of generations of inhabitants.

Hunters and gatherers had, at most, only one kind of domesticated animal: the dog. New World farmers and herdsmen domesticated no more than three or four species. The Old World's civilized peoples had herds of cattle, sheep, goats, pigs, horses, and so forth. They lived with their creatures, sharing with them the same water, air, and general environment, and therefore many of the same diseases. The synergistic effect of these different species living cheek by jowl – humans, quadrupeds, fowl, and the parasites of each – produced new diseases and variants of old ones. Pox viruses oscillated back and forth between humans and cattle to produce smallpox and cowpox. Dogs, cattle, and humans exchanged viruses or combined different viruses to produce three new maladies for each other: distemper, rinderpest, and measles. Humans, pigs, horses, and domesticated fowl in contact with wild birds shared and still share influenza, periodically and perpetually producing new virulent strains for each other. When humans domesticated animals and gathered them to the human bosom – sometimes literally, as human mothers wet-nursed motherless animals – they created maladies their hunter and gatherer ancestors had rarely or never known.[38]

And when the Sumerians and their successors invented such concomitants of civilization as long-range commerce and invasions – in general, the ebb and flow of peoples across deserts, mountain ranges, seas, and distances daunting to hunters and gatherers – they placed themselves in jeopardy from unfamiliar microlife and exposed immunologically innocent peoples to the bacterial flora peculiar to dense populations of humans and their animals. Ever since, the common individual's immune system, adjusted and tuned by heredity and experience to a particular environment, has been chronically obsolescent. One's immune system is tuned to one's part of the world, but human greed, aggression, curiosity, and technology chronically thrust one into contact with the rest of the world.[39]

In the literatures of the ancient Middle East are many references to pestilence. The first book of Samuel, for instance, tells us of the disease that afflicted the Philistines and Hebrews cited earlier, and it seems likely that some of the Mosaic plagues that scourged Egypt were caused by microorganisms. There are in the Pentateuch intimations of the beginnings of epidemiology, that is, an empirical knowledge of the circumstances that encourage the spread of infections. At the foot of Mount Sinai after the flight of the Hebrews from the pharaoh, God told Moses, "When you number the Israelites for the purpose of registration, each man shall give a ransom to the Lord, to avert plague among them during the registration."[40] It seems that God, or at least the author, knew that the coming together of the Israelites or of any large number of people who have been living in separate groups (in this case, separate groups scavenging in the wilderness for water and food) multiplies the chance of epidemics and that measures to deal with the problem must be taken.

Later, when Jehovah informed the Israelites of the many advantages he would bestow on them when they reached the land of milk and honey, provided they had obeyed his dictates, he vowed, "The Lord will take away all sickness from you; he will not bring upon you any of the foul diseases of Egypt which you know so well, but will bring them upon all your enemies."[41] People migrating out of the Nile Valley, probably the most densely populated area in the world at the time, into the relatively dry, less densely populated surrounding country were moving into territory that was safer vis-à-vis communicable disease and were carrying with them infections often unknown and quite possibly deadly to the scattered local peoples. The Israelites began their journey with the advantage of their infections, an immense advantage that goes far to explain how "civilized" peoples have so often conquered less advanced peoples so easily. (This process has been most clearly elucidated by William H. McNeill, and as a predictable factor in human history has been called McNeill's law.)[42]

Of all the cries to heaven for relief from pestilence that have come down to us from the ancient Middle East, none is more poignant than that of a priest of the Hatti land in the kingdom of Mursilis, a Hittite ruler of the fourteenth century before Christ. "For twenty years," the priest moaned, "men have been dying in my father's days, in my brother's days, and in mine since I have become a priest of the gods . . . The agony in my heart and the anguish in my soul I cannot endure any more."

Seeking in the invisibly infinite an antidote to the invisibly small (parasitic microorganisms), he worshiped in all the gods' temples, but to no purpose. He conducted careful inquiries to determine if anything had happened that was new or unusual when the pestilence first appeared, and when he found that the priests had stopped making offerings to the god of the river Mala about that time, he immediately made amends. The pestilence continued.

In his father's time, the Hittites had made a promise to their storm god pertaining to a war with Egypt, a war that the Hittites apparently won; but they had not fulfilled their promise. When the victors marched prisoners taken in the war back to Hatti land (i.e., from an alien disease environment of dense population to a disease environment of sparser and probably less cosmopolitan population), the new malady broke out among the doubtlessly undernourished, exhausted, and certainly overwrought prisoners, spread to their masters, and "From that day on people have been dying in Hatti land." Our priest made restitution to the storm god twenty times over, but the pestilence continued.

There was nothing to do but pray and pray again, respectfully pointing out to the gods that they were acting against their own self-interest:

The Hatti land, all of it, is dying; so no one prepares sacrificial loaves and libations for you. The plowmen who used to work the

· 33 ·

fields of the god are dead; so no one works or reaps the fields of the god at all. The grinding women who used to make the sacrificial loaves are dead; so they do not make the sacrificial loaves any longer. From whatever corral or sheepfold they used to select the sacrifices of sheep and cattle, the cowherds and shepherds are dead and the corral and sheepfold are empty. So it comes to pass that the sacrificial loaves and libations and the offering of the animals have stopped . . . Man has lost his wits, and there is nothing that we do aright. O gods, whatever sin you behold, either let a prophet rise and declare it, or let the sibyls and the priests learn about it . . . or let man see it in a dream . . . O gods, take ye pity on the Hatti land![43]

By 3,000 years ago, give or take a millennium or so, "superman," the human of Old World civilization, had appeared on earth. He was not a figure with bulging muscles, nor necessarily with bulging forehead. He knew how to raise surpluses of food and fiber; he knew how to tame and exploit several species of animals; he knew how to use the wheel to spin out a thread or make a pot or move cumbersome weights; his fields were plagued with thistles and his granaries with rodents; he had sinuses that throbbed in wet weather, a recurring problem with dysentery, an enervating burden of worms, an impressive assortment of genetic and acquired adaptations to diseases anciently endemic to Old World civilizations, and an immune system of such experience and sophistication as to make him the template for all the humans who would be tempted or obliged to follow the path he pioneered some 8,000 to 10,000 years ago.

The Old World Neolithic Revolution, diseases and all, rolled out from the centers of dense population, accreting an occasional new crop or weed, a few new domesticated animals and varmints, and a number of new diseases, such as malaria.[44] Written records have much to tell us of this revolution's initial arrival in the Americas and Australia, because that took place within the last 500 years, but its debut in all but a few enclaves of the Old World took place thousands of years ago, and in most cases the participants had no written language. What scribe observed the disembarkation of the first farmers and pastoralists in the British Isles 6,000 years ago, or the first herders of sheep and cattle to cross the Limpopo in South Africa 2,000 years ago?[45] Scribes of one kind or another often were on hand for arrival of the diseases of civilization, perhaps the last of the elements of the Neolithic Revolution to evolve and, in their dependence on the presence of a dense population, the most slow-footed. It is likely that the first crowd disease did not slip across the Channel to the British Isles until 664 A.D., when "a sudden pestilence first depopulated the southern parts of Britain and afterwards attacked the Kingdom of Northumbria, raging far and wide with cruel devastation and laying low a vast number of people." And it is probable that such did not arrive at the southern tip of Africa until 1713, the year in which smallpox came ashore at Cape Town and killed large numbers of the indigenes, the Khoikhoi. They blamed their fate on the foreigners, as perhaps the Britons had during their terrible initiation – conceivably even foreigners of the same origin. The Khoikhoi "lay everywhere on the roads . . . cursing at the Dutchmen, who they said had bewitched them."[46]

The impact of the Neolithic Revolution in most regions of the Old World is difficult to describe, because there were impacts, not a single impact, as the various elements of this collective phenomenon arrived one after another. Anyway, we know only about the final impacts. However, their effects have often been sufficient to give us an impression of what the cumulative and total effect, stretched over millennia, must have been. A good case for us to look at is that of

Siberia, which the Europeans conquered at the same time they invaded the Neo-Europes, and which is today populated in the great majority by Europeans.

Siberia is the Neo-Europe manqué. It is too much like old Europe to be a Neo-Europe. It is not far from Europe, but next door. Its native biota is not unlike, but rather almost identical with, that of northern Europe. Its native people are not descendants of the Paleolithic frontiersmen of humanity; almost all of them are close relatives of Mongols and other Eurasians and are similar in blood-type distributions to these peoples.[47] (More about this sort of thing later.) Indigenous Siberians are culturally like other Eurasians, and they contrast with the indigenes of the Neo-Europes in having received their first elements of the Old World Neolithic thousands of years ago: metals; agriculture; pastoralism – more often involving reindeer than temperate-zone animals, but pastoralism all the same.[48]

The glaring difference between Siberia and the Neo-Europes today is that the former does not produce collosal surpluses of food for export, despite enormous efforts to do so (the failure of one such effort helped bring down Nikita Khrushchev), whereas the latter do. This difference is primarily the result of Siberia's difficult climate; this land is simply too far north and too continental in weather to be a breadbasket. The winters of central Siberia are colder than those of the North Pole, and rainfall is undependable.[49] If Siberia were moderate in temperature and had plentiful and predictable rain, then farmers and pastoralists would have occupied it in great numbers thousands of years ago, at which time the final impacts of the Neolithic would have taken place – probably unrecorded.

The climate tended to repel intruders, and the Gobi Desert and simiarid steppes to the south and the marshes, mountains, and vacant expanses to the west walled them out. To the north and east are ice and oceans. The Roman and Han empires rose to glory and fell; Confucius, Buddha,

Christ, and Muhammad preached; the compass and gunpowder were invented; and Siberia remained frozen at the
first stage of the Neolithic. Then, in the sixteenth century,
men from the west – "with noses sticking out in front,"
according to the flat-faced Asians[50] – came through the
Urals seeking the furs that the upper classes and rising
bourgeoisie of western Europe were demanding.

The Westerners first crossed the Urals in force in 1580,
and in 1640 reached the Pacific – 5,000 kilometers in sixty
years.[51] By roughly 1700, the whites were already in the
majority in Siberia.[52] Some of the reasons for the swiftness
of the European takeover are obvious. Siberia's fierce
climate dictated that it would be mostly empty and would
be easier to pass through than similar but more pleasant and
more heavily populated lands, such as Canada. The invaders had firearms; the indigenes did not. The former were
better organized for conquest than the latter were for
defense, and they were infused with a single purpose – get
furs – whereas the latter had families, sacred traditions, and
all the confusing multiplicity of normal lives to deal with.
But initially the Westerners were few, the natives many;
and the reversal of that ratio was not automatically a matter
of armed European traders arriving and unarmed indigenes
falling supine before them.

The Westerners – let us call them Russians, though many
of them were Ukrainians and what have you – were the
standardbearers for the full platoon of the Old World
Neolithic. They must have carried with them some new
crops, though the principal grains suitable for Siberia were
there already. They must have contributed new weeds,
though most weeds associated with the principal grains had
probably arrived long before. They did not bring the first
horses and cattle, nor, in all likelihood, the first goats and
sheep, but they did bring the first domesticated cats and,
tardily, the first brown rats, to eat and foul food supplies.
(Peter Simon Pallas, the naturalist, found no rats there in

the eighteenth century, but they are certainly there now.)[53] They brought the first honeybees,[54] and that was all to the good, supplying wax, honey, and, in all probability, a better means of pollinating many crops in southern Siberia than had existed there before. Yet the Russians' Neolithic contribution was not a high percentage of Siberia's total of visible organisms.

The invaders brought pathogens of diseases never known before in thinly populated Siberia: smallpox, one or more kinds of venereal infection, measles, scarlet fever, typhus, and so forth.[55] Of these, the worst were the venereal diseases and breath-borne infections. The first took a heavy toll because many of the tribal peoples practiced a kind of sexual hospitality with strangers – "A woman is not food – she does not decrease"[56] – and smiled on sexual intercourse among the young prior to marriage; the second spread rapidly because the climate obliged Siberians to spend much of their time indoors rebreathing one another's air. Venereal disease, sometimes flatly called "the Russian Disease" by the indigenes, spread widely, killing some adults and many fetuses and babies, destroying fertility, and sending populations into steep decline.[57] The breath-borne infections were many; several of them, like measles, were mild childhood diseases to Europeans and Chinese, but deadly to peoples who had never known them before. The worst of them and the most feared of all the new diseases was smallpox, because of its swift spread, the high death rates, and the permanent disfigurement of survivors. It appeared for the first time in Siberia in 1630, crossing the Urals from Russia and passing through the ranks of the Ostyak, Tungus, Yakut, and Samoyed like a scythe through standing grain. The death rate in a single epidemic could soar past 50 percent. When it first struck Kamchatka in 1768–9, it killed two-thirds to three-fourths of the indigenes. Because of the sparse population in Siberia, the disease remained epidemic, rather than becoming endemic, as in Europe or China. This condition was the worse of the two possibilities because when smallpox did make its periodic depredations, every ten or twenty or thirty years, the young were totally susceptible, and an entire generation could be lost in a few weeks. "All that the population seems to gain in any of these intervals," said a late-eighteenth-century student of the Russian Empire, "is perhaps lost to a double amount by the havoc committed by the contagion at its return."[58] The Yukaghirs, who in the 1630s occupied vast areas of Siberia from the Lena basin east, and of whom there were only 1,500 at the end of the nineteenth century, have a legend that the Russians were not able to conquer them until the intruders brought smallpox in a box and opened the box. Then the land was filled with smoke, and the people began to die.[59]

Russians were slow to migrate to Siberia, depopulated or not; in 1724 there were only 400,000 of them there, at most. In 1858, after more than another century, the number had risen only to 2.3 million. By 1880, however, the peasant masses of Russia learned that opportunities were better east of the Urals than at home, where the population was growing rapidly and pressing on the land; between 1880 and 1913, over 5 million migrated into Siberia, where they multiplied at very rapid rates, making their new homeland nearly as white as their old. In 1911, Siberia's population was 85 percent Russian, and that percentage has increased greatly since then.[60]

The indigenes of Siberia have not succumbed and disappeared; in fact, today they are growing in numbers.[61] But they skirted close to extinction, and it is easy to understand why Kai Donner, who traveled in Siberia and stayed with one tribe for a considerable time shortly before World War I, would, remembering James Fenimore Cooper's most famous novel, call his hosts the "Samoyed Mohicans."[62]

If Siberia, where several of the most important elements of the Old World Neolithic were in place when the Europeans arrived, could be so profoundly changed by intruders bringing the rest of the Neolithic elements, what could be expected to happen in lands that knew nothing whatever of this very special revolution in human ways and human powers? What would be the fate of peoples for whom the full revolution would arrive, relatively speaking, in the twinkling of an eye, like doomsday?

3

❦

The Norse and the Crusaders

THEY WENT ASHORE AND LOOKED ABOUT THEM. The weather was fine. There was dew on the grass, and the first thing they did was to get some of it on their hands and put it to their lips, and to them it seemed the sweetest thing they had ever tasted.

—Vinland Sagas

HE [RICHARD THE LION-HEART] pursued the Saracens over the mountains, until following one of them into a certain valley, he transfixed him, causing him to fall dying from his horse. On his overthrow the King looked up and saw afar the city of Jerusalem.

—Itinerarium Ricardi

WHAT DATE SHALL we pick for completion of the Old World Neolithic Revolution in the lands of its origin? Suppose we have it terminate a neat 5,000 years ago with domestication of the horse – an arbitrary choice, perhaps, but a good approximation. Between that era and time of development of the societies that sent Columbus and other voyagers across the oceans, roughly 4,000 years passed, during which little of importance happened, *relative to what had gone before.*

Let us apply the technique of time-lapse photography to the four millennia following completion of the Old World Neolithic, exposing a frame only every half century or so. When we then view our film at normal speed, we are struck with the uneventfulness of this long period. Nothing in those four millennia compares in importance with the domestication of the horse, for instance. Indeed, very little happened that was truly new – just more of the same sort of thing. The epochal innovations of the Neolithic – cultivation of wheat, domestication of the pig, invention of the wheel – overshadow all that followed for scores of human generations. There are some new developments – invention of the arch, domestication of the camel, among others – but they are of minor significance *compared with what had gone before.* Old World civilization does not continue to innovate broadly nor attain higher levels of energy; it simply continues to spread. Empires pop up and down; few but the pharaonic, the Roman, and the Han last long enough to be clearly discerned as our film rolls through the projector. Higher cultures stir along the middle reaches of the Niger; the Javanese forget their old gods and build temples to worship Krishna and then Allah, as the waves of new influences sweep through the Indonesian archipelago from the mainland. At the other extreme of Eurasia, the English leave off painting their fundaments blue and take up debating the nature of the Trinity. The dominant theme in the Old World is emulation, not innovation.

The equivalent film for the Western Hemisphere is more eventful. The New World's Neolithic Revolution at last takes hold. Cities, or at least worship centers, appear on the Gulf Coast of Meso-America and in the river valleys sloping down from the Andes through the Peruvian drylands to the Pacific. Other high cultures appear, presumably stimulated by these first examples, and from the Ohio Valley to the Altacama Desert, Amerindians begin to gather themselves into larger and larger social units with elite groups of priests, politicians, and warriors; they start raising up temples, building states, inventing ways of preserving records in and on stone, skin, string, and forms of paper, that is, creating civilizations that are at least superficially similar to those of Sumeria and its immediate successors. There are, however, no equestrian statues of pre-Columbian Amerindian caesars, and although the Americans, like Old World peoples, invent the wheel, they use it only in a few toys, and then turn their attention elsewhere.[1] If we try time-lapse historiography on Australia, we see no jack-in-the-box empires, no pyramids, no advancing frontier of cultivated fields – only the slowly undulant flicker of Stone Age continuity. About 1000 A.D. the thylacine or pouched wolf disappears from Australia (but not from Tasmania, where it still lives), probably the victim of competition from the Aborigine and dingo. Otherwise, the Stone Age dreamtime continues.[2]

Four millennia rolled past. Gilgamesh journeyed in search of immortality, Quetzalcoatl disappeared over the eastern sea, and Dante trekked through hell, purgatory, and heaven before humanity's next quantum leap into the utterly unforeseeable. Then, in the second Christian millennium, the species bestirred itself again, radically and irrevocably altering its culture and the biosphere. This most recent meta-revolution – we are still too immersed in its turbulence to give it a proper name – was initially a Western European affair. (Here we speak of Western

Europe after the Roman Empire's decline. The subjects of Rome were members of a society more similar to the societies of the ancient Middle East than to the new societies with largely barbarian aristocracies that sprouted in the bared ground left by Rome's retreat.) This next great breakthrough after the Neolithic Revolution is most easily discerned as a matter of science and technology, but it was and is many, many things. None of these is of greater importance than the sixteenth-century crossings of the drowned seams of Pangaea that produced the rediscoveries of Australia and the Americas, eventually leading to creation of the Neo-Europes, the subject of this book. But before we consider that, let us at least glance at the earlier imperialistic ventures of the Europeans. Did their first colonies succeed or fail? Why? Perhaps an examination of their first overseas attempts at settlement will provide us with insights about later attempts or, at least, with intelligent questions to ask about them.

One cannot, of course, establish the birth date of a human society, but approximations are sometimes possible, and historians often find them necessary. In the year 1000 A.D. (or at least during the century or so in which that year falls), Western Europe ceased being the wrack left behind by the ebb of the Roman Empire and began being something new and vital. The dark centuries of barbarian wanderings and Carolingian false starts and general cultural infertility were over. Populations, towns, and trade began to revive, and trailing after them came the arts, philosophy, and engineering. And this was more than a simple revival. The Gothic cathedral, sublime product of the twelfth century, was more than a sign of rebirth. It marked the first birth of a society of remarkable energy, brilliance, and arrogance. Such societies are often expansionistic.

Europeans made two attempts to plant permanent settlements outside their home continent during the Middle Ages. In the first they sailed west to colonize the bleak islands of the North Atlantic and even to establish footholds in the New World. In the second they sailed and marched east to create Western European states among the anciently civilized peoples of the eastern Mediterranean. Some of these colonies, east and west, lasted for barely a season; others lasted for generations, and Iceland is with us yet.

While some Scandinavians were raiding and colonizing across the narrow waters between their homelands and the British Isles and the Continent in the last centuries of the first Christian millennium, others were turning away from Eurasia and launching into the North Atlantic to settle first the Faroe Islands and then, about 870 A.D., Iceland. Iceland is 1,000 kilometers from Norway, its motherland. It lies athwart – in fact, is a smoking, steaming product of – the Pangaean seam we call the Mid-Atlantic Ridge, and so it is the very antithesis of anything continental. Iceland was Europe's first large overseas colony and is her oldest by 500 or 600 years, or even more than that if we consider that the sprinkling of Irish holy men the Norse found there constituted a true settlement.

Then, late in the tenth century, Erik the Red led a fleet from Iceland to southern Greenland to found Europe's first colony beyond the Mid-Atlantic Ridge.[3] The Greenland colonists pastured their sheep and cattle on the sparse meadows between the icecap and the cold ocean, built homes and churches (in time, even brought a great bell from Europe for their cathedral at Gardar), and lived in Greenland for 500 years, about as long as Europeans and their descendants have lived in America since Columbus.[4]

In approximately the year 1000, Leif Eriksson, son of Erik the Red, made a reconnaissance voyage west and south of Greenland to lands that he named, as he sailed farther and farther from home, Helluland, Markland, and Vinland. A few years later, Thorfinn Karlsefni sailed from Greenland to Vinland with livestock, five women, and either 60 or 160 men, depending on which saga one reads.

This attempt at colonization was better led and planned than, say, the attempt at Jamestown, Virginia, 600 years later, but it failed nevertheless. The Norse made other trips to America: In 1172, for instance, no less a personage than Bishop Erik Upsi "went in search of Vinland," with unknown results; in 1347, Greenlanders sailed to Markland, probably for timber; and no doubt there were unrecorded voyages. But the Norse never established a foothold in America.[5] The fact is that this entire series of European sorties beyond the Mid-Atlantic Ridge, including the settlements in Greenland, might as well never have happened, except insofar as it has stimulated archeologists and scholars interested in the old sagas. The Norse achieved perfect failure in the western reaches of the North Atlantic. Why? Why does the continuum of European presence beyond the Mid-Atlantic Ridge not begin at the end of the tenth century instead of at the end of the fifteenth?

Before we examine the reasons for the failure of the North Atlantic Norse, let us look at some of the reasons they managed to accomplish as much as they did. First and foremost was their character, their own amazing courage and seamanship. One can easily picture them looking over their shoulders as they set out into the ocean, proclaiming "You could never do this, but we will!" And they did it. The Norse never sailed as far as the Pacific islanders did, but the latter accomplished their miracles in a warm ocean with dependable winds. The Norse sailors played out their heroics in one of the colder and more treacherous bodies of water in the world. The greatest advantage of the Norse in the Atlantic, in addition to their own amazing capabilities, was the ship they sailed. The *langskip* (longship) of the Viking raiders was too small and not sufficiently seaworthy for the open ocean. For that work, a true sailing ship was needed, not a galley with supplemental sailing capacity, but a true sailing ship with a broad beam to minimize rolling in heavy seas and to carry more cargo than the longships carried. The Norse merchantman, the *knörr* (pl. *knerrir*), was such a vessel. As buoyant and flexible as a longship, but a good deal broader, it carried twenty tons and fifteen to twenty people, and with a good following wind and a friendly sea it could sail at six knots, a respectable pace for a merchantman as recently as the Napoleonic Wars.[6]

The Norse were uniquely skilled in their day as ship-builders, but as farmers and herdsmen they were unsophisticated heirs to the innovations of the Old World Neolithic, without which they could never have survived on the North Atlantic islands. Not even an Icelander can live on fish alone. The rocky nature of these islands and the short northern growing season sharply restricted the productivity of farming, and, of necessity, the Norse were pastoralists. From Norway to Iceland to Greenland, herds of sheep and cattle were their most important sources of sustenance.[7] Their animals probably were runtier, hairier, and most surely woollier than those of Abel, son of Adam and Eve and heir to Sumeria, but they were of the same species – in some instances possibly direct descendants of Abel's flocks.

The Scandinavian livestock did well enough in Iceland and Greenland to sustain themselves and their masters, and they showed great promise in Vinland during their few seasons there. Grass in America was plentiful and lush, and the climate was certainly more moderate than they were accustomed to. Their horns and hooves apparently were adequate protection from New World predators – or perhaps the wolves and cougars did not have enough time to get over their shyness of the new critters.

It is worth noting for later reference that these Old World animals began to go wild in the Vinland wilderness, despite centuries on centuries of domestication. "Soon," reads the saga, "the male beasts became very frisky and difficult to manage."

The half-feral animals gave the Norse a special advantage over the Skraelings (the Norse term for both Eskimos and

Amerindians). The indigenes were understandably frightened of these large creatures that seemed to be so involved with and, sometimes at least, obedient to their masters. One day the bull that the Karlsefni expedition had brought from Greenland began to bellow and roar, and the Amerindians, who had come to trade, took to their heels. Later, when the newcomers with the blond hair and blue eyes had to fight what was apparently a superior force of Amerindians, the guileful Karlsefni took advantage of the Skraelings' fear. He sent ten men to draw an attack, and when the natives took the bait, he charged them with the bull "to the fore." The plan worked, and Karlsefni lived to die a farmer back in Iceland.[8]

One wonders what difference a horse or two, animals the Spanish used with enormous effect against the Aztecs and Incas a few hundred years later, would have made to Norse fortunes in Vinland. The Greenlanders did have horses – Erik the Red hurt his leg falling off one – but insofar as the sagas tell us, not one of these animals ever accompanied the Norse to Vinland.[9]

A very specific advantage of the Norse over the Skraelings, Eskimo or Amerindian, was the ability of their adults to gain nourishment from fresh milk. Scandinavians, like other northwest Europeans, are among the world's champion milk digesters, which perhaps had effects that might not be readily apparent.[10] One day (the day of the bellowing bull) when the Skraelings demanded weapons from the Norse in return for furs, the former refused and offered a novelty instead: milk. Soon the natives wanted nothing else. The outcome of the day's trading was that the Norse had furs to bring back home, and "the Skraelings carried their purchases away in their bellies."[11] We can be quite sure the latter were miserably sick within hours. What effect did that, along with the bull, have on Norse–Skraeling relations? Did it lead to the battle won by the bull?

The Norse needed the bull in that battle because they enjoyed only a slight technological advantage over the natives of Vinland. The Norse had the wheel and the Skraelings did not; and the Norse had metal and the Skraelings did not. This was all to the good from the point of view of the invaders, but in practice these advantages seem to have been irrelevant rather than decisive. A cart might be useful on a Greenland farm, but it is doubtful that Eriksson or Karlsefni ever carried such an awkward luxury across the North Atlantic to Vinland. And for what would they have used it once there? It is probable that Greenlanders used rollers to get logs to the beaches of Markland for shipment back home, but in the short run the wheel, the lever, the arch, and all the other examples of Old World cleverness – the alphabet, the Pythagorean theorem – made little difference beyond the Mid-Atlantic Ridge.

The Vinland Norse did have metal; archeologists have even unearthed a primitive ironworks, the very first in America, at the site of a Norse settlement in Newfoundland.[12] Norse swords and axes were less bulky and more durable and kept an edge longer than any Skraeling equivalents, and that must have given the invaders an appreciable advantage, but it was obviously not sufficient to assure victory. Metal is essential for firearms, but effective, if crude, clubs, ax heads, and projectile points can be made of stone. For example, Thorvald Eriksson, brother of Leif, received a mortal wound from a stone-tipped Skraeling arrow. (Worthy of the Norse tradition, he died while calmly choosing a site in Vinland for his grave: "I seem to have hit on the truth when I said that I would settle there for a while.")[13]

Flint points can pass between ribs as easily as metal, and a stone ax can crumple a shoulder or smash a skull quite as neatly as anything made of iron or steel. Metal weapons are better than stone, but in hand-to-hand combat between desperate men this may be only an example of the proverbial distinction without a difference. So much for Norse advantages over the Skraelings. The list of their disadvantages is much longer.

The Norse were not capable of mounting either many expeditions or large expeditions to America. The largest expedition to Vinland of which we have any record consisted of three vessels and only 65 or 165 people. Many of the post-Columbian expeditions from Europe to America were not much larger, but there were a lot of them, and even those that failed seem to have stimulated interest in new attempts. And some of the more important post-Columbian expeditions were quite large. The fleet that Columbus led to the West Indies in 1493 consisted of seventeen ships carrying 1,200 to 1,500 men. Britain's First Fleet to Australia – the year was 1788 – comprised eleven ships with nearly 1,500 men, women, and children on board. Endeavors of such size were beyond the capability of the medieval Norse of the North Atlantic. Greenland at its peak had not a great many more than 3,500 people. At the most, Iceland had about 100,000, and Norway perhaps 400,000.[14]

The number of Scandinavians on the islands of the North Atlantic was so small because their settlements were too poor to attract or maintain larger numbers. Norway itself was not comparable to the Byzantine Empire or even Carolingian France, but rather a cold, poor country a long way from the centers of Old World population and civilization. It attained unity and considerable influence in that part of the world in the period from the eleventh through the thirteen century, but it lacked the agricultural surplus, the large population, the capital, and most of the other ingredients for empire building. For most Icelanders and Greenlanders, Norway was not the anchor of an Atlantic empire, but a distant trading partner and an ancestral memory of a steep beach, rimed with frost, from which brave men and women had set out in search of a better life.

Anyway, Vinland's motherland was not Norway but Greenland, and Norse colonies in America could never have become viable unless the settlements in Greenland had first attained solid viability. This they never did, in spite of all the centuries the Norse were there. Grain would barely grow, and most Greenlanders had never so much as seen any. The island had no timber at all, except driftwood, and no iron. The islanders had no product – nothing like Virginian tobacco or West Indian sugar – permanently in demand in Europe, and thus no guarantee of unbroken contact with that continent. The strange truth of the matter is that a substantial colony in Vinland could have supported a colony in Greenland, but not vice versa.[15]

Conflict with the indigenes was not a problem in Greenland until the Eskimos came south (about which more presently), but in Vinland it was an insuperable problem from the first. There the Skraelings were hostile and numerous. Little wonder they were hostile: The Norse murdered eight of the first nine they met, and the ninth escaped only by luck and nimbleness. When the Skraelings came to trade with Karlsefni, the number of their boats was so great "that it looked as if the estuary were strewn with charcoal," and when they came to fight, their boats poured "in like a torrent." Karlsefni's followers coveted Vinland – the land was rich, game plentiful, the streams full of salmon, the grass to the taste of their livestock, and already one child, Snorri, son of their leader and Gudrid, had been born there – but the Norse realized they could never live in that land safely. Vinland was already thoroughly occupied.[16]

The Norse needed an "evener," something to compensate for their inferiority in numbers to the Amerindians. Their military technology was not it, as we have seen. They needed something with genocidal potentiality; they needed to have McNeill's law (cited in the last chapter) operating on their side. However, the biological weapons that had worked effectively for the dense populations of the Middle East were not available to the eleventh-century Norse. In fact, infectious diseases seem to have worked not for the Norsemen but against them.

The Norse in Iceland and even more so in Greenland were so remote from Europe that they rarely received the latest installments of the diseases germinating in European centers of dense settlement, and their tiny populations were too small for maintenance of crowd diseases. Epidemics of these would burn themselves out, condemning the next generation of islanders to the same vulnerability that had characterized their parents. Smallpox, for instance, which came ashore in Iceland for the first time in 1241 or 1306, swept the island again and again in the next two centuries, seemingly appearing whenever enough new susceptibles had been born. The longer the respite, the worse the blow when it came. When smallpox returned in 1707 after a long absence, 18,000 people, one-third of the entire population, died. A Briton familiar with the North Atlantic Norse has written that "The ravages committed by the small pox in Iceland have been such as to render this disease important even in the political history of the island." Fatal infections, off-loaded from European ships time and again, dealt blow after blow to these people for whom survival was difficult under the best of circumstances, knocking back population growth that might have led to healthy societies.[17]

Whatever chance might have existed for renewed colonization in Vinland and revival in Greenland during the late Middle Ages and the Renaissance was snuffed out by the Black Death. This very virulent strain of plague arrived in Italy in 1347, swept north and reached Norway in 1349 – 50, paused there for half a century, and sailed off to Iceland, disembarking in 1402 – 4. In Europe as a whole, this pandemic may have killed one-third of the population. In Norway and Iceland, two-thirds of the humans died, as famine followed the plague because the livestock, their winter forage ungathered, died of neglect. If the plague traveled as far as Greenland, then we need inquire no further about the steepness of the outpost's decline in the fifteenth century.[18]

All kinds of horrors can properly be blamed on the Black Death, but we cannot blame it for initiating Greenland's decline. That was well under way even before the plague got off the boat in Norway. In the fourteenth century, the European demand for North Atlantic products had waned, and fewer and fewer ships made the long voyage from Norway to Greenland. The trade between Norway and Iceland languished as well, and fifteenth-century Iceland suffered severely from neglect, almost to the point of demise. Greenland and Iceland had always been far out on a limb, and now the limb withered.[19]

As the number of *knerrir* sailing between Europe and its North Atlantic offspring decreased, nature seemingly maneuvered for the kill. The quantity and quality of good land in Iceland decreased as the imported livestock denuded its slopes and the Norse burned and cut away its forests, baring the land to the effects of water and wind erosion.[20] Hunger became chronic, and outright famines accompanied by pestilence swept the island again and again. Iceland, the strong link in the chain that connected Greenland and, potentially, Vinland to Europe, rusted and grew frail.[21]

The climate, decent enough in the first centuries after 1000 A.D. to tempt adventurers and their families to Iceland, and tolerable even in Greenland, grew colder. Cultivating grain became more and more difficult; glaciers advanced; drift ice reached Iceland's shores more and more often and heaped up across the entrances of the once hospitable Greenland fjords. Mariners sailing to the Greenland settlements had to detour south and west, and by the fifteenth century they could hope to reach the settlements only in August.[22] Greenland, never better than marginally Norse in climate, was becoming Eskimo country again, and the indigenes moved south to claim their birthright. In 1379, Skraelings attacked and killed eighteen Greenland Norse and carried off two boys. This was surely not the last of Eskimo raids.[23]

The last Norse Greenlander died in cold and abysmal loneliness sometime at the end of the fifteenth century.[24] Europe's first colony beyond the Mid-Atlantic Ridge flickered out at approximately the same time that Columbus, sailing west from the Canary Islands bound for Asia, renewed Europe's connection with America.

What were the Norse doing as far north as Greenland anyway? Why did they seek out shores even frostier than the parts of Norway from which most of them came? Vinland was vastly more attractive than the islands the Norse discovered and accurately named Iceland and, inaccurately, Greenland. Why did they not make a major effort to settle Vinland? "It is beautiful here," said Thorvald Eriksson. "Here I should like to make my home."[25] He made not his home but his grave in Vinland when a Skraeling arrow ended his life, and soon thereafter his fellow colonists departed for home. But why were they so quickly dissuaded? The peoples of the British Isles, France, and Russia offered resistance to Viking invaders at least as stiff as that of the Skraelings, and yet in those regions the invaders had brought in their relatives and started to build towns. If the oceanic Norse would stake their lives in attempts to settle even in ocean-lost islands with volcanoes and ice caps, then why did they not persist in the effort to colonize America?

Because it was simply too far away. They could reach it, but not grasp it. Of course, in the lower latitudes the fogs were rarer, the ice not so dangerous, the winds more predictable, and the North Star close enough to the horizon to have its altitude measured accurately, but at lower latitudes the ocean was wide and without landfalls, except for the Azores, which had not yet been discovered. There is no record of any Norse ship ever crossing directly from Europe to America or vice versa in medieval times, nor, for that matter, is there any mention of anyone making an intentional voyage from Iceland to America. The Norse did not span the Atlantic in one leap, but brachiated across from one island or at least from one indication of land – a gathering of clouds, a flocking of sea fowl – to another. Even so, *hafvilla* is a word that appears often in the sagas. It means the loss of all sense of direction at sea, a state that could last for days or even weeks, even, we may suppose, to death.[26]

Norse sailors minimized their risks, and so made few voyages of discovery. Only a fool with a new theory would sail off into an ocean without a very specific idea of where he was going; the Norse always had a specific idea. They sailed for Iceland only after holy men from Ireland had settled there and no doubt had told the Norse about it. Erik the Red did not discover Greenland; he was following up Gunnbjorn Ulfsson's report that he had seen land to the west of Iceland while off course. Leif, Erik's son, did not discover America; he was following up Bjarni Herjolfsson's report that he had seen land to the west and south of Greenland while he, too, was off course.[27]

The Norse sailors were conservatives; their *knerrir* made that compulsory. These ships were marvels of craftsmanship, but small, miserably wet and cold, and not very maneuverable. The ships of Erik, the Erikssons, and Karlsefni were less than thirty meters in length – probably a good deal less – and roughly one-fourth or one-third as broad in beam, and they were only half-decked at best. No doubt they took every wave as nimbly as a floating gull, but they must have shipped a lot of water in rough weather, most of which went into the bilge. There were no pumps; the bilge had to be bailed out by hand.[28] The Norse ships had no rudder as we understand its construction, but rather a steerboard, a very large and awkward oar that hung off the quarter, trailing like the broken wing of a bird. Propulsion was supplied by oars while in harbor and by a single square sail at sea. With a following wind, all was well, but these vessels could not tack into a headwind, and the only way to deal with "a dead muzzler" was to wait for it to change. They could manage some forward progress by use of their oars, of course, but it was not practical to row across an ocean. Some power could be sucked out of a beam wind by turning the square sail to catch it, but this was an awkward business. What the Norse needed was a fore-and-aft or lateen rig, about which more in Chapter 6.

To take a *knörr* to sea was to try to strike a bargain with the gods of the deep, and the best a sailor could reasonably hope for was that the gods would let him go where he wanted a lot of the time in return for his accepting courses they plotted some of the time. Shipwrecks were, of course, common, and *hafvilla* a chronic affliction; the sagas are full of tales of helpless drifting. For example, Thorstein Eriksson, another brother of Leif, set sail for Vinland, but saw nothing of America. He did see Iceland and then birds flying from Ireland, and then at long last the weather improved and allowed him to return home to Greenland. Thorhall the Hunter sailed for America with Karlsefni, but took an independent course, seeking Vinland on his own. He ran into headwinds and drifted with them right across the Atlantic to Ireland, where he died and his crew was enslaved.[29] Much of the time the Norse did go where they wanted to go, but their ships, rigging, and navigational techniques were only marginally adequate for the special difficulties of the North Atlantic. Leif and his fellow sailors performed miracles there – in the drift ice, in fearsome gales, in fogs like wet sheepskins – but empires have to be built of commoner stuff than miracles.

Some of the improvements in navigational techniques and gear, ship design, and rigging that Western Europeans needed to cross the Atlantic where it was safest but widest doubtless came to them from the Levant with returning Crusaders. Jacques de Vitry of the city of Acre in the Holy Land informed Europe in 1218 that "An iron needle, after it has made contact with the magnet stone, always turns toward the North Star, which stands motionless while the rest revolve, being as it were the axis of the firmament." Such a needle, he pointed out, "is therefore a necessity for those travelling by sea."[30]

Jacques de Vitry was a bishop of the Latin Christian church in a city in a region that had been the homeland of Christ and was still the home of many of his followers. Most, however, were not Latin but Greek Christians, Armenian Christians, Coptic Christians, and other miscellaneous kinds of Christians. Even more appalling to the bishop was the fact that all Christians of all the sects added together amounted to only a minority of the population. The majority were Muslims, followers of the awesomely heretical Muhammad, whose armies had swept over the Middle East in the seventh century, conquering Bethlehem and all the other places where the Savior had walked.

For several generations Europeans found this situation tolerable; after all, the heavenly Jerusalem, not the geographical one, was the one that mattered. Then, in the eleventh century, the concrete, actual Holy Land became increasingly important to Western Europeans (also known at the time as Latins or Franks, no matter how German or English they might be). Bishops, counts, peasants, and even many noble ladies journeyed to the Holy Land, "a thing which had never come to pass before."[31] A thought was stirring the mind of the coarse and powerful new society growing in Western Europe, a thought compounded of religious idealism, a desire for adventure, and, it turned out, rampant greed. When the emperor of Byzantium, frightened by the massive victories of the Seljuk Turks, asked Urban II for help, the pope delivered his famous call for a Crusade in 1095. And Latin Christianity answered with the First Crusade, a sort of banzai charge by hordes of the pious to rescue the Holy Sepulchre from the Muslims. Seven or eight other Crusades followed, depending on how one defines the term. Over the next two centuries, hundreds of thousands of Western Europeans marched and sailed to the eastern Mediterranean – to a region with peoples, cultures, biota, and diseases quite different from those to which most of them were accustomed – to fight the infidel and break his hold on the Holy Land.

The Crusades were the most spectacular manifestations of religious vigor in the history of European society. They were also the first massive attempts to permanently extend European power outside the boundaries of that continent, and they produced four new states in the biblical lands: Edessa, Antioch, and Tripoli in the north, and the Kingdom of Jerusalem, the largest of the four, in the south. Today, the only evidences left of these states are a few massive ruins, usually the stumps of castles. Western Europe's first imperialistic attempts in Asia failed, and failed because of factors similar to those that rendered later European extensions in Asia ephemeral. But before assessing those factors, let us first examine the European advantages, as we did with the Norse effort in the North Atlantic.

The ships and navigational capabilities of medieval Europeans were better suited for the Mediterranean (a sea that an American poet, with enormous but somehow appropriate exaggeration, has called "the blue pool in the old garden") than for the fearsome North Atlantic.[32] Initially the Muslims, or Saracens, as they were often called, were unable to unite against the Frankish invaders. Europe gave the Crusaders generous, even fanatical support for generations, and so they were able to mount and maintain efforts that dwarfed anything the Norse were ever able to do in the Atlantic. The Greenland Norse at their peak numbered perhaps 3,500, certainly no more than 5,000, whereas the Latin population of the Kingdom of Jerusalem at its apogee was well over 100,000.[33] The Crusaders were familiar with the peoples and lands they sought to conquer. They were not fighting Skraelings beyond the edge of the known world. They were not journeying away from the hearthlands of Old World civilization, but toward them, seeking ancient certitudes in ancient lands.

Yet medieval European imperialism flopped in the East, and in the end the Crusaders retained no more of the Holy Land than they inadvertently carried home in the chinks of their battered armor. The Norse at least retained Iceland, but the Crusaders ultimately lost even Rhodes and Cyprus. Constantinople fell to the Muslims in 1453 after a millennium as a Christian city. The Crusaders' failure was immaculate. Why?

First, the obvious: The Crusaders crawled out on a limb in order to get to Jerusalem. It was shorter and stouter than the one that reached from Norway to Vinland, but a limb all the same. Their position in the Levant could be sustained only by an unending supply of substantial aid from Europe. After a surge of fervor that went on for many years, that aid became episodic, diminished, and finally trickled to an end. Christian Edessa, Antioch, Tripoli, and Jerusalem languished and eventually disappeared.

As for more subtle matters, it is true that Latin nautical equipment and skills were adequate for the usual Mediterranean commerce, but they were not equal to the task of transporting large armies to the Holy Land and supplying them there. This inadequacy was especially significant in that it discouraged the mass migration from Western Europe to the Crusader states that would have ensured their viability.[34] The larger Crusader armies marched all or most of the way to the Levant, exposing the marchers to disease, to severe weather, to attacks by local predators of whatever religious persuasion, and to the temptation to idle away months or even years in the fleshpots of the East, to sack Constantinople, to make a profitable thing of a Crusade.

The disunity of the Muslims, essential to Crusader success or even survival, did not last. After the First Crusade, the invaders increasingly found themselves battling Saracens from the entire region. Egypt, with the largest population in the medieval world west of the Indus, raised or hired enormous armies and under the leadership of the Mamluks united much of the Middle East against the Franks. In contrast, the Christians in the Levant – Latin, Greek, Syrian, Coptic, and so forth – were rarely able to pull together to one purpose, even when that purpose was survival.

These problems of transportation difficulties and disunity were secondary compared with the simple and stark lack of sufficient Latin Christians in the Crusader states to make them viable. At the beginning, the Crusaders gloried in the odds: "Can there be anyone who does not marvel how we, a few people in the realms of so many of our enemies, could not only remain but could even thrive?" But reality soon proved such statements to be pure bravado.[35] Saladin, who won Jerusalem back for Islam in 1187, understood the Crusaders' problems perfectly and wrote a letter to Emperor Frederick Barbarossa recommending that he sit out the Third Crusade because

If you reckon up the names of the Christians, the Saracens are more numerous and many times more numerous that the Christians. If the sea lies between us and those whom you name Christians, there is no sea to separate the Saracens, who cannot be numbered; between us and those who will come to aid us, there is no impediment.[36]

(Moctezuma could have written such a letter to Cortés when the latter first set foot in Mexico, but then the situation rapidly changed.) The emperor ignored Saladin's reasonable advice and became one of those who fell victim to the West's maritime inadequacies. He marched his army from Germany across Hungary and the Byzantine Empire into Asia Minor, where he drowned in a river, after which event his army disintegrated.[37]

The Latin population in the Crusader states was at maximum no more than a quarter million in a region of many millions of cool friends and hot-blooded enemies. In the whole of the Kingdom of Jerusalem there were only fifty or sixty Latin settlements out of 1,200 centers of population. By rough estimate, only about one in five inhabitants of the Crusader states was a Latin. The Crusaders, perched in castles, fortified villages, and city quarters, remind one of British sahibs on the eve of the Sepoy Rebellion, never quite safe in their enclaves, and dependent on multitudes of native peoples for whom their presence was at best dully aggravating.[38] There were three possible solutions to the Crusaders' demographic woes: one, immigration of large numbers of Western Europeans; two, recruitment of large numbers of local non-Latin Christians by intermarriage, persuasion, conversion, or what have you; three, a birth rate among Crusaders higher, *much* higher, than their death rate.

Latins never migrated to the Crusader states in great numbers except at times of great enthusiasm, as during the First Crusade – and even then most of the survivors returned home afterward. They had succeeded in capturing Jerusalem, the holiest of all cities for Christians, but they were reluctant to settle even there. "There were not enough people to carry on the undertakings of the realm," complained William, archbishop of Tyre. "Indeed there were scarcely enough to protect the entrances of the city and to defend the walls and towers against sudden hostile attacks . . . The people of our country were so few in number and so needy that they scarcely filled one street." Baldwin I had to invite and cajole Eastern Christians to migrate from Jordan to provide the city with enough people to function at all, and the shortage of laborers remained a problem for as long as the Crusaders ruled within the walls of Jerusalem.[39]

The shortage of Latins in the East persisted despite economic attractions there. It was much easier for a ne'er-do-well knight to win a rich fief in the Levant by arms or political savvy than back home, where Latin Christians at least as pious as himself held all the land. Baldwin and the other Crusader leaders offered special advantages to knights who would settle in their realms, loosening the rigid rules of the patriarchal inheritance system to allow a knight's fee to go to daughters and collateral relatives, and even allowing women to hold fiefs under certain circumstances. As for immigrant commoners, it would seem likely that they, too, found that their opportunities for advancement were better in the East. They could at least count on being socially above Eastern Christians, even landowners, and vastly superior to Muslims.[40] "Those who were needy have here been enriched by God," wrote Raymond of St. Gilles' chaplain. "Those who have a few pennies, here possess countless bezants. He who had not a village, here possesses a God-given city. Why should one who has found the East like this return to the West?"[41]

A very good question, because they did return home by the droves. The Crusaders passionately wanted to seize the Holy Land, but they seemed not to want to hold it, and were therefore incapable of doing so. It was as if Cortés and his *conquistadores* had conquered the Aztec Empire and then packed up and gone home, leaving Mexico to return to Amerindian control.

The Crusaders did not solve their demographic problem by recruiting and intermarrying with local Christians because they found that the local Christians simply were not like Latins. Quite the contrary: They were "untrustworthy, double-dealers, cunning foxes even as the Greeks, liars, and turncoats" – in many ways as bad as the Saracens.⁴² There was, inevitably, some intermarriage between Western and Eastern Christians, the offspring of which were, by nature and nurture, the first real citizens of the Crusader states and the hope of their future. The Crusaders, unfortunately, held these people in contempt because they were indeed Eastern Westerners, comfortable in the Levant, at least bilingual, tolerant of different cultures and religions, and therefore interested in the pursuits of peace: "soft and effeminate, more used to baths than battles, addicted to unclean and riotous living, clad like women in soft robes . . . They make treaties with the Saracens, and are glad to be at peace with Christ's enemies."⁴³

The Crusaders were a small minority of conquerors presiding over a vast majority of peoples of ancient, confident, and in many ways superior cultures. The conquerors, taken collectively, were like a lump of sugar presiding in a hot cup of tea. For cultural survival they withdrew into themselves and practiced clannishness to the point of *apartheid*. When the bishop of Acre advocated converting the local people to Latin Christianity, he met opposition from the Crusaders. They were willing, in the words of the historian Joshua Prawer, "to fight and die for their religion, but not ready to convert even the willing!"⁴⁴

That left only natural increase as a means by which the Crusaders might have solved their manpower problems. They and the women they brought from the Latin West would have to produce offspring who would live to produce even more, and all this reproduction would have to go at a faster rate than Franks were dying, and much faster than the indigenous Christians, Jews, and especially Muslims were reproducing. The Latins lost the propagation race.

With few exceptions, Westerners throughout history who have gone to the eastern Mediterranean to fight wars have believed their chief problems to be military, logistical, and diplomatic, and possibly theological, but the truth is that their primary and immediate difficulties usually have been medical. Westerners often have died soon after arrival, and more often have failed to have children who have lived to maturity in the East.

It would be guesswork to say which Crusader died of what. In September and October of 1098, thousands of members of the First Crusade died of some sort of pestilence. It seems to have been infectious: An army of 1,500 Germans, freshly arrived, suffered rapid annihilation, which suggests infection rather than malnutrition, although the latter certainly could have contributed to the rapid rate at which they died. Rains fell almost continuously that autumn, and the Crusaders knew next to nothing about field sanitation. Perhaps typhoid or some sort of dysentery was the killer.[45] The chief killer during the Seventh Crusade, on the other hand, probably was malnutrition. The symptoms – sore mouth, rotting gums, stinking breath, skin "tanned as black as the ground, or like an old boot that has lain behind a coffer" – suggest a diagnosis of scurvy.[46] But such diagnostic hindsight is largely guesswork. The Crusaders' descriptions of their sicknesses are ambiguous, and no doubt many pathogens were operating at once. The Franks, when they traveled to the East, were subject to a new climate, exposure to all sorts of severe weather, a new diet, malnutrition and occasionally starvation, exhaustion, general disorientation – stress in a host of forms – in addition to new pathogens. When a hungry, scared, bone-tired, filthy man with one or more infections died, it was difficult to say specifically what killed him.

In contrast to the Franks, the Saracens fought on their own ground. Richard of Devizes noted enviously that "the weather was natural to them; the place was their native country; the labour, health; their frugality, medicine."[47]

When the Crusaders arrived in the Levant, they had to undergo what British settlers in the North American colonies centuries later would call "seasoning"; they had to ingest and build resistance to the local bacterial flora.[48] They had to survive the infections, work out *modi vivendi* with the Eastern microlife and parasites. Then they could fight the Saracens. This period of seasoning stole time, strength, and efficiency and ended in death for tens of thousands.

It is likely that the disease that affected the Crusaders the most was malaria, endemic in the Levant's low, wet regions and along the coast, exactly where the bulk of the population of the Crusader states tended to concentrate.[49] Crusaders from the Mediterranean and even from northern Europe may have brought with them a degree of resistance to malaria, because the disease was widely distributed in medieval Europe – indeed, it was still present as far north as the English fen country in the nineteenth century – but nowhere north of Italy, certainly, was it as virulent as continually and in so many varieties as in the eastern Mediterranean. Unfortunately for the Crusaders, a person immune to one kind of malaria is not immune to all, and immunity to malaria is not long-lasting.

The Levant and the Holy Land were and in some areas still are malarial. The sickle-cell and beta-thalassemia genes, which bestow resistance to severe attacks of malaria, are today common among the indigenes in this part of the world, solidly complementing the testimony of Hippocrates and contemporaries that malaria has existed in the eastern Mediterranean for well over 2,000 years. Such genes are extremely rare among Europeans north of the Alps, proving that the worst kinds of malaria, specifically falciparum malaria, have seldom or only fitfully been active there. Each new batch of Crusaders from France, Germany, and England must have been fuel shoveled into the furnace of the malarial East. The experience of Zionist immigrants to Palestine early in our own century may be pertinent: In 1921, 42 percent of them developed malaria in the first six months after their arrival, and 64.7 percent during the first year.[50]

Malaria seems to have most profoundly influenced the Third Crusade, the one led briefly by the poor drowned Frederick Barbarossa, diffidently by the king of France, and enthusiastically by Richard the Lion-Heart of England. Disease of some ambiguous nature (with malingering as a possible secondary infection) persuaded the king of France to give up the Crusade early in the campaign, and it almost killed King Richard in his first months ashore in the Holy Land in 1191. His was "a severe illness to which the common people gave the name Arnoldia, which is produced by a change of climate working on the constitution." After he recovered, he led his army along the coastal plain, an especially malarial region, and then inland toward Jerusalem. This first advance stumbled during the heavy rains of November, often the worst month for malaria in Palestine, and halted in January "as sickness and want weakened many to such a degree that they could scarcely bear up." Later, Richard, though his army was melting away, had another try at Jerusalem, with about the same results. He fell sick again, this time, whispered the doctors, with an "acute semitertian" (defined today as a combination of tertian and quotidian malaria); he threw in his cards and sailed away in 1192. Thereafter, Christians gained access to the Holy Sepulchre only with Muslim permission.[51]

English soldiers do not necessarily stumble in the East, however. The British army fought very successfully in Palestine in World War I, largely because its leader, General Edmund H. H. Allenby, prepared for the campaign by reading all he could on the Levant, including the Crusader accounts, and by listening to his medical officers carefully. "He was," said one of his admirers, "as far as I know, the first Commander in that malarial region in which many armies have perished to understand the risk and to take measures accordingly."[52] Even so, the British Expeditionary Force in Palestine in 1918 had 8,500 primary cases of malaria between April and October, and over 20,000 cases in the remaining months.⁵³

Longevity was not characteristic of Crusaders. Frankish women apparently did better than Frankish men in the East, but they often failed to produce healthy children, or any children at all.⁵⁴ It is pertinent to mention that malaria is a great threat to pregnant women, often causing abortions, and it is very dangerous for children.⁵⁵ The inability of the women to produce guarantees of the future made all efforts in the present irrelevant. The Crusader states died like bowls of cut flowers.

In 1291, the Muslims took Acre, the last major Crusader stronghold in the Holy Land. The first effort of Western Europeans at founding large settlements outside of Europe was over.⁵⁶ The attempt, for all its ineffectuality, did deeply influence later and more successful ventures. The Crusades probably served to hasten the spread of such Eastern contributions to ship design and navigation as the sternpost rudder and the compass, both crucially important to future European expansion.⁵⁷ The Crusaders were the first Western Europeans to develop a taste for that Asian product, sugar – "a most precious product, very necessary for the use and health of mankind," said one of them – and they carried both the taste and the plant westward. First it traveled from Palestine to the islands of the Mediterranean and to Iberia, and then, as we shall see, to Madeira and the Canaries, and thence beyond the seams of Pangaea.⁵⁸

As better times returned to Western Europe at the end of the Dark Ages, population, wealth, and ambition surged upward for the first time in centuries, and a specifically European imperialism surged forward for the first time in history. The expansions of the Norse westward and the Crusaders to the Middle East were its most sensational – if almost completely ephemeral – manifestations. The settlements in Greenland and Vinland failed because they were simply too far away to be sustained by a population with the technological, economic, political, and epidemiological characteristics of the Norse. Even the church, the central institution of medieval Europe, could not effectively reach across the Mid-Atlantic Ridge. As far as we know, not a single priest ever visited Vinland, with the possible exception of the one who appears and disappears from our story in one tantalizing sentence: "Bishop Erik went in search of Vinland."[59] The consolations of Christianity barely reached even so far as Greenland. *Erik's Saga* tells us that the dead often were buried without proper services in that land where priests were nearly as rare as trees. The laity placed the body in the ground, permafrost permitting, and then drove a stake into the earth over the chest of the deceased. When a priest finally arrived, he pulled out the stake, poured holy water into the hole, and tardily carried out the proper ceremony.[60] Not until Europe had ships and navigation aids equal to the challenge of crossing the Atlantic where it was warm, if wide, would Europeans establish permanent settlements on the western side of the Mid-Atlantic Ridge.

In the East, the Europeans tried to plant colonies among dense populations of high culture. Frankish imperialism had its decades of triumph, and the Crusader presence in the Holy Land lasted as long as or longer than European overlords held sway in Algeria and India in our era. But the Crusader states ultimately failed. Not even Latin Christian fanaticism could cancel out the numerical advantage of the indigenous peoples. Europeans might be able to temporarily conquer, but never permanently depose, the more numerous native populations, especially with the disease environment working against the invaders.

Iceland, where the European presence goes back well over a thousand years, is the one exception to the dismal record of European overseas imperialism in the Middle

Ages. Iceland is closer to Europe than Greenland or Vinland, and its climate is more moderate than that of Greenland. Furthermore – and this is as important as it is simple – Iceland had no Skraelings, no Greek Christians, no Muslims, nobody with the advantages of prior occupation and more nearly perfect physical and cultural adjustment to the environment, no human inhabitants but a handful of Irish anchorites, as easily deposed as the gulls and puffins.

4

❧～❧

The Fortunate Isles

THE FORTUNATE ISLES OR THE ISLES OF THE BLESSED "abound in fruit and birds of every kind . . . These islands, however are greatly annoyed by the putrefying bodies of monsters, which are constantly thrown up by the sea."
—*The Natural History of Pliny* (first century A.D.)

IN 1291, THE CRUSADERS LOST ACRE, the last Christian stronghold in the Holy Land, and, coincidentally, two Genoese brothers, Vadino and Ugolino Vivaldi, sailed out past Gibraltar into the Atlantic with the intention of circling Africa. Not surprisingly, they were never seen again. Their voyage, in and of itself, had little significance, but its implications were of transcendent importance. The Vivaldi venture was the beginning of the most important new development for the human and many other species since the Neolithic Revolution. European sailors and imperialists were now ready to try their luck in the latitudes where the Atlantic was warm, if deplorably wide.

The Vivaldis may not have died at sea or on the coast of Africa. Even in their unseaworthy craft they could have reached the Canaries, Madeiras, or Azores, all within a week or two of Gibraltar, given favorable weather. The Canaries, certainly, and the other two groups, possibly, had been known to the Romans and other sailors of the ancient Mediterranean world, and named by them the Fortunate Isles. However, Europe forgot or at least misplaced them during the centuries of Rome's decline and the Middle Ages. The sailors of Europe's Renaissance discovered or rediscovered them and made them laboratories for a new kind of European imperialism. The transoceanic empires of Charles V, Louis XIV, and Queen Victoria had their prototypes in the colonies on the islands of the eastern Atlantic.

In 1336, Lanzarote Malocello, following in the Vivaldis' wake, came upon the most northeasterly of the Canary Islands, which still bears his name, Lanzarote, where he settled and was killed by the native Canarians, the Guanches, some years later. During the fourteenth century, the Italians, Portuguese, Majorcans, Catalans, and, no doubt, other Europeans sent individual ships and expeditions to the Canaries and to the other archipelagos opposite Iberia and Morocco, the Madeiras and Azores, as they were discovered.[1]

Figure 4. The Atlantic, the first ocean learned by the *marinheiros*. Reproduced by permission from Francis M. Rogers, *Atlantic Islanders of the Azores and Madeiras* (North Quincy, Mass.: The Christopher Publishing House, 1979), endpapers.

The islands' heights are often craggy and rasp-edged, but there are broad areas of richly fertile volcanic soil. The all-enveloping ocean supplies most of that fertile soil with a plenitude of rain, although some of the less mountainous islands are parched, particularly the most easterly Canaries, which are too low to comb the moisture out of the trade winds. The temperature in the Azores is characteristically cool, and temperatures in the Madeiras and the Canaries are more moderate than their latitude would suggest they should be. The cold Canary Current and the trade winds render them Mediterranean in temperature and in the general nature of their flora and fauna as well, though many of their species are unique, as are oceanic island organisms everywhere. Geographers place both these island groups, though of Saharan latitude, in the same floral region with the Mediterranean littoral far to the north.[2] Here were lands only a few days' voyage from Europe, lands temperate and potentially fruitful, unlike the islands of the far North Atlantic, lands, it appeared, less dauntingly defended than Vinland or the Levant. There were no Azoreans nor Madeirans whatever to resist conquest, and the Guanches were infidels without armor, "nor any knowledge of warfare, and they can receive no help from their neighbors."[3]

We shall look at the histories of these archipelagos in ascending order of their degrees of influence on the course of European imperialism, beginning with the Azores. At first, these nine mid-Atlantic islands were no more than signposts in the deep – sail east from here to reach Portugal – and welcome places to water and revictual on the voyage home from the Canaries or West Africa. Soon the Europeans were altering them, "Europeanizing" them, for the sake of the transient mariners, "seeding" them with livestock, as they later did other islands and newly found mainlands. Sheep usually are too meek and mild to survive alone, but the Azores had neither large carnivores nor, in all probability, diseases to prey on them, and so passing ships put some rams and ewes ashore, and feral herds were grazing there at least as early as 1439. They apparently preceded the earliest permanent human settlers, because 1439 was the year that the king of Portugal made his first grant of the right to settle in the Azores.[4] The sheep, and then cattle and goats, found the vegetation of the slopes and valleys of the larger Azores nourishing and the environment salubrious. They reproduced enthusiastically.

European attempts to introduce crops marketable on the mainland turned up winners in wheat, shipped to Portugal by the end of the 1440s, and woad, a dye plant brought from France that also became a staple export; but the great money-maker of the age, sugar, languished in the Azores' cool winds. The archipelago's significance in history is not as a source of wealth, but as a way station on the routes to and from colonies that did grow money-makers.[5]

The Madeiran group consists of two islands – Madeira, a bit less than sixty kilometers in its longest dimension, and Porto Santo, only one-fifth as long – plus a few barren islets.[6] Both islands are rugged, Madeira much more so, rising to peaks of almost 2,000 meters. Its topography has been described as being like that of the skeleton of a reptile: a high backbone running the length of the island, with sharp ridges – the ribs – running off at right angles. There is little that can be called coastal plain, and some of the ridges terminate in cliffs that are among the highest in the world. Most of Madeira's cattle are born and raised, live and die, in sheds from which they are rarely allowed to emerge to graze for fear that they will slip and fall off their meadows.[7]

Porto Santo is the lower in altitude, as well as the smaller, of the two islands, and clouds often pass over without dropping any rain. Historically it has been more important for its livestock than for crops. Madeira's high country deflects the ocean winds to heights where their vapors condense, and the island has enough rain for cultivation of its rich soils, although the water runs off rapidly to be lost in the sea unless its plunge is interrupted. In the last eight centuries, fortunes have been made time and again in warm, fertile, well-watered colonies (Española, Brazil, Martinique, Mauritius, Hawaii, etc.) by raising tropical crops in demand in Europe. Crete, Cyprus, and Rhodes were the first of these in the Mediterranean. Madeira was the first in the Atlantic, and the bellwether for all those that came later.[8]

In the 1420s, the first settlers arrived from Portugal: fewer than a hundred plebeians and lower-rank nobles, all looking for fresh lands to increase their prospects for wealth and social advancement. Madeira and Porto Santo were virgin in the purest sense of the word: They were uninhabited and bore no mark of human occupation, Paleolithic or Neolithic or post-Neolithic. The newcomers set to work to rationalize landscape, flora, and fauna previously unaffected by anything but the blind forces of nature. Bartholomeu Perestrello, captain donatory of Porto Santo (and, incidentally, future father-in-law of Columbus), set loose on his island where the likes of such had never lived before a female rabbit and her offspring; she had given birth on the voyage from Europe. The rabbits reproduced at a villainous rate and "overspread the land, so that our men could sow nothing that was not destroyed by them." The settlers took up arms against these rivals and killed great numbers, but in the absence of local predators and disease organisms adapted to these quadrupeds, the death rate continued to lag far behind the birth rate. The humans were obliged to leave and go to Madeira, defeated in their initial attempt at colonization not by primeval nature but by their own ecological ignorance. Later they tried again and succeeded, but, even so, in 1455 it was noted that Porto Santo still swarmed with "countless rabbits." Europeans would make such mistakes over and over again, setting off population explosions of burros in Fuerteventura in the Canaries, rats in Virginia in North America, and rabbits in Australia.[9]

The rabbits of Porto Santo, if their history is anything like that of rabbits in similar circumstances elsewhere, ate not only the crops but just about everything gnawable. Native plants must have disappeared, and native animals must have died out for lack of food and cover. Wind and rain erosion followed, and then the empty econiches were occupied by weeds and animals from the continents. The Porto Santo of 1400 is as lost to us as is the world before the Noachian flood.

When Europeans first came upon Madeira, it was an island without "a foot of ground that was not entirely covered with great trees." Hence the name they gave it: *Madeira,* meaning wood. The timber proved to be a valuable export, but its forests were really too much of a good thing; the settlers wanted to clear space for themselves and their crops and animals faster than was being accomplished by commercial cutting. Therefore, they set a fire or fires, and the resulting conflagration almost burned them right off the island. At least one group "was forced, with all the men, women and children, to flee its fury and to take refuge in the sea, where they remained up to their necks in the water, and without food or drink for two days and two nights." The story goes that the fire lasted seven years, which perhaps we can interpret as meaning that the settlers continued burning off forests for that length of time.[10] One wonders about Madeira as one wonders about Porto Santo: What was it like in its primeval state? It seems probable that some Madeiran species, not adapted in such a climate to surviving holocausts, were lost to the world forever and that many of her present "native" species, popularly believed to have been present there forever, really arrived and spread after the great burn-off of the early fifteenth century.

At first the Madeira colonists had to scramble and scrape for a living, eating the native pigeons, so unused to humans they could be caught by hand, and exporting the wood of the native cedar and yew, and dragon's blood, a dye made from the resin of a local tree, but the island contained nothing precious enough to support the newcomers in the styles to which they aspired.[11] The path to prosperity lay in adding to the existing flora and fauna plants and animals that were in demand, in one form or another, in the ports of Portugal and beyond. Ideally, the Madeirans would find something in great demand that they could produce cheaper, better, faster, and in greater quantity than anybody else. They experimented, and soon pigs and cattle, some of them feral, were rooting and cropping there and, incidentally, making sure that Madeira's forests would never recover from the great fire. Honeybees, almost surely introduced rather than indigenous, were producing wax and honey for the colonists by the 1450s. Wheat from the mainland and grapevines brought all the way from Crete did well in the rich soil and warm sun, and they found good markets in Portugal.[12]

These products were enough to maintain the colonists at an Azorean level of prosperity, but they had not ventured into the Atlantic to remain peasants and down-at-the-heel aristocrats. They needed a crop as good as gold; they needed sugar. Porto Santo was too dry for sugarcane, but Madeira seemed ideal, and in all likelihood sugarcane was growing there before the middle of the fifteenth century. The experiment must have proved encouraging, for in 1452 the Portuguese crown authorized the first water-driven sugar mill on the island.

The first of a number of Atlantic successes, explosive successes, in the production of sugar followed. By 1455, Madeira's annual output was over 6,000 arrobas (an arroba equals eleven to twelve kilograms), and the first sugar was exported from the island to Bristol, England, the next year. By 1472, the island was producing more than 15,000 arrobas annually, and in the first decades of the next century about 140,000 arrobas per year. Scores and scores of ships were carrying her sugar to England, France, Flanders, Rome, Genoa, Venice, and even as far as Constantinople. Madeirans had plumped solidly for monoculture, had chosen to devote themselves utterly to pandering to Europe's sweet tooth.[13]

The population grew along with the sugar production. In 1455, Madeira had 800 people, and at the end of the century 17,000 to 20,000 or more, including at least 2,000 slaves.[14] These people transformed Madeira in a few decades into the world's greatest producer of what was considered an important medication and what was and is, for practical purposes, an addictive substance: sugar. Not even tobacco, the next quasi-addictive substance to come along and reshape the world, would exceed it as a money-maker.[15]

Raising sugar or wheat or what have you on Madeira is, in the words of T. Bentley Duncan, "a truely penitential labor."[16] The original preparation of the land for farming, the clearing and grubbing of the primordial growth, burned or not, must have been an Augean task. Much of the land was too steep for normal practices of cultivation and had to be terraced. Most back-breaking of all the tasks, and the most dangerous, was the creation of a vast and complicated irrigation system to bring water from the windy and sodden uplands to the cultivated fields far below: "Pharaoh had his pyramids; the Madeirense their man-made water courses."[17]

They are the *levadas,* a network of conduits and tunnels, some of mortar and some carved out of the living rock, that gird the mountains, collect the rainwater, and guide it along knife-edged ridges and yawning gorges down to the farms and gardens. Today its length is estimated at 700 kilometers, 700 kilometers on an island that is only 60 kilometers long.[18] The tale of its beginnings is obscure; apparently the first primitive sections were roughed out as early as the 1420s and 1430s. In 1461, the lord proprietor of Madeira appointed two water stewards, which suggests the *levada* network was already of considerable size as the sugar revolution began, an economic explosion that must have further expanded the system.[19]

Slaves are not unequivocally mentioned in the Madeiran record until 1466, but they must have been imported years before to do the initial work of remaking the island according to European desires. That work continued for generations as the plantations expanded and the demand for water multiplied. At the same time, there was a growing demand for workers to cultivate, harvest, and mill the sugarcane. By the end of the century, slaves were a subject of constant reference in the documents of the island, and we can discern in Madeira the basic pattern for plantation colonies for generations to come.[20]

Portugal's involvement in the slave trade along Africa's Atlantic coast did not begin until the 1440s; so Madeira's first slaves were in all probability not black. We can make an educated guess that some were Berbers, some Portuguese Christians who acted too much like Moors, some new Christians who acted too much like Jews, plus a few other marginal people. It seems probable that many of them, a plurality if not a majority, were Guanches, natives of the Canary Islands, who entered into the stream of European slavery some years before Madeira was first settled. There seem to have been captives from the Canaries in Majorca, for instance, as early as 1342. Their first appearance in Madeira is not recorded, but they must have been there early. Many of them were from islands nearly as rugged as Madeira, and they were famous for their nimbleness; they must have been very useful in chipping out *levadas* on the sheer cliffs. By the end of the fifteenth century there were so many of them on Madeira that the Madeirans were calling for regulations to limit their numbers. They were a dangerous lot.[21] The Atlantic slave trade, which we always think of as exclusively black, was in its very earliest beginnings largely white or, to be more precise as to complexion, "olive-colored . . . the color of sunburned peasants," that is, the color of the people of the Canary Islands.[22]

The Canary archipelago of seven islands is the largest in area, highest in altitude, and most complex biogeographically of the three archipelagos under consideration. (In fact, it is higher and has a greater variety of flora and fauna that even Iceland, though it is considerably smaller in area.) It lies nearer to the mainland – only about 100 kilometers off shore at the closest – than either the Azores or Madeiras, and it was the only one of the three with human inhabitants before the coming of the Europeans. The latitude is tropical and the climate hot, but not oppressive, thanks to the ocean and its winds. The two eastern islands are dry, but the others are relatively well watered because of their elevation. Tenerife and Gran Canaria, the highest and largest of these, have topographies rather like that of Madeira – good terrain for ambush, for lightning raids and swift escapes – and had the largest and fiercest populations of indigenes.[23]

As we have already seen, Renaissance Europeans went to the Canaries earlier than to the other mid-Atlantic islands, possibly as early as the 1290s and certainly no later than the first decades of the 1300s. There were several things on these islands the Europeans could gather and take back home to sell at a profit: skins and tallow from the Guanches' large herds of livestock; orchil, a dyestuff made from a kind of Canarian moss; and people – the Guanches themselves. There was a good market for people, especially after the Black Death swept away so many of southern Europe's peasants.

The Guanches deserve more attention than they have received. They were, with the possible exception of the Arawaks of the West Indies, the first people to be driven over the cliff of extinction by modern imperialism. Their ancestors had come to the Canaries from the African mainland over a period of many centuries, starting no earlier than the second millennium B.C., and the last arriving no later than the first centuries A.D. These people were seagoing contemporaries of the great Polynesian navigators, but unlike the Polynesians, they forgot whatever they knew of seamanship after their first salt-water venture. When the Europeans arrived, the Guanches had very few or, more likely, no boats whatever – certainly none capable of voyages to the mainland.[24] Like Darwin's Galapagos finches, they were in all likelihood descendants from a few ancestors and had evolved independently on their separate islands. The finches survived the coming of the Europeans and afforded biologists a great opportunity to learn about divergent biological evolution. The Guanches would have provided anthropologists with a classic example of divergent cultural evolution if they, too, had survived.

We know only a little about them. According to early accounts, some were rugged and some gracile, some swarthy and some light. Most were clearly related to the Berbers of the adjacent mainland. Tissue taken from their dried mummies informs us that none or very few of them had type B blood. In this characteristic they were like Amerindians, Aborigines, Polynesians, and a number of other historically isolated peoples.[25] When they arrived in the Canaries, the only animals present, it seems, were birds, rodents, lizards, and turtles or tortoises; and the islands' flora, though generally like that of the Mediterranean region, was similar in the mass of its specific details only to that of Madeira.[26]

The Guanches were not exceptions to the rule that migrating humans bring their plants and animals with them, and thereby tend to homogenize the world's biota. They were heirs to the Middle Eastern Neolithic Revolution, at least in part, and they brought from the mainland barley, probably wheat, beans and peas, as well as goats, pigs, dogs, and probably sheep. They had no cattle or horses. They also carried with them the knowledge of how to make pottery, but they did not spin or weave or make metal tools, weapons, or decorations. The Canaries had no deposits of metallic ores; so if the Guanches knew anything of metallurgy on arrival, they soon forgot it. Their lack of metal weapons was one of the several fatal gaps in the Guanche culture.[27]

The rude process of European conquest began in 1402, a date we might take as the birth year of modern European imperialism. The Moors still held southern Iberia, and the Ottoman Turks were advancing in the Balkans, but Europe had begun to march – or rather to sail – to world hegemony.

An estimated 80,000 Guanches stood in opposition to this initial sally, like pickets deployed out in front of trenches held by Aztecs, Zapotecs, Araucanians, Iroquois, Australian Aborigines, Maori, Fijians, Hawaiians, Aleuts, and Zunis.[28]

In 1402, a French expedition under Castilian auspices went ashore on the smaller of the two eastern Canaries, Lanzarote. Within a few months the Europeans won the island, in spite of their own internal squabbles and the resistance of about 300 natives. The invaders now had a secure base in the archipelago. Two other islands with small populations fell within the next few years.[29]

The Portuguese coveted the Canaries, as did the French and Spanish. Between 1415 and 1466, Portugal launched a number of minor assaults and at least four major assaults on the archipelago, including an expedition of 2,500 infantry and 120 horses in 1424. All failed, but these expeditions established a connection between Portuguese Madeira and the Canaries in the decades when colonists were shaping the former into a device for producing sugar. These expeditions almost always stopped at Madeira on their way to the Canaries, and when they returned to Portugal, they carried Guanche captives as part of the loot. At least some of the captives, we can assume, went to Madeira, the hungriest market for slaves in the environs of Portugal, where they applied their mountain-goat skills to the task of creating the *levadas*.[30]

While the Portuguese and their slaves were transforming Madeira, the Spanish were struggling to finish their conquest of the Canaries, a task they had taken over from the French knights. As of 1475 or so they had reduced the number of islands still under Guanche control to three: La Palma, Tenerife, and Gran Canaria. The first was one of the smaller of the Canaries, with only a few hundred fighting men, and would inevitably share the fate of the other two. On Tenerife, the largest of these islands, and on Gran

Plate 1. Two Guanches as remembered – or imagined – at the end of the sixteenth century. Reproduced by permission from Leonardo Torriani, *Die Kanarischen Inseln und Ihre Urbewohner* [1590], ed. Dominik Wolfel (Leipzig: K. F. Koehler, 1940), Pl. X.

Plate 2. A Flemish version of the machine with which the *marinheiros* changed the world: the three-masted ship, square-rigged on the foremast and mainmast, lateen-rigged on the mizzenmast, with a smaller vessel in sight. Reproduced by permission from H. Arthur Klein, *Graphic Worlds of Peter Bruegel the Elder* (New York: Dover, 1963), 63.

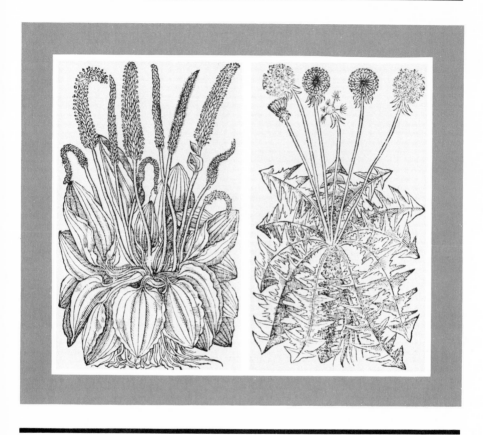

Plate 3. A late-sixteenth-century print of an Old World plantain, soon to be called "Englishman's foot" by North American Indians. From John Gerard, *The Herball or General Historie of Plants* [1597] (Amsterdam: Walter J. Johnson, 1974), Vol. I, 228.

Plate 4. The dandelion of the European Renaissance, now found in all the Neo-Europes. From John Gerard, *The Herball or General Historie of Plants* [1597] (Amsterdam: Walter J. Johnson, 1974), Vol. I, 338.

Plate 5. A twentieth-century Texas longhorn, certainly better fed than his feral ancestors, but in all likelihood just as cranky. Reproduced by permission from Baker Texas History Center, University of Texas.

Plate 6. Getting horses across the oceans required special equipment and special treatment, and still the death rate was high. Reproduced by permission from Robert M. Denhardt, *The Horse of the Americas* (Norman: University of Oklahoma Press, 1975).

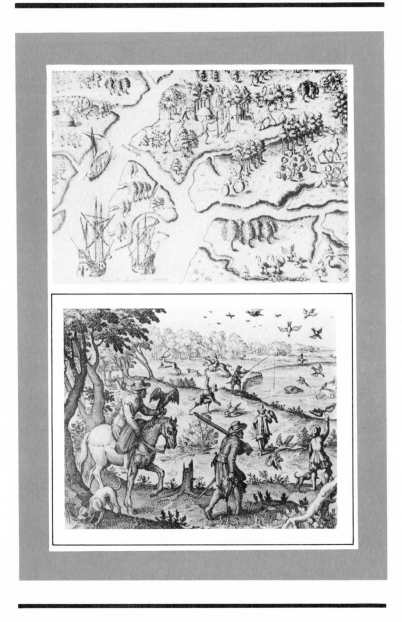

Plate 7. The French in Florida in the late sixteenth century. From *Discovering the New World, Based on the Works of Theodore de Bry*, ed. Michael Alexander (New York: Harper & Row, 1976), 21.

Plate 8. Englishmen and animals in Virginia in the early seventeenth century. From *Discovering the New World, Based on the Works of Theodore de Bry*, ed. Michael Alexander (New York: Harper & Row, 1976), 202.

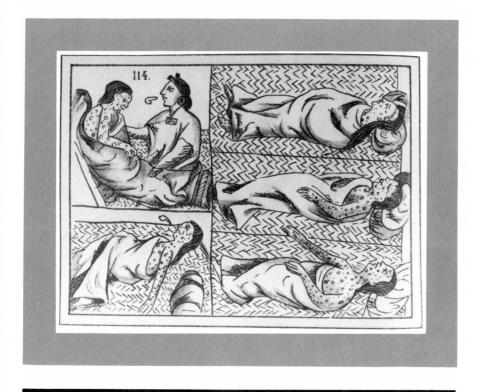

Plate 9. Aztec smallpox victims in the sixteenth century. From *Historia De Las Cosas de Nueva Espana*, Volume 4, Book 12, Lam. cliii, plate 114. Used with the permission of the Peabody Museum of Archaeology and Ethnology, Harvard University.

Plate 10. Buenos Aires in the late sixteenth century, a troubled settlement. Reproduced by permission from Ulrich Schmidel, *Wahrhafftige Historien einer wunderbaren Schiffart* [1602] (Graz: Akademische Druck- u. Verlagsanstalt, 1962), 17.

Plate 11. Indians and fauna of southern South America, as they struck the European Renaissance sensibility. Reproduced by permission from Ulrich Schmidel, *Wahrhafftige Historien einer wunderbaren Schiffart* [1602] (Graz: Akademische Druck- u. Verlagsanstalt, 1962), 24.

Plate 12. An Aborigine of the early nineteenth century, sketched with more sympathy than most white artists would extend to native Australians later. From Robert Hughes, *The Art of Australia* (Harmondsworth: Penguin Books, 1970), 43.

Plate 13. A family of Aborigines, still intact.

Plate 14. A sculptured tobacco pipe, an example of pre-Columbian art by a craftsman of the Mississippian culture. From Frederick J. Dockstader, *Indian Art in North America* (Greenwich, Conn.: New York Graphic Society, n.d.), 48.

Plate 15. An eighteenth-century Maori seacraft, probably quite like those that first brought Polynesians to New Zealand. From *The Endeavour Journal of Joseph Banks, 1768–1771*, ed. J. C. Beaglehole (Sydney: Angus & Robertson, 1962), Vol. II, Pl. 3.

Plate 16. A Maori as seen by an artist who sailed with Captain Cook. From *The Endeavour Journal of Joseph Banks, 1768–1771*, ed. J. C. Beaglehole (Sydney: Angus & Robertson, 1962), Vol. II, Pl. 6.

Plate 17. A sketch of one of the first New Zealanders ever to see a white man. From *The Endeavour Journal of Joseph Banks, 1768–1771*, ed. J. C. Beaglehole (Sydney: Angus & Robertson, 1962), Vol. II, Pl. 7. Plates 15, 16, and 17 are reproduced by permission from the Mitchell Library, State Library of New South Wales, Australia.

Plate 18. A Maori of the 1820s in his prime. From Auguste Earle, *Narrative of a Residence in New Zealand. Journal of a Residence in Tristan da Cunha*, ed. E. H. McCormick (Oxford: Clarendon Press, 1966), Pl. 12.

Plate 19. An Argentinian of the early nineteenth century, with bolas twirling, in pursuit of a rhea. From Emeric E. Vidal, *Picturesque Illustrations of Buenos Ayres and Montevideo* [1820] (Buenos Aires: Presas del Establecimiento Grafico F. G. Prufomo y hno., 1943), 50.

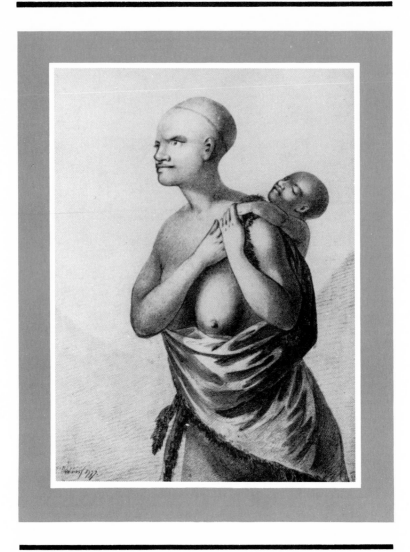

Plate 20. A mother and child of an extinct branch of humanity, the Tasmanians. Reproduced by permission from *The Journals of Captain James Cook on His Voyages of Discovery, 1776–1780*, ed. J. C. Beaglehole (Cambridge: Hakluyt Society, 1967), Vol. III, Part I, Pl. 12B. Reproduced by permission of the British Library [Add MS 15513, 5].

Canaria, the third largest, lived thousands of warriors. At the beginning of the century the French had said that the people of Tenerife were the hardiest of the Guanches: "they have never been run down or carried into servitude like those of the other islands." Their Gran Canarian brethren were so fierce that they earned their island its name, bestowed not for its size but for their valor and fighting skill.[31]

Europeans had several tries at invading Gran Canaria during the first three-quarters of the fifteenth century and always ended by taking to their boats, usually in a downpour of missiles. Then, in 1478, the struggle for the island and for the Canaries entered a new phase. Ferdinand and Isabella of Spain, covetous of the entire archipelago, sent to Gran Canaria an expedition of hundreds of soldiers with cannon, horses, and all the paraphernalia of European warfare. The campaign for the island lasted five bloody years. The Spanish quickly won the lowlands, but could not dig the Guanches out of the high country. The latter practiced guerrilla tactics and even made an alliance with the Portuguese, who sent some troops ashore and tried to cut the Spaniards' supply lines. Spain, however, made peace with Portugal, and although the Guanches could win skirmishes, they had no chance of winning a long war. The struggle ended in April of 1483, when 600 Guanche men, 1,500 women, and a number of children, besieged in the mountains, surrendered to the *conquistador* of Gran Canaria, Pedro de Vera. Friar Abreu de Galindo, the sixteenth-century historian of Gran Canaria, said that it cost more in labor and blood to reduce that island to the Catholic faith than any of the other Canaries, even Tenerife.[32]

Then only La Palma, the second smallest of the Canaries, and Tenerife, the largest, remained free. Alonso de Lugo invaded La Palma in September of 1492 and, astutely mixing military force, persuasion, and treachery, attained victory in the following spring.[33] Tenerife, a tougher nut to crack, took another three years.

The first generation of would-be conquerors of the Canary Islands had, by and large, avoided Tenerife. Its defenders, numerous and bellicose, embellished their reputation by pushing one set of invaders into the sea in the 1460s and another about 1490. Then, in 1494, Alonso de Lugo landed with 1,000 infantry, 120 horsemen, and artillery. It was an imposing army, but the Guanches ambushed a large part of it in the highlands, where they killed hundreds of the invaders. The battlefield was afterward called *La Matanza de Acentejo,* the massacre of Acentejo. Lugo retreated to La Palma to regroup, reconsider, and tend to his wounds.[34]

Lugo, a Spaniard of the same steel as Cortés and Pizarro, returned in November of 1495 with 1,100 men and seventy horses, plus firearms. Ten months later, the Guanches, hungry, appalled at the depth of the resources the invaders could draw on, and drastically depleted in numbers, surrendered. The Stone Age breathed its last in the Canaries at the end of September 1496.[35]

Was the Guanche defeat inevitable? In the long run, of course. But what about the short run? Was it preordained that the Spaniards would conquer the Canaries in less than twenty years once they decided to really try? It seems so now because of so many similar conquests in the following four centuries, but we are not talking here of Maxim guns versus spears, nor even of muskets versus spears. As in the European invasions of Mexico and Peru, the war for the Canaries was a matter of hundreds of Europeans with a few inaccurate, slow-firing, often misfiring guns, a larger number of crossbows, and lots of metal swords, axes, and lances versus what were at the start thousands of courageous warriors armed with weapons that, though made of mere wood and stone, were murderous enough.

The Guanches were fierce and numerous, and their

techniques of warfare were very effective in the extensive highlands of the larger islands, where they always took refuge when the invaders won the first battles. George Glas, an eighteenth-century British resident in the Canaries and translator of a history of the conquest of Gran Canaria, examined the terrain and marveled that the Spaniards ever won. All the islands, except Lanzarote and Fuerteventura,

are so full of deep narrow vallies, or gullies, high rugged mountains, and narrow difficult passes that a body of men cannot march into any of them the distance of a league from the shore, before they come to places where a hundred men may easily baffle the efforts of a thousand. This being the case, where could shipping enough be found to transport a sufficient number of troops to subdue such a people and in a country so strongly fortified by nature?[36]

No explanation can be found in the character of the defenders. The French, at the beginning of the conquest of the archipelago, noted that the Guanches "were tall and formidable" and that their Christian captors often were obliged to kill them out of self-defense. The Guanches' only projectile weapons were stones, but they made good use of them, especially in the mountains, where they usually arranged to hold the high ground. They hurled their stones, testified the invaders, with the velocity and accuracy of crossbows, "breaking a shield in pieces, and the arm behind it." And while the Europeans bumbled slowly among the crags and ravines, the defenders scrambled about with miraculous speed, as if they had acquired their nimbleness "in sucking the milk from their mother's breasts."[37]

Even communicating, much less marching, across the broken and cratered interiors of the Canaries was and is challenging. This probably explains how it was that the Guanches, most clearly those of Gomera, devised an actual articulated language, not just a simple system of signals, of very loud, finger-aided whistles. This enabled them to communicate across wide canyons and, it is likely, was of great help in the tumult of battle.[38]

The Guanche chiefs could whistle up armies of many hundreds, if not thousands, of men. In the middle of the fifteenth century, Gomes Eannes de Azurara estimated Tenerife to have 6,000 fighting men and Gran Canaria 5,000. His estimates for the other Canaries were much lower, but then most of these islands are much smaller or had already gone though the trauma of conquest.[39] No one, of course, actually counted the Guanches, and Azurara certainly was not of a statistical bent, at least not by our standards, but neither was he a fool. The natives of the Canaries were grain farmers, with a steady supply of animal protein and fats from shellfish and large herds of livestock, and they lived on large islands "abundant of all things necessary for the life of man."[40] We should not be surprised to be told that there were thousands of them.

Because of the scarcity of their speculation capital and their available shipping, the Spaniards could bring to bear in the Canaries armies of only a thousand or so, at maximum. Yet they did win, as they would in so many lands outside of Europe in the next century. Their advantages must have been considerable. What were they? Superior weaponry has already been mentioned, but we have decided that that is not a sufficient answer in and of itself, especially in the early stages of European expansion. Supremacy at sea gave the Europeans a sure means of retreat and access to greater resources than the Guanches, but just how available would those resources have been if Guanche resistance had been more effective? Lugo did find backing for his second invasion of Tenerife, but would he have found support for a third or a fourth, or a tenth? Is there any reason to believe that Europe would have been more patient with defeat in the Canaries than it had been in the Holy Land or than it would be in tropical Africa, where repeated failures would discourage invasions until the latter part of the nineteenth century?

Did the Europeans have allies we have not yet given credit? Were the Guanches weaker than we have noted? We have to realize that although the Guanches were numerous, they were never united. They lived on seven islands and lacked even the rudiments of seamanship. They spoke a number of different dialects and possibly different languages. The invaders were able to recruit natives from one island to join them in fighting the natives of another. On Tenerife, the invaders were even able to recruit allies from one part of the island against the people of the rest of the island.[41]

Disunited Guanches found it difficult to defend themselves against the Europeans, who took advantage of superiority at sea to wage, for all practical purposes, a war of attrition, that is, to raid the Canaries for slaves. We do not know how many people were taken off to the slave marts, but apparently the number was considerable. In 1385 and 1393, slavers seized at least several hundred Guanches from Lanzarote, a large and initially well-populated island, and put them up for sale in Spain, leaving only 300 behind to defend the island against the French in 1402.[42] Other island populations also suffered similarly, but Gran Canaria and Tenerife were probably too populous to be critically weakened by the slavers. Abreu de Galindo, however, offered the puzzling information that women far outnumbered men on Gran Canaria before the conquest, an imbalance that could have existed only if something were killing or taking off many more males than females. This is commonly the sexual bias of war, and often of slavers collecting workers for plantation labor.[43]

The success of the slavers was part and parcel of what may have appeared to the Guanches to be a general superiority of the Europeans. Their metals, their gear, their gods, and their very selves must have fascinated the indigenous Canarians and tended to sap their resolve to reject utterly – and violently, if necessary – all contact with these dangerous aliens. On Tenerife, the often inhospitable Guanches allowed the Spaniards to build a trading post, and there it remained, a source of miracles and puzzlement, until the Europeans used up all their welcome in one swoop by hanging several of the locals.[44] The people of Gran Canaria learned the wisdom of treating gold and silver with contempt, but they could not resist iron, which they beat into fishhooks. The Guanches must have wondered if superior fishhooks were an indication of superior gods, so to speak. On the island of Hierro, said the indigenes after their conquest, a wizard named Yone had lived who predicted that after his death and when his bones had crumbled into dust, a god called Eraoranzan would come in a white house, and they should not fight him or run from him but should worship him. The Europeans did take the island with little struggle.[45] The people of Gomera told of a Christian priest who had come to their islands before the conquest and baptized many of them, and who had persuaded them to accept conquest without resisting. The Gomerans, too, succumbed with a minimum of violence, although they did manage a revolt later with Portuguese help.[46]

The most famous example of – what should we call it? – cultural disorientation or reorientation of the Guanches prior to the conquest occurred on Tenerife. According to oral tradition, in 1400 or so the Virgin Mary appeared to Guanche shepherds of Guimar, a part of Tenerife. She left behind an image of herself, the statue ever after called Our Lady of Candelaria, which was involved in a number of miracles in the Canaries until its destruction in a flood in the nineteenth century. Around the hem of her mantle and on her belt were many letters spelling words that no one has ever been able to decipher satisfactorily: TIEPFSEPMERI, EAFM, IRENINI, FMEAREI. The thought occurs to the unbeliever that these words, if not necessarily the statue, were the products of a Guanche who had had sufficient contact with Europeans to realize the power, the *mana,* of the alphabet, but who remained illiterate. Our Lady's first celebrant on Tenerife, long before its conquest, was a Guanche who as a boy had been kidnapped by Europeans and trained as an interpreter. He received baptism and the name Anton Guanche, and then he escaped back to Tenerife, where he attended Our Lady of Candelaria for the rest of his life.[47]

Whatever may be the full truth about Our Lady of Candelaria, it is apparent that Christianity in some form existed in Guimar for several generations before the conquest. There the Europeans found friends, while the rest of the island was hostile, and there the invaders found warriors to fight alongside them in the final subjugation of Tenerife.[48]

The most important allies of the invaders were not, however, native Canarians. The Europeans brought with them fellow life forms, their extended family of plants, animals, and microlife – descendants, most of them, of organisms that humans had first domesticated or that had first adapted to living with humans in the hearthlands of Old World civilization. In addition, no doubt, there were new acquisitions brought to the Canaries by slavers and traders working the African coast.

The Europeans crossed the waters to the Canaries, as to the Azores and Madeiras, with a scaled-down, simplified version of the biota of Western Europe, in this case of the Mediterranean littoral. This portmanteau biota was crucial to their successes in these island groups and to their successes – and failures – later and elsewhere. Where it "worked," where enough of its members prospered and propagated to create versions of Europe, however incomplete and distorted, Europeans themselves prospered and propagated.

The organisms that had "worked" on such Mediterranean islands as Crete, Sicily, and Majorca did so in the Canaries as well. The most obvious example is the horse. Guanches were intimately familiar with smaller livestock – goats and pigs, for instance – but they had never seen any animals as large as horses, nor any that carried men on their backs and obeyed orders in battle. Soldiers on horseback played a vital role in the conquest of the last two of the Canaries to fall, and probably the others as well. The European centaur was worth a score and more of his pedestrian brethren. For example, consider the story of Lope Fernández de la Guerra, a knight, and mounted, of course. He went out on reconnaissance alone in the final stages of the Tenerife campaign and found himself ambushed by fifteen or twenty Guanches. An infantryman would have been swarmed over and killed instantly, but Lope Fernández

put spurs to his horse, as the spot where he was appeared to be dangerous, until he reached an open space. There he turned with his horse, so as not to show cowardice, and having knocked over six of the natives, the rest fled towards the woods. Feeling that he had done little unless he got one of them into his hands to make him disclose the designs and intentions of the others, he got in front of a fugitive in a narrow place, got hold of him by making the horse knock him down, secured him, and brought him into the camp, where Lope Fernández was well received.[49]

One hopes the horse was welcomed, too, and got a good rubdown and an extra half hour in the meadow.

The Guanches sensibly surrendered all flat and open country (and therefore, one might guess, most of their grain fields and their flocks) as soon as they learned of the power of horsemen. "It was the mounted soldiers," said Friar Alonso de Espinosa, historian of Tenerife, "that the natives feared most, and this was the main strength of their enemies."[50]

Christian chroniclers paid much less attention to the other members of the portmanteau biota than to horses and their riders. We, who are more interested in, say, rabbit propagation than in manifestations of Our Lady of Candelaria, must resort to inference from scanty information, inferences suggested by what we know of the influence of later European arrivals on other remote islands – dodos plunging to extinction on Mauritius, mongoose swarmings in Hawaii, epidemics raging among the native peoples of Samoa, and so forth. In these islands, and surely in the Canaries, too, the coming of Europeans set off wild ecological oscillations.[51]

As noted earlier, the number of women on Gran Canaria unnaturally exceeded that of men before the conquest, for whatever reason and with whatever influence on family structure and birth and death rates we cannot be sure. Abreu de Galindo reported that a few years before the conquest, births on the island so exceeded death rates that population growth outstripped the food supply. Did an improvement in the food supply suddenly boost the birth rate and lower the death rate? He also reported that the Majorcans, who came early to the island, brought the fig tree or perhaps a new variety of fig tree with them. The Guanches liked the fruit and planted its seeds, and the tree also spread by natural means, extending over the entire island; figs became the principal food of the people of Gran Canaria.[52] Such an addition to the food supply might well set off a population explosion, but we shall never know the truth. Perhaps the whole tale of the increased birth rate is a garbled version of a simpler truth that something happened to so reduce the food supply as to present the Guanches with the problem of an abruptly excessive population. For whatever reason, the problem did arise, and the Guanches, to avoid or at least to limit famine, began to kill all new babies or all new female babies (the two accounts differ on this point), except the firstborn of each mother.[53]

Mother nature always comes to the rescue of a society stricken with the problems of overpopulation, and her ministrations are never gentle. The Guanches had lived for a very long time alone with what we can assume was a narrow selection of parasitic organisms, macro and micro. The native Canarians could not have numbered much more than 100,000, and no more than a few score thousand per island. Their contacts with the mainland were nil, and their island ecosystems simple, relative to those of Europe and Africa. It is very unlikely that they suffered anything like the range of parasites and pathogens that preyed on humans in Europe or Africa. At the opening of the fifteenth century, the French invaders noted with delight the salubrity of the Canaries: "during all the long time that Bethencourt and his company remained there, no one suffered from sickness, which surprised them greatly."[54] They were enjoying much the same advantage the rabbits were to have on Porto Santo a few years later.

Every Eden has its snake, and that is the role Europeans played in the Canaries. Any group from the advanced societies of the Old World, whatever their attitude toward the Guanches, would have played the same role. We do not know when, where, or how the first diseases from the mainland arrived, or how many they infected and killed. All that history and science tell us of the epidemiology of isolated populations suggests that waves of new illnesses may have troubled the Guanches as early as the fourteenth century. The first that was recorded rolled through the Gran Canaria Guanches not long before their conquest. The Spaniards considered the epidemic heavenly punishment for the Guanches' sinful practice of infanticide. God "sent among them *la peste,* which in a few days destroyed three-quarters of the people" – so says Leonardo Torriani, one of the two earliest sources we have on the event. Friar Abreu de Galindo, the other, tells approximately the same story, putting the death rate at two-thirds.[55]

Alonso de Lugo's first invasion of Tenerife, 1494, ended in disaster, the worst the Guanches ever dealt the Europeans. His second, 1495, began with Spanish victories and then settled into a stalemate as both sides waited for the end of the winter rains and snows. The season was excessively wet and cold, and both invaders and defenders suffered from hunger, because the hostilities had prevented sowing and therefore harvesting. The Guanches, in greater numbers than the Spaniards, and isolated in the misty highlands for fear of the Europeans' horses, must have suffered more severely. God, as ever on the side of the Spaniards and offended by the number of Christians the Guanches had killed at *La Matanza de Acentejo,* visited a pestilence on the defenders of Tenerife, a disease called *modorra.* "A woman of the island announced the pestilence from a precipitous rock, making signs to the Spaniards, and when they came near enough, declaring it to them; asking why they did not come up and occupy the land, for there was no one to fight, no one to fear – all being dead." The Spaniards advanced warily and found confirmation of her words in the bodies of the fallen. In fact, there were so many corpses that the Guanches' dogs were feeding on them, and Guanches caught by nightfall between their mountain strongholds had to sleep in trees for fear of the feral animals. "The mortality was so great," said Friar Espinosa, "that the island remained almost without inhabitants, they having previously numbered 15,000."[56] The final battle took place the following September, and the mopping-up took three years more. "If it had not been for the pestilence," Espinosa said, "it would have taken much longer, the people being warlike, stubborn and wary."[57]

What were Gran Canaria's *peste* and Tenerife's *modorra?* We have no detailed description of their symptoms or of the patterns of their spread, and thus few clues to their identities beyond their names. *Peste* means bubonic plague, but, like "plague" in English, it has been used to refer to any and every pestilence. *Modorra* is a word of even less specificity. As an adjective it means drowsy, sleepy, or pulpy. As a noun it refers today to a disease of sheep. Dr. Francisco Guerra of the medical faculty of the Universidad de Alcalá de Henares, Madrid, suggests typhus as the most likely human infection to be lurking behind this vague word.[58] Fortunately, we do not have to identify the maladies. Many, perhaps most, of the diseases available in, say, Seville, could have done the job. We do have to decide if the death rates claimed for the two epidemics were accurate, plus or minus 20 percent. If they were, then the diseases were possibly the decisive factors in the final defeat of the Guanches. The answer to the question is quite probably yes. Virgin-soil epidemics (as outbursts of communicable diseases among previously untouched peoples are called) have the following effects: the impact of the infection on individuals is extreme, and death often occurs; nearly every person exposed falls ill, so that the death rate among the sick is the death rate for the entire population; very few are well enough to care for the ill, and many people die who might very well have recovered with minimal care; and crops are neither planted nor harvested, and flocks go untended. The mundane business of providing for future nourishment and warmth goes undone.[59] It had all happened in Iceland when the Black Death arrived from Europe. It happened again in the Canaries when *peste* and *modorra* arrived from Europe.

As soon as Europeans conquered a given island in the Canaries, they set about transforming it in accordance with their plans to become wealthy. They sold off the orchil to the European market, and as much grain, vegetables, timber, skins, and tallow and as many Guanches as could find buyers. They "Europeanized" their island, importing species of Old World plants and animals that were already doing well in Mediterranean lands. Several of the more important of these species – dogs, goats, pigs, and probably sheep, barley, peas, and probably wheat – were already present. The Europeans added cattle, asses, camels, rabbits, pigeons, chickens, partridges, and ducks, as well as grapevines, melons, pears, apples, and, most important of all, sugar.[60]

Most of the newcomers did very well, the animals spectacularly so. They helped to assure that seedlings would not grow into trees to replace the thousands cut down in answer to European needs in the islands and elsewhere. La Palma had rabbits "without number" by the 1540s. By the end of the century, Hierro had even more, and the pasturage on both islands was showing the effects of multitudes of hungry rabbits. Fuerteventura, large and relatively flat, became a vast ranch dotted with herds of several species of animals from the continents. In the last decades of the sixteenth century these included camels, 4,000 of them, and braying multitudes of wild asses. The asses were consuming so much of the grass and herbage that they threatened the island's value to other immigrant species, especially the European humans. In 1591, the humans struck back, killing 1,500 asses and leaving them for the ravens. The humans recruited two other species to assist in the slaughter: horses, which they rode, and dogs (greyhounds), which helped in locating and running down the overabundant species.[61]

The honeybee (as differentiated from other kinds of bees) was another immigrant that apparently spread widely and rapidly. This Old World insect may have lived in the islands before the coming of the Europeans, but it seems more likely that the invaders brought hives of bees from Iberia. Honeybees seldom swarm farther than ten kilometers, never as far as the distance from the mainland to the Canaries, and transporting them for long distances is a tricky business, almost impossible to accomplish by accident. Tenerife is supposed to have been without them, at least in the fifteenth century, obliging Our Lady of

Candelaria to produce by miracle the beeswax for the candles needed for church ceremonies. La Palma and Hierro proved to be especially good bee country and in the sixteenth century contributed greatly to the Canaries' exportation of large quantities of honey.[62]

During the Renaissance, Europe's chief source of sweetness was honey, but this role was usurped by sugar in the following centuries, a revolution the Canaries helped to accomplish. The *conquistador* of Gran Canaria, Pedro de Vera, was probably the man who introduced the sugar industry to the archipelago. He built his first mill for grinding the cane on his conquered lands in 1484. Other invaders followed his example, and sugar became the most important crop and export of the whole island group.[63]

Sugar was the catalyst of social and ecological change. The Canaries' new elite imported thousands of laborers, some free and many slave, from Europe and Africa to work in the cane fields and mills, and they transformed the Canarian ecosystem in the drive to produce sugar. The archipelago's forests gave way to cane fields, pasture, and bare slopes as the trees fell before the need for timber for the many new buildings and especially for fuel to boil the fluid squeezed from the harvested cane. The cut cane stalks, explained an Englishman familiar with the Canaries, "are carried to the sugar house called Ingenio, where they are ground in a mill, and the juyce thereof conveyed by a conduct to a great vessell made for the purpose, where it is boiled till it waxe thicke." The appetite of the *ingenios* was insatiable; said our Englishman about Gran Canaria, an island of thick forests in Guanche times, "Wood is the thing that most wanteth." That appetite was such on Tenerife that the government there began issuing – in vain – regulations to protect the forests from the lumberjacks as early as 1500.[64]

Deforestation encouraged erosion, made the flow of streams a matter of flood or famine, and, said Christopher

Columbus, and many since, reduced the rainfall in the Canaries, as it had in the Madeiras and Azores. He may have been right, insofar as ocean mists congeal on trees, particularly pines, and then fall as "fog drip," a process that cannot occur without trees. For whatever reasons, watercourses on Fuerteventura that the French at the beginning of the fifteenth century had judged to be likely power sources for mills have been dry gullies for much of the time since.[65]

Foreign plants, often weeds by European definition, rushed onto the lands bared by European ax, plow, and herds and by what can accurately be called European erosion. Most of the plant pests of the Canaries came from the mainlands, especially from southern Europe and North Africa. Only two on the list of the Canaries' worst weeds today are natives. Currently, the very worst is probably the Mediterranean bramble or blackberry, *Rubus ulmifolius,* a plant in all probability of post-Guanche importation. There is no doubt as to its origin – the Mediterranean littoral – nor to its spread over the traumatized lands of the Canaries.[66]

The Guanches declined even faster than the forests, and their replacements spread as fast as the weeds. Some of the native Canarians ran to the mountains and lived as rustlers and bandits and occasionally rose in rebellion, but this sort of behavior soon dwindled and ceased. Resistance in some form probably lasted as long as did the pure-blooded Guanches, but that was not long. In the 1530s, Gonzalo Fernández de Oviedo y Valdés wrote that very few of them were left. Girolamo Benzoni, a wandering Italian who visited the islands in 1541, found the Guanches to be "nearly all at an end." At the end of the century, Friar Espinosa recorded that on Tenerife a few still survived, but they were all mixed-bloods.[67]

The Guanches died off from a multitude of causes. They lost their land, and with it their ways of making a living. When the Spaniards allocated the lands and flocks that were theirs by right of conquest, they granted very little to their Guanche allies, and then only the least desirable. Of the 992 allocations of land made in Tenerife, only 50 went to Guanches of various descriptions, and few of the 50 grants stayed long in native hands.[68]

Some Guanches, seeing that there was little hope for them at home, joined the ranks of Spanish migrants to fight and work in America, Africa, and elsewhere, and soon disappeared from history. They died without reproducing, or they scattered their seed in alien wombs or gave birth to strangers.[69]

They left home "voluntarily" because for most Guanches leaving was inevitable. The *conquistadores* deported many in order to stymie rebellion and sold many others as slaves to work the plantations in Madeira and elsewhere. Whether in the long run or the short run, only one fate awaited most of the Guanches who left their home islands: Exiles from the Canaries were well known for their high death rate. We can assume that families were broken up in the processes of exile and enslavement, which certainly would have tended to increase the death rate and sharply decrease the birth rate of pure Guanches. In the 1480s and 1490s, a flood of slaves departed the Canaries, but thereafter there was only a trickle, not because of a decline in demand, but rather a decline in supply.[70]

Many baleful influences converged on this frail strain of humanity to eliminate it from the Canaries and the world, and each influence amplified the effects of the others. There can be no simple explanation for their extinction, but no single influence can have been more destructive than disease, which works its way through a susceptible population irresistibly, taking advantage of every flaw, choking out lives day and night, season after season, spreading like a noxious weed over bare and fertile soil. *Modorra* returned again and again, dysentery was common, and *dolor de costado* ("pain in the side" – pneumonia?) carried off many

Guanches. European males, we can sadly and safely assume, exploited the Guanche women, infecting them with venereal diseases, especially syphilis, an epidemic of which swept Europe in the 1490s and early sixteenth century. That curse and the other diseases *d'amour* not only shortened the women's lives but also diminished their fecundity.[71]

Some Guanches surely died of the psychological trauma of subjugation, the loss of so many kin and friends, the decline of their language, the swift obliteration of their way of life. One of the leaders of the resistance on La Palma, a captain called Tanausu, exiled to Spain soon after the European conquest of his island, died there of despair and self-imposed starvation, "a thing very common and ordinary." When Girolamo Benzoni visited La Palma in 1541, he found only one Guanche, an eighty-year-old, who stayed drunk all the time. The Guanches had become a paltry few, stumbling along the edge of doom, numbly observing their own extinction.[72]

Today, Guanche genes must survive among the inhabitants of the Canaries, but so slight is the Guanche strain that it probably would not be credited but for nostalgia among the present-day citizens for what is unique about their islands and their history. This alleged genetic evidence, some ruins, mummies, and pottery shards, a number of words, and nine sentences of the Guanche language are all we have as proof that the Canary Islands once had a native race.[73] Very few experiences are as dangerous to a people's survival as the passage from isolation to membership in the worldwide community that included European sailors, soldiers, and settlers.

The uninhabited Azores and Madeiras became European by default when the first European sailors unshipped their oars and waded ashore. The Azores have remained almost purely European ever since. The Madeiran planters imported many thousands of non-European slaves, but the proportion of Europeans always stayed high enough (along with the slaves' death rate) to assure an overwhelmingly European society. In the Canaries, a new population appeared by 1520 to fill the niche left by the Guanches. The new Canarians were a mixed lot, but clearly European in the great majority.[74] Within a few generations they began to take pride in their islands not as colonies but as a part of Europe.[75]

These three archipelagos of the eastern Atlantic were the laboratories, the pilot programs, for the new European imperialism, and the lessons learned there would crucially influence world history for centuries to come. The most important lesson was that Europeans and their plants and animals could do quite well in lands where they had never existed before, a lesson that the Norse experience had never made completely clear and that the Iberians had never had the opportunity to learn from them, anyway. The other great lesson was that indigenous populations of newly discovered lands, though fierce and numerous, could be conquered, despite all their initial advantages. In fact, they could even, on the eve of battle, or, most aggravatingly, when they were needed for labor after the war, fade away like messages drawn in sand at the edge of a rising tide; but then heartier laborers could be imported from Europe and Africa. The islands of the eastern Atlantic provided precedents for both settlement colonies and plantation colonies beyond the seams of Pangaea.

So much for the lessons these islands taught the Renaissance Europeans. What have they to teach us about the general nature of European imperialism? Why were these colonies so much more successful than the Norse settlements in the North Atlantic and the Crusader states in the eastern Mediterranean? Textbooks inform us that Renaissance Europe was institutionally and economically stronger than medieval Europe, and better able to seize and sustain colonies. It is also clear that European technology was significantly more advanced in the fifteenth century than ever before. The invaders' possession of firearms, though not decisive in the Canarian campaigns, must have had some significance. Fourteenth- and fifteenth-century European innovations in shipbuilding, rigging, and navigation made long blue-water voyages safer, faster, and therefore more attractive for Renaissance sailors than they had been in medieval times. All this is unquestionably true, but the histories of the Azores, Madeiras, and Canaries have more to tell us than that. The Europeans who sailed off to these islands had biological advantages that the Norse and the Crusaders had not enjoyed.

The Norse Atlantic colonies were almost too cold and too far north for the plants and animals of the Old World Neolithic Revolution. They did well in Vinland, but that made no difference, because the people who brought them did not. In the Holy Land, these plants and animals also did well, as they had been doing for thousands of years, but most of them provided for the enemies of the Europeans. In the Azores, Madeiras, and Canaries, the invaders' wheat, sugar, grapes, horses, cattle, asses, pigs, and so forth, prospered famously, and exclusively for Europeans and their slaves.

The Norse colonies were so remote that contact with Europe was a tenuous matter, and therefore the arrival of ships from the mainland could and did set off deadly epidemics. In the north, disease worked against the European colonists. (In Vinland, it seems to have played little role at all, but it certainly did not help the invaders.) When Europeans went east as Crusaders, they moved into a region inhabited by dense populations of high culture who had lived there for millennia. These peoples exceeded the invaders in quantity, and in many ways outclassed them in quality – quality of diplomacy, literature, textiles, and quality of epidemiological experience – and thousands of Crusaders died of their inferiorities. The Europeans who went to the Azores and Madeiras initially had no such problems – there was no one there to be inferior or superior – and those who went to the Canaries had the advantage of moving from an area of relatively dense and cosmopolitan population to islands inhabited by people who had been isolated for many generations. In the Canaries, disease worked for the Europeans. José de Viera y Clavijo described the Guanches in their decline as "watered with their tears and infested with *modorra*."[76]

The islands of the eastern Atlantic suffered periodic epidemics after the conquest, as did Europe itself, but they were not devastating. The new islanders' contacts with the mainland occurred often enough to keep their antibody levels high enough to protect them from true virgin-soil infections. In the sixteenth, seventeenth, and eighteenth centuries, their epidemiological experience was not like that in the newly discovered lands beyond the oceans.[77]

A brief analysis of the record of European attempts to found colonies during the medieval and Renaissance periods suggests the following as essential for successful planting of European colonies of settlement beyond the boundaries of the home continent: First, the prospective settlement had to be placed where the land and climate were similar to those in some part of Europe. Europeans and their commensal and parasitic comrades were not good at adapting to truly alien lands and climates, but they were very good at constructing new versions of Europe out of suitable real estate. Second, the prospective colonies had to be in lands remote from the Old World so that there would be no or few predators or disease organisms adapted to preying on Europeans and their plants and animals. Also, remoteness assured that the indigenous humans would have no or few such servant species as horses and cattle; that is, the invaders would have the assistance of a larger extended family than the natives, an advantage probably more important than superior military technology – certainly so in the long run. Likewise, remoteness assured that the indigenes would be without defenses against the diseases the invaders inevitably would bring with them. The Canary Islands, though not more than a few days' voyage from the mainland, met the qualification of remoteness, because the Berbers of the mainland opposite knew little about seamanship, and the Guanches less. This bizarre flaw in the Guanche culture kept them in the Stone Age, a disadvantage when they met European iron and steel, and it left them naked to their worst enemies: horses and the pathogens of *peste* and *modorra* and surely a number of other mainland diseases.

The great weakness of the Guanches derived from their ignorance of how to cross a short distance of ocean. The source of weakness for almost all the other peoples usurped or replaced by Europeans in the next four centuries (Amerindians, Aborigines, etc.) was the enormous distance their ancestors had put between themselves and the hearthlands of the Old World civilizations. The penchant of their ancestors for migration, along with the melting of the Pleistocene glaciers and the rising levels of the oceans, left them, as their sad histories in the last few centuries testify, on the losing side of the seams of Pangaea.

5

⤛⤜

Winds

"Ah! why cannot men be content with the blessings
Providence places within our immediate reach, that they must
make distant voyages to accumulate others!"

"You like your tea, Mary Pratt – and the sugar in it, and your
silks and ribbons that I've seen you wear; how are you to get such
matters if there's to be no going on v'y'ges? Tea and sugar, and
silks and satins don't grow along with the clams on 'Yster Pond"
– for so the deacon uniformly pronounced the word 'oyster.'

Mary acknowledged the truth of what was said, but changed
the subject.

—James Fenimore Cooper, *The Sea Lions*

IF THE OLD WORLD expansionists were to be able to take full advantage of the global opportunities for ecological imperialism prefigured by the European successes in the islands of the eastern Atlantic, they would have to cross the seams of Pangaea – the oceans – in large numbers, along with their servant and parasite organisms. That great endeavor waited on five developments. One of the five was simply the emergence of a strong desire to undertake imperialistic adventures overseas – a prerequisite that may seem too obvious to bother mentioning, but not one we can omit, as the Chinese case, to which we shall refer presently, proves. The other four developments were technological in nature. Vessels were needed that were large enough, fast enough, and maneuverable enough to carry a worthwhile payload of freight and passengers across thousands of kilometers of ocean, past shoals, reefs, and menacing headlands, and back again in reasonable safety. Equipment and techniques were needed to find courses across oceans while out of sight of land for weeks, even months, on voyages far longer than any the Norse ever survived. Weaponry was needed that was portable enough to be carried on board ship and yet effective enough to intimidate the indigenes of the lands across the oceans. A source of energy was needed to drive the vessels across the oceans. Oars would not do: Neither freemen nor slaves could row without fresh water and plenty of calories, and a galley large enough to carry sufficient supplies for an oar-powered crossing of the Pacific would, paradoxically, be too large to row anywhere. Wind, of course, was the answer to this last requirement, but which winds, where, and when? The explorer who puts to sea in the faith that there will always be a wind to carry him where he listeth will find that the wind will carry him where *it* listeth. The births of the Neo-Europes had to wait for the sailors of Europe, who rarely ventured beyond the continental shelf, to become blue-water sailors.

To make short work of a long story that has been well

told elsewhere by such historians as J. H. Parry and Samuel Eliot Morison,[1] most of the foregoing requirements were met no later than the 1490s, the decade of the triumphs of Columbus and Da Gama. In many ways, they had been met three or four generations before. Chinese maritime technology was sufficiently advanced at the beginning of the fifteenth century for Cheng Ho, chief admiral and eunuch of the Ming emperor, to despatch to India and all the way to East Africa fleets of scores of vessels armed with multitudes of small cannon and manned by thousands of crewmen and passengers. It is this admiral, rather than, say, Bartholomeu Dias, who should be credited as the first great figure of the age of exploration. If political changes and cultural endogeny had not stifled the ambitions of Chinese sailors, then it is likely that history's greatest imperialists would have been Far Easterners, not Europeans.[2]

But China chose to turn its back to the oceans, leaving history only two possibilities for the role of the greatest imperialists: the Muslims, led by their sailors, and the Europeans, led by theirs. (There were other expansionistic peoples, but none both as powerful and as experienced on the high seas.) As of 1400, the mariners of these two sets of prospective imperialists still lagged behind the Chinese, but their ships, though smaller than those of Cheng Ho, were seaworthy and adequate in size; some were fitted with cannon, and more soon would be, and their navigators had compasses and crude instruments with which to estimate speed and latitude. Neither the Muslims nor the Europeans could accurately judge longitude, but neither could anyone else until the invention of an accurate chronometer in the eighteenth century. Meanwhile, they made do with what they had and guessed about longitude – exactly as Columbus was to do in his time. Science made its great contributions to navigation after the fifteenth century.[3]

The unsolved problem was the wind. It was not that they did not understand how to tap its force: Christian square sails and Muslim lateen sails, used in combination more and more frequently as the century went on, could have carried Magellan across the Pacific about as well in 1421 as in 1521. The problem was that in 1421 no one knew much about where and when the winds blew over the major oceans, with the exception of the Indian Ocean. The Indian Ocean was certainly vast enough to get lost in, but it was land-locked on three sides, and its winds were under the discipline of the monsoon, a seasonal weather system that could be comprehended from land. The lessons the Indian Ocean taught its indigenous sailors were only imperfectly applicable elsewhere, and that may have had something to do with their general inferiority to European sailors outside the waters of monsoon Asia. It is also true that the fifteenth century was one in which the attention of Muslims was fully engaged on land, or, if on water, then on that sea-of-the-lands-around-it, the Mediterranean. The very placement of the Indian Ocean discouraged curiosity. Beyond its known waters lay primitive peoples and more and more ocean. How different from the Atlantic: Beyond it lay Aztecs, Incas, and the lush Americas.

The history of the closing of the seams of Pangaea is a European story – not completely, of course; for the essential compass was Chinese, and the lateen sail that enabled ships to beat into the wind, a necessity for exploration of unfamiliar coasts, was Muslim – but the actual ships, owners, bankers, interested monarchs and noblemen, cartographers, mathematicians, navigators, astronomers, masters, mates, and common seamen were Europeans or their servants. They led humanity into its greatest adventure since the Neolithic. John H. Parry has called that adventure not "the discovery of America," for that was only one of its chapters; he has named it "the discovery of the sea," which is to say, the discovery of the where and when of the oceanic winds and the currents they drive before them.[4]

When the sailors of the Mediterranean and Iberia first

ventured into the pelagic waters beyond Gibraltar, they were familiar with only the winds of their home waters. They knew nothing whatever about those that glide and gust (spin, whirl? blow straight up?) beyond the continental shelf. These mariners did inherit – at many removes, because they were not, most of them, of a scholarly bent – what the savants of the ancient world and their latter-day disciples had to say on the general nature of the world. There was a tradition, raised almost to the level of revealed truth by Aristotle, that climates and therefore a lot of other things would be found spread out in latitudinal strata from the North Pole to the equator, and then, in reverse order, to the South Pole.[5] Hence, in 1492, Columbus was not surprised that the people of the Bahamas and Antilles were tawny, because that was the color of the Guanches, who lived in the same latitude.[6] The theory was, of course, an oversimplification, and it led, for instance, to the false assumption that there would be an enormous southern continent, a *Terra australia incognita,* to balance the masses of land north of the equator, but the theory was not entirely wrong-headed. It is valid, generally speaking, and for many practical purposes, in regard to the winds of the Atlantic and Pacific – which is all the fifteenth- and sixteenth-century explorers, who crossed oceans as if playing blindman's buff, asked.[7]

The winds of the Atlantic and Pacific flow in gigantic wind wheels. In each ocean north of the equator, one airy carousel revolves clockwise, and south of the equator another spins counterclockwise. The poleward edges of the carousels are the prevailing westerlies of the temperate zones, north and south. In the tropics, between the wind wheels, broad bands of moving air swing out and plunge obliquely toward a belt of low pressure steaming under the vertical equatorial sun. These are the famous trade winds, called such in English because of the obsolete meaning of "trade" as a course or track. The low-pressure belt is the

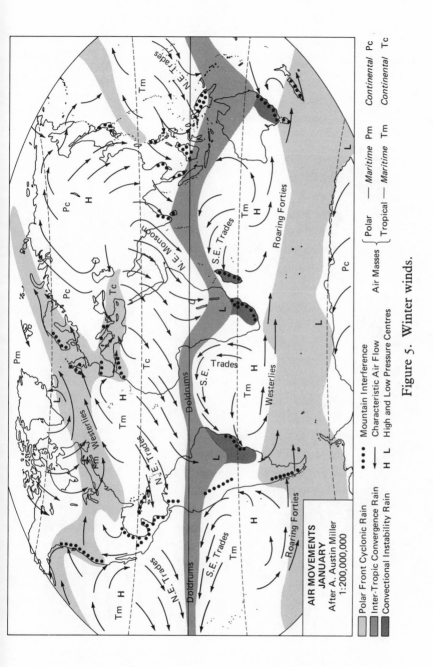

Figure 5. Winter winds.

Figure 6. Summer winds. Source for Figures 5 and 6: *The Times Atlas of the World, Mid-Century Edition*, ed. John Bartholomew (London: The Times Publishing Co., 1958), Vol. I, Pl. 3.

detested doldrums, source of so many horror stories of thirst and starvation for those becalmed in their sweaty clasp. The whole vast system – westerlies, trades, doldrums, and all – rocks gigantically north and south with the seasons, cuing on the annual veering of the vertical sun back and forth between the Tropic of Cancer and Tropic of Capricorn. The latitudinal nature and rough predictability of the system (very rough, because local variations are legion, and every so often the whole system shuts down for a while) contain the key to sailing across the seams of Pangaea from Europe to new worlds.

The sailors of southern Europe who in their historical prime were to discover America, round the Cape of Good Hope, and circumnavigate the globe went to primary school in the Mediterranean and to secondary school in the next best thing to a closed sea: a large spread of open ocean with reasonably predictable winds and enough islands for the navigator to practice his skills without losing his life the first time he lost his bearings. This watery expanse the historian Pierre Chaunu has shrewdly called "the Mediterranean Atlantic." It is that wide wedge of the Atlantic west and south of the Iberian peninsula that has as its far boundary stones the archipelagos of the Canaries and the Azores and includes the Madeira group, and over which firm northerlies blow during the warmer months. Southerlies are rare any time, and the general flow of air commonly comes from the west only in the temperate Azorean latitudes.[8] The Vivaldi brothers disappeared into the Mediterranean Atlantic in 1291, but the majority of those who followed survived. They familiarized themselves with these waters, and in doing so became blue-water sailors, true mariners – *marinheiros,* to use the most appropriate language, Portuguese. The key to understanding what they learned and how they learned it is the Canaries. It is that island group that tempted Portuguese sailors (plus Genoese, Majorcan, Spanish, and others, many sailing for the Portuguese) far out into the Atlantic and into their historic roles as Europe's first oceanic sailors after the Norse. The voyage to these islands down the trades was an easy one of a week or less, with the archipelago almost too wide and its peaks too high to miss. "In the Island of Teneriffe," said a Dutch traveler in the sixteenth century, "there is a hill called Pico de Terraira, which is thought to be the highest hill that ever was found, for it may easily be seene at the least threescore miles in the sea."9 And at the end of a voyage in this cozy patch of the Atlantic lay profit in the Canaries: animal skins, dyestuffs, and slaves.

Getting from Iberia to the Canaries was not the problem; getting back was the problem. In solving that puzzle, the sailors of Europe certainly sharpened and perhaps even invented some of the skills that enabled them to sail to America, to India, and around the world, and to bind up the seams of Pangaea. The course from Iberia to the Canaries is often about as straight as a sailor can sail, because usually both current and wind carry him to his destination, perhaps with not so much as a squall, if he has chosen the season rightly. Square sail, lateen sail, or perhaps, with luck, no sail at all will suffice; but to return by anything approximating the same route he must tack to and fro, to and fro, for many days, sliding backward every time the vessel comes about, and gaining little on the best reach, because the current is relentlessly contrary. If he sails conservatively, his only hope is to shave the coastline, taking full advantage of the shore winds that blow from the south and southwest during the hours immediately before and after dawn. Then, at midday, he must tack back toward the coast, praying to gain some northing, or at least not to lose any, before anchoring or before the shore winds pick up again. Much of the real hope for northing lies in the strength in the backs of his oarsmen, but where on that inhospitable coast is there food and water to keep them going? A good guess as to the fate of the Vivaldi brothers is that they sailed perhaps as far as the Canaries, perhaps farther, and then found their sails inadequate for the voyage back, and the task of rowing against the Canary Current too much for their thirsty rowers. Perhaps they died of deprivation and exhaustion, or perhaps, in attempting to finesse their way home by means of the shore winds, they were hit by a squall and, lacking sea room, were flung on the shoals of Morocco.[10]

When faced with strong contrary winds, European sailors prior to the *marinheiros* – even the Norse – either gave up and went home or took down their sails until the wind changed, busying themselves with the housekeeping chores that always need doing on a vessel. There was no other way to buy a passage from a relentless headwind. The Europeans who sailed the Mediterranean Atlantic found a new way. If they could not sail close enough to a contrary wind to gain against it, then they had to try "to sail around the wind," that is, steer as close to the wind as they could, holding their course for as long as it took to find a wind they could use to get them where they wanted to go. Sailors of the Mediterranean Atlantic pinned in the Canaries by the southward rush of air and water had to steer northwest into the open ocean and steadily sail farther and farther away from their last landfall, perhaps without gaining a centimeter toward home for many days, until they finally sailed far enough out of the tropics to tap the prevailing westerlies of the temperate zone. Then they could steer for home. They had to have faith in their knowledge of the winds, turn their backs to land, and become, possibly for weeks, creatures of the pelagic deeps. They had to become true *marinheiros*. The Portuguese, who perfected this strategy, called it the *volta do mar,* the returning by sea or the veering out and around by sea.[11]

This alternating use of the trade winds on the outward leg, then the *volta* (the crabwise slide off to the northwest) to the zone of the westerlies, and then the swoop home with the westerlies as following winds – this pattern of voyaging and this pattern of prevailing winds made the gambles of Columbus, Da Gama, and Magellan acts of adventure, not acts of probable suicide. These sailors knew they could sail out on the trades and back on the westerlies, and with this faith, as the Jesuit José de Acosta put it, "men have indangered themselves to undertake strange Navigations, and to seeke out farre Countries unknowne."[12]

It is doubtful that the sailors of the age of exploration thought about the *volta* in any sort of formal way. It is improbable that they learned the technique as a principle; they were, after all, not searching after laws of nature but simply groping out to sea for a favorable wind. But prevailing patterns of thought grew up to match the patterns of prevailing winds, and Iberian sailors used the *volta* as a template with which to plot their courses to Asia, to the Americas, and around the world.

In the fifteenth century, Portuguese navigators continued past the Canaries down the African coast, feeling their way along desert and then jungle shores, and learning the tricks of trading with the Africans for gold, pepper, and slaves. About 1460, they colonized the Cape Verde Islands and then sailed on farther, south and round the bulge of Africa. There they found themselves in dangerous and confusing waters. Near shore during the summer months they were hostages to the violent doings of the West African monsoon. The continent, baking under the vertical sun, sucks the relatively cool ocean air inland, and the prevailing winds back around to the southwest, carrying vessels toward a coast that is almost without harbors. If the *marinheiros* stood out to sea away from monsoon weather, they sailed right out of the zone of the northeast trades into the doldrums, where the superheated air rises vertically, producing calms alternating with dangerous storms. The worst large expanse of ocean in the world for thunderstorms lies off the coast of Africa from the Senegal River to the

Congo River.[13] Often it takes the longest to drift out of the doldrums not far south of the Cape Verdes. Columbus strayed into this buckle on the doldrums belt on his third voyage: "There the wind failed me and the heat grew so great that I was afraid my ships and crew would be burnt."[14]

In the Atlantic off the southwest "corner" of the bulge of Africa, the *marinheiros* set courses and sails according to the season and the educated guess; but sail on they did, due east to the rich islands of Fernando Po and São Tomé, which the Portuguese came upon in the 1470s and soon transformed into new Madeiras staffed with black labor.[15] East of these islands, the coast turned south again; the secret of the passage to India was not to be come by easily. King João II, who came to the throne in 1481, spurred the *marinheiros* forward, and soon they were at the estuary of the Congo River, but south of the mouth of the Congo they met new but oddly familiar obstacles: the Benguela Current, southern counterpart of the Canary Current, and the southeast trades, southern counterpart of the northeast trades.[16]

In 1487, Bartholomeu Dias pushed south beyond the Congo along the coast of southwest Africa, today's Namibia, fighting the adverse current and wind. He was in the same dilemma as the first *marinheiros* a century before trying to sail back to Europe along the coast of Morocco. Somewhere south of the Orange River, the present border of the Union of South Africa, he ran into stormy weather, and there he made a sensible change in course, sensible for a *marinheiro*. He put out to sea, close-hauled, in search of sea room and a favorable wind. Perhaps he turned as simply as a sheep turns away from the rain, but more likely he turned southwest on the basis of the old tradition that God or the gods like symmetry: If there are trade winds off Morocco slanting from the northeast toward the equator, with westerlies prevailing to their north, and if there are trades off Namibia, slanting from the southeast toward the equator, then there must be westerlies beyond them, too. Perhaps Dias realized that the wind system of the South Atlantic is much like that of the North Atlantic and that the *volta* template, flipped upside down to match the upside-down conditions of the bottom half of the world, would work as well south of the Orange River as north of the Senegal River.

Dias ran into westerlies well south of the southern tip of Africa, and he ran with them east and north to the verge of the Indian Ocean. There, unrest among his crew turned him around somewhere in the vicinity of the Great Fish River and sent him back to Portugal. A nautical Moses, he had seen the Promised Ocean but was never to enter it. He brought home with him two precious bits of knowledge: one, there was a passage to the Indian Ocean from the Atlantic; two, the wind patterns of the South Atlantic were, according to his experience, very much like those of the North Atlantic, only upside-down.[17]

For reasons we do not fully understand, the Portuguese paused for several years before capitalizing on Dias's findings. The next master of the *volta* to prove himself was not even Portuguese, but rather a Genoese mapmaker named Christopher Columbus working for the Spanish. Dias had turned the *volta* upside down; Columbus stretched it sideways.

Columbus, as every schoolchild knows, was interested in sailing west to Asia, believing that would be a shorter route than around Africa. His obvious course was due west from Spain to Cipangu (Japan), but he and every other *marinheiro* knew that the prevailing westerlies in those latitudes made that choice a foolish one. He dropped south to the Canaries, and in September of 1492 turned west with the trades blowing over his starboard quarter and filling the sails of his small fleet. At that season he was on the far northern edge of the trades, where the winds often are not dependable (on his other voyages to America he always dropped farther south before turning west), but 1492 was his lucky year, and he had a splendid voyage to the West Indies. His choice of a course to America was so nearly optimal for sailing craft that navigators, even those from ports in northern Europe, followed it, with a few adjustments such as those he later made himself, for generations. The English expedition that founded the Virginia colony 115 years later and the Dutch fleet that founded New Amsterdam two decades after that both sailed to America via the general vicinity of the Canaries.[18] The Spanish called the warm and dependable trades *las brisas* and named the expanse of the Atlantic between the Canaries and Cape Verdes on one side and the West Indies on the other the *Golfo de Damas,* the Ladies' Gulf.[19]

Columbus bowled down the trades to the Bahamas, to the Greater Antilles, and to immortality. Then he faced the old nagging question of the Mediterranean Atlantic: How to return home against the trades? Beat against them for the thousands of kilometers between Española and Spain? He started the return voyage by noodling about in the waters of Española for a few days, trying to find a crack in the relentless *brisas* to slip through – much like a man looking for a way through a thick hedge – and then did the only sensible thing. He resorted to the *volta do mar,* sidling northeast through the Sargasso Sea (where the weed was so thick his sailors worried it might hold them fast) to the latitudes of the westerlies, and then sailed east to the Azores and back to Spain.[20]

Columbus himself did not quite believe in his own brilliance as a sage of the winds. When in 1496 he made his second trip back from the West Indies to Spain, he again tried to butt his way through the trades. Headwinds and horse-latitude calms reduced him and his crew to starvation rations and the thought of eating their Carib captives before they whistled up a fair wind. Since then, no one but a fool has bucked the North Atlantic trades. As an English scholar of the *marinheiros* said in the early seventeenth century: "For such is the statute of the windes, which all Shipping in that Sea must obey: they must goe one way and returne another."[21]

The first great prize earned by using the *volta* strategy fell to the Spaniards. The next prize justly fell to the Portuguese. Vasco da Gama's fleet set sail from Lisbon in July 1497 and dropped south to the Cape Verdes. Beyond those islands he faced the problems of the doldrums, the dangerous weather of the Gulf of Guinea, and the adverse southeast trades. He dealt with all three by means of an innovation so extravagant that many historians, despite a total lack of direct evidence for their assumption, have surmised that the Portuguese must have made secret reconnaissance voyages in the South Atlantic in the years immediately after Dias's return to learn the wind patterns of that ocean.

South and east of the Cape Verdes, Da Gama ran into severe thunderstorms, such as are often met there, lost a main yard, and then, according to the very sparse documentation of this voyage, took up a course close-hauled to the southwest with the southern trades on his port beam, angling *away from* the southern tip of Africa. He rode the southeast trades right out of the tropics into the zone of the prevailing westerlies of the Southern Hemisphere, and then steered for the Indian Ocean. Even so, he still fetched up on the west coast of southern Africa and had days of struggle to finally round the ultimate cape, but nothing compared with the trouble he would have had if he had not swerved out into the South Atlantic on his magnificent *volta*. His vast half circle from the Cape Verdes to his first South African landfall took eighty-four days to accomplish, and in distance and duration dwarfed Columbus's longest voyage.[22]

Da Gama's course – an extravagant exaggeration of Dias's course – was and is the most practical route for a sailing ship bound from Europe to the Indian Ocean: south to the Cape Verdes or thereabouts, then a great curve southwest until nigh the coast of Brazil, and then southeast round the Cape of Good Hope. It was the course of choice, recommended by both the British Admiralty and the United States Hydrographic Office, for as long as sails ruled the oceans.[23]

Da Gama solved the conundrum of the South Atlantic, and then found himself with a whole new set of mysteries. Beyond the mouth of the Great Fish River he was in waters unfamiliar to all Europeans. In the thirteenth century, Asians had told Marco Polo that the current sweeping south along the southeast coast of Africa was so powerful that vessels dared not enter it from the Indian Ocean for fear of never returning, and now Da Gama was breasting that very flood. They had also told Polo that the waters in which the Portuguese now sailed had islands with birds so large they killed elephants for food by carrying them aloft and dropping them.[24] This was an exaggeration: The elephant bird (*Aepyornis maximus*) of Madagascar (now extinct, but then possibly still living) was only three meters high and no more than 500 kilograms in weight and could not fly at all.[25] Even so, Vasco Da Gama was obviously a long way from Christendom.

The voyage from Europe to the Indian Ocean had started with the Vivaldi brothers and had taken two hundred years. Now there was the whole east coast of Africa to creep along and an entire new ocean with a whole new set of winds and currents to decipher – work for another two centuries, one might think. But Da Gama rounded the Cape at the turn of the year and arrived in India in May.

Europeans entering the Indian Ocean had two advantages. One was the dependability of the monsoon winds and currents. In some ways the Indian Ocean was a simpler place than the Atlantic: A ship could go out and come back on the same course. Second, around this unfamiliar ocean lived advanced maritime peoples who knew its winds and currents better than the Europeans knew those of the Atlantic. To cross the Indian Ocean, Da Gama had only to tap the existing sources of knowledge.[26]

When Da Gama's fleet rounded the Cape and turned north into the Indian Ocean, it instantly became the most powerful naval force in that or any of the other Asian seas beyond. The Turks had ships armed with cannon, but they were in the Mediterranean. Large vessels and cannon gave Da Gama the trump card wherever he sailed in the East, as his king may have known before dispatching him. The explorer made free use of his firearms and taught the East Africans, as a bit later he taught the Indians, to fear him as an enemy and value him as an ally. His *artilheria* so impressed the headman at Melindi, in what is now Kenya, with the advantages that might come with Portuguese friendship that he presented Da Gama with what the explorer wanted most: an expert on the subject of getting from East Africa to India across the mysterious Indian Ocean.[27]

There is good evidence that this expert was the famous Ahmad Ibn Majid, a Gujarati who was one of the greatest experts on the Indian Ocean. Whoever he may have been, he had a map of the Indian coasts with plenty of meridians and parallels to sooth European fears, and he knew how to read the monsoon shift and perhaps even how to cheat on it a little. In spite of leaving Melindi on a date that seems a bit early – at least it would be for most years – Da Gama was on the coast of India twenty-odd days later.[28] Ahmad Ibn Majid, if indeed that is who he was, in his way played a role like that of Malinche in the Spanish conquest of Mexico. She gave the Europeans the means to surmount the language barrier, and he gave them the means to surmount their ignorance of the winds and currents that were confounding their efforts to reach the riches of India.

The Indian Ocean (and the China Sea, as well) functions in a very different manner than does the Atlantic, and so must those who sail her. Marco Polo, who had sailed both the Indian Ocean and the China Sea, told Europeans that there were only two winds that blew over those waters: one that carried sailors out from the continent and one that carried them back, the former blowing in the winter and the latter in the summer.[29] He was reminiscing about the Asian monsoon, the world's most colossal.

The monsoon of southern Asia is much like that of West Africa, but a lot larger in the area it affects. Here the land bulk, frying in summer, and most of it freezing in winter, is Asia, the largest of all continents, and its temperature extremes run all the way from a high of blood heat plus in India's summer to a low in Siberia's winter cold enough to shatter rubber. The continental summer sucks the southern trade winds all the way to the base of the Himalayas, and the winter reverses the flow, with the northern trades ranging south to the latitude of Madagascar. To sailors carried this way and then that by these vast currents of air – and of water, too, because the winds are so powerful they oblige the seas to flow in parallel – the system seems to have little in common with those of the other great oceans, and they do not talk of contrasting trade winds in Asian waters, but of the awesome monsoon shift.[30]

For much longer than there have been Christians and Muslims, the sailors of Asia have been riding the monsoon winds and currents from India and the Middle East to Africa and Southeast Asia in winter and back in summer. If all goes well, they always have a fair wind. If all goes well, navigation is simply a matter of keeping the wind abaft the beam and veering to port or starboard depending on destination. All does not always go well, but a wisely scheduled voyage between, for instance, Melindi and India can be as easy in both directions as riding *las brisas* from the Cape Verdes to the West Indies.

Ignorance and arrogance, however, can lead to disaster. Da Gama had made a swift passage from Melindi to India, with his pilot's help, but on the return voyage he was on his own, and spent ninety-five days crossing back to East Africa. So many of his crew sickened and died that there were barely enough men to operate the ships.[31] Beyond the Cape of Good Hope he was in waters he understood, and his course from the southern tip of Africa to Portugal was a crude opposite of that taken on the voyage out: "such is the statute of the windes, which all Shipping in that Sea must obey: they must goe one way and returne another." His outward and return courses in the Atlantic make a titanic figure eight, scrawled from latitude $40°$ N to nearly $40°$ S.[32] The voyage from Lisbon to Calicut, India, and back cost two of four ships and the lives of 80 to 100 men, about half those who had embarked, most of them victims of scurvy. The cargo of spices brought back made the voyage a profitable one.[33]

Da Gama had sailed a distance almost equal to that of a voyage around the world. The next great figure of the age of exploration, Ferdinand Magellan, a Portuguese who sailed for Spain, tried to make that voyage, and although he died before the voyage was completed, his ship and surviving crew did circumnavigate the globe. He and his successor, Juan Sebastián Elcano, drew on all the lessons of the winds learned by the anonymous sailors of the Mediterranean Atlantic, by Dias, Columbus, and Da Gama, and by the unknown ancients who first sailed the Asian seas.

Magellan's fleet of five vessels cleared the Spanish port of San Lucar in September 1519 and sailed the trade winds to the Canaries, arriving in six days. From there they sailed to and past the Cape Verdes, and off Sierra Leone they ran into the doldrums at their worst; for sixty days it rained, with winds feeble and varying and alternating with dead calms. There were birds without anuses and birds without feet, whose females laid their eggs on the backs of the males in flight – or so said the chief chronicler of this voyage.[34]

Eventually the ships floated loose, caught the trades, and in a rough approximation of the first half of Da Gama's *volta* to the Cape, crossed the Atlantic to South America. Here was the obstacle – Brazil and whatever lands might lie to its south – around which they had to find a passage. They coasted along the continent, stopping occasionally to frolic and exchange strains of venereal disease with the Amerindians, to ferment their own mutinies and execute mutineers, and to lose one ship in shoal water. In October they came upon the straits named after their leader. In the last days of November, after losing another ship (this one to successful mutineers, who turned about and sailed home) and after weeks of the most difficult kind of navigation, they emerged into the largest body of liquid water in our solar system. Magellan ordered that thanks be offered to God, and he set a course to the north "to get out of the cold."[35]

He was then in waters that no Old World human had sailed before – no Phoenician or Viking, no Arab, not Cheng Ho, not even St. Brendan. Europeans had some acquaintance with the Asian side of the Pacific, and Magellan himself had been in the East Indies, but that part of the world's greatest ocean was now well over one-third of the globe's circumference away. Magellan was in a part of the world a good deal less familiar to him than the far side of the moon is to us; yet he immediately set sail to the north to the trade-wind zone and then steered west. "He could have done no better," said historian and sailor Samuel Eliot Morison, "had he enjoyed full information about the great ocean's winds and currents."[36]

Another on-the-button guess by another Renaissance seaman in another *mare incognita!* Magellan sought the spice islands of the East Indies, the Moluccas, which lie just south of the equator, but he chose a course that curved ten degrees north of the line and brought him to the Philippines, due north of his target. Such a course was his best bet, but how could he have known that? Did he simply sail a course that the prevailing winds dictated? Yes and no. Winds dictate what courses one cannot take, but not which of the others one will take. Magellan could have veered off on any course within an arc of no less than 150 degrees or so. He did not have to select the best route across the Pacific; he could have taken some dreadfully wrong ones, all with favorable winds.

He must have learned something of the wind patterns of the western Pacific, the monsoon Pacific, during his time in the East Indies, and this knowledge would have recommended to him the route he did trace across the great ocean.[37] What he surely did not know was the width of that ocean. He no doubt expected to reach the Philippines in winter, well before March, when he in fact did arrive. A winter landfall would have placed him there with time to refit and to ride the monsoon winds flowing out of frigid Asia for an easy descent on the spice islands.

It is also obviously true that he sailed north from the Straits of Magellan to get to the zone of the trade winds. If one wants to cross the Pacific from east to west, whatever the season, one seeks, as in the Atlantic, *las brisas*. Surely, Magellan may have reasoned, a benign and consistent God would so order the world that the wind patterns of the central Pacific would resemble those of the more familiar ocean. In any case, what other hypothesis did he have to work with?

Magellan sailed north to the tropics and bowled west through some of the emptiest water in the world, week after week without sight of any land. He had indeed chosen the right course, but for three months and twenty days he and his men had no fresh food and little enough of any kind of food, and they suffered the agonies of the damned.[38] The one saving grace was the weather: fair winds and stormless seas. "Had not God and His blessed mother given us so good weather we would all have died of hunger in that exceedingly vast sea. Of a verity I believe no such voyage will ever be made again."[39] Nineteen Europeans and an Amerindian they had taken on board in Brazil died of scurvy on that plain of Pacific waters beneath the dazzling sky and the measured march of the fiery cumuli.

In March, ninety-nine days from the Straits of Magellan, they sighted Guam and other nearby islands and went ashore for food and supplies. Refreshed, they sailed on to the Philippines, where Magellan, probably looking for allies to provide Spain with a beachhead in the East, involved himself in local squabbles and was killed for his trouble. He was not a diplomat, but a *marinheiro,* and a shipmate wrote of him, "He endured hunger better than all the others, and more accurately than any man in the world did he understand sea charts and navigation."[40]

Magellan and those who survived him had, as had Da Gama, reached the monsoon waters of Asia exclusively by means of their own skills. Now they (or at least those who survived Magellan) could turn, as had Da Gama, to native pilots and sea lore older than civilization in that part of the world. Barriers of culture, language, and religion being what they were, the Europeans felt they had to resort to kidnapping to obtain pilots, and they did so with success. (One of their pilots escaped and swam to freedom, but his son, unable to hold on to his father's shoulders, drowned.)[41]

Soon the Europeans were at the Moluccas, the almost mythic spice islands that were the source of Europe's cloves. They took on cargo and made plans for the voyage home, deciding that the *Trinidad* and the *Victoria,* the only two surviving ships of the fleet that had set out from Spain (a third had been scrapped in the Philippines for lack of crew to man her), should part in order to increase the chances of getting some of this valuable cargo home. The *Trinidad* was to sail back across the Pacific to New Spain (Mexico), about which more later. The *Victoria,* captained by Juan Sebastián Elcano (certainly the least publicized of all the great captains of the age of exploration), was to continue around the world.[42]

Nine months of torment equal to that suffered in the mid-Pacific passed before Elcano and the *Victoria* reached home. He mistimed the monsoon; he swung too far south around Africa and ran headlong into fierce westerlies – later sailors would call these latitudes the Roaring Forties. Then came the not particularly eventful, but long, laborious passage north through the Atlantic. Dead Christians, consigned to the deep, sank face upward. Infidels, of which a few had joined in the East Indies, sank face downward.[43] By skill or luck, *Victoria* slipped through the doldrums without long delay; then it was north to the Canaries, the classic *volta* to the Azores, and finally fair winds for home.

On Monday, 8 September 1522, the *Victoria* dropped anchor near the quay at Seville and fired all her cannon. The first circumnavigation of the world was completed. The next day, "we all went in shirts and barefoot, each holding a candle, to visit the shrine of Santa María de la Victoria, and that of Santa María de l'Antigua."[44]

Five ships and 240 or so men had left Spain to sail around the world in 1519. Three years and one month later the voyage was done. Only the *Victoria* made the entire circumnavigation. Of the total crewmen, 210 had been at their posts when the fleet, diminished by mutiny, had passed through the Straits of Magellan into the Pacific. Of these, 36 reached home again by various routes and at various times. Of this number, only 18, plus 3 Indonesians of the 15 who had joined in the East Indies, were on the *Victoria* when it reached Seville. It also brought back a cargo of cloves, cinnamon, mace, and nutmeg that paid the costs of the entire enterprise, plus a little profit.[45]

What the *Victoria*'s officers and men brought back in their heads was more important than the cargo of spices. They knew more about the winds and currents of the major oceans, and more about world geography in general, than anyone short of God. They knew a way around America. They knew that the Pacific Ocean and therefore the world was a great deal larger than previously believed. They knew that there was a way across that ocean and around the world, that the trade winds were as dependable in all but the western Pacific as in the Atlantic. Only continents and monsoons interrupted or radically altered their flow; and Asian pilots held the key to using the monsoons to good purpose.

As of 1522, Europeans had a sketchy but reasonably accurate comprehension of how the ocean winds of the world worked between the Arctic Circle and about 40° S in the Atlantic, and from the northern coasts of the Indian Ocean to about 15° S, and they knew that the trades offered a passage across the Pacific from east to west. They also knew a good deal about the winds off southern Africa and had made a beginning on learning how the winds functioned off southern South America.

Now to implement, consolidate, build empires, and, in general, make money from what the *marinheiros* had learned. That meant commerce, for which round trips across oceans would be necessary. The shifting monsoon made going and returning across the Indian Ocean and the China Sea easy – in fact, almost compulsory. The secret of sailing east across the Atlantic had been known since Columbus's 1493 return trip, but clawing northward through the trades to the zone of the westerlies was long and laborious. In 1513, Ponce de León discovered Florida and, although he did not know it, the easy way to get to the westerlies from the West Indies: the Gulf Stream.

The trade winds continually pile water from the central Atlantic into the Gulf of Mexico, which consequently is higher than the main ocean, and this enormous body of water has one surface vent – the straits between Florida on one side and Cuba and the Bahamas on the other – through which it rushes like a herd of stallions loosed from a corral. No wonder De León found himself moving backward in spite of a fair northerly wind in the vicinity of present-day Miami, a bulge of shore he named *El Cabo de los Corrientes,* the Cape of Currents.[46]

Six years after De León's discovery, his pilot, Antonio de Alaminos, sailing from the Indies to Spain, passed not south of Cuba, as was customary, but north and through the Florida Straits, tapping the enormous thrust of the Gulf Stream to sling his ship to the latitude of the westerlies.[47] This innovation completed the development of the classic route from Iberia to America and back. The entire course, out and back, is a skewed parallelogram from Cádiz to the Canaries or Cape Verdes, then to Havana, and then back via the Gulf Stream and the westerlies, all in accordance with the titanic wheeling of the winds and currents around the weedy vacancy of the Sargasso Sea.

This utilization of the Gulf Stream was a matter of improving on what was already known. In the Pacific, a generation after Magellan, the passage from Asia to America was still unaccomplished. When he died, his ships departed the Philippines, went to the Moluccas, and loaded with spices. Then the surviving leaders of the expedition decided that the *Victoria* should continue on around the world, and the *Trinidad* should sail back across the Pacific to Mexico. The *Trinidad,* contrary to all the experience the voyage westward across the Pacific should have taught the Spaniards, set off into the teeth of the trades. Relentless headwinds in the tropics, and then, when they finally did turn north, storms and cold, plus scurvy – thirty died among a crew of fifty-three – forced the *Trinidad* back to the East Indies, where the Portuguese, zealous to protect their trade monopoly there, seized the ship and imprisoned its crew.[48]

The first step toward achieving Hispanic round trips across the Pacific was to obtain an eastern terminus somewhere on or near the Asian mainland. In the mid-1560s, a Spanish expedition under the command of Miguel López Legaspi sailed from Mexico and invaded the Philippines. Manila, with trading connections all over the Far East, was to be the center, the Havana, of the Spanish Orient. Legaspi quickly established a foothold in the Philippines and then turned to implement the rest of the plan, of which Manila was only a part. It seemed sensible to hope that westerlies blew north of the tropics in the Pacific, as in the Atlantic. Two great *marinheiros* raced to be the first to trace with the keels of their vessels the largest *volta* of them all.

The winner was Lope Martín, a better navigator than gentleman. He deserted Legaspi in the Philippines and sailed off in a tiny vessel with a crew of twenty and no extra sails or provisions. He steered north, caught the westerlies and rode them to the coast of California, and then sailed south to Mexico, arriving 9 August 1565. The voyage was marked by scurvy, near mutinies, and executions by drowning. Its success was more a product of luck and bravado than wisdom, and it seemed a weak precedent for annual exchanges between the Philippines and New Spain.

The credit for showing humanity how to cross the great waters from Asia to America is usually given to Andrés de Urdaneta, who had been Legaspi's pilot and chief adviser during the invasion of the Philippines, and whom Legaspi commissioned to sail to Mexico. (The nominal leader of the expedition was Legaspi's nephew, but everyone knew who the real leader was.) The *San Pablo* cleared Cebu on 1 June 1565, ran with the monsoon winds out of the Philippines, and crawled northwest across the Pacific to between 37°N and 39°N latitude, where the westerlies filled its sails and carried the ship to California waters. On 8 September it reached Acapulco, from which Urdaneta traveled on to Spain to tell his king of the treachery of Martín. The voyage of the *San Pablo* across the North Pacific took 129 days, and during that time sixteen men lost their lives.[49]

There was much more to learn: For instance, not until the seventeenth century did Europeans, specifically the Dutch, harness the westerlies of the Roaring Forties to carry them under the monsoon zone to the East Indies, and as a natural consequence learned a lot about Australia by underestimating longitude and blundering into that continent's west coast.[50] And not until Captain Cook returned from the Pacific did Europeans know anything about Australia's east coast or much of anything about New Zealand beyond the fact of its existence. But all that was relatively unimportant, icing on the cake, after Urdaneta.

In 1492, *marinheiros* had crossed the Atlantic. In the 1520s they had circumnavigated the globe for the first time, and the chief chronicler of the voyage had expressed doubt that it would ever be done again. But by 1600 even a private citizen could make that trip by taking passage on merchantmen, traveling most of the way by annually scheduled voyages. Francesco Carletti, who did it himself, described how: Embark from Spain for America with the West Indian fleet in July, and make a leisurely journey across Mexico to Acapulco, arriving in time to catch the Manila Galleon in March. From Manila, take passage to Japan and then Macao, and sail from the latter to Goa in India on a Portuguese merchantman, debarking in March. In Goa, sadly, there is a layover of months, waiting for the monsoon shift. But in December or January, board one of the giant Portuguese carracks for the annual six-month voyage to Lisbon. The circumnavigation, including all the delays for collecting cargoes and waiting for suitable winds, took four years. Going round the other way might take longer, westerlies being less dependable than the trades, but it, too, could be made entirely or almost entirely on commercial vessels under Spanish or Portuguese flags.[51]

The seams of Pangaea were closing, drawn together by the sailmaker's needle. Chickens met kiwis, cattle met kangaroos, Irish met potatoes, Comanches met horses, Incas met smallpox – all for the first time. The countdown to the extinction of the passenger pigeon and the native peoples of the Greater Antilles and of Tasmania had begun. A vast expansion in the numbers of certain other species on this planet began, led off by pigs and cattle, by certain weeds and pathogens, and by the Old World peoples who first benefited from contact with lands on the other side of the seams of Pangaea.[52]

The *marinheiros*, albeit unintentionally, were at the work of gods. Samuel Purchas, an early seventeenth-century English clergyman who collected and edited many of their accounts, asked a rhetorical question of his readers and posterity, of us:

who ever tooke possession of the huge Ocean, and made procession round about the vast Earth? Who ever discovered new Co nstellations, saluted the Frozen Poles, subjected the Burning Zones? And who else by the Art of Navigation have seemed to imitate Him, which laies the beames of his chambers in the Waters, and walketh on the wings of the Wind?[53]

The answer, of course, is *os marinheiros!*

6

⚜

Within reach, beyond grasp

. . . WHERE THE VITAL SUBSTANCE fermenting as it were into life by the heat of the sun, breaks forth precipitately from its matrix, and spreads with a kind of fury over the whole land.
—John Bruckner, *A Philosophical Survey of the Animal Creation* (1768)

WHEN CIVILIZED NATIONS come into contact with barbarians the struggle is short, except where a deadly climate gives its aid to the native race.
—Charles Darwin, *The Descent of Man* (1871)

MASTERY OF THE WINDS brought all oceanic coastlines and their hinterlands between Arctic and Antarctic ice within the European reach, but as history makes clear, not all were within the power of the Europeans to grasp, to occupy in numbers and displace the indigenous populations. Almost all the lands beyond the boundaries of Europe that are Neo-European today are those that most nearly meet the criteria cited at the end of the last chapter: similarity to Europe in such fundamentals as climate, and remoteness from the Old World. These are the Neo-Europes, the most visible residues of the age when Europe exclusively ruled the waves. Their history is the burden of the rest of this book, but first we must deal, if only briefly, with the lands that do not meet these criteria and that today are not Neo-European, though many were European colonies for long periods.

We can be brief about Pacific Asia north of the Tropic of Cancer. In China, Korea, and Japan, the Europeans had to deal with dense populations with traditions of strong central governments, resilient institutions, and cultural self-confidence, as well as with crops, domesticated animals, microlife, and parasites quite like those of Europe. In fact, the East Asians were very much like Europeans in most of the important ways, with a crucial but temporary deficiency in technology. The white imperialists never established colonies of settlement in this part of the world; the European quarters in such ports as Macao, Nagasaki, and Shanghai were only spigots tapped into the flank of Asia to draw off some of its wealth.

Middle Easterners were as well defended as the East Asians vis-à-vis the Europeans in the matters cited earlier, and they were actually expanding the area they controlled while the *marinheiros* were accomplishing their conquest of the oceans. The Ottoman Turks, with Janissaries and dervishes in attendance, controlled the Middle East, the Balkans, and North Africa for several centuries, and even after their decline, European colonies of settlement were impossible in the Islamic world except on its edges: for example, Algeria and Kazakstan.

Europeans tried hard to establish settlements in the torrid zone, but generally failed, often spectacularly. Let us divide this enormous area into three types of tropics, each with its different history of European residence. Europeans seldom coveted the arid tropics, except for their minerals, and so rarely migrated to them in large numbers. They were attracted to the relatively moist and often cool highlands, but even there the invaders were seldom able to replace the indigenes. The qualities of the highlands that attracted the whites had attracted multitudes of indigenes before the whites arrived, and the natives commonly occupied the high valleys and plateaus in numbers too great to be obliterated. To illustrate, considerable numbers of Spaniards migrated to the high central valley of Mexico; yet they did not replace, but rather interbred with, the Aztecs and other Amerindians. Mexico is a *mestizo* country, not a Neo-Europe.

Other Europeans also headed for the hills in the tropics – for the White Highlands of Kenya, for instance – but usually their stay was brief. There are exceptions: The great majority of Costa Rica's people live in its highlands and are of European descent, and that nation fits the definition of a Neo-Europe – but it is no more than an exception to the rule, and a tiny one at that. Its total population is less than 2.5 million. The rule (not the law) is that although Europeans may conquer in the tropics, they do not Europeanize the tropics, not even countrysides with European temperatures.

The areas of the tropics that attracted European imperialists first and that they have never ceased to covet are the hot, well-watered areas. The torrid zones in Africa and America did or obviously could produce dyewoods, pepper, sugar, slaves, and other cash crops; southern Asia included large expanses of fertile soil on which lived millions of disciplined, skilled people accustomed to turning out surpluses for indigenous and invader elites. Europeans did succeed in enriching themselves enormously in both the Old World and New World tropics, but seldom were they successful in establishing permanent European communities there. In the long run, the humid tropics proved to be a mouthful for which Europe had the teeth, but not the stomach.

Most of tropical Asia, as one would expect, was too hot and wet for European tastes, but more important than its propensity for making invaders sweat was the teeming presence of minute enemies. The Asians and their plants and animals had existed in and around thousands of villages and cities for thousands of years, and along with them had evolved many species of germs, worms, insects, rusts, molds, and what have you attuned to preying on humanity and its servant organisms. The victims had evolved along with their attackers and were reasonably well adapted to living and reproducing despite these parasites. In contrast, the Europeans and their servant organisms were babes in the woods in south Asia. The first to arrive, the Portuguese, found themselves attacked by agues, fluxes, poxes, piles, and "secrete diseases." "Mordexijn" (cholera?), for example, was rife in India: "it weakeneth a man and maketh him cast out all that he hath in his body, and many times his life withall." (The malady was especially dangerous in Goa because of the "unsatiable lustes" of the local women, whose demands on a man could "grinde him to powder, and sweep him away like dirt.")[1]

Indeed, women were central in the difficulties European settlers faced in the East – not Eastern women, but rather Western women. When the latter learned of the heat, sickness, exotic foods, and so forth, awaiting them in the East and of the ease with which European men acquired concubines there, few were willing to make the dangerous voyage around the Cape of Good Hope to raise families in Asia. Some European males might yearn for the life east of Suez, "Where there aren't no Ten Commandments an' a man can raise a thirst," but why would a prospective wife and mother want to go out there? European offspring in Asia usually were half Asian. (There was a snide saying in British India that necessity is the mother of Eurasians.) As for making good little Portuguese, Dutch, or British citizens of these children, they usually took up the cultures and languages of their mothers with greater facility than those of their fathers; and Europeans had little trust or understanding of Eurasians, anyway.[2]

The problems of European intruders in tropical Asia were similar to those of the Crusaders in the Holy Land a half millennium before. The desirable regions were already thoroughly occupied by humans in much greater numbers than Europe could ever send east, humans of physical endurance and sinewy culture. Like Europeans, these Indians, Indonesians, Malaysians, and so on, planted and consumed the small grains (especially rice, which had not arrived in Europe until the Renaissance), depended on approximately the same animals (though in much smaller numbers per human being), and struggled to maintain health against the same pathogens and parasites, plus several venomous species unknown in Europe. Despite all the differences between Easterners and Westerners, both were obviously children of the Old World Neolithic Revolution, and therefore the European advantage over the Asians was ephemeral. Even the great cities Singapore and Batavia, created at the command of the white imperialists, were in essence only gigantic trading posts, and their white inhabitants little more than sailors and supercargoes on extended shore leave, though they might stay for decades.

Only some of the elements of the Old World Neolithic (e.g., farming, large settlements, and iron) were present in hot, wet Africa when the Europeans arrived, and so in theory the Europeans should have conquered the Africans more more easily than the Asians. The conquest, however, was not accomplished until the end of the nineteenth century; the African ecosystem was simply too lush, too fecund, too untamed and untamable for the invaders until they added more science and technology to their armaments.

Europeans did not have the gear or concepts equal to the Pleistocene challenge of the rain forest. According to the chronicler of a 1555 expedition to West Africa to obtain, among other things, ivory,

This day wee tooke thirtie men with us to seek Elephants, our men being all well armed with harquebusses, pikes, long bowes, crossebowes, partizans [a kind of battle-ax], long swordes, and swordes and bucklers: wee found two Elephants which we stroke divers times harquebusses and long bowes but they went away from us and hurt one of our men.[3]

Only one? They were lucky to have come upon deferential elephants on first try. The whites simply were not equipped to impose their will on Africa until the nineteenth century and the age of cheap and plentiful quinine and repeating rifles. Their crops did poorly, falling victim to rot, insects, and all kinds of hungry animals (including elephants). If the plants survived all that, then the unvarying length of the day in the tropics gave them the wrong cues or no cues at all as to when to blossom and seed, and they died of anomie. On São Tomé, the early Portuguese found that wheat "will not produce in full ear, but runs to leaf and grows high without having any grain in the ear."[4]

European livestock in West Africa did no better. The local parasites and diseases, most importantly trypanosomiasis, almost entirely excluded domesticated animals. West Africa had some cattle when the whites arrived on its coasts, but they were a runty lot, their meat "dry and lean," and their milk production so meager that twenty or thirty were "scarce sufficient to supply the Director-General's table" at the Dutch outpost there in the seventeenth century. Of horses there were none on the coast or in the immediate hinterland unless imported. They did not last long nor reproduce in the wet, torrid climate, and the Portuguese made a good thing of bringing them down the coast to exchange for gold, pepper, and slaves. Some horses did live deep in the interior, probably on the edge of the sudanic grasslands, but they were "so very low that a tall man sitting on their Backs may very near touch the ground with his feet."[5]

West Africa's most effective defense against Europeans was disease: blackwater fever, yellow fever, breakbone fever, bloody flux, and a whole zoo of helminthic parasites. Examples of their ravages, early and late, are legion. King João II (1481–95) sent a squire of his household, a gentleman of the spurs, and a crossbowman of the king's chamber, plus servants (eight men in all), to Africa and up the Gambia River to see the king of Mandi. All died but one, he "being more accustomed to these parts."[6] In the early nineteenth century it was common that each year more than half the British troops stationed on the Gold Coast would die.[7] Two generations later, Joseph Conrad, then working – and nearly dying – in King Leopold II's mad enterprise to exploit the Congo, reported fever and dysentery of such high incidence that most of his fellow employees were sent home before their terms of duty were finished, "so that they shouldn't die in the Congo. God forbid! It would spoil the statistics which are excellent, you see! In a word, it seems that there are only seven per cent who can do their three year service."[8]

Africa was a prize well within European reach, but it seared the hand that tried to hold it. João de Barros, who was on the Guinea coast in the sixteenth century, eloquently expressed the frustration of all imperialists who gazed on Africa, opulent, tantalizing, and impossible:

But it seems that for our sins, or for some inscrutable judgement of God, in all the entrances of this great Ethiopia that we navigate along, He has placed a striking angel with a flaming sword of deadly fevers, who prevents us from penetrating into the interior to the springs of this garden, whence proceed these rivers of gold that flow to the sea in so many parts of our conquest.[9]

Until the beginning of the twentieth century, colonies of outsiders in tropical Africa tended to sizzle and die. When the American Revolution canceled Britain's right to transport convicts to Georgia, some were sent to the Gold Coast, but that sentence so frequently proved fatal that it was equivalent, said Edmund Burke, to imposition of the death penalty after "a mock display of mercy."[10] Britain exiled its convicts instead to that germ cell of a new Neo-Europe, Botany Bay, where they, relatively speaking, thrived.

In the late eighteenth and nineteenth centuries, liberal whites in Britain and the United States tried to hurry along the emancipation of slaves and to head off racial conflict by shipping freed blacks to colonies in West Africa: Sierra Leone and Liberia. In doing so, the abolitionists proved that even African genes, sans an African childhood, provided only a flimsy shield against African pathogens. In the first year of the Province of Freedom, Sierra Leone, 46 percent of the whites died, but so did 39 percent of the black settlers. In Liberia between 1820 and 1843, 21 percent of all immigrants, presumably all or almost all of them black or mulatto, died during their first year of residence.[11]

Most of the problems that existed for Europeans in Africa also existed in tropical America, but usually to a lesser degree. In the West Indies, complained José de Acosta in the sixteenth century, the wheat "comes up well, and is presently greene, but so unequally, as they cannot gather it; for the seede sowen at one instant, some is spindled, some is in the eare, one in the grasse and another in the graine."[12] Only in tropical America's mountains and high plateaus would wheat and a number of other Middle

Eastern plants grow in accordance with Judeo-Christian tradition. In the American lowlands, as in the African lowlands, Europeans were often obliged to adopt local crops – cassava, maize, sweet potatoes, and others – which, of course, served Europeans no better than they served the other races.

The story of European domesticated animals in the West Indies and elsewhere in tropical America contrasts sharply with the fate of many Old World plants there. This was particularly true of pigs and cattle; horses sometimes proved more finicky, taking many years to adjust to the environments of Brazil's grasslands and the llanos. Even so, European livestock succeeded in torrid America while failing in Africa in the same latitudes, and this provides one obvious explanation for the contrasting histories of the colonies in the two areas.[13]

Disease organisms, most of them apparently from the Old World, took a heavy toll among Amerindians in the tropics, eliminating most of them in the lowlands and islands and opening these areas up for white settlement. But the specifically African pathogens treated the whites almost as severely, crippling their colonial enterprises. Between 1793 and 1796, the British army in the Caribbean theater lost about 80,000 men, over half of them to yellow fever alone, for a total greater than the Duke of Wellington lost in the entire Peninsula War.[14] Even between 1817 and 1836, a time of peace, the annual death rate among British soldiers in the West Indies ranged from 85 to 130 per thousand, whereas in their home islands it was only about 15 per thousand. (In West Africa, we should note, it was over 500 per thousand in these years.)[15] European colonies of settlement in the American tropics were understandably rare, and even more rarely successful. For instance, the upshot of a Scottish attempt at Darien at the end of the seventeenth century and of a French attempt in Guiana about sixty years later was simply thousands of deaths and a few score huts damply crumbling into mold.[16] A European colony in hot and moist America often consisted of a small white managerial class, a number of free blacks and mulattos, and an enormous mass of African slaves. The latter, almost invariably malnourished, often overworked, and living in a disease environment not as inimical for them as for whites but significantly different from that in their homeland, also died at a lively rate; however, they could be and were continually replaced.[17]

Disease was the most important factor dictating that hot, wet America would be a land of racial mixture. Amerindians melted away, and European immigrants survived with difficulty; so the entrepreneurs of Atlantic commerce brought millions of Africans to replace Amerindian labor in the humid American tropics. The results are today's Neo-African and mixed societies: not temperate Montreal, where the ranges of race and culture are as narrow as the channel the English call English and the French call *la Manche*, but tropical Rio de Janeiro, where mulattos and *zambos* and allegedly pure Portuguese dance the African samba on the eve of Lent.

Yet, despite all we have said, Europeans can create Neo-European societies in the hot and humid tropics – indeed, they have done so – but the prerequisites are stiff. It is a valuable lesson in biogeography to examine them. Let us look at the early history of Queensland, the white and remarkably healthy state in tropical northeastern Australia. It had several special dispensations from fate, enabling it to become a Neo-Europe in an area quite as steamy as many where European colonies died of mildew, rot, and malaria. Ultimately, the problem of European settlements in the wet tropics was not the heat *per se* or the humidity *per se*, although these did contribute massively to the difficulties; the problem was contact with tropical humans, their servant organisms, and *attendant parasites,* micro and macro.

Queensland had as much moisture and warmth as an *Anopheles* or *Aëdes* mosquito or a tsetse fly or a hookworm or any other kind of worm could want, but it did not have a large population of indigenes and their animals and plants teeming with tiny malevolent occupants. The Queensland Aborigines were few in number, and therefore they had fewer kinds of parasitic organisms; they had no crops and only one animal, the dingo, to provide a medium for the evolution of germs and what have you to prey on immigrant plants and animals. When the white invaders imported laborers to work their sugar plantations (Queensland was one of the very last examples of the Madeira type), they brought them in from the relatively healthy Pacific islands, not from the disease-ridden continents. The "kanakas," as these contract workers were called, did bring some tropical infections with them, as did the few Chinese who came and British soldiers from India, but all together they did not arrive with as rich a selection of pathogens and parasites as, for instance, the Africans carried to Brazil and the Caribbean. Malaria established itself in Queensland, but not firmly. The government prohibited further immigration of nonwhites (for a variety of reasons, economic, humanitarian, and racist), greatly reducing the inflow of disease organisms, and the white Queenslanders accepted and applied the lessons of the sanitationist and bacteriological revolutions of the nineteenth and twentieth centuries to protect themselves, their livestock, and crops. Malaria faded away, and Queensland became, as it remains, one of the healthiest areas on earth, inside or outside the torrid zone. This has cost a great deal of money, which Australia, by one means and another, has supplied.[18] Queensland's neo-European society is not as artificial as the one the United States created in the Panama Canal Zone, but neither is life there as cool, comfortable, and easy as in southern and *temperate* Australia, where a reincarnated William Wordsworth could observe "the young lambs bound as to the tabor's sound," and in some locations might be flimflammed into thinking himself home in the Lake Country.

In the second decade of the seventeenth century, a small group of English Dissenters in exile in the Netherlands, struggling with poverty and fearful that their children were growing up Dutch, tried to decide where to go to found a godly and English society. They carefully considered Guiana; they considered northern Virginia. Their analysis of the advantages and disadvantages of each was valid then, and, barring the investments mentioned above vis-à-vis Queensland, remains so. Guiana, they judged,

was both fruitful and pleasant, and might yield riches and maintenance to the possessors more easily than the other; yet, other things considered, it would not be so fit for them . . . Such hot countries are subject to grievous diseases and many noisome impediments which other more temperate places are freer from, and would not so well agree with our English bodies.[19]

So off they sailed to North America, where half the Pilgrims, as we have come to call them, died of malnutrition, exhaustion, and cold during their first winter in New England. But the rest, as they believed to be their due, received benefits like unto those promised Abraham by the Lord: "I will bless you abundantly and greatly multiply your descendants until they are as numerous as the stars in the sky and the grains of sand on the sea-shore. Your descendants shall possess the cities of their enemies. All nations on earth shall pray to be blessed as your descendants are blessed."[20] If the Pilgrims had gone to Guiana –

persuaded, perhaps, by Sir Walter Raleigh's vision of that land: "for health, good air, pleasure and riches I am resolved it cannot be equaled by any region east or west"[21] – they would have entered an environment inimical to Europeans and their servant organisms because of its heat, humidity, predators, parasites, and pathogens. The Pilgrims would have left little more behind them than shallow graves in wet ground.

7

Weeds

WE HAVE THE APPARENT DOUBLE ANOMALY, that Australia is better suited to some English plants than England is, and that some English plants are better suited to Australia than those Australian plants were which have given way before English intruders.

—Joseph Dalton Hooker, 1853

IT IS REALLY NOT SURPRISING that Europeans failed to Europeanize Asia and tropical Africa. They did better in the New World tropics, but fell far short of founding congeries of Neo-European societies under the blazing American sun. In fact, in many areas they did not even try, but concentrated on creating plantation colonies staffed with non-European peons, slaves, or contract laborers. What is amazing is that Europeans were able to establish themselves in large numbers in the Neo-Europes, and indeed to thrive and multiply there "as the stars in the sky, and as the grains of sand on the seashore." This the white imperialists achieved despite the remoteness of the Neo-Europes and their many bizarre aspects – bizarre by Old World standards. Quebec may be like Cherbourg today, but in 1700 it certainly was not. San Francisco and Montevideo and Sydney may be European today, but a few – really a very few – generations ago they were without masonry or streets, and they were inhabited by Amerindians and Aborigines jealous of their lands and rights. What enabled the white intruders to make Neo-European cities of these harbors and shorelines?

Any respectable theory that attempts to explain the Europeans' demographic advance has to provide explanations for at least two phenomena. The first is the demoralization and often the annihilation of the indigenous populations of the Neo-Europes. The obliterating defeat of these populations was not simply a matter of European technological superiority. The Europeans who settled in temperate South Africa seemingly had the same advantages as those who settled in Virginia and New South Wales, and yet how different their histories have been. The Bantu-speaking peoples, who now overwhelmingly outnumber the whites in South Africa, were superior to the American, Australian, and New Zealand indigenes in that they possessed iron weapons, but how much more inferior to a musket or a rifle is a stone-pointed spear than an iron-pointed spear? The Bantu have prospered demographically not because of their numbers at the time of first contact with whites; they were probably fewer per square kilometer than, for instance, the Amerindians east of the Mississippi River. Rather, the Bantu have prospered because they survived military conquest, avoided the conquerors, or became their indispensable servants – and in the long run because they reproduced in greater numbers than the whites. In contrast, why did so few of the natives of the Neo-Europes survive?

Second, we must explain the stunning, even awesome, success of European agriculture in the Neo-Europes. The difficult progress of the European agricultural frontier in the Siberian *taiga* or the Brazilian *sertão* or the South African *veldt* contrasts sharply with its easy, almost fluid advance in North America, for instance. Of course, the white pioneers of the United States and Canada would never have characterized their progress as easy; their lives were filled with danger, deprivation, and unremitting labor. But as a group they always succeeded in taming whatever portion of temperate North America they wanted within a few decades, and usually a good deal sooner. Many individuals among them failed – they were driven mad by blizzards and dust storms, lost their crops to locusts and their flocks to cougars and wolves, or lost their scalps to understandably inhospitable Amerindians – but as a group they always succeeded, and in terms of human generations, very quickly.

These phenomena were so vast that they strike one as suprahuman, as manifestations of forces impinging on human affairs that are more powerful, undeviating, and pervasive than human will – forces that are to will as the persistent and inexorable progress of a glacier is to the rush of an avalanche. Let us look at human migration between Europe and the Neo-Europes. Tens of millions of Europeans left home and went to the Neo-Europes, where they reproduced voluminously. In stark contrast, very few indigenes of the Americas, Australia, or New Zealand ever went to Europe and had children there. Now, it is not startling that the flow of human migration was almost entirely from Europe to the colonies, nor is it very enlightening. Europeans controlled overseas migration, and Europe needed to export, not import, labor. But this pattern of one-way migration is significant in that it reappears in the history of the migration of other species between Europe and the Neo-Europes. We cannot take all the migrant species into consideration, and the spread overseas of such Old World crops as wheat and turnips, for instance, is the obvious and uninformative concomitant of the spread of European farmers. Let us consider three general kinds of life forms that often passed over the seams of Pangaea and usually prospered in the colonies, not with but often without help and even despite European actions: weeds, feral animals, and pathogens associated with humanity. Is there a pattern in the histories of these groups that suggests an overall explanation for the phenomenon of the demographic triumph of Europeans in the Neo-Europes, or that at least suggests new paths of inquiry?

First, it is necessary to define "Neo-Europe" more narrowly than we have thus far. Not all parts of the United States, Argentina, Australia, and so forth, attracted great numbers of Europeans. There are, for instance, few whites in Australia's Great Sandy Desert, and if all of Australia were arid, then that continent would be no nearer to being a Neo-Europe than is Greenland. Where the hottest, coldest, driest, wettest, and, in general, the most inhospitable parts of the Neo-Europes have white populations today, it is because great numbers of white immigrants were attracted to the more hospitable regions, and then spread out from there. These regions are the arenas in which native and alien species had their most significant competitions in the post-Columbian and post-Cookian era, and in which the results made possible the Europeanization of the whole lands. It is on these arenas that we shall be focusing our attention. The eastern third of the United States and Canada, where half the population still lives, though it has been over three and a half centuries since the founding of Jamestown and Quebec, is the Neo-European seedbed of North America. The counterpart in Australia is its southeastern corner, bounded by the seas and a line drawn from Brisbane to Adelaide, plus Tasmania. All of New Zealand, minus its high cold country and the west coast of the South Island, falls into this alluring category. The Neo-European core of southern South America is the humid grassland at whose center lies the city of Buenos Aires. It is an enormous territory, most of it flat as a board, that lies within a half circle scrawled from Bahía Blanca in the south to Córdoba in the west to Pôrto Alegre on the Brazilian coast. This vast tract of upwards of a million square kilometers includes a fifth of Argentina and all of Uruguay and Brazil's Rio Grande do Sul. There live two-thirds of Argentina's people and all those of Uruguay and Rio Grande do Sul, the largest concentration of population in the world south of the Tropic of Capricorn.[1]

Having set the scenes, let us introduce into them "the tramps of our flora," as Sir Joseph Dalton Hooker called them: weeds.[2] "Weed" is not a scientific term in the sense of species, genus, or family, and its popular definitions are protean; so we must pause to define it. In modern botanical usage, the word refers to any plant that spreads rapidly and outcompetes others on disturbed soil. Before the advent of agriculture, there were relatively few of these plants representing any given species; they were the "pioneers of secondary successions or colonizers," specializing in the occupation of ground stripped of plants by landslides, floods, fires, and so forth.[3]

Weeds are not always unlikeable. Rye and oats were once weeds; now they are crop plants.[4] Can a crop plant shift the other way and become a weed? Yes. Amaranth and crab-grass were prehistoric crops in America and Europe, respectively, both treasured for their nourishing seeds, and now both have been demoted to weeds. (Amaranth may be on its way back to respectability in the crop category again.)[5] Are weeds, while in that category, always a bane and torment to everyone? No, indeed. Bermuda grass, one of the most irrepressible tropical weeds, was extolled a century and a half ago as a stabilizer of levees along the lower Mississippi at the same time that farmers not far from that river were calling it devilgrass.[6] Weeds are not good or bad; they are simply the plants that tempt the botanist to use such anthropomorphic terms as aggressive and opportunistic.

Europe had plenty of weeds long before the *marinheiros* set out into the Mediterranean Atlantic. As the Pleistocene glaciers retreated, species of weeds evolved to take over the bare earth left behind. As Neolithic farmers moved into Europe, they carried with them their crops, their livestock, and Middle Eastern weeds. Some of these opportunistic plants probably crossed the Atlantic to Vinland, but lasted no more than a season or two longer than the Viking settlements there. Mediterranean weeds were no doubt the first successful crossers among colonizing plants, making the short jump to the deforested slopes of the Azores, Madeiras, and Canaries, and then the long voyage to the West Indies and tropical America.

We know very little about weeds in America in the fifteenth and sixteenth centuries. The *conquistadores* paid little attention to farming, less to weeds as such, and the historians who traveled with or followed after Cortés and the rest rarely took notice of the *malas hierbas,* but we know they were there. European crops and other desirable plants flourished in the Indies even when disgracefully neglected by farmers gone crazy for gold and conquest; so we can be sure that the imported weeds, which thrive on neglect, did very well indeed.⁷ Even trees sank to the level of weedy behavior. When, at the end of the sixteenth century, José de Acosta asked who had planted the forests of orange trees through which he walked and rode, the answer was "that oranges being fallen to the ground, and rotten, their seeds did spring, and of those which the water carried away into divers parts, these woods grew so thicke." Two centuries and a half later, Charles Darwin found islands near the mouth of the Paraná thick with orange and peach trees, sprung up from seeds carried by the river.⁸

The imported weeds must have taken over large areas in the West Indies, Mexico, and other places, because the Iberian conquest created enormous areas of disturbed ground. Forests were razed for timber and fuel and to make way for new enterprises; burgeoning herds of Old World animals grazed and overgrazed the grasslands and invaded the woodlands; and the cultivated fields of the declining Amerindian populations reverted to nature, a nature whose most aggressive plants were now exotic immigrants. Friar Bartolomé de las Casas told of large herds of cattle and other European animals in the West Indies eating native plants down to the roots in the first half of the sixteenth century, followed by the spread of ferns, thistles, plantain, nettles, nightshade, sedge, and so forth, which he identified as Castilian and yet stated were present when the Spanish arrived.⁹ It is impossible that the same species would have developed in both Castile and Española, and unlikely that they made the trans-Atlantic passage in pre-Columbian times. It is much likelier that they were Old World colonizing species moving in with the explorers and advancing as fast as or faster than the friars.

The weeds must have advanced at least as fast in central Mexico, as colossal herds of Spanish cattle and other animals, tame and feral, grazed and overgrazed and, by the end of the sixteenth century, began in some areas to starve in the midst of the vacancies they had made.¹⁰ Old World colonizing plants had not had such an opportunity since the invention of agriculture. At least as early as 1555, European clover was so widespread that the Aztecs had a word of their own for it. They called it Castilian or *Castillan ocoxichitli,* naming it after a low native plant that also prefers shade and moisture.[11] It is probable that central Mexico's weed flora by 1600 was largely what it is today: mostly Eurasian with a predominance of Mediterranean plants.[12]

Perhaps we can reconstruct to an extent what happened in Mexico in the sixteenth century by examining the record of weed spread in California (upper California) in the late eighteenth and nineteenth centuries. We do not have a firsthand description of the aboriginal condition of California's grasslands, but botanists with a taste for history have gathered together such evidence as does exist in the way of tiny relict meadows in neglected corners and a few oblique references in written sources. They have hypothe- sized a flora dominated by bunch grasses subjected to only the light grazing of pronghorns and such. The buffalo did not flow through the Sacramento and San Joaquin valleys in all their millions, any more than through central Mexico.

This Californian flora was as fatally vulnerable to Eur- asian invaders as were California's aboriginal peoples, but isolation protected the flora, as it did the people, for two and a half centuries after the first coming of the Spanish to America. California, separated from Europe by a continent and an ocean, and from the population centers of Spanish Mexico by deserts and the northerly winds and currents that flow along the coasts of both upper and lower Califor- nia, remained one of the most remote regions in any of the European empires until the last decades of the eighteenth century. As late as 1769, according to the evidence of plant materials embedded in the adobe bricks of California's oldest colonial buildings, only three European plants were growing there: curly dock, sow thistle, and red-stemmed filaree.[13] The latter was in particular the pioneer of an assemblage of Mediterranean weeds tolerant of hot weather with seasonal droughts.

When, in the middle eighteenth century, Russian fur traders and imperialists became active on the northwest coast of America, the Spanish reacted by dispatching soldiers and missionaries to the wild California frontier. They took with them, whether they intended to or not, the forage plants and weeds of the Mediterranean – the three named earlier, plus wild oats, common foxtail, chess, bromes, Italian ryegrass, and others – and these accompanied them and in some cases may even have preceded them along the coastal hills and into the San Joaquin and Sacramento valleys and beyond.[14] Some of these plants had tagged along with the agricultural frontier all the way from the hearthlands of Old World civilization. Black mustard, the tiny seed of which, according to Jesus Christ, is like the kingdom of God, because it "groweth up, and becometh greater than all herbs, and shooteth out great branches; so that the fowls of the air may lodge under the shadow of it," arrived in California with the Franciscan friars.[15]

A few of these plants trickled in, and then more and more, as their pioneers pressed on ahead. As John Charles Frémont, an explorer from the United States, was coming down along the *Río de los Americanos* into the Sacramento Valley in March of 1844, he found red-stemmed filaree, an Old World immigrant like himself and his mounts. It was "just now beginning to bloom, and covering the ground like a sward of grass." The horses consumed it "with avidity," and even the squaws he met ate it "with apparent relish," indicating by sign language that what was good for the animals was good for them, too.[16]

A number of weeds came into California during the late Spanish era, probably more during the Mexican years after 1824, and more yet after annexation by the United States, as Anglo-Americans brought plants with them across the plains from the eastern seaboard. The gold rush of 1849 produced an immense demand for beef and therefore severe overgrazing, which was followed by extensive floods in 1862 and then an intensive two-year drought. When the rains came again, the introduced plants sprouted first and fastest, and California's grasslands became what they had been becoming for a century, that is, Eurasian. Without the opportunistic invaders, the loss of topsoil would have impoverished thousands of hectares of the most valuable agricultural land in the world today. By 1860 there were at least ninety-one alien weed species naturalized in the state. A twentieth-century reconnaissance of the San Joaquin Valley revealed that introduced plants "constituted 63 per cent of the herbaceous vegetation in the grassland types, sixty-six per cent in the woodland, and fifty-four per cent in chaparral."[17]

We have to guess about the early history of Old World colonizing plants in Mexico, extrapolating backward from more recent examples of their spread, but not in Peru, thanks to the Jesuit Bernabé Cobo and the half Amerindian, half Spanish nobleman Garcilaso de la Vega. They did not write specifically about plants that were unequivocally weedy in behavior – such plants did not deserve the attention of distinguished men – but they did write about respectable plants that went wild and defied attempts to keep them out of cultivated fields, citing turnips, mustard, mint, and camomile as among the worst offenders. Several of these "have overgrown the original names of the valleys and imposed their own as in the case of Mint Valley on the seacoast, which was formerly called Rucma, and others." In Lima, endive and spinach grew taller than a man, and "a horse could not force his way through them."

The most expansionistic European weed in sixteenth-century Peru was *trébol,* a clover or clovers that took over more of the cool, damp country than any other colonizing species, providing good forage but smothering crops as well. The former subjects of the Inca, who had abruptly found themselves with a new elite and a new God to support, now discovered themselves in competition with *trébol* for crop land.[18] What was *trébol?* Most of it, in all likelihood, was white clover, which performed the same role of pioneer and *conquistador* in North America.

England, which spawned most of the colonies in northern America, had, according to John Fitzherbert's *Book of Husbandry,* "divers maner of weeds, as thystels, kedlockes, docks, cockledrake," and others,[19] and they are as thick in Shakespeare's language as they no doubt were in his gardens at Stratford-upon-Avon. His duke of Burgundy informs Henry V not that times are hard in France, but that, "darnel, hemlock and rank fumitory" are growing there. His Hotspur wins literary immortality by promising that "out of this nettle, danger, we pluck this flower, safety." Poor mad Lear roams the fields

> Crowned with rank fumiter and furrow-weeds,
> With hardocks, hemlock, nettles, cuckoo-flowers,
> Darnel, and all the idle weeds that grow
> In our sustaining corn.[20]

It is a sure bet that English weeds were rooted in North American soil while Shakespeare was alive. John Josselyn, who visited New England in 1638 and 1663, scores of years after the first European fishermen began summering in Newfoundland and environs, and in all likelihood planting small gardens, made a list "Of Such Plants as have sprung up since the English Planted and kept Cattle in New-England."[21] He was not a professional botanist and may have been mistaken in a few of his identifications, but surely was accurate in most.

Couch grass	Shepherd's purse
Dandelion	Groundsel
Sow-thistle	Wild arrach

Night Shade, with the White Flower	Nettles stinging
Mallowes	Plantain
Black henbane	Wormwood
Sharp-pointed dock	Patience
Bloodwort	Adder's tongue
Knot-grass	Cheek-weed
Compherie, with the white flower	May-weed
The great clot-bur	Mullin, with the white flower

Nettles were the first of these plants to be noticed in New England, either because they were the first to spread or because they do indeed sting. Plantain, which figures in *Romeo and Juliet,* Act I, Scene II, as a medicinal herb ("Your plantain leaf is excellent for that. What? For your broken shin.") was called "Englishman's foot" by the Amerindians of both New England and Virginia, who believed in the seventeenth century that it would grow only where the English "have troden, & was never known before the English came into this country."[22]

What was the first European weed in the southern colonies of North America? A candidate that does not come first to mind is the Old World peach, but it was as quick to take up residence in North America as José de Acosta's orange trees in tropical America. When the English first penetrated into the interior of Carolina and Georgia, they found peach trees flourishing in Amerindian orchards, and many growing wild. The indigenes, some of whom believed peaches to be as American as maize, dried the fruit in the sun and baked it into loaves for winter consumption. The trees were so quick to sprout from the stone that John Lawson wrote from Carolina in the early eighteenth century that "eating peaches in our orchards makes them come up so thick from the kernel, that we are forced to take a great deal of care to weed them out, otherwise they make our land a wilderness of peach trees."[23] The probable explanation for the Old World peach preceding the English pioneers, and also for the odd fact that the Amerindians initially had more varieties of the fruit than the English, is that the Spanish or French had introduced it into Florida in the sixteenth century. From there, the Amerindians spread it northward, where, as their populations declined and their orchards went wild, the peach became naturalized.

Plants more commonly rated by Europeans as weeds than the peach probably arrived as early, but, as befitted their stature, less ostentatiously. In 1629, Captain John Smith reported that most of the woods around Jamestown, Virginia, had been cut down and "all converted into pasture and gardens; wherein doth grow all manner of herbs and roots we have in England in abundance and as good grass as can be," but he did not trouble us with specific names.[24] The champion pioneers among the European weeds in North America were forage forbs and grasses gone wild. Native American grasses east of the Mississippi, never having had to survive the enormous herds of quadrupeds that grazed the Great Plains, had few of the attributes that enable plants to live in the same fields with cattle, sheep, and goats. The indigenous grasses disappeared from all but the niches and crannies of British and French North America after the arrival and spread of those animals.[25]

Among the imported forage crops, the champions were white clover (the probable champion of colonizing plants in Peru) and the Eurasian plant Americans have arrogantly named Kentucky bluegrass. The two mixed together were called English grass. They were quite English in their preference for cool, damp climates; if peaches preferred the southern tier of European colonies in North America, English grass preferred the northern.[26] Either or both the clover and grass were being sown intentionally in North America at least as early as 1685, when William Penn tried some in his courtyard. Their desirability as forage and their own aggressive natures soon spread them widely in the thirteen colonies and in Canada along the St. Lawrence. When English pathfinders topped the Appalachian and proceeded into Kentucky in the last decades of the eighteenth century, they found white clover and bluegrass waiting for them. The plants either had crept over the mountains clinging to the coats of traders' horses and mules from Carolina or, more likely, had entered with the French in the late seventeenth or eighteenth century.[27]

White clover and Kentucky bluegrass continued west until the rain petered out on the other side of the Mississippi, hustling along to keep up with the frontier of the new United States and even striking off on their own.

Illinois, 1818: Where the little caravans have encamped as they crossed the praries, and have given their cattle hay made of these perennial grasses, there remains ever after a spot of green turf for the instruction and encouragement of future improvers.[28]

From those green spots, ripples of nourishing forage and nearly ineradicable weeds spread out over the Midwest, in time to be carried across the semiarid plains to renew their wild spree of expansion in the cool, moist lands of the Far West.[29]

Right behind white clover and Kentucky bluegrass on the list of the most aggressive floral imports were barberry, Saint-John's-wort, common hemp, corn cockle, and chess, plus all those on Josselyn's list, plus many more. In January of 1832, Lewis D. de Schweinitz, after much research, announced to the Lyceum of Natural History of New York that the most aggressive plants in the northern states of the United States were the foreign weeds, and he provided a list of 137 of them. The situation in the South was in all probability similar.[30]

The weeds whose presence he and Josselyn and the others east of the Mississippi recorded seemed to lose their aggressiveness as they neared the center of North America. Buffalo grass and grama grasses and the other native flora of the plains were able to resist the invaders effectively, except when humans made an earnest effort to assist the exotics, as in obliterating the Manitoba and Dakota grasses and planting wheat. Later we shall return to the question why the Great Plains flora was so resistant to invasion.

Meanwhile, let us turn to another success story, this one some eighty degrees of latitude to the south-southeast. There sprawls the pampa, a plain that in its well-watered portions succumbed to Old World invaders about as thoroughly as equivalent parts of the San Joaquin Valley in California. The pampa is an enormous level area, well watered in the east, and less and less so as one moves away from the Atlantic and the Río de la Plata toward the Andes. The moist and fertile pampa was four centuries ago a vast grassland, "barren and flat and without trees, except along the rivers," said the first Spaniards to see it. Dominating the flora were the swaying needlegrasses, and grazing on them and moving through them were outlandish humpless camels and giant flightless birds.[31]

The usurpation of the native biota of the pampa must have been under way by the end of the sixteenth century, as domesticated animals from Europe arrived, thrived, and propagated into enormous herds. Their eating habits, trampling hooves, and droppings, and the seeds of the weedish plants they carried with them, as alien to America as they were themselves, altered forever the soil and flora of the pampa. That alteration must have been swift, but there is little in contemporary documents on the subject until the eighteenth century. A visitor, Félix de Azara, recorded in the 1780s that the vast numbers of livestock and the practice of burning off the dead grasses annually were eliminating delicate plants and the taller grasses, and the resulting vacancies were not going begging. Wherever the European or half-breed pioneer threw up his little hut, mallows and thistles and such sprang up, even if there were no other such plants for thirty leagues. And it was enough

that the frontiersman frequent a road, even though alone
with his horse, for these plants to rise up along its edges.
The pioneer of the pampa was a sort of botanical Midas,
changing the flora with his touch.[32]

The story of the flora of the pampa, in at least its most
spectacular features, becomes clearer in the nineteenth
century. The wild artichoke, *cardo de Castilla,* common in
Buenos Aires in 1749, continued to spread, and when
Charles Darwin visited this part of the world eighty years
later, he found it in Argentina and Chile and so luxuriant in
Uruguay that it rendered hundreds of square miles impen-
etrable by horse or man. "I doubt," he wrote, "whether
any case is on record of an invasion on so grand a scale of
one plant over the aborigines."[33]

W. H. Hudson, as a child in mid-nineteenth-century
Argentina, saw thickets of wild artichoke that stretched
bluish and gray green as far as the eye could see, but he was
more impressed with the imported giant thistle, a Mediterranean biennial that grew as high as a mounted man. In
"thistle years" it sprang up everywhere, and when it dried
there was great danger of fire:

At such times the sight of smoke in the distance would cause
every man who saw it to mount his horse and fly to the
danger-spot where an attempt would be made to stop the fire by
making a broad path in the thistles some fifty to a hundred yards
ahead of it. One way to make the path was to lasso and kill a few
sheep from the nearest flock and drag them up and down at a
gallop through the dense thistles until a broad space was cleared
where the flames could be stamped and beaten out with horse-
rugs.[34]

The evidence we have on the floral changes in the
grasslands of the Río de la Plata region is anecdotal, spotty,
far from scientific, but we can take the enormous spread of
these two alien weeds in the nineteenth century as certain
proof that the ecosystem of the pampa had been trauma-

tized by the whites and their animals. The herds caused changes nearly everywhere between the snow line on the Andes and some similar line in Patagonia, but nowhere was the transformation as profound as in the core of the grasslands: the well-watered, fertile, and, all in all, rather European region 300 and more kilometers across that has as its kernel the city of Buenos Aires. As Darwin in 1833 crossed into that core from the outside, he noticed a change from "coarse herbage" to "a carpet of fine green verdure." He attributed this transformation to some change in the soil, but "the inhabitants assured me that . . . the whole was to be attributed to the manuring and grazing of the cattle."[35]

In 1877, Carlos Berg published a list of some 153 European plants he had found in the province of Buenos Aires and in Patagonia, including among the most plentiful such European familiars as white clover, shepherd's purse, chickweed, goosefoot, red-stemmed filaree, and curly dock. Also included is *llanten,* as it is known to the Spanish, or plantain to the English, or Englishman's foot to the Algonkins in North America.[36] According to field botanists, only one quarter of the plants growing wild on the pampa in the 1920s were natives.[37] W. H. Hudson bemoaned the plight of the European of the pampa, surrounded by his weeds "that spring up in his fields under all skies, ringing him round with old-world monotonous forms, as tenacious of their undesired union with him as the rats and cockroaches that inhabit his house."[38] Yet without these plants, what would have – what could have – replaced the native species disappearing under the hooves of the exotic herds?

If it were true that the degree of difference between European life forms and the native life forms of a colony correlates with the vulnerability of the latter to invasion by the former, then Australia – with its distinctive grasses and forbs, forests of unique eucalypti, black swans, giant flightless birds, and pouched mammals – should today be another Europe. It has not become so, of course, because it was saved by its hot, arid, and entirely un-European interior, and by the tight grip on existence that characterizes organisms living in the environments that shaped them. But there have been changes, considerable changes. The Europeans and their portmanteau biota have altered the Australian environment irreversibly.

The British who came to New South Wales in 1788 to found a colony intentionally brought many kinds of plants with them – over two hundred by March of 1803 – and, of course, others unintentionally. Some of those brought on purpose immediately took up the ways of the weed – purslane, for one – and their success indicates the vulnerability of the Australian flora to Old World invasion.[39] White clover barely held its own in the rather dry site of the original settlement at Sydney, but advanced rapidly in the moist climate of Melbourne, "often destroying other vegetation."[40] Sow thistle seemed to thrive everywhere in and around the latter city, even growing on roofs. Other weeds also spread rapidly in Victoria, including knotgrass and red sorrel, pushing less aggressive grasses right out of some pastures. Tasmania, whose climate is very like that of northwestern Europe, was also hospitable to the new weeds, and knotgrass and snakeweed kept pace with the colonizing humans.[41]

The weeds could move into the interior with amazing speed, sometimes bounding ahead of the settled frontier. In the same general period in which Frémont found filaree along the *Río de los Americanos* in the foothills of California's Sierras, Henry W. Haygarth found wild oats, a weed common in Europe since the early Iron Age, along the Snowy River where it flows down from the Australian Alps:

Horses are excessively fond of this plant, so much so, that in the early part of the spring, when it shoots up sooner than other vegetation, they will not hesitate to swim over the river in quest of it. The waters at that time are frequently so much swollen as to prevent any one from crossing, so that the stockkeeper, after losing the track of his saddle-horses upon the river's edge, has the mortification of seeing them quietly grazing upon the other side.[42]

In the middle decades of the last century, according to a careful census of naturalized plants around Melbourne and a few scattered reports from elsewhere, 139 aliens were growing wild in Australia, and almost all of them of European origin.[43] In the state of South Australia, settled later than Victoria or New South Wales, the climate is drier than around Melbourne, and, as in California, Mediterranean weeds have a special advantage. As of 1937, the state had 381 species of naturalized plants. Of these, the great majority were Old World species, and 151 were Mediterranean species.[44] One of the more widespread was the red-stemmed filaree that Frémont found in the valley of the *Río de los Americanos*.[45]

Today, most of the weeds of the southern third of Australia, where most of the continent's population lives, are of European origin. There the climate is most nearly European, and there the impact of imported animals, particularly the sheep, has been greatest. The native grasses – kangaroo grass or oat grass, for instance – often are toothsome and nourishing for livestock, but are intolerant of heavy grazing and of the direct sunlight that burns down on them after the forests are cleared. Kangaroo grass, initially described in some places as up to the "very flaps of the saddle," was on the retreat as early as 1810, and in many localities it now survives only in railroad embankments, cemeteries, and other protected refuges. As the native plants faded and the settlers, arrogant and ignorant about Australia's periodic droughts, burdened her grasslands with excessive numbers of animals, ecosystems frayed, and erosion followed, opening even more land to the opportunistic plants. In 1930, the botanist A. J. Ewart stated that in the previous two years, alien species had been establishing themselves in Victoria at a rate of two per month.[46]

Not all weeds, by our definition, are obnoxious, but those that plague the farmer tend to get the most scientific attention, and our statistics for them are plentiful and dependable. Let us revert for a moment to the common definition of weeds for the sake of these statistics, on the basis of which we can generalize about the success in the Neo-Europes of weeds in the broader definition. Sixty percent of the more important farmland weeds in Canada are European.[47] Of the 500 equivalents in the United States, 258 are from the Old World, 177 specifically from Europe.[48] The total number of naturalized plant species in Australia is about 800, and despite contributions from the Americas, Asia, and Africa, the majority came from Europe.[49] The situation vis-à-vis naturalized plants in the Río de la Plata region is approximately the same.[50] For each one of these triumphant tramps, there is at least one other exotic flourishing in the Neo-Europes that is loved, not hated, and therefore is not included in these statistics.

The naturalized floras of the Neo-Europes overlap to a considerable extent. Of the 139 European plants listed as being naturalized in mid-nineteenth-century Australia, at least 83 had already attained that status in North America.[51] Of the 154 European plants listed as naturalized in the province of Buenos Aires and Patagonia in 1877, no fewer than 71, and probably more, were also growing wild in North America.[52]

The onslaught from Europe troubled American naturalists, though most of them were of the same origin as the plants in question. Charles Darwin did not let pass the opportunity to tease his American country cousins a little on the subject. "Does it not hurt your Yankee pride," he asked in a letter to the botanist Asa Gray, "that we thrash you so confoundedly? I am sure Mrs. Gray will stick up for your own weeds. Ask her whether they are not more honest, downright good sort of weeds." She countered nicely, answering that American weeds were "modest, woodland, retiring things; and no match for the intrusive, pretentious, self-asserting foreigners."[53] Thus, she proved herself both a patriot and an observant botanist.

It was more than a matter for joking. Research on the distribution of life forms – we call it biogeography today – was leading biologists further and further away from orthodoxy and into the environs of evolutionary theory. This affair of the migratory weeds was obviously a spectacular biogeographical phenomenon going on right under their noses, and they did not understand it.[54] The premier British botanist of the Victorian age, Joseph Dalton Hooker, who witnessed the advance of European weeds in Australia and New Zealand circa 1840, opined "that many of the small local genera of Australia, New Zealand and South Africa, will ultimately disappear, owing to the usurping tendencies of the emigrant plants of the northern hemisphere, energetically supported as they are by the artificial aids that the northern races of man afford them." But European weeds were doing very well in North America, too; so it seems that his interpretation of the mystery was in part faulty.[55]

Something approaching an equal exchange of weeds between mother Europe and her colonies – or at least something in proportion to the sizes of their floras – is what nineteenth-century scientists expected. Indeed, it is what we would expect: Old World crabgrass for American ragweed, for instance. But the exchange has been as one-sided as that of human beings. Hundreds of Old World weeds packed up, weighed anchor, set sail for the colonies, and prospered there, but the American and other Neo-European plants that crossed the Pangaean seams in the other direction usually pined away and died unless given special quarters and pampering at such homes for exotica as Kew Gardens.

A few American plants did manage in Europe by themselves. The Canadian waterweed, which first attracted notice in Britain's waterways in the 1840s, had them nearly clogged solid in a decade, and Canadian fleabane and annual fleabane gained a foothold in Europe by the last third of the nineteenth century. But most of the native weeds rated as fiercest in North America (ragweed, goldenrod, milkweed, etc.) could not even get started in Europe. And as of the middle of the nineteenth century, not one Australian or New Zealand plant had attained naturalization in Britain, nor, as far as we know, anywhere else in Europe.[56]

Some naturalists muttered obscurely about the greater "plasticity" of Old World plants. Meaning what? Variability? Others talked about European flora having the advantage over American flora because of being older, and still others because of its being younger.[57] The whole matter was clouded in mystery. "It appears," wrote Professor E. W. Claypole of Antioch College in Ohio, "as if some invisible barrier existed preventing passage Eastward, though allowing it Westward."[58]

The obvious explanations do not hold water. It is true that crop seeds and therefore (and unintentionally) weed seeds were exported from Europe to the colonies in quantity, but the ships that carried them returned to Europe with bales and barrels of tobacco, indigo, rice, cotton, wool, timber, hides, and, increasingly, enormous quantities of wheat and other grains, and all this cargo, inside and out, was a vehicle for seeds from the Neo-Europes. The bales of raw hides that Buenos Aires shipped to Cádiz by the millions must have carried innumerable American seeds with them, but no American equivalent of the wild artichoke ever swept over the backcountry of Granada. One tuft of fluff caught on a splinter of a log shipped from Portsmouth in New England to Portsmouth, Great Britain, could have set off an epidemic of milkweed in the south of England, but it never did. And sailors with Sydney mud and chaff still in the cracks of their best boots clumped down the gangway onto Liverpudlian quays, but only European, never Australian, weeds sprouted between the pilings. It seemed contrary to nature that Australian plants could not even get a toehold in Britain, whereas British plants were spreading wildly in Australia. Scientists who were moving toward a theory that species adapt to their environments, taking hundreds of generations to do so, found the contrast inexplicable. Joseph Dalton Hooker sputtered at "this total want of reciprocity in migration."[59]

Let us consider why weeds in general do so well, and where and when. They reproduce rapidly and in great quantity. Mayweed, one of those John Josselyn saw in seventeenth-century New England, produces 15,000 to 19,000 seeds each generation. Others he saw – shepherd's purse, for instance – produce fewer per generation, but compensate by producing several generations per season. Many weeds reproduce not by seed or not by seed alone, but from bulbs, pieces of root, and so forth. Mow them before they come to seed, and they are discouraged not at all. Wild garlic, a bane of wheat farmers in colonial North America, propagates in six different ways, most of which would require more explanation than we can provide here. It is no wonder that weeds are so difficult to eradicate and can reproduce in solid masses. To cite two extreme examples, broadleaf filaree in the San Joaquin Valley has been found in concentrations of 13,000 young plants to the square meter, and fescue up to 220,000 per square meter.[60]

Weeds are, as well, very efficient at getting themselves, particularly their seeds, distributed. This is essential, because 220,000 plants in one place are their own worst enemies. Some weeds produce seeds so light – down to

0.0001 gram – that they float away with any movement of air. Some, like Josselyn's sow thistle and dandelion, provide their seeds with sail-like filaments to further their travels down wind.[61] Other weeds produce seeds that are sticky or have hooks to grab fur and clothing to hitchhike to new places. Others produce their seeds in pods that dry and explode, flinging their seeds out and away. Many have tasty leaves and fruit, plus seeds that easily survive digestion, and so are deposited, with fertilizer, at distant points. White clover seed ambled from campground to campground right across North America in this fashion. In Australia, the settlers realized very early that their most important distributor of this plant was the sheep they drove before them into the interior.[62]

Weeds are very combative. They push up through, shade out, and shoulder past rivals. Many spread not by seed as much as by sending out rhizomes or runners along or just below the surface of the ground, from which "new" plants sprout.[63] Plants of this kind – Josselyn's couch grass, for example – can advance in solid mats, smothering every other plant in their way. The leaves of weeds often grow out horizontally, pushing back and suppressing all other vegetation. The dandelion, a bright spring flower in all the Neo-Europes, is such an efficient usurper that a large one can produce a bald spot a third of a meter across on a lawn, bare except for its own expansive self.[64]

Weeds are very good at doing what many of them evolved to do when the Pleistocene glaciers retreated: grow profusely in miserable micro-environments. Henry Clay, the perennial Whig candidate for the American presidency and gentleman farmer from Kentucky, said of Kentucky bluegrass that "you will find no better time to sow it, than to scatter it upon the snow in the month of March."[65] Weeds sprout early and seize bare ground. Direct sun, wind, and rain do not discourage them. They thrive in gravel beside railroad tracks, and in niches between slabs of concrete.

They grow fast, seed early, and retaliate to injury with awesome power. They will even take root in the cracks in an old shoe; not much hope there, but perhaps the shoe will be thrown into the midden out back, and then they can burgeon and swallow the whole yard.

To sum up the weedy qualities of weeds, let us turn again to plantain, the Englishman's foot. The average plant produces 13,000 to 15,000 seeds, 60 to 90 percent of which germinate. Some have been known to sprout after forty years. It thrives in meadows and in hard-packed pathways, where it suffers little from being stepped on. Its leaves spread wide, shading out and pushing aside other plants. Its undergound structure enables it to survive even weather that freezes its leaves. Cut it off at ground level and it produces lateral shoots, and new plants appear. It has been with us for a very long time: Its seeds have been found in the stomachs of ancient Danes disinterred from peat bogs. It was one of the nine sacred herbs of the Anglo-Saxons, and Chaucer and Shakespeare cited its medicinal qualities. It grows wild today in all the continents but Antarctica, as well as in New Zealand and a number of islands. It rates as one of the very hardiest of weeds in the world, and it will be with us forever, apparently.[66]

It is probably necessary at this point to explain why the entire land surface of the globe is not covered with plantain and the like. Colonizing plants – weeds – can survive nearly anything but success. As they take over disturbed ground, they stabilize the soil, block the baking rays of the sun, and, for all their competitiveness, make it a better place for other plants than it was before. Weeds are the Red Cross of the plant world; they deal with ecological emergencies. When the emergencies are over, they give way to plants that may grow more slowly but grow taller and sturdier. In fact, weeds find it difficult to elbow into undisturbed environments, and they will usually die out if disturbance ceases. A botanist interested in weeds calculated the proportion of introduced plants – weeds – in three fields, one that had been undisturbed for two years, another for thirty years, and another for two hundred years. The percentages of weeds, respectively, were 51 percent, 13 percent, and 6 percent. Weeds thrive on radical change, not stability.[67] That, in the abstract, is the reason for the triumph of European weeds in the Neo-Europes, concerning which we shall have more to say in Chapter 11 in a general discussion of the success of Old World species overseas.

What has all this about weeds to do with European humans in the Neo-Europes, beyond providing latter-day investigators with a model for the success of other exotic organisms – humans, for instance? The simple answer is that the weeds were crucially important to the prosperity of the advancing Europeans and Neo-Europeans. The weeds, like skin transplants placed over broad areas of abraded and burned flesh, aided in healing the raw wounds that the invaders tore in the earth. The exotic plants saved newly bared topsoil from water and wind erosion and from baking in the sun. And the weeds often became essential feed for exotic livestock, as these in turn were for their masters. The colonizing Europeans who cursed their colonizing plants were wretched ingrates.

8

❧

Animals

We have a bellyfull of victuals everyday, our cows run about, and come home full of milk, our hogs get fat of themselves in the woods: oh, this is a good country.
—J. Hector St. John de Crèvecoeur, *Letters from an American Farmer* (1782)

THE *MARINHEIROS* TAUGHT their apprentices how to cross the oceans, and the latter did so, taking large numbers of people with them. Then the passengers, landsmen and women, had to make homelands of their new lands. The task was not beyond the range of their capabilities – they could have managed, given enough time – but it was beyond the range of their preferences. They were Europeans, not Americans or Australasians, and would never have adapted voluntarily to the new lands in their pristine condition. The migrant Europeans could reach and even conquer, but not make colonies of settlement of these pieces of alien earth until they became a good deal more like Europe than they were when the *marinheiros* first saw them. Fortunately for the Europeans, their domesticated and lithely adaptable animals were very effective at initiating that change.

The prospective European colonists were livestock people, as their ancestors had been for millennia. The founders of the Neo-Europes were descendants, culturally and often genetically, of the Indo-Europeans, a west central Eurasian people who spoke the ancestral language of most of the tongues of Europe (English, French, Spanish, Portuguese, German, Russian, etc.), a people who were practicing mixed farming, with heavy emphasis on herding, 4,500 years before Columbus.[1] The Europeans who founded the first transoceanic empires were also mixed farmers and pastoralists (they would have understood the Indo-Europeans' way of life more readily than our own), and the success of their animals was, generally speaking, their success.

The Europeans brought with them crop plants, which gave them a very important advantage over the Australian Aborigines, none of whom farmed, and who were slow to take it up. But the Amerindians possessed a number of productive, nourishing plants whose value the invaders quickly acknowledged by cultivating themselves. Cassava is one of the staples of Euroamericans in the tropics, especially in Brazil, and maize is a standard food of Euroamericans nearly everywhere, as it was of Australian colonists in the late eighteenth and early nineteenth centuries.[2] The European advantage over the indigenes of their overseas colonies was not so much a matter of crop plants as of domesticated animals.

The Australian Aborigines had only one domesticated animal, the dingo, a knee-high dog of the size the English used for chasing foxes.[3] Amerindians also had dogs, plus llamas, alpacas, guinea pigs, and several kind of fowl, but that was all. For almost every purpose – for food, leather, fiber, or carrying or pulling burdens – the domesticated animals of America and Australia were inferior to those of the Old World. If the Europeans had arrived in the New World and Australasia with twentieth-century technology in hand, but no animals, they would not have made as great a change as they did by arriving with horses, cattle, pigs, goats, sheep, asses, chickens, cats, and so forth. Because these animals are self-replicators, the efficiency and speed with which they can alter environments, even continental environments, are superior to those for any machine we have thus far devised.

Let us begin with what is possibly the "weediest" of all the large domesticated animals, the pig. Pigs convert one-fifth of what they eat into food for human consumption, as compared with one twentieth or less for beef steers. (These statistics pertain to tweintieth-century livestock, which are larger than in past centuries, but we can assume that as a matter of proportion, the difference in the food-producing efficiencies of pigs and steers was in the colonial period approximately what it is today.) Pigs, unfortunately for hungry humans, eat concentrated carbohydrates and proteins, foods that are often fit for direct human consumption, which reduces the value of swine to us. Even so, there is no doubt of their importance, especially in the early years of a given colony when there was often an abundance of carbohydrate and protein and few settlers to exploit it.[4]

Swine are omnivorous, and there were more kinds of nourishment available to them in the early colonies across the seas than to any of the species of imported animals that were to be of prime importance economically.[5] They ate practically anything of organic origin: nuts of all kinds, windfall fruit, roots, grass, any animal too small to defend itself. They especially fancied peaches in Carolina and Virginia, where "large Orchards are planted of them to feed Hogs with, which when they are satiated of the fleshy Part, crack the Shells and eat the Kernels only."[6] In New England they learned to root for and thrive on clams: "they will not faile at low water to be with them."[7] In Sydney, wrote an early visitor, the pigs "are allowed to run in the bush during the day, just giving each a cob of maize to bring it home in the evening . . . They feed on grasses, herbs, wild roots and native yams, on the margins of rivers and marshy grounds, and also on frogs, lizards, etc. which come their way."[8]

Pigs did not prosper in the very cold regions of the colonies, for obvious reasons, nor in bare, hot country, because they cannot tolerate strong, direct sunlight and unmitigated heat; they must have easy access to water and cover in the tropics. But in most of the early colonies in the Americas and Australasia there was enough moisture and shade to satisfy pigs, plus an abundance of roots and mast – and soon after the arrival of the whites a great plenty of pigs. The great exceptions to the rule that pigs did magnificently in the early colonies were the grasslands – too bare, too sunny – yet even in the pampa they swarmed along the watercourses.[9]

Healthy sows have large litters, up to ten or more piglets apiece, and with an abundance of food, pigs can increase at the velocity of funds deposited at high compound interest.

Within a few years of Española's discovery, the number running wild was "*infinitos*," and "all the mountains swarmed with them."[10] They spread to the other Greater Antilles and to the mainland in the 1490s, where they continued to multiply rapidly. They followed in the footsteps of Francisco Pizarro (who allegedly began life as a swineherd) and were soon doubling and redoubling their numbers in the area of the conquered Incan empire. Their rate of increase on the mainland was probably lower than in the West Indies because of the former's carnivores, but pigs soon increased to many, many thousands on the continents – *infinitos* again. Every last one of these swarms of pigs, said the saintly Las Casas, were descendants of the eight pigs that Columbus had bought for seventy *maravedis* each in the Canaries and brought to Española in 1493.[11]

The swinish multitudes rooting through the swamps, jungles, and savannas of Brazil by the end of the sixteenth century presumably had other origins, as did the pigs of Port Royal, Nova Scotia, France's first successful American colony, where they multiplied and often slept out-of-doors in the winter of 1606–07.[12] Some of those in early Virginia could have been descendants of the Columbian eight, picked up in the West Indies on those voyages that took the English colonists across the Atlantic in the trade-wind belt. Whatever their origin, they thrived in Virginia, and circa 1700 did "swarm like Vermaine upon the Earth, and are often accounted such, insomuch that when an Inventory of any considerable Man's Estate is taken by the Executors, the Hogs are left out, and not listed in the Appraisement. The Hogs run where they list and find their own Support in the Woods without any Care of the Owners."[13]

Pigs were the favorite choice of explorers, pirates, whalers, and sealers for "seeding" remote islands to assure a supply of meat on the hoof for the next set of transient Europeans or Neo-Europeans to come along. As a result, pigs were already running wild on islands in the Río de la

Plata, on Barbados and Bermuda, on Sable Island off Nova Scotia, on the Channel Islands off California, and on islands in the Bass Strait between Tasmania and the mainland when mention of those patches of land first appears in the written record.[14]

In Australia, pigs swept inland from Sydney, keeping pace with or trotting along in advance of the frontier. They were almost as much a part of the usual station (ranch) as the sheep, scavenging the environs for kilometers around. On the more sloppily run establishments they might be seen no more often than once a month. Many, of course, were not domesticated even to that extent.[15] In the twentieth century, the wild pigs of Australia, though thousands have been shot, poisoned, and electrocuted, have a range that includes most of the eastern third of the continent.[16]

After a few generations, feral pigs revert to a type very different from what we are accustomed to seeing in the barnyard. Long-legged and long-snouted, slab-sided, narrow-backed, fast and vicious, and equipped with long, sharp tusks, they earned the same name in both North America and Australia: razorback.[17] The razorback is a bad-tempered beast, especially the boars, an Argentinian example of which nearly robbed us of *Green Mansions* and several good books on the pampa by almost unhorsing the young William H. Hudson, after which the animal almost certainly would have sabered and eaten the prospective author.[18]

Today, wild pigs, except in a few remaining frontier areas, are at best game animals and at worst a nuisance and danger, but from the Antilles in the 1490s to Queensland in the late nineteenth century they were a very important source of food. They provided for themselves – completely, if given the opportunity – and their meat was flavorful, nourishing and free. The first generations of European settlers in most of the colonies in America and Australasia ate pork more often than any other flesh.

Cattle have, from the human point of view, at least two advantages over pigs: They are equipped with more efficient thermoregulating systems and are more tolerant of heat and direct sunlight; they specialize in turning cellulose – grass, leaves, sprouts – that humans cannot digest into meat, milk, fiber, and leather, in addition to serving as draft animals. These characteristics, added to the natural self-reliance of cattle, make them a species as good at taking care of themselves in open grassland as pigs are in forest and jungle. The cattle that Columbus carried from the Canaries to Española in 1493 certainly had that capability, as did their descendants who were living as breeding herds in the West Indies by about 1512, in Mexico in the 1520s, in the Incan region in the 1530s, and in Florida in 1565. By the end of the century they were in New Mexico, and in 1769 they arrived in Alta California.[19] Their story is not one of uniform success everywhere. In steamy Brazil and the Colombian and Venezuelan llanos, Iberian cattle took generations to adapt; but in the higher country they exploded in numbers, dropping calves at what the colonists thought amazing rates. At the end of the sixteenth century, the cattle herds in northern Mexico may have been doubling every fifteen years or so, and one French visitor wrote his king of the "great, level plains, stretching endlessly and everywhere covered with an infinite number of cattle."[20] They were completely naturalized, as permanent a part of the fauna as the deer and coyotes, and still advancing north. A century and three quarters later, Friar Juan Agustín de Morfí, traveling through that part of Mexico called Texas, saw "amazing" numbers of wild cattle.[21]

What happened to cattle on the pampa was even more amazing. The first European settlement at Buenos Aires failed, but the Spanish tried again, successfully, in 1580. By that date, European quadrupeds, descendants of the first settlement's strays or of feral animals that drifted in from other European outposts, were already present in large numbers. The origins of the feral herds east of the Río de la Plata in what is now Uruguay and Rio Grande do Sul are also obscure. The Spanish or the Portuguese or the Jesuits may have introduced livestock first, and all three groups brought in cattle and horses eventually. The first solid date we have is 1638, when Jesuits abandoned a mission in the area, leaving 5,000 head of cattle behind.[22] We can be sure the freed animals propagated at high rates, as did all the herds of the pampa. In 1619, the governor of Buenos Aires reported that 80,000 cattle per year could be harvested for their hides without decreasing the wild herds.[23] The trustworthy Félix de Azara, who told us about weeds in the pampa in the last chapter, estimated the number of cattle in that grassland between 26°S and 41°S circa 1700 at 48 million, feral cattle in numbers comparable to those of buffalo on the Great Plains in their heyday.[24]

The cattle on the pampa were never properly counted until late in their history, and so a caveat should accompany Azara's estimate: 48 million, plus or minus how many? A quarter, even a half? The bovine multitudes inspired not statistics, but awe. William Hudson, in his autobiography, remembered plantations and orchards in mid-nineteenth-century Argentina with walls

built entirely of cows' skulls, seven, eight, or nine deep, placed evenly like stones, with the horns projecting. Hundreds of thousands of skulls had been used thus, and some of the old, very long walls, crowned with green grass and with creepers and wild flowers growing from the cavities of the bones, had a strangely picturesque but somewhat uncanny appearance.[25]

The majority of the cattle of the Americas from the sixteenth to the nineteenth century were probably feral. As with the pigs, their environment rendered them fast, lean, and mean – the kind of cattle that meat packers describe as "eight pounds of hamburger on eight hundred pounds of bone and horn" – animals that when fully grown could take on nearly any challenge. In the viceroyalty of Río de la Plata, according to Father Martin Dobrizhoffer, the cows could not be milked unless their feet were tied and their calves were present, and the cows and bulls alike moved "with a sort of ferocious arrogance," holding their heads high like stags, which they almost equaled in speed. When Anglo settlers began moving into Texas in the 1820s, they found these cattle more difficult to catch and more dangerous to handle than mustangs.[26]

The cattle that came to French and British North America were not so agile, so fearsomely equipped with long horns, nor so vicious when accosted as the Iberian cattle, but they, too, were a hardy lot. A cattle frontier preceded the European farmers as they moved west from the Atlantic, even though forests were thick and broad expanses of meadow uncommon.[27] Not until the Neo-Europeans moved onto the vast grasslands of middle North America in the nineteenth century were the numbers of their cattle comparable to the herds of colonial Ibero-America, but there were enough of them in the eighteenth century to impress Europeans who had never visited the southern steppes. Shortly after 1700, John Lawson remarked that the stocks of cattle in Carolina were "incredible, being from one to two thousand Head in one Man's possession."[28]

Some of the English cattle were feral, some tame, and all of them hardy. Within thirty years of the founding of Maryland, the settlers were complaining that their stocks of cattle were being "molested by reason of severall heards of wilde Cattle resorting amonge their tame."[29] Two human generations later, cattle on the South Carolina and Georgia frontier were migrating west "under the auspices of cowpen keepers, which move (like unto the antient patriarch or the modern Bedowin in Arabia) from forest to forest as the grass wears out or the planters approach."[30] We, of course, can make an educated guess as to what replaced the worn-out native grasses.

To maintain a measure of control over these frontier cattle and the other semidomesticated animals that roamed the woods from Nova Scotia to the lower Mississippi, one easily obtained item was needed: salt. A stockman would locate his herd by listening for the bell hung round the neck of the herd leader and then approach with a cake of salt in his outstretched hand. While the animals licked the salt, he could harness or yoke or select for slaughtering those he wanted.[31]

These herds of only semidomesticated animals wandering in the forests and canebrakes had no easy time of it. The full trough, the warm barn, the attentive herdsman were unknown to them. Their weakest went to feed the cougars and wolves, died foundering up to their withers in bogs, froze in blizzards, "pined and starved." But the survivors made up the losses and more in the months of warmth and lush forage, and continued to mosey farther into the North American wilderness.[32]

In the nineteenth century, Australia established itself as one of the chief wool and mutton producers in the world, but nature did not foreordain that sheep should dominate in the antipodes. The mechanization of Europe's textile industry did that, and without that influence, feral cattle might have taken over as thoroughly as they did, for instance, in Texas.

The colonizing First Fleet arrived in Australian waters in 1788 with a discomforting number of livestock on board, obtained at Cape Town, South Africa. The master's mate on the *Sirius* declared that the ship looked like a livery stable. Among the animals were two bulls and six cows. Within the first few months at Sydney, these eight animals strayed off or, some said, were driven off by a surly convict named Edward Corbett.[33] The settlers assumed that the Aborigines had killed them. When spotted next, seven years later, the cattle numbered sixty-one head and they were grazing in an area soon called Cowpastures. The governor, John Hunter, went out to see them, and he and his party were "attacked most furiously by a large and very fierce Bull, which rendered it necessary for our own Safety, to fire at him. Such was his Violence and Strength, that six Balls were fired through, before any Person dared approach him."[34]

The governor, who may have been familiar with the story of feral livestock on the pampa, decided to leave the cattle alone so that "they may become hereafter a very great Advantage and Resource to this Colony." By 1804, the feral herds ("mobs," to be properly Australian) numbered 3,000 to 5,000 head. The Australians in time would become fine livestock handlers, but they were not yet, and the best they could do with these fierce African animals was to shoot some and salt them down, and capture a few of the calves. The rest confounded those who pursued them by "running up and down the mountains like goats." The herds had become a nuisance and worse, providing a source of food for escaped convicts living in the wild – the famous and infamous "bushrangers." Furthermore, the wild cattle were occupying, and were unshakably resolved to continue occupying, some of the very best land between the sea and the Blue Mountains.[35] The government, convinced that humans, not cattle, had been ordained to be the dominant species in New South Wales, reversed its policy toward the wild cattle and in 1824 ordered the last wild descendants of the strays of 1788 destroyed.[36]

In the second decade of the new century, the Australians found a way through the Blue Mountains into the grasslands beyond and passed through with their livestock; there, according to all appearances, cattle increased faster in proportion to their original number than either sheep or horses.[37] Most of these cattle were now of European rather than South African ancestry, but that did not mean docile animals. The calves were as wild as deer and nearly as fast, and many – "Kangaroos, as we term them" – could leap a two-meter fence.[38] By 1820, the number of cattle in the tame herds of New South Wales was 54,103; ten years later it was 371,699. In another human generation, Australia would have millions.[39] No one knew the number of the feral cattle, some of which preceded the frontiersmen and women, some even the explorers. In 1836, Thomas L. Mitchell, trekking through the wilderness near the Murrumbidgee River, came upon cattle trails around the water holes so wide and hard-packed that they resembled roads, "and at length the welcome sight of the cattle themselves delighted our longing eyes, not to mention our stomachs." The animals were so unused to people that "we were soon surrounded by a staring herd of at least 800 head of wild animals."[40]

Even the so-called tame cattle on the frontier saw so few humans – most cattle stations consisted of no more than two or three stockmen and a "hut-keeper" – that one wonders to what extent the animals realized that men were their masters. The bulls were especially imperious. They stayed with the herds most of the time, but drifted off to spend the winters in solitude, returning in the spring to battle for females. One of the memorable sounds of the Australian frontier was the returning bull's challenging bellow, "now sullen and deep, then rising into a shrill scream, clear as a bugle . . . awakening the echoes for miles around, through the deep glens, and pathless solitudes."[41]

Horses died out in the Americas some 8,000 to 10,000 years ago, and returned again only when Columbus carried several to Española in 1493. The Iberians, initially a minority wherever they went in the New World, found horses effective, indeed an absolute necessity, in fighting the Amerindians, and so they brought the animals with them everywhere.[42] The horses propagated rapidly in most of the colonies – not with the wild abandon of pigs, perhaps, but rapidly.[43] Even in coastal Brazil, where the climate is too hot to be ideal for horses, there were plenty of them by the end of the sixteenth century, and the settlers were shipping them to Angola.[44] Given the same latitudes and climates, horses died in Africa and bred in America.

In northern Mexico, horses thrived and went wild in multitudes. In 1777, Friar Morfí found feral *mesteños* (the Mexican word for horses of the northern plains, which North Americans corrupted into "mustangs") beyond counting near El Paso, Texas. The horses, wild, of course, were so plentiful that the plain was crisscrossed with their paths, so many paths that this empty land seemed "the most populous country in the world." They had eaten and worn away the grass from large expanses, which immigrant plants were moving in to occupy. Around the water hole at San Lorenzo he found a great abundance of the plant called *uva de gato* in Spain and stonecrop in England, "which gladdened the landscape with its greenness." It may have been one or more of the European species of the genus *Sedum,* highly valued today as ground cover, that have spread widely since the *marinheiros* learned to read the oceanic winds.[45]

The story of the mustang in North America, of its spread north across the Great Plains into Canada before the end of the eighteenth century, is well known, and we shall not repeat it here.[46] That migration was largely the work of Amerindian raiders and traders, but it was the Spaniards who drove the first horses into Alta California in the 1770s. There the animals took up the ways of their ancient ancestors of the mid-Asian steppes. When the gold rush began in 1849, there were so many wild horses that ate so much of the grass that livestockmen with an eye for the profit that other stock could make out of the same grass drove the horses off the cliffs at Santa Barbara by the thousands.[47]

Some of the ancestors of the horses of the Atlantic seaboard colonies were of Mexican origin, brought eastward by traders from the midcontinental grasslands,[48] but most came directly from Britain and France, arriving in Virginia as early as 1620, in Massachusetts in 1629, and in New France in 1665. John Josselyn found plenty of horses in seventeenth-century Massachusetts, "and here and there a good one." Their owners let most of them scavenge the wilderness for their own feed in wintertime, though the practice, he said, brought the animals "very low in flesh till the spring, and so crest fallen, that their crests never rise again." He was from Europe, where horses were very expensive, and worth taking good care of. In North America they were relatively cheap and wandered free, often with little more evidence of their connection with humanity than a collar with a hook at the bottom to catch on fences as they tried to leap over them to get at the crops. Hogs, incidentally, were collared with triangular yokes so that they would not push through fences.[49] Fences were not for keeping livestock penned in, but for keeping livestock out.

Having hardy mounts for no more than the effort of catching them was a boon for the frontiersman, but there were so many of them in some places than they actually became a nuisance. (How unthinkable in Great Britain on both counts.) By the end of the seventeenth century, feral horses were pests in Virginia and Maryland. Runty stallions made so much trouble by impregnating valuable mares that statutes were passed requiring their penning or gelding. In Pennsylvania, anyone finding a stallion under thirteen hands running free had the legal right to geld him on the spot.[50]

Thousands of feral horses are still with us in the western parts of North America, where there is still a lot of open country. Despite drought and blizzard, epizootics, the gluttonous pet-food industry, and periodic cullings by men looking for free mounts, in 1959 mustangs were still roaming a dozen or so western states and two Canadian provinces.[51]

As mentioned earlier in reference to cattle, the first European settlements on the pampa did not succeed, but large herds of feral horses were grazing there when the Spanish returned to Buenos Aires in 1580. They were increasing at what was perhaps an unprecedented rate for large herds, and at the opening of the next century there were wild horses in Tucumán "in such numbers that they cover the face of the earth and when they cross the road it is necessary for travellers to wait and let them pass, for a whole day or more, so as not to let them carry off tame stock with them." The grasslands around Buenos Aires were overrun with "escaped mares and horses in such numbers that when they go anywhere they look like woods from a distance."[52] Such reports trigger skepticism, but are probably accurate. The pampa, east and west of the Río de la Plata, was a paradise for horses; even in the nineteenth century, after many of the advantages the animals enjoyed initially had dissipated, herds set apart as sources of cavalry mounts and protected from human harvesting increased at a rate of one-third per year.[53]

The Jesuit, Thomas Falkner, found the number of horses on the pampa in the eighteenth century to be "prodigious," and the going price of a two- or three-year-old colt was half a dollar. Sometimes, he wrote, the pampa was empty, the feral horses over the horizons, and other times they were on all sides.

They go from place to place, against the current of the winds; and in an inland expedition which I made in 1744, being in these plains for the space of three weeks; they were in such vast numbers, that, during a fortnight, they continually surrounded me. Sometimes they passed by me, in thick troops, on full speed, for two and three hours together; during which time, it was with great difficulty that I and the four Indians, who accompanied me on this occasion, preserved ourselves from being run over and trampled to pieces by them.[54]

Horses in such profusion, tame or feral, existed nowhere else on earth. Their abundance shaped the societies of the pampa more firmly and more permanently than the discovery of gold would have. The metal would not have lasted long. The enormous herds of wild horses, the indispensable element of gaucho culture, lasted for two and a half centuries.

Seven horses came to Australia in 1788 with the First Fleet. The governor reported next winter that "the horses do very well," but that was not true, or not for long, at least.[55] Only two of them survived the first years, and not until good South African mares arrived in 1795 did the number of horses really begin to increase. In 1810 there were 1,134, a decade later four times as many, and the settlers were even starting to export a few.[56] Many were already roaming free. In Australia they were known not as mustangs but as brumbies. The word may be derived from the Aboriginal term "baroomby," meaning wild, or from Baramba, the name of a creek in Queensland, or from the name of James Brumby, who came to New South Wales about 1794 as a private, settled on a hundred acres where he grazed stock, and then went off on an expedition to Tasmania in 1804. Before leaving, the story goes, he mustered (rounded up) his animals, but missed a few horses, and they strayed off to found dynasties of brumbies.[57]

Brumbies once ran by the tens and scores of thousands in the interior of Australia, and in 1960 there were still 8,000 to 10,000 of them living in Western Australia, "by spur and bridle undefiled." They are not lovely animals; 150 years ago they were so narrow in the chest and shoulders that saddles intended for them had to be made narrower than those for European horses, and in 1972 an expert on brumbies declared that "they have a great bloody head like a bucket." But they are amazingly durable and need no more feed than what they can find for themselves, summer or winter. They make excellent horses for working stock, intelligent and able to "turn on a cabbage-leaf."[58]

As elsewhere, horses thrived so famously in Australia that the Neo-Europeans forgot what a miracle it was to have mounts for next to nothing, and cursed the excess of their own good fortune. The brumbies were pests, sweeping past and carrying tame horses off with them, "leaving their owner to chew the cud of mortification." Worst of all, they drank and ate water and grass needed for profitable animals: sheep, cattle, and obedient horses.[59] Between the 1860s and 1890s, brumbies were a major nuisance in New South Wales and Victoria, "a very weed among animals." Many were killed for their skins – so many that in 1869, horsehides brought only four shillings each in Sydney. Some Australians simply fenced off the water holes in dry times and got rid of the animals that way. Other settlers, not willing to wait for thirst to work, devised methods of knifing or shooting the brumbies so that they would run a long way before dying, thus preventing noisome accumulation of dead horses at a single point. In the 1930s, when bounties were offered for horse ears, two men shot 4,000 in one year on the Innamincka. A little later, one man shot 400 horses in a single night.[60]

So much for domesticated quadrupeds gone wild. There is no value in belaboring the point that they adapted marvellously well to the Neo-Europes, and vice versa. We could go on at length about goats, dogs, cats, even camels, and go on further to point out that domesticated birds – chickens, for instance – prospered in the Neo-Europes, but the point has already been made: Old World livestock prospered in the Neo-Europes. In fact, they did amazingly better in the Neo-Europes than in their homelands – a paradox. Let us examine the story of what might be described as the Neo-Europes' only domesticated insect, the honeybee. If this Old World insect did as well in the Neo-Europes as did pigs, cattle, and horses, then the forces behind the success of Old World immigrants must have been pervasive indeed.

There are many kinds of bees and other insects producing honey all round the world, but the one insect that combines high production of honey with being amenable to human manipulation is the honeybee, a native of the Mediterranean area and the Middle East. There humans collected honey (and wax, for many peoples more important than the sweet product) long before written history began, and there Samson created one of the Old Testament's most striking images when he found "bees and honey in the carcass of a lion."[61]

In the fifteenth and sixteenth centuries, the sailors of western Europe became *marinheiros,* with many and diverse results, among them enormous expansions in the ranges and numbers of honeybees. These bees may have been in the islands of the Mediterranean Atlantic before the arrival of the Europeans, but if so, then not in all the islands. If they had been in Tenerife before Our Lady of Candelaria, then why would she have been obliged to produce wax for her candles by miracles? It appears that they arrived late in Latin America, and in many cases came from North America, not from Europe. In tropical America, the indigenes were collecting honey from bees long before Cortés and continued to do so; and for long after Cortés sugar was plentiful and cheap in Latin America. Both factors tended to discourage the importation of honeybees. Today Argentina is one of the world's top producers of honey, but that is a relatively recent development. In contrast, honey was an essential sweetener in North America, and the honeybee arrived early.[62]

The first honeybees brought to North America arrived in Virginia in the early 1620s, where honey became a common food in the seventeenth century. In Massachusetts, bees came ashore no later than the 1640s, and by 1663 they were thriving "exceedingly," according to John Josselyn. The immigrant insects did as well as or better than the Europeans themselves in seventeenth-century British America.[63]

To an extent, their advance was due to human intervention, humans with hives on their rafts and wagons moving into Indian territory, but in most cases the avant-garde of these Old World insects moved west independently. They were naturalized in the seaboard colonies in the seventeenth century and widespread there by 1800,[64] but the Appalachians were a real barrier for them. Some were carried across by people, and some reputedly blown across by a hurricane. They did get across and then seem to have spread even more rapidly in the Mississippi basin than they had east of the Appalachians. In the campaign that climaxed with the battle of Tippecanoe in 1811, the advancing United States forces found many beehives in hollow trees in the Indiana wilderness, and one man recorded that he and his friends found three bee trees in an hour.[65] The first honeybees west of the Mississippi are supposed to have settled in Mme. Chouteau's garden in St. Louis in 1792.[66]

One of the favorite recreations of rural North Americans was to seek out and steal the honey from the hives of wild bees. A whole system of techniques grew up: how to find foraging worker bees, how to follow their beeline back to the bee tree while cracking shins and falling into creeks, and how to smoke out the bees and chop down the tree – all without being stung any more than was absolutely necessary. Then came the reward, as witnessed by Washington Irving on the Oklahoma frontier in the 1830s. The unbroken honeycombs were placed in kettles to take back to camp or settlement, and

those which had been shivered in the fall were devoured upon the spot. Every stark bee-hunter was to be seen with a rich morsel in his hand, dripping about his fingers, and disappearing as rapidly as a cream-tart before the holiday appetite of a schoolboy.[67]

Honey was a blessing to the North American indigenes, who had previously had only maple sugar for a strong sweetener, but the "English fly" was for them a dismal portent of the approach of the white frontier. St. Jean de Crèvecoeur wrote that "as they discover the bees, the news of this event, passing from mouth to mouth, spreads sadness and consternation in all minds."[68]

Australia has small stingless bees, which the Aborigines valued for their very sweet product, but it was as innocent of true honeybees as America. These arrived in Sydney on 9 March 1822 on the ship *Isabella,* along with 200 convicts.[69] Once established in New South Wales, the bees propagated and swarmed with the same vigor as in America. They were introduced in Tasmania in 1832 or shortly before, and the first hive there swarmed either twelve or sixteen times the first summer ashore, according to which account one accepts.[70] It seems that several of the eucalypti, native to Australia, are among the best of all honey sources in the world.[71] When Anthony Trollope visited Australia in the early 1870s, he found the alien bee much more plentiful than the native, and honey to be "a customary delicacy with all the settlers."[72] A hundred years later, Australia is one of the world's largest producers and exporters of honey.[73]

The creatures we have discussed thus far went to the colonies because the colonists wanted them, but others crossed the seams of Pangaea without invitation. These varmints pose a very interesting set of animals for us, because whereas it can be argued that the barnyard organisms succeeded overseas because the Europeans worked for their success (not necessarily true, but let us accept that argument for the moment), no one would argue that rats, for instance, succeeded because the settlers wanted them for neighbors. On the contrary, Neo-Europeans have made gargantuan efforts to exterminate them. If they have thrived in the Neo-Europes, then the forces encouraging the success of Old World creatures in the colonies must be truly powerful.

The common rat of Europe is really two rats: the black and the brown, the former smaller and the better climber, and the latter larger, fiercer, and a better burrower. The rat mentioned in colonial sources is probably the former (often called the ship rat) most of the time, but the chronicles speak only of "rat." Either animal or both will do for our purposes, so we shall use the single word for both. To make matters more confusing, the colonial Spanish often used the same word for mice and rats.

Rats shipped as stowaways with the Iberians everywhere they went in America, but the accounts of the *conquistadores* omit mention of them. We do, however, know a little about their early years on the Pacific coast of South America, thanks (as with weeds) to Bernabé Cobo and Garcilaso de la Vega. There were several indigenous species of rodents in Peru and Chile, but none equal to the immigrant rats in adapting to the ways of European civilization. It was the latter, in all likelihood, that were the protagonists in the three plagues of rats (and of mice, too) that swept Peru between the arrival of Pizarro and 1572. "They bred in infinite numbers," said Garcilaso de la Vega, "overran the land, and destroyed the crops and standing plants, such as fruit trees, by gnawing the bark from the ground to the shoots." Afterward they remained in such numbers on the coast "that no cat dare look them in the face."[74] Rats and/or mice (possibly indigenous, probably imported) afflicted Buenos Aires almost from its first beginnings as a viable settlement, swarming among the grapevines and the wheat. The colonists called upon Saint Simon and Saint Jude for divine intervention and sang masses pleading for mercy. Two hundred years later, at the beginning of the nineteenth century, the rats were so numerous that at night people stumbled over them in the streets: "Every house swarms with them, and graneries are dreadfully taxed. Indeed, the increase in that species seems to have kept pace with the cattle in those regions."[75]

Immigrant rats almost extinguished Jamestown, Virginia. In 1609, when the colony was barely two years old, the settlers found that their stores of food had been consumed by "the many thousands of rats" from the English ships. The settlers were reduced to dependence on their own meager skills as hunters, fishermen, and farmers for nourishment, and to dependence on Amerindian generosity.[76] At about the same time, the French at Port Royal, Nova Scotia, were also doing battle with multitudes of rats that they, too, must have inadvertently introduced. The Amerindians nearby were victims as well, beset with this entirely new kind of four-legged varmint that had come "to eat or suck their fish oils."[77]

The story was much the same in the early days of Sydney. In 1790, rats (conceivably native marsupials, but almost certainly rodents the settlers had brought with them) overran the food stores and the gardens as well. The governor estimated that they were the cause of the loss of "more than 12,000 weight" of flour and rice.[78] And the rats continued to arrive. Early in the nineteenth century, a Tasmanian newspaper grimly announced that "the number of rats leaving the convict ship now tied up in the Bay has to be seen to be believed."[79] Today, Old World rats infest Australia's ports and waterways and have even left the immediate vicinity of humanity to go wild in the bush, reverting to a way of life they have practiced little in thousands of years.[80]

Neo-Europeans did not purposely introduce rats, and they have spent millions and millions of pounds, dollars, pesos, and other currencies to halt their spread – usually in vain. The same is true for several other varmints in the Neo-Europes – rabbits, for instance. This seems to indicate that the humans were seldom masters of the biological changes they triggered in the Neo-Europes. They benefited from the great majority of these changes, but benefit or not, their role often was less a matter of judgment and choice than of being downstream of a bursting dam.

Were there animals from the Neo-Europes that swarmed over Europe and the Old World? Was the exchange anything like even? The answer, which the reader must be expecting by this time, is no. The American turkey did go to the Old World, but it did not go wild there and has not swarmed like locusts over the face of Africa or Eurasia. In much of Great Britain the relatively large and aggressive North American gray squirrel has replaced the Old World red squirrel, decimated early in this century by an unknown epidemic disease. And the American muskrat, first released in Bohemia in 1905, has spread widely since, helped along by other ill-advised introductions. By 1960 its range extended from Finland and Germany to the headwaters of several of the tributaries of the Ob River far to the east.[81] Still and all, nothing has happened in the Old World approaching the deluge of Old World domesticated animals gone feral in the Neo-Europes. The exchange of animals, tame or feral or wild, between the Old World and New World has been as one-sided as the exchange of weeds, and Australasia seems to have contributed nothing of importance to Europe in this category. As with weeds, the reasons why will be discussed in Chapter 11.

There is an old American folksong of the frontier in which a certain Sweet Betsy from Pike County, Missouri, crosses the mountains, presumably the Rockies or Sierras, "with her lover, Ike, with two yoke of oxen, a large yellow dog, a tall shanghai rooster, and one spotted hog."[82] Betsy was heir to a very old tradition of mixed farming, and whereas it must be pointed out that her oxen were castrated and the other animals without mates, Betsy's party was not the only one to cross the mountains; wagon trains had bulls and cows, plus hens and dogs and pigs of genders opposite to those of her animals. (Betsy herself had the foresight to bring Ike.) Rapid propagation of the colonizing species would be the rule on the far side of the mountains. Betsy came not as an individual immigrant but as part of a grunting, lowing, neighing, crowing, chirping, snarling, buzzing, self-replicating and world-altering avalanche.

9

⚜

Ills

THE COLONY OF A CIVILIZED NATION which takes possession, either of waste country, or of one so thinly inhabited, that
the natives easily give place to the new settlers, advances more
rapidly to wealth and greatness than any other human society.
—Adam Smith, *An Inquiry into the Nature and Causes of the
Wealth of Nations* (1776)

OLD WORLD GERMS were entities having size, weight, and mass, just like Sweet Betsy, her Ike, and their animals; germs required transportation across the oceans, which the *marinheiros* unintentionally supplied. Once ashore and lodged in the bodies of new victims in new lands, their rate of reproduction (as often as every twenty minutes) enabled them to outperform all larger immigrants in rapidity of increase and speed of geographical expansion. Pathogens are among the "weediest" of organisms. We must examine the colonial histories of Old World pathogens, because their success provides the most spectacular example of the power of the biogeographical realities that underlay the success of European imperialists overseas. It was their germs, not these imperialists themselves, for all their brutality and callousness, that were chiefly responsible for sweeping aside the indigenes and opening the Neo-Europes to demographic takeover.

Until recently, the chroniclers of human history had no knowledge of germs, and most believed epidemic disease to be supernatural in origin, something to be piously endured but rarely chronicled in detail. Therefore, the epidemiological history of the European colonies beyond the seams of Pangaea is like a jigsaw puzzle of 10,000 pieces, of which we have only half – enough to give us an idea of how large the original was and of its major features, but not enough for a neat reassembly. We bemoan the spottiness of our information; yet so great is its quantity and so neatly does it parallel accounts of the modern experience of what happens to isolated peoples when they are dragooned into the world community that we cannot doubt its general validity. Before we approach the history of Old World pathogens in the Americas and Australasia, let us take a look at a few recent examples of what science calls virgin soil epidemics (rapid spread of pathogens among people whom they have never infected before), in order to accustom ourselves to the possibilities of epidemiological catastrophe. When in 1943 the advance of the Alaska Highway exposed the Amerindians of Teslin Lake to fuller contact with the outside world than they had ever had before, they underwent in one year epidemics of measles, German measles, dysentery, catarrhal jaundice, whooping cough, mumps, tonsillitis, and meningococcal meningitis. When in 1952 the Amerindians and Eskimos of Ungava Bay, in northern Quebec, had an epidemic of measles, 99 percent became sick, and about 7 percent died, even though some had the benefit of modern medicine. In 1954, an epidemic of the same "minor" infection broke out among the people of Brazil's remote Xingu National Park. The death rate was 9.6 percent among those of the afflicted who had modern medical treatment, and 26.8 percent among those who did not. In 1968, when the Yanomamas of the Brazilian-Venezuelan borderland were struck by measles, 8 or 9 percent died despite the availability of some modern medicines and treatment. The Kreen-Akorores of the Amazon basin, contacted for the first time a few years later, lost at least 15 percent of their people in a single brush with common influenza.[1] The evidence is that when isolation ceases, decimation begins; hence the reasonable belief of the Yanomamas that "white men cause illness; if the whites had never existed, disease would never have existed either."[2]

The isolation of the indigenes of the Americas and Australia from Old World germs prior to the last few hundred years was nearly absolute. Not only did very few people of any origin cross the great oceans, but those who did must have been healthy or they would have died on the way, taking their pathogens with them. The indigenes were not without their own infections, of course. The Amerindians had at least pinta, yaws, venereal syphilis, hepatitis, encephalitis, polio, some varieties of tuberculosis (not those usually associated with pulmonary disease), and intestinal parasites, but they seem to have been without any experience with such Old World maladies as smallpox, measles, diphtheria, trachoma, whooping cough, chicken pox, bubonic plague, malaria, typhoid fever, cholera, yellow fever, dengue fever, scarlet fever, amebic dysentery, influenza, and a number of helminthic infestations.[3] The Australian Aborigines had their own infections – among them trachoma – but otherwise the list of Old World infections with which they were unfamiliar before Cook was probably similar to the list of Amerindian slaughterers. It is worth noting that as late as the 1950s it was difficult to get a staphylococcal culture from Aborigines living in the sterile environs of the central Australian desert.[4]

Indications of the susceptibility of Amerindians and Aborigines to Old World infections appear almost immediately after the intrusion of the whites. In 1492, Columbus kidnapped a number of West Indians to train as interpreters and to show to King Ferdinand and Queen Isabella. Several of them seem to have died on the stormy voyage to Europe, and so Columbus had only seven to display in Spain, along with some gold trinkets, Arawack finery, and a few parrots. When, less than a year later, he returned to American waters, only two of the seven were still alive.[5] In 1495, Columbus, searching for a West Indian commodity that would sell in Europe, sent 550 Amerindian slaves, twelve to thirty-five years of age, more or less, off across the Atlantic. Two hundred died on the difficult voyage; 350 survived to be put to work in Spain. The majority of these soon were also dead "because the land did not suit them."[6]

The British never shipped large numbers of Australian Aborigines to Europe as slaves or servants or in any other category, but in 1792, two Aborigines, Bennilong and Yemmerrawanyea, did sail to England as honored pets. Despite what we can assume was good treatment, they did no better than the first Amerindians in Spain. Bennilong pined and declined and showed indications of a pulmonary infection, but he did survive to return to his home. His companion succumbed to the same infection (perhaps tuberculosis, which was very widespread in Western Europe at the end of the eighteenth century) and was buried beneath a stone inscribed "In memory of Yemmer-rawanyea, a native of New South Wales, who died on the 18th of May, 1794, in the 19th year of his age."[7]

We have some idea of the source of the Aborigines' morbidity and mortality: pulmonary infection. But what killed the Arawacks in 1493 and 1495? Maltreatment? Cold? Hunger? Overwork? Yes, and no doubt about it, but could this be the entire answer? Columbus certainly did not want to kill his interpreters, and slavers and slaveholders have no interest whatever in the outright slaughter of their property. All or almost all of these victims seem to have been young adults, usually the most resilient members of our species – except in the case of unfamiliar infections. The hale and hearty immune system of one's prime years of life, when challenged by unprecedented invaders, can overreact and smother normal body functions with inflammation and edema.[8] The most likely candidates for the role of exterminator of the first Amerindians in Europe were those that killed so many other Arawacks in the decades immediately following: Old World pathogens.[9]

We shall turn now to the colonies, but obviously we cannot include within the limits of this chapter even a cursory epidemiological history of all of Europe's overseas colonies or even of the Neo-Europes alone. Let us restrict ourselves to the peregrinations of one Old World pathogen in the colonies, the most spectacular one, the virus of smallpox. Smallpox, an infection that usually spreads from victim to victim by breath, was one of the most communicable of all diseases and one of the very deadliest.[10] It was an old human infection in the Old World, but it was rarely of crucial importance in Europe until it flared up in the sixteenth century. For the next 250 to 300 years – until the advent of vaccination – it was just that, of crucial importance, reaching its apogee in the 1700s, when it accounted for 10 to 15 percent of all deaths in some of the western European nations early in the century. Characteristically, 80 percent of its victims were under ten years of age, and 70 percent under two years of age. In Europe, it was the worst of the childhood diseases. Most adults, especially in the cities and ports, had had it and were immune. In the colonies, it struck indigenes young and old and was the worst of all diseases.[11]

Smallpox first crossed the seams of Pangaea – specifically to the island of Española – at the end of 1518 or the beginning of 1519, and for the next four centuries it played as essential a role in the advance of white imperialism overseas as gunpowder – perhaps a more important role, because the indigenes did turn the musket and then rifle against the intruders, but smallpox very rarely fought on the side of the indigenes. The intruders were usually immune to it, as they were to other Old World childhood diseases, most of which were new beyond the oceans. The malady quickly exterminated a third or half of the Arawacks on Española, and almost immediately leaped the straits to Puerto Rico and the other Greater Antilles, accomplishing the same devastation there. It crossed from Cuba to Mexico and joined Cortés's forces in the person of a sick black soldier, one of the few of the invaders not immune to the infection. The disease exterminated a large fraction of the Aztecs and cleared a path for the aliens to the heart of Tenochtitlán and to the founding of New Spain. Racing ahead of the *conquistadores,* it soon appeared in Peru, killing a large proportion of the subjects of the Inca, killing the Inca himself and the successor he had chosen. Civil war and chaos followed, and then Francisco Pizarro arrived. The miraculous triumphs of that *conquistador,* and of Cortés, whom he so successfully emulated, are in large part the triumphs of the virus of smallpox.[12]

This first recorded pandemic in the New World may have reached as far as the American Neo-Europes. The

Amerindian population was denser than it was to be again for centuries, and utterly susceptible to smallpox. Canoeists of the Calusa tribe often crossed from Florida to Cuba to trade in the early sixteenth century, and certainly could have carried smallpox home to the continent with them; and peoples in at least sporadic contact with each other ringed the Gulf of Mexico from areas where the disease was rife all the way around to the thickly populated regions of what is now the southeastern part of the United States. The Mississippi, with villages rarely so much as a day's journey apart along its banks, at least as far north as the Ohio, would have given the disease access to the entire interior of the continent. As for the pampa, the pandemic certainly spread through the Incan Empire to present-day Bolivia, and from there settlements with easy access to each other were sprinkled across Paraguay and down along the Río de la Plata and its tributaries to the pampa. Smallpox may have ranged from the Great Lakes to the pampa in the 1520s and 1530s.[13]

Smallpox is a disease with seven-league boots. Its effects are terrifying: the fever and pain; the swift appearance of pustules that sometimes destroy the skin and transform the victim into a gory horror; the astounding death rates, up to one-fourth, one-half, or more with the worst strains. The healthy flee, leaving the ill behind to face certain death, and often taking the disease along with them. The incubation period for smallpox is ten to fourteen days, long enough for the ephemerally healthy carrier to flee for long distances on foot, by canoe, or, later, on horseback to people who know nothing of the threat he represents, and there to infect them and inspire others newly charged with the virus to flee to infect new innocents. To give one example (a precise rather than sensational example), most of the Abipones with whom the missionary Martin Dobrizhoffer was living in mid-eighteenth-century Paraguay fled when smallpox appeared among them, some as far as eighty kilometers. In some instances this quarantine-by-flight worked, but often it simply served to spread the disease.[14]

The first *recorded* epidemic of smallpox in British or French North America erupted among the Algonkins of Massachusetts in the early 1630s: "Whole towns of them were swept away, in some not so much as one soul escaping Destruction."[15] William Bradford of Plymouth Plantation, a few miles south, provided a few more details on just how hard the Algonkins nearby were hit, and how the death rates could soar to such heights in these epidemics. Some of the victims, he wrote

fell down so generally of this disease as they were in the end not able to help one another, no not to make a fire nor fetch a little water to drink, nor any to bury the dead. But would strive as long as they could, and when they could procure no other means to make fire, they would burn the wooden trays and dishes they ate their meat from, and their very bows and arrows. And some would crawl out on all fours to get a little water, and sometimes die by the way and not be able to get in again.[16]

The disease raged through New England, on west into the St. Lawrence – Great Lakes region, and from there no one knows how much farther. Smallpox whipsawed back and forth through New York and surrounding areas in the 1630s and 1640s, reducing the populations of the Huron and Iroquois confederations by an estimated 50 percent.[17]

After that, smallpox never seemed to stay away for more than two or three decades at a time.[18] The missionaries, Jesuit and Mennonite, the traders from Montreal and Charleston – they all had the same appalling story to tell about smallpox and the indigenes. In 1738 it destroyed half the Cherokee, in 1759 nearly half the Catawbas, in the first years of the nineteenth century two-thirds of the Omahas and perhaps half the entire population between the Missouri River and New Mexico, in 1837–8 nearly every last one of the Mandans and perhaps half the people of the high plains.[19] Every European people to establish major settlements in North America – the English, French, Dutch, Spanish, and Russian – recorded, sometimes in gloom, sometimes in exultation, the horrors of smallpox running loose among Americans who had never known it before.

The disease often spread far beyond the European frontier, often to people who had barely heard of the white invaders. Smallpox probably reached the Puget Sound area on the northwest Pacific coast in 1782 or 1783, a part of the world then as distant from the main centers of human population as any place on earth. When the explorer George Vancouver sailed into the Sound in 1793, he found Amerindians with pockmarked faces, and human bones scattered along the beach at Port Discovery – skulls, limbs, ribs, backbones – so many as to produce the impression that this was "a general cemetery for the whole of the surrounding country." He judged that "at no very remote period this country had been far more populous than at present." It was an assessment that he could accurately have extended to the entire continent.[20]

Smallpox may have reached the pampa as early as the 1520s or 1530s, as suggested earlier. In 1558 or 1560, smallpox appeared again (or for the first time) in the grasslands of the Río de la Plata and killed, says a hearsay account, "more than 100,000 Indians."[21] We have only one source for this, but the explosion of smallpox in Chile and Paraguay at about the same time and in Brazil from 1562 to 1565, killing masses of indigenes, provides strong support for this report of the disease afflicting the people of the lower reaches of the Río de la Plata.[22]

From the last decades of the sixteenth century and into the second half of the nineteenth century, smallpox swept the southern steppes and adjacent areas again and again, seemingly arising whenever enough susceptibles had been born since the last epidemic to support a new one. The seventeenth century opened with the government at Buenos

Aires asking the Spanish crown for permission to import more black slaves, because smallpox had struck down so many of the Amerindians. That city alone had at least four epidemics of smallpox in less than a hundred years (1627, 1638, 1687, and 1700), and many others followed in the next two centuries. The first solid reference to the disease in Rio Grande do Sul did not appear until 1695, but this firestorm of a disease must have swept that province, contiguous to both Portuguese and Spanish areas where epidemics blazed up again and again, long before the end of the seventeenth century.[23]

The death rates could be very high. In 1729, two churchmen, Miguel Ximénez and a priest named Cattaneo, started out from Buenos Aires for the missions in Paraguay accompanied by 340 Guaraní. Eight days up the Río de la Plata, smallpox appeared among the latter. All but forty contracted the infection, and for two months the disease raged, at the end of which 121 were convalescing and 179 were dead. The Jesuits, a group more given to numerical precision than most, reckoned that 50,000 had died in the Paraguayan missions in the 1718 smallpox, 30,000 in the Guaraní villages in 1734, and 12,000 in 1765. Out of how many at risk? We shall have to leave that to the demographic historians.[24]

We shall never know how many died among the tribes roaming the pampa. Their ability to flee at short notice must have saved them from some epidemics, but the longer they avoided the infection, the more pulverizing its impact when it did strike. For instance, there is the case of the Chechehets, in 1700 one of the more numerous of the peoples of the grasslands, and therefore probably a tribe that had dodged the worst epidemics. When this tribe acquired smallpox near Buenos Aires early in the eighteenth century, it suffered near obliteration. The Chechehets tried to fly from this danger, which this time only increased their losses: "During the journey they daily left behind them their sick friends and relations, forsaken and alone, with no other assistance than a hide reared up against the wind, and a pitcher of water." They even killed their own shamans "to see if by this means the distemper would cease." The Chechehets never recovered as an autonomous people. By the end of the century, even their language was gone. Today we have fifteen of their words and some place names, barely as much as we have of the language of the Guanches.[25]

This disease continued to periodically ravage the pampean tribes, terminating only with the spread of vaccination and the destruction, incarceration, or expulsion of the last peoples of the Argentine steppe. Doctor Eliseo Cantón, physician, scientist, and medical historian of Argentina, stated flatly that the extermination of the Amerindians as an effective force on the pampa was due not to the Argentinian army and its Remingtons, but to small-pox.[26]

The medical history of Australia begins with smallpox, or something very much like it. The First Fleet arrived in Sydney harbor in 1788, and for some time thereafter the problems of infections among either the thousand colonists or the Aborigines were minor. Scurvy was causing trouble among the settlers, but even so they produced fifty-nine babies by February of 1790.[27] The Aborigines were a healthy lot, at least so far as the English could see. Then, in April of 1789, the English began finding on beaches and rocks around the harbor the bodies of dead Aborigines. The cause was a mystery until a family of natives with active cases of smallpox came into the settlement. In February, an Aborigine who had recovered from the disease told the whites that fully half his fellows in the general vicinity of Sydney had died and that many of the others had fled, carrying the infection with them.[28] The sick left behind rarely lived long, perishing for want of food and water. "Some," wrote John Hunter,

have been found sitting on their haunches, with their heads reclined between their knees; others were leaning against a rock, with their head resting upon it: I have seen myself, a woman sitting on the ground, with her knees drawn up to her shoulders, and her face on the sand between her feet.[29]

The disease spread far up and down the coast and inland, raging on for an undetermined period, raking back and forth through the native populations. It passed through the Blue Mountains, attacked the Aborigines along the interior rivers long before they had ever seen whites, and then flowed through the riverine peoples to the sea, nearly depopulating the banks of the Murray River for more than 1,600 kilometers. For scores of years after, old Aborigines with the pocks and scars of the disease kept turning up here and there in the deep hinterlands of New South Wales, Victoria, and South Australia. The pandemic may even have reached the northeast and western coasts of the continent. There was nothing to stop it so long as there were fresh Aborigines to infect.[30] Three times in the nineteenth century, smallpox returned to spread extensively among the Aborigines, but the first pandemic was surely the greatest single demographic shock the native peoples of Australia ever received. It may have killed, said Edward M. Curr, the great nineteenth-century expert on the Aborigines, one-third of their population, leaving only the tribes in the northwest quarter of the continent untouched. These did not get their dose of smallpox and associated devastation until 1845 and later.[31] For generations the Aborigines shuddered whenever they spoke of smallpox, giving expression to a "genuine horror, as it is impossible for any other evil to elicit from their inherent stolidity." In 1839, old men of the Yarra, Goulburn, and Geelong tribes, when asked how they got their pocks, answered, "Big long time Dibble Dibble come, plenty kill him black fellow."[32]

The impact of smallpox on the indigenes of Australia and the Americas was more deadly, more bewildering, more devastating than we, who live in a world from which the smallpox virus has been scientifically exterminated, can ever fully realize. The statistics of demographic decline are cold, the eyewitness accounts at first moving, but eventually only macabre. The impact was so awesome that only a writer with the capabilities of a Milton at the height of his powers could have been equal to the subject, and there was no one like him on Española in 1519 or in New South Wales in 1789. We are obliged to turn not to the witnesses but to the sufferers for enlightenment, and they made legends, not epic poems. The Kiowa of the southern Great Plains of North America, who suffered at least three and probably four epidemics of smallpox in the nineteenth century, have a legend about the disease. Saynday, the mythic hero of the tribe, comes upon a stranger dressed in a black suit and a tall hat, like a missionary. The stranger speaks first:

"Who are you?"
"I'm Saynday. I'm the Kiowa's Old Uncle Saynday. I'm the one who's always coming along. Who are you?"
"I'm smallpox."
"Where do you come from and what do you do and why are you here?"
"I come from far away, across the Eastern Ocean. I am one with the white men – they are my people as the Kiowas are yours. Sometimes I travel ahead of them, and sometimes I lurk behind. But I am always their companion and you will find me in their camps and in their houses."
"What do you do?"
"I bring death. My breath causes children to wither like young plants in the spring snow. I bring destruction. No matter how beautiful a woman is, once she has looked at me she becomes as ugly as death. And to men I bring not death alone but the

destruction of their children and the blighting of their wives. The strongest warriors go down before me. No people who have looked at me will ever be the same."[33]

The whites took a sunnier view of imported diseases. John Winthrop, first governor of Massachusetts Bay Colony and a lawyer by training, noted on 22 May 1634, "For the natives, they are neere all dead of small Poxe, so as the Lord hathe cleared our title to what we possess."[34]

Smallpox was only one of the diseases the *marinheiros* let loose on the native peoples overseas – perhaps the most destructive, certainly the most spectacular – but only one. We have not dealt at all with respiratory infections, the "hectic" fevers so often prevalent among the indigenes after contact with the strangers from over the horizon. To cite one piece of evidence, in the 1960s, 50 to 80 percent of central Australian Aborigines examined in one study had coughs and abnormal breath sounds, the higher percentages being among those most recently come in from the desert.[35] We have said nothing of enteric infections, which unquestionably have killed more humans in the last few millennia than any other class of diseases, and still are doing so. Cabeza de Vaca, staggering lost and desperate across Texas circa 1530, unintentionally presented his Amerindian masters with some sort of dysenteric disease that killed half of them and elevated him and his comrades to the status of priestly physicians, ironically saving their lives.[36] We have said nothing of the insect-borne diseases, though in the nineteenth century, malaria was the most important sickness in the entire Mississippi Valley.[37] We have said nothing of the venereal infections, which depressed the indigenes' birth rates as they raised death rates from Labrador to Perth in western Australia. Old World pathogens in their dismal variety spread widely beyond the seams of Pangaea and weakened, crippled, or killed millions of the geographical vanguard of the human race. The world's greatest demographic disaster was initiated by Columbus and Cook and the other *marinheiros,* and Europe's overseas colonies were, in the first stage of their modern development, charnel houses. Afterward, mixed European, African, and indigene societies quite unlike any that had ever existed before grew up in the colonies in the torrid zone, with the single major exception of northern Australia. The temperate-zone colonies developed less distinctively; they became Neo-European, with only minorities of non-whites.[38]

We accept that Mexico and Peru were full of indigenous peoples prior to European arrival, because their ancient monuments of stone are too huge to ignore and because their descendants still live in these lands in large numbers. But to imagine the Neo-Europes, now chock-full of Neo-Europeans and other Old World peoples, as once having had large native populations that were wiped out by imported diseases calls for a long leap of historical imagination. Let us examine one specific case of depopulation of a Neo-Europe.

Let us select a Neo-European region where indigenous agriculturalists of an advanced culture lived: the portion of the eastern United States between the Atlantic and the Great Plains, the Ohio Valley and the Gulf of Mexico. By the time Europeans had quartered that region, had traversed it up and down, back and forth, often enough in search of new Aztec Empires, routes to Cathay, and gold and furs to have acquainted themselves with its major features – by 1700 or so – the native inhabitants were the familiar Amerindians of the United States history textbooks: Cherokee, Creek, Shawnee, Choctaw, and so forth. These and all the others, with only one or two exceptions, were peoples without pronounced social stratification, without the advanced arts and crafts that aristocracies and priesthoods elicit, and without great public works comparable to the temples and pyramids of Meso-America. Their

populations were no greater than one would expect of
part-time farmers and hunters and gatherers, and in many
areas less. Very few tribes numbered in the tens of thousands, and most were much smaller.

The scene in this part of North America had been very
different in 1492. The Mound Builders (a general title for a
hundred different peoples of a dozen different cultures
spread over thousands of square kilometers and most of a
millennium) had raised and were raising up multitudes of
burial and temple mounds, many no more than knee or hip
high, but some among the largest earthen structures ever
created by humans anywhere. The largest, Monks Mound,
one of 120 at Cahokia, Illinois, is 623,000 cubic meters in
volume and covers six and a half hectares.[39] Every particle
of this enormous mass was carried and put into place by
human beings without the help of any domesticated animals. The only pre-Columbian structures in the Americas
that are larger are the Pyramid of the Sun at Teotihuacán
and the great pyramid at Cholula. Cahokia, in its heyday,
about 1200 A.D., was one of the great ceremonial centers of
the world, served by a village with a population estimated
by some archeologists as upward of 40,000. (The largest
city in the United States in 1790 was Philadelphia, with a
population of 42,000.)[40] Graves at Cahokia and other such
sites contain copper from Lake Superior, chert from Arkansas and Oklahoma, sheets of mica probably from North
Carolina, and many art objects of superb quality. They also
contain, in addition to the skeletons of the honored dead,
those of men and women apparently sacrificed at the time of
burial. One burial pit at Cahokia contains the remains of
four men, all with heads and hands missing, and about fifty
women, all between eighteen and twenty-three years of age.
Surely this assemblage is evidence for a grim religion and a
severely hierarchical class structure – this last a key factor
in the origins of civilization everywhere.

When whites and blacks settled near the site of Cahokia

and similar centers (Moundsville, Alabama; Etowah, Georgia) in the eighteenth and nineteenth centuries, the local Amerindian societies were relatively egalitarian, their population sparse, their arts and crafts admirable but no longer superb, their trade networks regional; these people knew nothing of the mounds and ceremonial centers, abandoned generations before. The whites credited them to Vikings, or to the lost tribes of Israel, or to prehistoric races now gone from the earth.[41]

The builders of the mounds had been Amerindians, of course, in some cases, no doubt, the ancestors of the people who were living near the sites when the Old World settlers arrived. These ancestors had been alive in large numbers when the Europeans first approached the coasts of the Americas. They were the people through whose lands and bodies Hernando de Soto hacked a path from 1539 to 1542 in his search for wealth equal to what he had seen in Peru. His chroniclers give us a clear impression of regions of dense population and many villages in the midst of vast cultivated fields, of stratified societies ruled with an iron hand from the top, and of scores of temples resting on truncated pyramids, which though often stubby and made of earth rather than masonry, remind one of similar structures in Teotihuacán and Chichén Itzá.

Where in the images of North American native societies that we share today is there a place for De Soto's wily opponent, the "Señora of Cofachiqui," a province that probably contained the present site of Augusta, Georgia. She traveled by sedan chair borne by noblemen and was accompanied by a retinue of slaves. For a distance of a hundred leagues "she was greatly obeyed, whatsoever she ordered being performed with diligence and efficacy."[42] Seeking to deflect the greed of the Spaniards away from her living subjects, she sent the former off to sack a burial house or temple that was thirty meters long and twelve or so wide, with a roof decorated with marine shells and fresh-water pearls, which "made a splendid sight in the brilliance of the sun." Inside were chests containing the dead, and for each chest a statue carved in the likeness of the deceased. The walls and ceiling were hung with art work, and the rooms filled with finely carved maces, battle-axes, pikes, bows, and arrows inlaid with fresh-water pearls. The building and its contents were, in the opinion of one of the grave robbers, Alonso de Carmona, who had lived in both Mexico and Peru, among the finest things he had ever seen in the New World.[43]

The Amerindians of Cofachiqui and of much of what is now the southeastern United States were impressive country cousins of the civilized Mexicans, perhaps comparable to the immediate predecessors of the Sumerians in general culture, and there were a lot of them. The latest scholarly work estimates that the population of one marginal area, Florida, may have been as high as 900,000 at the beginning of the sixteenth century.[44] Even if we skeptically subtract half from that figure, the remainder is impressively large. The southeastern United States, relative to what it had been, was vacant circa 1700 when the French came to stay.

Something eliminated or drove off most of the population of Cofachiqui by the eighteenth century, as well as a number of other areas where heavy populations of people of similar cultural achievements had lived two centuries before: along the Gulf Coast between Mobile Bay and Tampa Bay, along the Georgia coast, and on the banks of the Mississippi above the mouth of the Red River. In eastern and southern Arkansas and northeastern Louisiana, where De Soto had found thirty towns and provinces, the French found only a handful of villages. Where De Soto had been able to stand on one temple mound and see several villages with their mounds and little else but fields of maize between, there was now wilderness. Whatever had afflicted the country through which he had passed may have reached far to the north as well. The region of southern Ohio and northern Kentucky, among the richest in natural food resources on the continent, was nearly deserted when whites first penetrated from New France and Virginia.[45]

There had even been a major ecological change in the regions adjacent to the Gulf of Mexico and for tens of kilometers back from the coast, a change paralleling and probably associated with the decline in Amerindian numbers. In the sixteenth century, De Soto's chroniclers saw no buffalo along their route from Florida to Tennessee and back to the coast, or if they did see these wonderful beasts, they did not mention them – which seems highly improbable. Archeological evidence and examination of Amerindian place names also indicate that there were no buffalo along the De Soto route, nor between it and salt water. A century and a half later, when the French and English arrived, they found the shaggy animals present in at least scattered herds from the mountains almost to the Gulf and even to the Atlantic. What had happened in the interim is easy to explain in the abstract: An econiche opened up, and the buffalo moved into it. Something had kept these animals out of the expanses of parklike clearings in the forest that periodic Amerindian use of fire and hoe had created. That something declined or disappeared after 1540. That something was, in all likelihood, the Amerindians themselves, who naturally would have killed the buffalo for food and to protect their crops.[46]

The cause of that decline and disappearance was probably epidemic disease. No other factor seems capable of having exterminated so many people over such a large part of North America. The dismal genocidal process had already begun before De Soto arrived in Cofachiqui. A year or two before, a pestilence had threshed through that province, killing many. Talomeco, where the Spanish raided the burial temple mentioned earlier, was one of several towns without inhabitants because an epidemic had killed and driven off so many. The intruders found four large houses there filled with the bodies of people who had perished of the pestilence. The Spanish judged Cofachiqui heavily populated, but its citizens said their number had been much greater before the epidemic. De Soto entered Cofachiqui on the heels of a medical disaster, just as he had with Pizarro in Peru.[47]

How could this pestilence have reached so far into the interior from European settlements, presuming that it was an Old World importation? Any epidemic in Mexico could have swung around the Gulf through the medium of the coastal tribes and plunged inland along the thickly populated waterways. A number of ships riding the Gulf Stream from Havana were driven by hurricanes onto the shoals along the Florida coast, and their survivors, struggling ashore, could have brought infectious disease with them. And there were whites, a few of them, living on the mainland already. De Soto obtained one as an interpreter at the beginning of his invasion in Florida, a survivor of the same abortive expedition that had left Cabeza de Vaca to wander off across Texas. De Soto's men found in Cofachiqui a Christian dirk, two Castilian axes, and a rosary, which presumably had found their way there via Amerindian trade routes from the coast or even from Mexico. Infectious disease can tag along with commerce just as effectively as with any other kind of human intercourse. The Old World and many of her creatures had already penetrated the interior of North America by the time De Soto's men sprang into the surf and dragged their boats ashore.[48]

The epidemics continued to arrive and to do their work of extermination, as they did in every part of the Americas we know anything about in the sixteenth and seventeenth centuries. To cite but one, in 1585–6, Sir Francis Drake led a large fleet to the Cape Verdes, where his men picked up a dangerous communicable disease, and then sailed off to raid the Spanish Main, but so many of the English were sick and dying that the venture failed miserably. Seeking redress, he attacked the Spanish colony at St. Augustine, Florida, infecting the local people with the Cape Verde epidemic. The Amerindians, "at first coming of our men died very fast, and said amongst themselves, it was the English god that made them die so fast." Presumably the disease proceeded on into the interior.[49]

When the French penetrated into the hinterlands behind the coast of the Gulf of Mexico, where De Soto had fought so many battles with so many peoples, they found few to oppose their intrusion. And the decline in Amerindian numbers continued; indeed, it probably accelerated. In six years, the last of the Mound Builders, the Natchez, with their pyramid-top temples and their supreme leader, the Great Sun, diminished by a third. One of the Frenchmen wrote, unintentionally echoing the Protestant, John Winthrop, "Touching these savages, there is a thing that I cannot omit to remark to you, it is that it appears visibly that God wishes that they yield their place to new peoples."[50]

The exchange of infectious diseases – that is, of germs, of living things having geographical points of origin just like visible creatures – between the Old World and its American and Australasian colonies has been wondrously one-sided, as one-sided and one-way as the exchanges of people, weeds, and animals. Australasia, as far as science can tell us, has exported not one of its human diseases to the outside world, presuming that it has any uniquely its own. The Americas do have their own distinctive pathogens, those of at least Carrion's disease and Chagas' disease. Oddly, these very unpleasant and sometimes fatal diseases do not travel well and have never established themselves in the Old World.[51] Venereal syphilis may be the New World's only important disease export, and it has, for all its notoriety, never stopped population growth in the Old World.[52] *Niguas,* as Fernándo de Oviedo called the tropical American chigger causing barefoot Spaniards so much trouble in the sixteenth century, reached Africa in 1872 and spread across the continent as an epidemic of lost toes and fatal secondary infections of tetanus, but it has since retreated to the nuisance category and has never changed the Old World's demographic history.[53] Europe was magnanimous in the quantity and quality of the torments it sent across the seams of Pangaea. In contrast, its colonies, epidemiologically impecunious to begin with, were hesitant to export even the pathogens they did have. The unevenness of the exchange (the product of biogeographical factors discussed in Chapter 11) operated to the overwhelming advantage of the European invaders, and to the crushing disadvantage of the peoples whose ancestral homes were on the losing side of the seams of Pangaea.

10

❦

New Zealand

THE VARIETIES OF MAN seem to act on each other in the same
way as different species of animals – the stronger always extirpat-
ing the weaker. It was melancholy in New Zealand to hear the fine
energetic natives saying, that they knew the land was doomed to
pass from their children.
—Charles Darwin, *The Voyage of the Beagle* (1839)

A VIRGIN COUNTRYSIDE cannot be restocked; the vicissitudes
of its pioneers cannot be re-enacted; its invasion by alien plants,
animals and birds cannot be repeated; its ancient vegetation
cannot be resuscitated – the words terra incognita have been
expunged from the map of little New Zealand.
—H. Guthrie-Smith, *Tutira, the Story of a New Zealand Sheep
Station* (1921)

WE HAVE DISCUSSED the American and Australian Neo-Europes topically – weeds, then animals and germs – in order to tease out evidence of the ecological factors underlying the success of European colonies there, but we have not tried to reweave the history of, say, the pampa into a narrative. The stories of all the continental Neo-Europes are too long and complicated to tell within the limitations of this book. Therefore, we turn to New Zealand, insular and comparatively small, whose history is the briefest and most fully documented among all the Neo-Europes. New Zealand is a palimpsest written on by only a few people, and only recently. It would be better for our purposes if New Zealand's indigenes had been Paleolithic or New World Neolithic when the *marinheiros* first came – purely non–Old World Neolithic, to be clear about it, like those of all the other Neo-Europes. They were not, but they were nearly so, because the long migrations of their Asian and Polynesian ancestors across the Pacific had stripped them of all but a few Neolithic elements, as we shall see later. They almost fit our needs perfectly, and whatever difficulties the said few elements may make for us are compensated for by the fact that the Europeans came to New Zealand so late that they made their first and most important additions to its biota while under the perceptive scrutiny of scientists and scientifically minded men of the generations of Cuvier and Darwin.

New Zealand calved off Australia 80 to 100 million years ago and has been in splendid isolation ever since.[1] It consists of two large bodies of land – the North Island and South Island – and, off the southern end of the latter, the much smaller Stewart Island. New Zealand, 1,600 kilometers from balmy Cape Reinga to the cool reach of the South Cape, is the only piece of continental crust above water and of significant size between the Bering Strait and Antarctica, and between Australia and Chile. It is geologically youthful, with active volcanoes, a profusion of mountains, and an

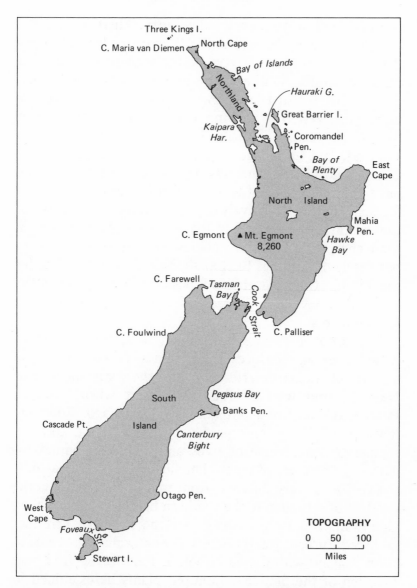

Figure 7. New Zealand. Source: *Hammond Ambassador World Atlas* (Maplewood, N.J.: Hammond, 1966), 101.

abundance of broken, rumpled country. There is some flat land, but only one broad and level expanse, the Canterbury Plain, built up by the rivers, milky with rock flour, that careen down the Southern Alps and wander to the Pacific.

Like the British Isles, New Zealand sits in the path of prevailing westerlies flowing over an ocean that never freezes; its weather is warm to cool and as soggy as that of England, and its foliage as green, though often a darker green (almost black on cloudy days) than the native English have known since pre-Celtic and Celtic farmers culled her forests. There are relatively dry areas in the rain shadow of the mountains, particularly the Southern Alps, but even there the precipitation is sufficient for the Western European style of farming. In climate, New Zealand is ideal for the kinds of agriculture and pastoralism, especially the latter, that have been characteristic of Europe for the last few millennia.

The kind of climate best suited to Europe's kind of mixed farming produces thick stands of timber in the absence of human interference, and the great majority of New Zealand was covered with forest when humans, Polynesians, arrived about a thousand years ago. However, it was not a European-type forest; rather, it was and is a temperate-zone jungle of trees and epiphytes bound together by a variety of vines. The history of New Zealand's native flora is very different from that in Europe. It is the product of evolution in the southern half of Pangaea, called Gondwanaland by geologists, not the northern half that included Europe. Joseph Banks, the naturalist who came to New Zealand with Captain Cook in 1769, recognized only fourteen of the first four hundred plants he examined in New Zealand. An amazing 89 percent of its native flora is exclusive to New Zealand. Ferns and their allies amount to one-eighth of the flora, as compared with a mere twenty-fifth in Britain.[2] In and on and with this unique flora lives one of the most distinctive of all faunas. When the Polynesians came, there were no land mammals but the bat. Zoologists call New Zealand's fauna "depauperate," and although that may be true in terms of the numbers of orders and families, it also includes some of the most unusual creatures on earth. For instance, there is a worm a half meter long and an insect, the giant weta, that is so large, upward of ten centimeters, that it fills the econiche that mice fill elsewhere. The tuatara, a medium-sized reptile not so long as a man's arm, is the world's only representative of *Rhynchocephalia,* an order that had its salad days while Pangaea was whole. Most impressive of all the creatures that met the Polynesians were the flightless birds, most of them now extinct. The largest of these filled the niche of the mammalian browsers that the islands lacked until the coming of cattle, sheep, and goats. These birds, the moas, included the tallest and nearly the heaviest birds that have ever lived. The largest commonly attained three to three and a half meters and had legs much more like an elephant than a sparrow.[3] All in all, the indigenous biota of New Zealand is bizarre by the standards of the lands where humans have spent most of their time on this planet, and at least as different from that of Europe as any on earth.

That biota was as unfamiliar to the Polynesians when they came to New Zealand as it was to the Europeans eight centuries later. The Maori (as the Polynesians of New Zealand are called) must have found it more difficult to adjust to their new home than did the British, because the former came from the central Pacific, where the climate is tropical, whereas the latter, though half a world from home, were accustomed to New Zealand's kind of weather. The Maori's transition from torrid zone to temperate zone and their lengthy voyage, thousands of kilometers long, filtered out many of their customary ways of obtaining the necessities of life. They could raise taro, the staple of Polynesia, in only small amounts, and they lost their pig, so important elsewhere in the Pacific. The Maori's only domesticated animal was their dog, a food source more than a companion, but too small to be a satisfactory substitute for the pig. They did bring a kind of Amerindian sweet potato with them, the kumara, which in time became their most important crop.[4]

When the Europeans arrived and penetrated into the interior of New Zealand, the moas were gone, killed off and much of their habitat burned out by the Maori, and the Maori were raising large quantities of kumara and some amounts of a few other crops in the islands' warmer regions: the North Island and the northern end of the South Island. There the human population was densest, but on the whole the Maori were still heavily dependent on wild sources of food, animal and plant. This does not mean they were poor farmers; indeed, these, the southernmost farmers in the world, were hard workers and skillful, but their crops were only marginally suitable for New Zealand, and they were isolated and had no opportunities to obtain others.

When the *marinheiros* first came – Abel Tasman in 1642 for just long enough for the Maori to kill four of his men at Murderers' Bay, and James Cook in 1769 to stay for half a year[5] – the landscape and the flora and fauna were profoundly un-European, one might almost say anti-European, at least in appearance. Maori farmers and torch-wielding hunters had altered the plant cover in certain areas in the North Island and in most of the eastern side of the South Island, replacing forest with scrub, fern, and grassland, but fully half of the islands' surface (not excluding large areas above the tree line) was still covered with a forest as dense in many places as that of Amazonia.[6] There were only four kinds of land mammals in New Zealand: the bat, the Maori, their dog, and a kind of small rat, called the Maori or Polynesian rat, which they had unintentionally brought across the Pacific with them. There was agriculture, but no grains – indeed, no crops familiar in Europe whatsoever, except insofar as the sweet potato was cultivated in a few places in Mediterranean Europe. There were no domesticated animals except the dog, a small and unimpressive animal that howled rather than barked. The Maori's only other sources of red meat, besides each other – they were enthusiastically cannibalistic – were the rat, which they prized highly, seals, and an occasional beached whale.[7] Even so, New Zealand supported at least 100,000 Maori, and in all likelihood a great many more.[8] They were physically large and powerful and extremely bellicose. Speak to a Maori of war, said the first of that race to visit Europe, and he will open his eyes "as wide as a teacup."[9]

Surprisingly, Captain Cook, normally a shrewd man, decided that this land would be an excellent place for a colony: "Was this Country settled by an Industrus peple they would very soon be supply'd not only with the necessarys but with many of the luxuries of life." The Maori might object to interlopers, of course, but they were not united, and by "kind and gentle usage the Colonists would be able to form strong parties among them."[10]

An observer who knew nothing of Neo-European histories would have judged Cook's prophecy a silly one. New Zealand, as it existed in 1769, seemed a poor candidate for transformation into a European colony. It was already stuffed to the gunnels with indigenous plants, animals, microlife, and scores of thousands of people. There was no room, so to speak, for organisms from the continents, unless, with elbows flying, they made room for themselves. But such aggressors would never get to New Zealand unless carried there by the only organisms among them who commanded the seas, the *marinheiros* and their students. What would attract these Europeans to make repeated trips halfway around the world to these ocean-lost islands?

New Zealand as it existed in 1769 did have a few things Europeans would go out of their way to get: the seals on its beaches and rocks, and the whales plentiful in its waters.

Sealskins and whale oil were in demand on the world market. There was also New Zealand's native flax, which the Maori had learned how to extract from a native agave, and which might become a substitute for hemp for maritime ropes and cables. There was also New Zealand's magnificent timber, trees strong, tall, straight, and eminently suitable for masts and spars. And there were the Maori themselves: their souls needful of washing in the blood of the Lamb and their bodies in need of exploiting.

Nearly a quarter century passed before Cook's news of New Zealand's multitudinous seals tempted William Raven, in command of the *Britannia,* to land a party of sealers at Dusky Sound in the South Island. After that, a number of sealing parties, made up of Europeans, North Americans, a few Australian Aborigines, and what have you, came to New Zealand's cool southern coasts. They often employed, mingled with, and fought with the Maori, and their influence on the indigenes was considerable. But there were never more than a few score of these intruders, and they killed off almost all the seals by the 1820s and either left or found other vocations.[11]

Some of them probably joined the shore whalers to prey on the huge mammals whose migrations brought them to New Zealand waters every year. Shore whaling stations, manned by the same kind of motley collections as the sealing camps, sprouted along the coasts, especially along Cook Strait and in the far south, in the 1820s. Some of these stations lasted for a number of years, and their crews established long-lasting relationships with the Maori, usually by acquiring women; but there were only a few hundred of these aliens, and they, too, destroyed their own livelihood and thus shortened their stay and minimized their influence. It was their practice to harpoon calves and drag them into shallow water, where the trailing mother, potentially the source of several calves, would go aground and be easy to kill. By the latter 1840s, shore whaling was in sharp decline.[12] Shore whalers, like sealers, were ephemera, except insofar as they introduced exotic organisms into New Zealand, which events, however momentous, went unrecorded.

Sealing and whaling brought pakeha to New Zealand, but seldom farther inland than the reach of the sound of the surf. ("Pakeha" is a handy Maori term for whites, European and Neo-European, that has been in common usage in New Zealand by both peoples for over 150 years.) Lumbering tempted the intruders inland, often far up the rivers into the magnificent forests for that perfect mast tree, the kauri, and, a bit later, for its industrially valuable gum. Yet lumbering per se attracted only a few whites to New Zealand, and even fewer stayed there long. Australia, the nearest market, had its own timber, however unsatisfactory the colonists considered it to be at first, and the European market was simply too far away. Besides, most of the actual work of felling the trees and moving them to rivers and then to the shore was accomplished by cheap and plentiful Maori labor, obviating the need for immigrant lumberjacks.

As for the flax trade as a lever that might pry open New Zealand, the product never did compete successfully with hemp outside of the southwest Pacific, and whites never went ashore in large numbers to reap and process the fiber. Like North American fur traders, the flax traders collected what they wanted from the indigenes, and there were never more than a few of these collectors. Large numbers of Maori along the coasts became involved in the trade, but by no means all Maori, and only for the few years that the trade flourished. It was largely a thing of the past by 1840.[13]

Maori souls, heathen and forever barred from heaven unless shown the Light, attracted white Christian missionaries, who intentionally and thoughtfully introduced all kinds of European ideas, tools, machines, and organisms. But missionaries in comparable numbers have done so in a variety of lands over the past half millennium, of which very few became Neo-Europes. The missionaries were a white drop in the vast brown Maori mass, and, incidentally, they converted not one Maori "in full health and the pride of life" for a decade and a half after arrival.[14]

Maori as hired help were an attractive item, and some of them were quite willing to take jobs with the pakeha, at shore or at sea. They made excellent seamen and were common on board the pelagic whalers in the Pacific, and a few even found their way to Nantucket and other whaling ports of the North Atlantic. Herman Melville, who knew whaling and the "Mowree," rated them as valuable ship-mates, especially for the most dangerous jobs: "Game to the marrow, these fellows are generally selected for harpooners; a post in which a nervous timid man would be rather out of his element."[15] Hundreds of New Zealand indigenes served on pakeha vessels, but these were only a tiny number out of their total population, and many never returned home. Maori women who became involved as servants, compan-ions, and prostitutes for the pakeha certainly served as a conduit carrying European influence into New Zealand, but their number, of course, was in proportion to the number of pakeha men coming to New Zealand, and a few hundred or even a few thousand blue-eyed Maori babies would not render the islands Neo-European. In fact, in other lands, such mixed offspring often became the shrewd-est of their mother race in thwarting European advance.

There is no doubt that New Zealand, inhabited by Maori of the Stone Age, would eventually have fallen prey to pakeha of the age of steam and steel, but European conquest does not necessarily render a land a Neo-Europe. For that, a demographic takeover is necessary, and New Zealand had little to attract large numbers of pakeha, with their attendant organisms. Possessed of no more than New Zealand appeared to have in 1769, it would have become another Papua New Guinea, a land acquired by European empires only late in the nineteenth century, and more because the empires were in fierce competition than because New Guinea itself was intrinsically desirable. Papua New Guinea today is populated and governed by its indigenous people. In contrast, New Zealand, in terms of population and culture, is the most British of all the lands that were once major colonies of England.

The pakeha ships, starting with Cook's *Endeavour,* accomplished that end by sailing to New Zealand and depositing there the tools, weapons, gewgaws, and ideas, and, most important, the organisms, of the continental societies. These ships were like giant viruses fastening to the sides of a gigantic bacterium and injecting into it their DNA, usurping its internal processes for their own purposes. The purposes (often unconscious) of the owners and crews of the ships were to Europeanize New Zealand: make it like home, which would attract more pakeha, which would make it even more like home. The transformation was not accomplished in full – even today, New Zealand, after over 200 years of change, is unquestionably not Europe – but the changes have been sufficient to make it attractive to hundreds of thousands of European migrants, and to make it a Neo-Europe.

Europeanization was not an inevitable process, though it often seemed so to both intruders and indigenes. At least three requirements had to be met before the process could become self-sustaining and irreversible. First, something was needed to attract the Europeans and their associated organisms in quantities large enough to disrupt the indigenous ecosystem and therefore Maori society. Second, large numbers of foreigners must somehow find themselves close enough to remote New Zealand to be attracted there. Europe and its colonies, including Australia, either filled their own needs or were so far from New Zealand that extensive commerce there was extremely unlikely. Third, something was needed to motivate the Maori to work very hard to provide what the foreigners wanted. For the process of Europeanization to work efficiently, the Maori would have to become active, even enthusiastic, participants in the transformation of their country into a land in which, inevitably, they would be a minority.

We shall look for these three factors in New Zealand's first post-Cook century, by the end of which the captain's prophecy was fulfilled. The story of that century falls into three chapters: 1769 to 1814, the momentous first years of contact between the pakeha and Maori, for which, maddeningly, there is an inverse (no, perverse) correlation between the significance of what was happening and the amount of information available today; 1814 to 1840, the period from the arrival of the missionaries and large numbers of whalers to the British annexation; 1840 to the 1870s, during which time the pakeha arrived by the tens of thousands, Maori resistance flared and waned, and New Zealand joined the ranks of the Neo-Europes.

1769–1814

Tasman came and left New Zealand like a musket ball glancing off the granite of Murderers' Bay. Cook came like a visitor from another planet, shattered Maori isolation forever, stayed for a number of months, and left ideas and organisms behind that initiated the transformation of New Zealand into a Neo-Europe. The Maori observed the British and their ship, both previously unimaginable, their metal tools and weapons, their muskets and cannon. The new weeds and crops also impressed the Maori, an insular people unused to the idea of "new" plants – probably impressed them even more than the Europeans, a nascently industrial people, were attuned to notice. Canary grass, a Mediterranean plant whose seeds have tiny wings for riding the wind, made its way ashore and was there in 1773 for Georg Forster, a naturalist with Cook on his second visit to New Zealand, to collect. The weed spread widely in the warm north, where it was often found in Maori fallow fields early in the nineteenth century, and where it spread widely in pakeha fields thereafter.[16] Wild cabbage also arrived early, and by 1805 it had spread so widely in the Bay of Islands region of the North Island that it seemed to be indigenous.[17]

Cow-itch (according to twentieth-century dictionaries, a woody vine) was another early and opportunistic immigrant. The Maori said that the French explorer Marion du Fresne left it in 1772, along with his carcass and those of a number of other French sailors who underestimated Maori tempers.[18]

We can be sure that several other European weeds arrived in these first post-Cook years, but we do not know their identities or if they achieved naturalization this early. They must have been introduced, because the explorers, like so many visitors later, were convinced that random sowing of Old World seed could only benefit botanically depauperate New Zealand, and they sowed with abandon. This practice, in an age when seed were always very "dirty" (i.e., included a lot of weed seeds), guaranteed the propagation of "these tramps of the flora." Julien Crozet, who took charge of the French expedition after Marion du Fresne's murder, recorded that "I planted stones and pips wherever I went – in the plains, in the glens, on the slopes, and even on the mountains; I also sowed everywhere a few of the different varieties of grain, and most of the officers did the same."[19] It did not occur to any pakeha for decades and decades that spilling and strewing alien organisms into an ecosystem can be like lighting a candle in order to lessen the gloom in a powder magazine.

The rapid spread of the weeds was matched by – in fact, was a concomitant of – the speed with which the Maori took to the new crops the pakeha offered. Most of the important exotics adopted in the eighteenth century were, interestingly, Amerindian in origin. The Maori liked the Amerindian maize, but their long experience with root crops, kumara and taro, predisposed them to like the new tubers most. The pakeha brought a new variety of the sweet potato that outproduced the kumara, and, more important than all the other new plants, they brought the white potato, for which New Zealand's climate and soils were nearly ideal, introduced first in the 1770s by Cook or Marion du Fresne. This American plant was enormously productive; unlike anything the Maori had known before, it thrived not only in the warm north but also all the way to the southern tip of the Maori world. The Maori gained with the white potato the means to produce large surpluses of food for foreign buyers. The Maori gained with the potato the means by which to enmesh themselves in something inconceivable to them in 1769: the world market that the Europeans were, willy-nilly, creating.[20]

Moderate climate, plenty of shade and moisture, and an almost inexhaustible supply of succulent fern roots made New Zealand a swinish paradise. Captain Cook first introduced pigs – the wild ones are still called Cookers – but naturalization of the species may not have taken place until the 1790s. Be that as it may, large feral populations appeared along the North Island coasts by 1810, and they were present seemingly everywhere on the island within a few more years.[21] With the pig, the Maori gained their first large land animal, wild or domesticated, and a means of producing large quantities of protein and fat for sale.

The new crops enriched both visitor and native; the new diseases operated preferentially. The Maori were like the Guanches, Amerindians, and Aborigines in their absence of B-type blood, an indication of long isolation and therefore epidemiological inexperience. They were unlike the Guanches and the others in having come to their present homeland abruptly from a different climate, a tropical one. Perforce, they must have left behind many of their ancient macroparasites and microparasites, the most obvious exception being their rat; and they came to a land in which there were almost no mammals, and therefore few parasites of whatever size preadapted to prey upon mammals, much less human beings. The Maori were in a fine state of "hilth," as Cook put it. Those through whom he shot holes in order to discourage them from attacking British sailors, and who survived the experience, healed with miraculous speed, confirming his assessment of their physical condition and suggesting absence of the bacteria that would have infected the wounds of a European. The Maori were as unprepared for continental pathogens as Adam and Eve were for deceitful serpents.[22]

The vulnerability of the New Zealanders to infectious disease was cultural, as well as immunological. For them, as for most peoples until very recently, the source of disease was supernatural, and preventive and curative medicine the province of priest and magician. It was usual to immerse the sick in cold water to purify them, which surely encouraged many secondary infections of pneumonia, and a common practice to purposely neglect the sick as being, almost by definition, beyond all hope. The custom of gathering the whole tribe together to honor dead nobility assured that infections would have access to every susceptible tribal member.[23]

The Maori culture was particularly defenseless against venereal disease. The Maori practiced polygamy, at least some of them; they accepted premarital sexual intercourse as normal and practiced what we might call sexual hospitality: the presenting of important male visitors with female partners, a common custom in many parts of the world when the *marinheiros* arrived.[24] Venereal disease can be decisively important in the history of a people in jeopardy, because it cripples their ability to reproduce, to win in the next generation what they may lose in this generation. If a people are already using some form of population control, venereal infection will multiply its effect, and the plunge in the birth rate can be very steep. The Maori practiced infanticide, a means of population control serviceable enough in periods of danger or dearth for the individual woman or family, but genocidal if the entire race is threatened.[25]

The Maori, an isolated and relatively diseaseless people, met in the Europeans perhaps the least isolated people on earth. The latters' homelands were the markets for a worldwide system of commerce and included the capitals of a half dozen transoceanic empires. Most of humanity's major diseases, excluding as a group only those like yaws that must have a very hot climate, were endemic or at least occasionally epidemic in Europe. Great Britain, which would be New Zealand's chief point of contact with the Old World, was especially fecund bacteriologically, because urbanization and the diseases associated with it were proceeding very rapidly there. Tuberculosis, soaring to unprecedented heights in Western Europe in the last years of the eighteenth century and early years of the nineteenth century, was endemic in British industrial cities and ports.[26] The connective medium between those ports and the Maori was made up of cold, wet ships, crewed by malnourished, often poorly clothed, often maltreated men who, as sailors in the slow age of sail, had no possibility of a normal family life. Tuberculosis and venereal infections were for them occupational diseases.

Captain Cook and his men carried many pathogens to New Zealand, none worse than those of tuberculosis, which killed three of his crew during his first voyage to the Pacific,[27] but there is no unequivocal evidence of the spread of any important imported disease among the Maori in their very first years of contact with the pakeha, with the exception of venereal disease.[28] In 1769 the British saw nothing of it ashore, but in 1772 the French found it among the indigenes at the locations on the New Zealand coast where the British had touched. Indeed, the French acquired the infection left behind for them by their fellow Europeans. Cook, retracing in part his own course in 1773, found venereal disease widespread in Charlotte Sound, and several of his men contracted it from the "fine jolly girls."[29] Thus was the ax laid to the root of Maori existence.

If Maori oral tradition is to be trusted, then pathogens other than those of tuberculosis and venereal disease – more immediately lethal pathogens – circulated in New Zealand in the years around the turn of the nineteenth century. The Maori told stories, years after the fact, of something called *rewa-rewa* that spread through the North Island and even to the South Island, killing enormous numbers. How many and how far it reached we shall never know. *Tiko-tiko* broke out in Mercury Bay. There was an epidemic called *papareti,* which is the name of a sort of Maori toboggan. The survivors compared the dying of so many to the swift slide of the *papareti.*[30] Before discounting these stories, collected from "primitives" perhaps decades after the alleged events, note that they echo many similar and often documented experiences of other peoples – Guanches, Amerindians, Aborigines – isolated until contacted by the *marinheiros.* The Hawaiians, jerked into the world community by the same Captain Cook who ushered in the Maori, underwent their initiation in an epidemic they called *okuu,* possibly the archipelago's worst, not long after *rewa-rewa.*[31]

Identification of the diseases of these semimythical epidemics, whether in Hawaii or New Zealand, is impossible, but we can be sure that they were not smallpox, the scourge of the Americas and Australia. None of the early European visitors saw any pockmarked indigenes, nor did the latter tell any tales of supernatural wrath turning a large proportion of the population into oozing horrors. Remoteness still defended the Polynesians.

The history of New Zealand between Cook's first appearance on its horizon and 1814 is one of more shadows than light. A few more explorers arrived: Jean François Surville in 1769, right on Cook's heels; Marion du Fresne in 1772; Cook again in 1773–4 and 1777; George Vancouver in 1791, and others. The early sealers, whalers, and sawyers came and went. A few exotic weeds established themselves, and the Maori experimented with pigs, new crops, and a few metal tools and marched up and down holding on high a few of the most fantastic of all pakeha devices: muskets. Venereal disease and other new infections took their perhaps considerable toll. But the integrity of the New Zealand biota and the Maori lease on the country were still solid. What the pakeha ships had thus far injected could be absorbed without precipitating drastic changes. In 1805, surgeon John Savage, ashore at the Bay of Islands, found the Maori currently "sound and healthy." He did, however, predict horrors for them in the next generation, basing his prediction on what he knew of the Amerindian and Aboriginal experience.[32]

1814–1840

If a giant were to pick up New Zealand, he would probably grasp it by its handle, the long peninsula called Northland that stretches out northwest from the bulk of the North Island. This is where the pakeha first took hold of New Zealand, establishing settlements of outsiders who learned how to live in New Zealand and live with the Maori. The Maori near these villages and outposts became increasingly alienated from their own traditions and served to carry European ideas, techniques, devices, and vices deeper into New Zealand. It was in Northland that the plants, animals, and pathogens of the pakeha entered most freely, changing it year by year into a land in which the pakeha increasingly felt more at home and the Maori less so.

The first pakeha settlers came not as giants but as supplicants. In 1814, the Ngapuhi of the Northland's Bay of Islands, a broad expanse of water with about 150 islands and an abundance of coves and protected anchorages, granted a small party of Church of England missionaries entrée to the tribal territory. In return, the Ngapuhi wanted not Christianity, for which the Maori at that time had no use at all, but the missionaries' knowledge of and access to European goods, gear, and power. For twelve axes, the missionaries bought two hundred acres of land, the beginning of the considerable landholdings of the church in Maori country, later to become a source of trouble.[33] During the next quarter century, other missionary stations were founded, most of them Anglican, several Wesleyan, and one Roman Catholic, but none were ever as influential on the Maori and the history of New Zealand as those in the vicinity of the Bay of Islands, which the missionaries and, treading on their heels (and the Ten Commandments, as well), the whalers made the most important Neo-European center in the entire country.

It would be over ten years before the missionaries would convert their first Maori, but their early influence was enormous – and deeply ironic in its secondary effect. They multiplied New Zealand's attractiveness to the pakeha by accelerating the process of Europeanization, an acceleration that would put many heathen in the way of sin before they had much of a chance to choose virtue. The Christians brought plants and animals with them – wheat, various vegetables and fruit trees, horses, cattle, sheep, and other animals – and instructed the Maori in how to raise them and benefit from them. The Maori did need help: At first they pulled up the wheat to see how its tubers were growing, and they were confused as to which end of a grazing cow was the front.[34] But they learned fast, and New Zealand's exportable surplus grew. But who would buy it?

The Maori found customers because of the demand for whale oil, which was burned to light the night for the citizens of Europe and its settlements overseas. At the end of the eighteenth century, European and Neo-European whalers from North America rounded Cape Horn and discovered the rich whaling grounds of the Pacific. Within a generation, thousands of men from Britain, the United States, and France, plus a number from Australia, were plying the Pacific, searching for sperm whales. These whalers needed food, preferably of familiar kinds, as well as sweet water, protected anchorage, and timber for repairs and fuel, and they were not averse to a bit of fun, if available. In the central Pacific, the best harbor for their purposes was Honolulu. In the South Pacific, their best port of call was the Bay of Islands. They would and did sail thousands of kilometers for the pork, potatoes, maize, cabbage, onions, and – a lagniappe – women of the Bay of Islands. The whalers were the force that drove the Europeanization process for two decades. The missionaries looked on in horror: "Here drunkenness, adultery, murder, etc. are committed . . . Satan maintains his dominions without molestation."[35]

What would motivate the Maori to chase down thousands of pigs, burn off and strip whole hillsides to cultivate tubers, grains, cabbages, and other vegetables for these customers who had crossed half a world to seek them out? The usual truck – blankets, calico, mirrors, beads, tobacco, and whiskey – was insufficient to turn a Maori into the Economic Man so dear to contemporary British economists. Muskets did that.

From the early 1770s on, the Maori openly coveted metal tools and weapons. In 1814 they would exchange one or even two large hogs for a small ax. That same year they exchanged 150 baskets of potatoes and eight pigs for one musket.[36] A tribe had to have muskets, at first for the mystical power of them, the *mana,* and then for their firepower. Possession of muskets could make a chief the owner of many slaves. Lack of guns would surely make him a dead man and his people slaves.

Until the 1830s, most of the guns streaming into New Zealand entered through the Bay of Islands, where whalers used them as currency to pay for what they needed and wanted. The greatest of the Maori leaders in that area was Hongi Hika, chief of the Ngapuhi, who went to England in 1820 to obtain muskets and a double-barreled gun, this last being the greatest possession a man could have on this earth.[37] He returned with his guns, plus a suit of chain armor – a present from George IV – and set off on the bloodiest series of military campaigns in the history of the land. He fought in his armor, firing five muskets loaded and reloaded for him by servants. He received a musket ball through the lungs in 1827 and lived for a year more with a hole in his chest, through which air whistled hoarsely, to his amusement.[38] Under his leadership, the Ngapuhi and allied tribes, strengthened by the prestige deriving from association with the pakeha, even with the missionaries, and, above all, armed with muskets provided by the whalers, inflicted terrible losses on their rivals, killing thousands and taking the survivors for slaves, the women to rent to the whalers. Hongi Hika made muskets a necessity for the Maori, and within a few years his musketeers had spread the gunpowder infection from the Northland through the entire island, and then, with fleets of war canoes, to the South Island, where people with spears and clubs in their hands waited to defend against others with muskets in theirs.

In 1830 and 1831 together, Sydney exported to New Zealand, where there were still no more than a few hundred whites, over 8,000 muskets and over 70,000 pounds of gunpowder.[39] In the new decade, the tempo of warfare slowed, as the muskets, now entering New Zealand in quantity from a number of coastal centers in addition to the Bay of Islands, spread more and more widely. The tribes eventually attained a rough sort of balance of terror, which, of course, sustained the demand for firearms. How else could a tribe participate successfully in the balancing act?

Starting around the Bay of Islands, the Maori planted hundreds of fields with alien crops to pay the pakeha for arms and other manufactured items, tearing breaches in the native ecosystem, opening the way to foreign plant aggressors. Charles Darwin, who visited the bay in 1835, noticed weeds "which, like the rats, I was forced to own as countrymen," particularly a kind of leek, brought by the French, and common dock, which "will, I fear, for ever remain a proof of the rascality of an Englishman, who sold the weeds for those of the tobacco plant."[40] Exotics that had not seemed particularly weedy in Europe were acting so in New Zealand. In 1838, Joel S. Polack, a resident in the Bay of Islands with close ties with the Maori, recorded that turnips, radishes, garlic, celery, cress, and even (as in the Carolinas in North America circa 1700) peach trees were growing wild. He bought a farm with two peach trees growing on it and found that a hundred more had sprung up around the parent pair.[41]

In the 1820s and 1830s, the kinds of pakeha animals ashore increased, and seemingly all kinds thrived, but none had as great an influence on the Maori economy and the New Zealand ecosystem – nor, in the long run, on the history of the pakeha in New Zealand – as the stalwarts of the Old World barnyard: pigs, horses, and cattle. The Maori kept great numbers of pigs to sell, and myriad others ran in the forests, some of them monsters up to 140 kilograms in weight, rooting up huge expanses, opening the way for exotic seeds. No matter how many pigs were harvested, there seemed unlimited quantities left. Animal protein was to be had for the taking, which certainly was not the case in Europe.[42] We know little of horses in the 1820s and 1830s beyond the fact that they foraged for themselves and bore strong and healthy foals, and that the Maori adored these huge quadrupeds for the power and mobility they could provide. There is nothing in the record about feral herds of horses this early; New Zealand would not have such until the last half of the century. Cattle, which find it easier to adapt to forest browsing than horses, may have done better in the North Island than horses, but there are few reports on them, none with statistics, and we can be sure that they were not propagating with pampean abandon. New Zealand's great grasslands lie not in the North but in the South Island. Even so, some cattle went wild, and both the tame and wild increased fast enough to impress the Maori, who, jealous of the high birth rates of the missionary families, accused the Christians of multiplying like the cattle.[43]

The total number of horses and cattle in New Zealand was small, but growing. The number was perhaps still small not only because of the lack of pasturage – the North Island is much better pig country than horse or cattle country – but also because so little time had passed since their first introduction. Geometric progression does not appear overwhelmingly greater than arithmetic until after the first series of multiplications.

One of the greatest of the few obstacles to the increase of these large exotic quadrupeds was the short supply of grasses. The North Island had much for the animals to graze on, especially the ferns, but few of its native plants can survive heavy grazing for long, native grasses being a case in point. To the pakeha in the North Island it seemed that sheep would never be important to New Zealand (which today has in excess of 60 million of them) because there simply was not enough feed.[44] The pakeha did their best to deal with the problem in the manner of Crozet, filling their pockets with grass seed and scattering them in the woods; some of what they planted flourished, but grass does not usually flourish in heavy shade, and most of the pasturage of the North Island today dates from the second half of the nineteenth century or later, when immigrants and Maori hired hands slashed and burned the forest over hundreds and hundreds of square kilometers.

Some of the phenomena that had been automatic in the other Neo-Europes hung fire in New Zealand because its biota was smaller and simpler than theirs. Let us consider the story of white clover, the champion weed of Peru and North America. When the missionaries imported and sowed white clover seed in New Zealand, it grew up thick and green and succulent, as one would expect in a humid, moderate climate. But it refused to seed itself. In New Zealand, which of all the Neo-Europes is perhaps most similar to England in climate, this champion weed had to be replanted every season. The problem was New Zealand's lack of an effective insect pollinator. It matters not how fast a plant is capable of propagating nor how thick a rug of growth it can create unless something carries its pollen from stamen to pistil. Maori New Zealanders could thrive and had thrived for centuries without such a something, but pakeha New Zealanders could not.[45]

In 1839, a Miss Bumby, the sister of a missionary, introduced the honeybee into New Zealand at Opononi, Hokianga Harbor, North Island. The two hives, carried all the way from England, were placed in the mission graveyard, "this place being considered the most free from possible disturbance through the curiosity of the Natives, who had never previously seen the bee." Further introductions followed in 1840 and 1842. The imported insects gloried in their new environment, swarming five and ten and even twenty-five times annually, producing abundant honey and wax, and pollinating millions of clover plants, which immediately began to live up to their American reputation. Thereby they helped immeasurably to make New Zealand hospitable to European livestock and the pakeha.[46]

The Maori were not innocent fools in regard to the pakeha and their unrelenting advance. Hongi himself worried about white soldiers coming from Australia to seize his

country,[47] but the pakeha threat was not so crudely imperialistic as that. The most dangerous threat was not soldiers
from the outside world, but germs from the outside world.

Maori who went abroad seemed to have a looser hold on
life than those who had stayed at home. The great Bay of
Islands chief Ruatara worked his way to London, returning
home in 1814 as the missionaries' protégé and, potentially,
the great Maori statesman of the age: "I have now introduced the cultivation of wheat in New Zealand. It will
become a great country, for in two years more I shall be
able to export wheat to Port Jackson [Sydney] in exchange
for hoes, axes, spades, and tea and sugar." But shortly after
coming home, he died of an infection incurred while
abroad, possibly tuberculosis complicated by dysentery.
The Reverend Samuel Marsden, overseer of the missionary
effort in New Zealand, and Ruatara's mentor, was stunned:
"I could scarcely bring myself to believe that the Divine
Goodness would remove from the earth a man whose life
appeared of such infinite importance to his country." With
his death, the only real rival to Hongi Hika as the most
important chief in Northland disappeared. When Hongi
went to Britain for his muskets and armor, he, too,
contracted a dangerous chest ailment, but recovered. The
dangers of infection the Maori faced abroad were so great
that in the 1820s the missionaries stopped sending Maori
protégés to Europe or even to Australia; the policy was
proving to be murderous.[48]

Meanwhile, morbidity and mortality in the Maori homeland were soaring. In 1838, measles hit the South Island,
with unknown effects,[49] but distance still served as an
effective shield against smallpox. There were, unfortunately, killers that were better travelers. Diarrhea seems to
have been chronic, but because it is often a symptom of
another disease rather than uniquely itself, its presence
does not tell us much. The Maori suffered no obvious
epidemics of typhoid until the last half of the century.[50]

Respiratory disease was a leading cause of sickness and death among the Maori in the 1820s and 1830s. Their tropical heritage had not prepared them for such a danger; the pakeha foods and tobacco may have lowered their resistance, and the crowded, dark, and airless huts in which they lived were perfect for the cultivation and transmission of breath-borne diseases. "Catarrh" (a vague Victorian term, but safer to use than to try to differentiate between colds, influenza, bronchitis, pneumonia, and what have you circulating a century and a half ago) swept through the tribes again and again after 1814. The wave afflicting the Bay of Islands Maori in 1827 and 1828 was particularly fatal for the very old and very young. The indigenes blamed it on the pakeha and were probably correct, because the same sort of sickness was raging in Sydney. Whooping cough, often deadly among people who have not known it before, also came ashore in those years. There was such an abundance of respiratory diseases for the next two decades and after that it is not helpful to try to draw lines between the alleged end of one epidemic and the beginning of the next. "Catarrhs and cold universally prevail," said Joel Polack in 1840.[51]

Nothing outdid tuberculosis and venereal disease as enemies of the Maori. These two afflictions provided the ground bass for Maori history in the nineteenth century. The first arrived with Captain Cook, but we see no more of it until, possibly, Ruatara's death in 1815. Five years later, the pakeha on the *Dromedary,* visiting the North Island to take on a cargo of spars, agreed that some infection or phalanx of infections was attacking the Maori. Dr. Fairfowl diagnosed it as "pneumonia in its acute stage, and also . . . consumption, inflammation of the bowels, cholic, dysentery, rheumatism, etc." One might hazard a guess that miliary tuberculosis was fulminating through the North Island Maori, granting, of course, that their trouble could easily have been a baker's dozen of imported infections.[52]

By the 1820s, the diagnosis becomes easier. Auguste Earle, an artist who lived in the Bay of Islands in 1827 and 1828, saw women who were "living skeletons," women who a few months before had been in perfect health. Galloping consumption, as it was commonly known in the nineteenth century, fit neatly into Maori preconceptions about the supernatural causes of death: "It is Atua, the Great Spirit, coming into them, and eating up their inside; for the patient can feel those parts gradually go away, and then they become weaker and weaker till no more is left; after which the Spirit sends them to the Happy Island."[53]

The Bay of Islands was a happy port of call for the whalers, and the effect of their presence was to change sexual hospitality into rampant prostitution; venereal disease became a ubiquitous plague. The chiefs, who at first had offered only female slaves, soon began to offer members of their own tribes and, according to some witnesses, members of their own families. The French, often more candid about sexuality in that age than the British, are our best source on the trade. When the *Coquille* dropped anchor in the Bay of Islands in 1824, 150 women swarmed over the ship and its crew of seventy in search of customers. "The captain tried to get rid of this lascivious livestock, but to no avail – for every ten females who left from one side of the ship twenty more clambered up the other; we were obliged to give up trying to enforce a measure that so many people were concerned to infringe."[54] Surgeon John Watkins, at the Bay of Islands at the end of 1833 and beginning of 1834, testified that he knew one man who habitually took pigs and women together to visiting ships, and sold the pigs and the use of the women "all in one Lot." He had the impression that not one woman in fifty at the bay was free of venereal infection.[55]

For the pakeha as a race, this meant little of general importance, because the women on whom the future of that race depended lived without direct contact with the fleshpots of the Bay of Islands and the shore whaling stations, and even, considering what can almost be called the segregation of sailors from "decent" society, apart from most indirect contact. For the Maori, in contrast, the situation meant calamity, because the fleshpots were in their own land, and their sexual mores permitted venereal infections to spread to all levels of their community. As early as 1820, some of them had a great dread of the venereal malady and considered it in some way to be a European god.[56]

The Maori of Northland, especially Hongi's Ngapuhi, won triumph after triumph in the 1820s, but the early 1830s found them in a world in which their enemies had as many muskets as they, a world in which their numbers were plunging and their ancient values melting away, and pakeha values were beyond understanding. The Maori wore pakeha blankets until they were matted with filth, and they smoked tobacco throughout all their waking hours – and the missionaries sniffed and the whalers snickered. The Bay of Islands indigenes fell into depression and apathy. Not their children, but the pakeha, they told Darwin, would inherit the land.[57]

Some of the Maori turned their backs on the whites, blaming the intruders for their troubles. "They charge us," reported one missionary, "as the authors of their evils, as having introduced among them many diseases. Till we came among them, they say, young people did not die but all lived to be so old as to be obliged to creep on their hands and knees. Our God, they say, is cruel; therefore, they do not want to know Him."[58]

Some of the Maori sought a remedy for confusion in synthesis. A new cult, founded by Papahurihia, also called Te Atua Wera, appeared in the Bay of Islands in 1833. It was a blend of Maori and Judeo-Christian traditions, and it taught that its followers were the children of Israel, adopting the Jewish rather than Christian sabbath. This perhaps was a product of the missionaries' conjecture that the Maori were descendants of the ten Lost Tribes of Israel. It mixed pakeha and Maori symbols – the snake of Genesis and the ngarara, the Maori lizard spirit form, for instance – and taught that heaven was a land filled with everything a Maori wanted: ships, guns, sugar, flour, and sensual pleasure. It also may have included as recreation what the missionaries absolutely forbade: combat and killing.[59]

In the late 1830s, the cult declined – it might be more accurate to say went underground – overwhelmed by the massive effort of the Maori majority to deal with the challenge represented by the pakeha by adopting his ways, his religion, his learning. The Northland Maori put on the white man's clothes, often upside down and backward, made a valiant and unfortunately successful effort to like alcohol and tobacco, and seized Christianity and the Bible with a passion. So it was that the gunpowder infection, as it swept southward from the Bay of Islands, was followed at a distance of a few years by a wave of Christianity and literacy.

The missionaries supplied much of the impetus by the example of their mission stations, where they introduced the Maori to positive aspects of pakeha culture: faith and hope, advanced agriculture with beasts of burden and plows, and simple technology. In 1835, at North Waimate, about a day's hike from the Bay of Islands, Charles Darwin found a mission station with fields of barley, wheat, potatoes, and clover, gardens with all kinds of European vegetables, orchards of apples, pears, apricots, and peaches, a barnyard with pigs and poultry, and a substantial water mill, where five years earlier there had been only fern. "The lesson of the missionary," he wrote, "is the enchanter's wand. The house had been built, the windows formed, the fields ploughed, and even the trees grafted by the [native] New Zealander. At the mill, a New Zealander was seen powdered white with flour, like his brother miller in England." In the evening, the missionary children and the mission Maori gathered together to play cricket.[60]

The missionaries, all but a few of them Protestants who viewed literacy as a major virtue, flung themselves at the problem of Maori illiteracy as if it were the boulder to be rolled away from Christ's tomb. They learned the Maori tongue, devised an alphabet for it, and in 1837 published the entire New Testament in Maori. By 1845 there was at least one copy of that publication for every two Maori in the country.[61]

The missionaries offered the Maori a new religion, new skills, new tools, and the magic of the alphabet, but it was the Maori themselves who accepted (no, seized) the opportunities offered. The most effective transmitters of Christianity and literacy were the prisoners taken by the Ngapuhi and allies – the lowest of the low, the slaves – who embraced the new religion with the greatest fervor, and then, as the wars waned and they were freed, returned home bearing the Word with them. When the missionaries penetrated the southern central districts of the North Island, they found the Maori there already clamoring for instruction and books, and often village schools under Maori teachers already in operation.[62]

There were no Maori conversions up to 1825, and only a few – usually of the moribund – between 1825 and 1830. Ten years later, the Anglicans alone claimed 2,000 communicants and thousands more, adult and child, under instruction in Christianity and the basic skills of literacy.[63]

One might supinely accept conversion, but literacy was hard work. As Thomas Tuhi put it after an 1818 visit to a pottery in England, where he made a few cups, "Yes, I say, very soon learn with fingers, but book very hard."[64] When he made that remark, no more than a few Maori could read, and most of them were probably in Australia or on the high seas. In 1833, something like 500 could read. Within a year or so, 8,000 to 10,000, according to the transient Edward

Markham, could "Read, write and do sums" – probably an exaggeration, possibly a wild exaggeration, but when each reader teaches two, who teach four, and so on, extraordinary acceleration of at least crude learning can take place, especially if the learning rides the tide of religious zealotry. Ernst Dieffenbach, a scientist who traveled extensively among the Maori circa 1840, expressed concern for their health, because instead of constantly exercising, they had become sedentary, having "become readers."[65]

We can wonder just how profound were the Maori conversions and literacy. The Reverend J. Watkins recorded that some Maori believed that the missionaries had a book called *Puka Kakari* that would render the possessor invulnerable to club or bullet. Others had it that the pakeha possessed a book that would restore the dead to life if placed on the chest of the deceased. Watkins found one of these books at Waikouaite; it turned out to be a publication called *Norie's Epitome*.[66] But we are carping if we make much of Maori superstition. Whatever their confusion about the nature of the new religion and books, the fact remains that they did not succumb to barren cultism or alcoholism or apathy, but took hold of Christianity and literacy with the same enthusiasm with which they had picked up the musket.

But it did them little good in any immediate sense. As they tried to Europeanize themselves in order to retain control over their lives, the rate at which they were losing the battle accelerated. New Zealand was becoming alien under their feet – more desirable than ever before, possibly, but as desirable to the increasingly powerful pakeha as to the declining Maori. More and more whalers came to the Bay of Islands – in 1836, for instance, no fewer than ninety-three British ships, fifty-four American, and three French[67] – and on occasion there could be as many as a thousand whites ashore, most of them drunk or intent on becoming so. More and more enterprising pakeha were moving in to try to make money out of the situation. Some bought land around the bay; some moved on and obtained land elsewhere, often to hold in the hope of selling later after increased immigration had raised land values. The land shark, a common figure in most colonies, had arrived in New Zealand. The missionaries continued their good works, which also entailed gaining land, and continued to stun the Maori with their birth rates. In 1839, according to the Reverend Henry Williams, over one thousand pakeha were resident – not transient, but resident – in New Zealand. The situation was, he complained, anarchic: "The whole White Population is free from any constraint of the law." Without a recognized source of authority, matters could get dangerously out of hand, as when in August of 1839 a mob of American sailors, ashore in the Bay of Islands, conceived the thought that they had been misused, unfurled Old Glory, and, in an excess of righteousness, pulled down the house of a British subject.[68]

The Maori were foundering in a situation not only out of their control but also increasingly beyond their comprehension. If a man with two wives should become a Christian and give one wife to another man, what exactly were the obligations of each man, especially if she and her relatives objected? Who was liable if pigs got into cultivated fields and damaged the crops, the owner of the pigs or the man who had been too lazy to fence his field? What if, as was sometimes the case, slaves with newly acquired skills or position should exalt themselves above their masters? "These only are the Things which cause us to err; Women, pigs and fighting one with another."[69]

The governor of New South Wales, the nearest fount of European law, sent a British Resident to New Zealand to bring things to order, but he had no real authority and less power. In 1837, two hundred missionaries and settlers petitioned the crown of Great Britain for protection.[70] The obvious next step, hallowed by many repetitions, was for

Britain to intervene to add New Zealand to the empire. There was pressure in London for such a move; it would head off possible French ambitions in that part of the Pacific and provide Britain, just entering the era of Chartist rumblings, with somewhere to send its alleged surplus people. But the current government was more interested in saving money than in gaining more bits of land in the antipodes. Was annexation really a necessity? Was New Zealand worth having in the long run?

The debate about annexation per se contains little of interest to us, but there are some interesting answers given to ministers and Parliamentary committees curious as to New Zealand's potential as a site for viable Neo-European societies. If Britain took on responsibility for this exotic place on the other side of the world and sent off shiploads of emigrants there, would the colony be self-sustaining, or would it be a drain on England's resources forever? In our terms, would it make a good Neo-Europe? The experts, the men who had been there, answered positively. Indeed, they said, New Zealand had already proved itself. Its climate was ideal, that is, very like England's, only better. Wheat, said one enthusiast, became biennial there, possibly perennial, springing up again from the root![71] As for livestock, Robert Fitz Roy, who had captained Darwin's *Beagle* and was to become a governor of New Zealand, announced that horses, cows, sheep, and deer, if turned out into the interior of New Zealand, would increase greatly in numbers. He was, of course, eminently correct. The New Zealand Land Company, which was trying to persuade Britons in migrate to New Zealand, summed it all up in 1839 and, unlike many land companies, stuck to the truth: "in whatever part of either Island [of New Zealand] they have been planted, European vegetables, fruits, grasses, and many sorts of grain, flourishes remarkably, but not more than the different animals which have hitherto been imported, such as rabbits, goats, swine, sheep, cattle, and horses." The stock assessment of the country was that of Thomas McDonnell, who owned, he said, 150 square miles in Hokianga: "No; a person must be uncommonly hard pushed if he cannot get a living in New Zealand, it being the best poor man's country in the world."[72]

The one outstanding fly in the New Zealand soup was the Maori: at least 100,000 stalwart indigenes, with a strong military tradition, ample supplies of muskets and ammunition, and already in occupation of the land. They could, at the very least, involve Great Britain in an expensive war, with supply lines stretched half the circumference of the world. How were they to be dealt with? The experts' answer was disarmingly simple: They really would not have to be dealt with; they were fading away. Their chief problem, the witnesses agreed, was glandular infections: scrofula, the tubercular infection of the lymph nodes, especially those in the neck.[73] The British Resident, James Busby, stated his judgment of the Maori condition in a letter to the colonial secretary, dated 16 June 1837: Yes, the Maori were in steep decline, in part because of venereal disease and deaths incurred in their wars, but the full story was more complicated and irreversibly dismal – from their point of view:

Disease and death prevail even amongst those natives who, by their adherence to the missionaries, have received only benefits from English connections; and even the very children who are reared under the care of missionaries are swept off in a ratio, which promises, at no very distant period, to leave the country destitute of a single aboriginal inhabitant. The natives are perfectly sensible of this decrease; and when they contrast their own condition with that of the English families, amongst whom the marriages have been prolific in a very extraordinary degree of a most healthy progeny, they conclude that the God of the English is removing the aboriginal inhabitants to make room for them; and it appears to me that this impression has produced amongst them a very general recklessness and indifference to life.[74]

Busby's opinion was similar to that of many of the most knowledgeable Maori. The chiefs of the North Island, paralyzed by tribal rivalries and stumbling in a world filling with devices, practices, and people more strange than anything in their mythologies, watching their own kin and their people sliding toward oblivion, turned to the pakeha again for help. In 1840, several hundred Maori met at Waitangi in the presence of William Hobson, the new British Resident and their prospective first governor, who offered annexation as a way out of their troubles. Some argued vehemently for rejecting the offer. They knew, for some of them had probably seen at first hand, what had happened to the Australian Aborigines, and they feared that the pakeha would reduce them, too, to peonage and beggary. Te Kemara, chief of the Ngatakawa, pointed to the Reverend Henry Williams, the self-styled friend of the Maori, and shouted, "Thou, thou, thou, thou bald-headed man, thou has got my lands."[75]

The tide of the debate ran for rejection of the treaty until Tamati Waaka Nene, a Wesleyan convert who as a young man had been one of Hongi's lieutenants, spoke. He knew the magnitude of the change that the pakeha had brought on the Maori, a change too great ever to be reversed. They were already enmeshed in the world community. He first addressed his fellow chiefs, asking them for their alternative to what Hobson offered. If they rejected it,

What then shall we do? Say here to me, O ye chiefs of the tribes of the northern part of New Zealand, how are we henceforward to act? Friends, whose potatoes do we eat? Whose were the blankets? These spears [holding up his *taiaha*] are laid aside. What has the Ngapuhi? The pakeha's gun, his shot, his powder. Many months has he been in our *whares* [houses]; many of his children are our children. Is not the land already gone? Is it not covered, all covered with men, with strangers, foreigners – even as the grass and herbage – over whom we have no power?

Then he turned to Hobson as to the only available source of authority: "Do not go away from us; remain for us a father, a judge, a peacemaker. You must not allow us to become slaves. You must preserve our customs, and never let our land to be wrested from us."[76]

About fifty chiefs signed or placed their *moko* (drawings of their distinctive facial tatoos, almost as distinctive as fingerprints) on the treaty by which they surrendered their sovereignty in return for a guarantee of their lands – or so said the English version. The Maori version said that they surrendered their governorship in return for a confirmation of their chieftainship. Scores of other chiefs signed later; the treaty went by ship to London, where the government confirmed it, and New Zealand became part of the British Empire.[77]

1840–1870s

Nene's hopes (hopes, not expectations, for he was a wise man) were largely disappointed. The processes of change, which he recognized to be much more profound than simply political, did not stop but accelerated and became more pervasive. There had been one Bay of Islands; now there were many, starting with full-scale pakeha settlements at Auckland, Wellington, and New Plymouth in the North Island, and, for the first time, real settlements in the South Island at Nelson, Christchurch, and Dunedin. The pakeha of the Bay of Islands had been sinful men, whereas those of the new settlements often were churchgoing people; but that made no difference at all compared with the fact that there had been hundreds of whites in New Zealand before 1840, and soon after there were thousands. They actually began arriving in Wellington the month before the chiefs met Hobson at Waitangi. Te Wharepouri had agreed to the sale of land to them beforehand because he had not believed they could possibly come in larger numbers than he and his people could control. When they disembarked, he realized he had been utterly wrong: "I see that each ship holds two hundred, and I believe now that you have more coming. They are all well armed; and they are strong of heart, for they have begun to build their houses without talking. They will be too strong for us; my heart is dark."[78] On the first day of 1840, there were no more than 2,000 pakeha in New Zealand; in 1854, there were 32,000, and the Europeanization of New Zealand accelerated proportionately.[79]

In June of 1841, Ernst Dieffenbach, exploring the center of the North Island on behalf of prospective colonists, arrived at Lake Rotorua, where the Maori were so unused to whites that they were astonished at the sight of him, and there he found plantain, chickweed, and other familiar European weeds, whose seeds had no doubt been carried into the interior unintentionally by Maori traders and by wild pigs and birds.[80] A half year later, in winter, William Colenso, New Zealand's first resident scientific botanist, found in the North Island "certain spots abounding in the rankest vegetation, but without a single indigenous plant. The new comers appear to vegetate so fast, as quite to exterminate and supersede the original possessors of the soil."[81] Joseph D. Hooker, Britain's premier botanist and one of the great scientists of that time, was in the antipodes on an expedition about that same time and was as astonished by the success of adventitious plants in New Zealand, as in Australia. A decade later, he published a list of naturalized plants of New Zealand, an incomplete list, he was sure. There were sixty-one, of which thirty-six were from Europe, including red-stem filaree (which Frémont met in California in the same decade as Hooker did in the antipodes), curly dock, dandelion, chickweed, sow thistle, and others that John Josselyn had found in seventeenth-century Massachusetts.[82]

Old World pigs, sheep, cattle, goats, dogs, cats, chickens, geese, and so forth, continued their takeover in the North Island, but the most spectacular biological explo-

NEW ZEALAND

sions were occurring in the South Island, where thousands
of pakeha and their organisms were moving into a nearly
empty land. What happened in the South Island in the
1840s and 1850s was, in proportion to the size of its
territory, much like what had happened in the pampa two
and a half centuries before. There were few Maori, because
they had only recently acquired the plants and animals to
enable them to live in the cool south in large numbers, and
there were no predators but wild dogs, and strychnine took
care of most of them. Immigrant shepherds, accustomed to
predators, were obliged to invent at least one native sheep-
eater, the kea, a large parrot with raucous voice. It was
supposed to swoop down, fix itself on the back of a sheep
such that the sheep could not defend itself, and then peck
the poor animal to death! If such happened once, it was
certainly remarkable; if twice, fantastic.[83] Livestock diseases were rare unless imported with the quadrupeds, and
the only one of significance for many years was sheep
scabies, a curse, but not a disaster.[84]

As before, let us begin with pigs. They apparently had
begun to spread into the South Island not long before the
Waitangi treaty and were rapidly increasing as the new
colonists arrived. As usual, we have only impressionistic
reports and no statistics, but according to these the numbers
of swine in at least the northern end of the island were greater
than anywhere else thus far in New Zealand. In the 1850s, the
Wangapeka Valley in Nelson was home for thousands upon
thousands, who literally plowed the soil by the hectare. In
twenty months, three men killed not less than 25,000 pigs
there, and still left thousands more to propagate.[85]

The larger quadrupeds had their population explosions
farther south, in Canterbury, an Anglican colony dating
from 1853, and in Otago, founded by Presbyterians in
1848, where there was little but vast expanses of tussock
grasses nodding in the winds from the Southern Alps. By
1861, 600,000 sheep, 34,500 cattle, and 4,800 horses were

· 254 ·

grazing the hills of Otago, and in Canterbury nearly 900,000 sheep, 33,500 cattle, and 6,000 horses,[86] not counting the wild livestock.

It is probable that something resembling the situation on the pampa circa 1650, with vast numbers of wild stock being preyed on by bands of mounted Maori, would have evolved if the pakeha, like the first Spanish settlers in Buenos Aires, had departed and not come back for half a century. However, the pakeha stayed and kept up with their herds, and so the histories of the pampa and the South Island are very different. Even so, the environment was so well suited to cattle and sheep that both went wild in numbers sufficient to make trouble for the settlers. Some of the feral cattle far back in the mountains even became longhorns, as in America. There were even considerable numbers of wild sheep, "disreputable with their long tails and torn trailing fleeces of six or seven years growth." Better proof of the absence of predation could not be had.[87]

The huge herds altered the flora in New Zealand as they had that in the pampa. Exotic weeds took over both sides of all the roads through the plains. Cow grass, often called knotgrass, grew luxuriantly, some of the plants spreading out until they were as much as a meter and a half in diameter. Dock spread out along the banks of every river and far up along the streams into the mountains. Sow thistle appeared everywhere, growing thick at elevations as high as 2,000 meters. Watercress clogged the rivers, and the new city of Christchurch had to spend six hundred pounds per year to clear it out of the Avon River for the sake of navigation. White clover, presumably ably assisted by honeybees, elbowed in everywhere, growing so thick that it smothered out the native grasses and lived up to the reputation it had made in the New World. The native plants, wrote the naturalist W. T. L. Travers to Hooker from Canterbury, "appear to shrink from competition with these more vigorous intruders."[88] Travers explained the success of Old World plants in New Zealand by pointing, a little vaguely, to the same forces "which have led to such changes in the Canary and other Islands long colonized by Europeans."[89]

Life was as good for the newly arrived pakeha in the middle years of the nineteenth century as it was for their attendant organisms. When the newcomers said, as they often did, that New Zealanders died only from drowning or drunkenness,[90] they were talking about themselves. For the Maori, the path downward steepened. In 1840, the year of the treaty of Waitangi, the pakeha who knew most about New Zealand, missionaries and officials, all estimated the indigenes at 100,000 or perhaps 120,000. In 1857–8, the year of the first real Maori census, the number was 56,000.[91] The pakeha were not slaughtering the Maori, and intertribal genocide was a thing of the past. Infanticide, alcoholism, poor diet, and despair were having their blighting influence, but they served only to confirm and amplify the work of the chief killers: infectious diseases.

Measles arrived for the first time in the North Island in 1854, killing 4,000, according to one witness.[92] After that time, there were fewer well-delineated disease epidemics, because most of the diseases that could maintain themselves through a long ocean voyage had already arrived, and New Zealand's remoteness still protected it from the others, which had to wait on the age of the transoceanic steamship. Smallpox did arrive, but it did not spread, a miracle for which the Maori can be eternally thankful. In November of 1840, the *Martha Ridgeway* put into Wellington harbor with smallpox on board. It was clumsily but successfully quarantined, and before the malady came ashore again, most of the Maori had been vaccinated. Luck saved New Zealand from the fate of Hawaii, where smallpox got loose in 1853, killing thousands, perhaps 8 percent of the population, in spite of quarantining and considerable vaccinating.[93]

The pathogens that had killed so many in 1820 and 1830 and 1840 continued seeping into every last Maori village. At the end of the 1850s, Dr. Arthur S. Thomson, one of the most dependable of all sources on New Zealand in the nineteenth century, stated flatly that scrofula was "the curse of the New Zealand race." He saw in some districts 10 percent of the population bearing the marks of this kind of tuberculosis, and in others 20 percent, and he pointed out that by no means do all sufferers of scrofula bear such visible stigmata. "Scrofula is," the physician wrote, "the predisposing and remote cause of much of the sickness among the New Zealanders; in childhood it causes marasmuses, fevers, and bowel complaints; in manhood, consumption, spinal disease, ulcers and various other maladies."[94] It is worth noting that in 1939, tuberculosis still accounted for 22 percent of all Maori deaths.[95]

Venereal disease was by then surely spreading through all but the most remote tribes; such, at least, was the pakeha's impression. There are at last some statistics: At the end of the 1850s, Francis D. Fenton, in the process of making a census of the entire Maori population, gathered data on 444 Maori wives, presumably a representative sample, that strongly suggested that venereal disease was destroying the procreative powers of the whole race. Of the 444, only 221 had any living children, and 155 were completely barren. Fenton described the Maori of that time as being in a "state of decrepitude."[96] In the same decade, a Dr. Rees, colonial surgeon at Wanganui, noted that among a sample of 230 Maori women, 124 either had no children or had no living children.[97] There are many possible explanations for the Maori barrenness – infanticide, particularly female infanticide, was probably still being practiced – but the worst villain in the tragedy was surely venereal disease. It kills parents, kills fertility, kills fetuses, kills children, and erases the desire for children.

Our account of the influence of alien pathogens on the Maori is far from complete – indeed, it is little more than a sketch – but it indicates that the impact was devastating. One would, however, like a few more statistics, especially statistics that would enable us to see how the Maori fared as compared with, say, contemporary Europeans, who were not a very healthy lot either by our standards. Dr. Thomson provided something like what we want on page 323 of his invaluable work *The Story of New Zealand: Past and Present – Savage and Civilized*, published in 1859 (Table 10.1).

This table is far from what we would like to have. How representative of the population of Great Britain were the 19,866? How representative of the native population of New Zealand were the 2,580? Surely the Maori who presented themselves at hospitals included few from the remote backcountry, who were probably the healthiest of all the race. What does the grab-bag category "Fevers" represent? To what does "Diseases of the brain" refer? Emotional disorders? The chart is not totally satisfactory, but it is far more precise that the usual kind of impressionistic data that history gives us concerning health and disease, and it confirms remarks made by Dr. Thomson, Dr. Peter Buck (Te Rangi Hiroa), and many others. A greater proportion of Maori than of pakeha fell sick with infections in the respiratory, gastrointestinal, and venereal categories, as well as with scrofula. The contrast between the morbidity rates for the two races, plus the obvious implications of New Zealand's geographical position in the Pacific, remote from the Old World, plus the general record of Maori health and population decline in the century following Cook's first visit – all these tend to support the hypothesis that they were unacquainted with a number of the infections brought by the pakeha. The native Polynesians of New Zealand dropped from perhaps 200,000 and certainly no less than 100,000 in 1769 to 42,113, according to the census of 1896[98] (Table 10.2).

Table 10.1. *Comparative frequencies of different classes of diseases among the inhabitants of a large town in England[a] and among the natives of New Zealand[b]*

Classes of diseases	Number of cases presenting themselves for treatment in an English infirmary	Number of cases presenting themselves for treatment in the New Zealand Hospitals	Proportion among each race; out of a thousand cases of disease there were among the:	
			English	New Zealanders
Fevers	390	190	20	74
Diseases of the lungs	2,165	435	109	169
Diseases of the liver	228	—[c]	12	—[c]
Diseases of stomach and bowels	1,418	304	71	119
Diseases of brain	1,031	15	52	5
Dropsies	451	2	23	—[c]
Rheumatic affections	2,365	495	119	191
Venereal	86	99	4	38
Abscesses and ulcers	2,195	278	111	108
Wounds and injuries	1,952	89	92	34
Diseases of the eyes	703	91	35	35
Diseases skin	801	181	45	70
Scrofula	1,173	210	59	82
All other diseases	4,908	191	248	75
Total	19,866	2,580	1,000	1,000

[a] Compiled from a synopsis of cases admitted into the Sheffield Infirmary during twenty-two years, by R. Ernest, M.D. Farr's "Annuals of Medicine, 1837."
[b] Compiled from returns obtained from Dr. Ford, Bay of Islands; Dr. Davies, Auckland; Dr. Fitzgerald, Wellington; Dr. Rees, Wanganul; and Dr. Wilson, New Plymouth.
[c] Data not available.

Table 10.2. *Size of the Maori population of New Zealand, 1769 to 1921*[a]

Year	Population
Estimates:	
1769	100,000–200,000
1814–15	150,000–180,000
1830s	150,000–180,000
ca. 1837	"Does not exceed" 130,000
1840	100,000–120,000
1846	120,000
1853	56,400–60,000
Census:	
1857–8	56,049
1874	47,330
1886	43,927
1896	42,113
1901	45,330
1911	52,723
1921	56,987

[a] The statistics for the years 1769 to 1853 range in quality from the wild guess to the educated guess and are subjects for argument. Consult Pool, *Maori Population*, 234–7, for the statistics per se, and pages 48–57 for the arguments. After 1853, the numbers are relatively dependable, i.e., satisfactory for most historians, if not for demographers.

The treaty of Waitangi brought the Maori no succor, only more pakeha. In their agony the Maori turned round and round, as desperate as a baited stag with the hounds slashing from all sides. Some simply tried harder to become like the pakeha. In the 1840s, over half of them were active Christians, and half of them could read.[99] In 1849, Governor George Gray stated that in his judgment, a larger proportion of Maori were literate than of any population in Europe.[100] Dr. Thomson tells us that he knew of Maori who were literate and bilingual, who could navigate with a compass, play chess, and "calculate the area of a plot of ground so as to sow two bushels of wheat to the acre, or the live weight of a pig, and its value at three pence a pound, deducting one fifth as offal."[101]

Some tribes flung themselves into farming and pastoralism, and even the beginnings of industrialism, selling not only to settlers, who often needed all the help they could get in their first years ashore, but all the way to Australia, then reinvesting the proceeds in more horses, sheep, and schooners, and, beginning in the late 1840s, in a flour-mill craze. "Each little petty Tribe must have a Mill," sniffed one missionary. "Two good Mills would grind all the Wheat on the Waipa and Waikato rivers, and there are now Six already erected."[102] In 1857, the Maori of the Bay of Plenty, Taupo, and Rotorua, about 8,000 of them, had 3,000 acres in wheat, 3,000 in potatoes, 2,000 in maize, and perhaps 1,000 in sweet potatoes. They owned nearly 1,000 horses, 200 cattle, and 5,000 pigs. They owned ninety-six plows, forty-one coasting vessels of about twenty tons each, and four water-powered mills.[103]

In 1849, King George Te Waru and John Baptist Kahawai sent Queen Victoria a sample of flour from wheat grown in their own fields and ground in their own mill in the center of the North Island. The Maori had built the mill largely with their own hands under the direction of a pakeha, whom they paid 200 pounds sterling, which they had saved over a period of a year by selling pigs and flax. "O the Queen," went the message they sent with the flour, "we are anxious to live in peace, to cultivate wheat, and breed cows and horses, in order that we may become assimilated to the white people."[104]

James E. Fitzgerald, a resident journalist, politician, and humanitarian without the usual winner's contempt for losers, stated flatly that he knew "of no race, at any period of the world's history, which had made in so short a period so great a stride."[105] He may very well have been correct, but nothing the Maori did halted their slide downward, and the pakeha were not interested in assimilation. Of greatest immediate danger was the loss of land. That matter, already volatile when Te Kemara pointed his finger at Reverend Williams at Waitangi, became the flash point between the Maori and pakeha. The trouble was worst in the North Island, where the greatest number of Maori lived. The island was currently occupied by two peoples: the Maori, in decline in every way, but still in the majority as late as 1860, and with a collectivistic and almost mystic sense of land ownership; the pakeha, a people advancing in every way, and with an individualistic and utterly simple sense of land ownership. The European concept was called fee simple: I, a single person, own this piece of land, or you, a single person, own it, and you by yourself can sell it to me totally and forever. By one means or another – legal or illegal, but always legalistic – the land flowed from the Maori to the pakeha. As the Maori wielded their paddles on the Waikato River, they sang:

> Like a creeping thing,
> The Land is moving;
> When gone, where shall man
> Find a dwelling?[106]

The Maori did not accept defeat without war first. Resistance to pakeha encroachment on Maori lands heated up as the years passed, and occasionally flared into violence, each incident serving to make clear that scattered opposition would be useless. The Maori took one more leaf from the pakeha book: nationalism. In the 1850s, a number of the tribes of the North Island tried what would have been unthinkable a few years earlier: to set aside forever their tribal rivalries and unite under a single leader. They utilized many of the pakeha symbols of nationhood, creating a king, a throne, a flag, a parliament – all legitimized with ceremonies and trappings from Maori tradition. The first Maori king was installed in 1858: Te Wherowhero, who called himself Potatau I. Two Maori printers who had learned their trade in Vienna set up a Maori press. A Maori newspaper appeared, called *Te Hokioi* after a mythical bird never seen but known by its scream, a bird that is an omen of war or pestilence. That paper helped to unite and inform the Kingites and, incidentally, issued what may have been the first call for conservationism in New Zealand. In a land where the Maori had practiced slash-and-burn farming for centuries, and where the sky was often darkened by the smoke of tremendous fires set by the pakeha to clear away bush and tussock for pakeha plants and animals, *Te Hokioi* asked its readers not to set fire to the forests, "lest there be no trees for our descendents. Do not either set fire to the scrub on the waste lands lest the manuka [a kind of bush] and the eel-weirs be destroyed and the land spoilt."[107]

The Kingites called for a halt to land sales, for the revival of old ways, and for strict separation from the pakeha. "Let the mad drunkards set off to Europe," they sang, "The King shall encircle the whole island."[108] The inevitable war hung fire for months in 1860, the desperation of the Maori's situation emphasized by an epidemic, alleged to be influenza, that swept the Waikato, laying low half the population and killing the first Maori king. His death may actually have hurried the war along, because he was a man of two minds: He died calling on his followers to be good Christians and on his pakeha friend, Sir William Martin, to be "kind to the niggers."[109]

The time for conciliation probably had already passed when he died. In the war that followed, the Maori fought with great skill and immense courage, adjusting admirably to fighting British regulars and pakeha irregulars in the tangled bush, ridges, and ravines of the North Island. But they were not truly unified: Many of the Maori ignored the call for war, thinking, rightly, that war could only make things worse, and others even aided the pakeha. And the tribes who waged the war lacked the one element crucial for victory, for they could not do what the British Empire and

New Zealand pakeha could do: sustain a war effort for years and years, seemingly forever, if necessary.

In the mid-1860s, the war ceased to be one of formal confrontation and became one of guerrilla and counter-guerrilla, with all the bestiality that kind of warfare usually entails. As the Maori situation worsened, a faith reminiscent of Papahurihia's cult of the 1830s spread among the most militant Maori. Again a strange blend of Christianity and Maori beliefs arose: The angel Gabriel appeared to the prophet Te Ua Haumene and told him to set up tall flagstaffs, the *niu,* and worship there as at an altar. In return there would be miracles: All the material things that the Maori wanted of the pakeha would be theirs, plus instantaneous knowledge of the English language, but the pakeha would be defeated and would depart; the faithful would be invulnerable to bullets if they held up their arms in a certain way and said certain words; and so on. Their chants were pitifully nonsensical streams of Maori and pakeha phrases, all connotation and no denotation:

Mountain, big mountain, long mountain, big staff, long staff –
 Attention!
North, north-by-east, nor'-nor'-east, no'-east-by-north, north-east colony –
 Attention!
Come to tea, all the men, round the *niu* – Attention!
Shem, rule the wind, too much wind, come to tea – Attention![110]

The most fanatic of the followers of the new cult, the Hauhau (their name derived from the words they repeated in battle to deflect bullets) revived cannibalism from the past, and in their desperation they devised rites as hideous as imagination could conceive – and may actually have shortened the war by flinging themselves into the line of fire, confident of their invulnerability.

Nothing the Maori could do would serve to cancel the pakeha soldiers' advantage in numbers and perseverance.

Maori power waned, pakeha security increased, and in 1870 the last British regiment withdrew. The colonists fought on with increasing effectiveness as they learned the nasty trade of irregular warfare, and the war dwindled to an end. For long afterward, no pakeha in the interior of the North Island felt secure away from his gun, but by 1875 there was no longer any question about who owned New Zealand. New Zealand was Neo-European.

The Maori had continued the war long after it was lost. Perhaps they had even begun it after it was lost. In 1870 – one century after a British citizen had first seen New Zealand, a land that had had only one kind of mammal when Charlemagne was crowned emperor, and that had only four when Cook arrived – this land had 80,000 horses, 400,000 cattle, and 9,000,000 sheep, and a pakeha population of a quarter million, as against one-fifth as many Maori. During the war, gold had been discovered in the South Island, and in two years the population of Otago increased by about as many whites as there were Maori in all of New Zealand.[111]

In 1770, Captain Cook made his statement that New Zealand would make an excellent European colony, implying a great similarity between New Zealand and Europe, or, at least, Great Britain. Yet, paradoxically, there is in the next century no evidence that any New Zealand organisms, plant or animal, micro or macro, achieved naturalization anywhere in Europe. In contrast – and in consonance with the captain's statement – a great many species of Old World organisms settled in New Zealand and propagated by the billions in that hundred years. The pakeha did not go ashore alone. If they had, their fate might have been like that of the gallant cavalier, superbly trained and equipped, who makes the fatal error of charging the enemy lines by himself.

The parallel between the widespread usurpation of New Zealand's biota and the decline of the Maori was not one missed by the indigenes. Years before the treaty of Waitangi, the Maori recognized the link between their fate and that of the ecosystem in which they had participated for forty generations before the coming of the pakeha. They identified themselves closely with the Maori rat, their age-old companion and the center dish in many festival meals. The Old World black rat or ship rat probably achieved naturalization in New Zealand very early, and without causing much disruption, in contrast to the brown or Norwegian rat, big and aggressive, when it came ashore about 1830. Within two years, this animal, considered inedible by the Maori, annihilated the Maori rats in much of Northland and then proceeded south, driving its native rivals before it. In the next decade or so, the intruder exterminated the Maori rat all over the North Island, except for a few crannies and islets. Pakeha lumbermen, when angered with the Maori, told them that the whites would eliminate them just as the new rat had the old rat, an idea already circulating among the Maori as their situation worsened. Ernst Dieffenbach said in 1843 that "it is a favorite theme with them to speculate on their own extermination by the Europeans, in the same manner as the English rat has exterminated the indigenous rat."

In the 1850s, with the avalanche of pakeha and associated species pouring ashore, more models for Maori extinction appeared. Exotic weeds ran like quicksilver along the roads into the bush. Native birds retreated as exotic cats, dogs, and rats advanced. The inadvertently imported Old World housefly proved to be so effective at driving back the native bluebottle fly, hated by the pakeha because it learned to lay eggs in the flesh of sheep, that herdsmen took up the practice of carrying their own kind of flies along with them into the backcountry in jars. The brown rats swept through the South Island, again exterminating all but a trace number of the Maori rats, and in the 1860s were deep into the Southern Alps and growing to enormous sizes. Julius von Haast, a geologist who arrived in New Zealand in 1858, wrote Darwin that there was a proverb among the Maori that "as the white man's rat has driven away the native rat, so the European fly drives away our own, and the clover kills our fern, so will the Maoris disappear before the white man himself."[112]

Pakeha with scientific training observed the same phenomena as the Maori and reached similar conclusions. Darwin was amazed at the one-sidedness of the exchange of life forms between Britain and New Zealand and in *The Origin of Species* stated his conclusion that "the productions of Great Britain stand much higher in the scale than those of New Zealand. Yet the most skillful naturalist, from an examination of the two countries, could not have foreseen this result."[113] Ten years later, exactly 100 years after Cook had first appeared off the shores of New Zealand, W. T. L Travers, pakeha naturalist and New Zealand politician, observed that the islands' ecosystem "had reached a point at which, like a house built of incoherent materials, a blow struck anywhere shakes and damages the whole fabric." He was sure that "if every human being were at once removed from the Islands . . . the introduced would succeed in displacing the indigenous fauna and flora." Nor were the Maori standing up to the European competition; the result was inevitable and tolerable:

If, by the intrusion of the vigorous races of Europe, smiling farms and busy marts are to take the place of the rough clearing and hut of the savage, and millions of a populous country, with the arts and letters, the matured policy, and the ennobling impulses of a free people, are to replace the few thousands of the scattered tribes now living in an apparently aimless and unprogressive state, even the most sensitive philanthropist may learn to look with resignation, if not with complacency, on the extinction of a people which, in the past had accomplished so imperfectly every object of man's being.[114]

Neither the despondent Maori nor the amazed Darwin nor the complacent Travers proved to be completely or even mostly correct. The Maori hit bottom demographically in the 1890s, with a nadir of little more than 40,000, but since then they have recovered much of their morale and all their numbers and more. In 1981, there were 280,000 New Zealanders who called themselves Maori.[115] Nor has the native biota of New Zealand disappeared. Any station owner will maintain that the indigenous flora is ineradicable and will leap to take back any pasture from which livestock are withdrawn. The fauna, like the flora, has been ravaged, but it, too, has come through the last hundred years better than expected. The kiwi still noodle through the humus for insects and grubs.

Even so, we cannot say that the Maori, Darwin, and Travers were fools. The forces they observed reshaping New Zealand did not maintain their headlong pace and make a Europe out of New Zealand, but they did confirm it as a Neo-Europe. In 1981, New Zealand had 2,700,000 pakeha, 70,000,000 sheep, and 8,000,000 cattle and produced 326,000 metric tons of wheat, 152,000 of maize, about 7,000 of honey, and – for old times' sake – 10,000 of kumara.[116]

11

𝓍𝓸𝓻𝓮𝓵

Explanations

"PERHAPS IT IS the very simplicity of the thing which puts you at fault."
—Edgar Allan Poe, "The Purloined Letter"

IF WE CONFINE the concept of weeds to species adapted to human disturbance, then man is by definition the first and primary weed under whose influence all other weeds have evolved.
—Jack R. Harlan, *Crops and Man* (1975)

As CONSTITUTED AT PRESENT, New Zealand's biota and society, as well as those of the other Neo-Europes, are largely products of the runaway propagation and spread of what I call the portmanteau biota, my collective name for the Europeans and all the organisms they brought with them. Understanding its success is the key to understanding the puzzle of the rise of the Neo-Europes.

Adam Smith said of the success of one of the portmanteau biota's more prominent organisms, "In a country neither half-peopled or half-cultivated, cattle naturally multiply beyond the consumption of its inhabitants."[1] He was among the wisest of men, but neither a historian nor an ecologist, and we might want to ask him why said country is so lightly populated and farmed, and, further, to point out that in most places and most times, with or without humans present, the increase of cattle and indeed all organisms is naturally kept within decent bounds by the actions of predators, parasites, pathogens, and hunger. Events to the contrary were in such profusion in Smith's time as to dazzle his common sense.

The triumph of the portmanteau biota has been massive in the Neo-Europes, but most of the extreme predictions of such nineteenth-century naturalists as W. T. L. Travers have proved to be exaggerated. Very few of the indigenous life forms of the Neo-Europes have become extinct, and in North America and Australasia the native peoples are now increasing faster in number than the descendants of their conquerors. Yet the indigenes are only small fractions of the total populations, and there is no scoffing at the number of invading organisms that have thrived and swarmed across the Neo-Europes. The present-day biotas of these lands are very different from what they were a few human generations ago. The magnitude of the change has been more accurately assessed by its human victims than by its human beneficiaries. At the end of the nineteenth century, the Amerindians of the plains and western mountains of

North America, facing absolute defeat in their long struggle with the whites, fashioned a new religion that foretold an immediate change as great as that of the preceding three hundred years: A whole new world, with the Amerindian dead come alive again and the buffalo and the wapiti and all the game in their former profusion, would come up from the west and slide over the surface of the present world, and the Amerindians who were dancing the Ghost Dance would be carried upward by their sacred dance feathers and would then descend to alight on this renewed world, and after four days of unconsciousness would awake to find everything as it was before the coming of the Europeans.[2] The *marinheiros* and their portmanteau biota had made a revolution more extreme than any seen on this planet since the extinctions at the end of the Pleistocene, and the losers could imagine its reversal only by means of a collosal miracle.

What underlay and underlies this biological revolution? Let us return to the C. Auguste Dupin technique recommended in the first chapter. Let us consider the most obvious factor: geographical position. The Neo-Europes are all in climatic zones similar to that of Europe, an advantage for organisms of European origin that does not need belaboring. They are also all very far from Europe, at the very least on the other side of the Atlantic Ocean, and some even on the other side of the world. Monsieur Dupin puffs on his meerschaum and advises "*cherchez* the traces and effects of remoteness and isolation."

The seams of Pangaea slipped and spread scores of millions of years ago, and after that the biota of the Old World, including Europe, and those of the Neo-Europes evolved separately. This trend was interrupted now and again by the appearance of broad land bridges over which species were exchanged, but by and large the histories of the life forms of these regions have been significantly different.

The several separate biotas did not develop in ways that

were intrinsically better or worse or higher or lower – these terms have no scientific content – but the biotas of the Neo-Europes-to-be may have been simpler in the sense of having fewer members than that of Europe, which was a part of a much larger geographical whole than were those of its future overseas colonies. This difference – we might better say alleged difference when we compare Europe and North America – is one from which we must be wary of drawing too many conclusions. It was much more apparent when the *marinheiros* arrived than it was when the Neo-Europes first became human habitats thousands of years earlier. This recent amplification of the differences between the native biota of the Old World and those of the Americas and Australasia is a matter that provokes curiosity.

Before we consider that, let us tick off the most obvious consequence of the isolation of the Americas and Australasia from the Old World. Neither humans nor anthropoids are native to the former two regions; when humans set foot there they were moving into ecosystems in which they were profoundly alien. No native predators, parasites, or pathogens adapted to preying on them existed in the new lands. Carnivores, being creatures with brains and wills, might learn fast enough, but microorganisms would take a while. As far as we know, no major human diseases have originated in Australasia, and there are very few of American provenance, and their pathogens have never adapted fully enough to humans to have established themselves anywhere outside the Americas – with the possible exception of the spirochetes of venereal syphilis.

We must not ignore the probability that these first humans to reach the Americas and Oceania brought pathogens and parasites with them, but they could not have had too many deadly or debilitating passengers. The carriers were nomads, following herds across the tundra from Siberia to Alaska, island-hopping across the Indonesian archipelago, sailing from volcanic outcropping to atoll to atoll across the Pacific. All but the most hearty succumbed, and the sickly were abandoned. As for the nomads' vermin, by moving periodically these people left most of their garbage and therefore most of their vermin behind. The Maori were probably an especially healthy lot, because they must have sloughed off a whole menagerie of tropical insects, vermin, and pathogens – those of yaws, for instance – when they sailed from the hot islands of central Polynesia to cool New Zealand.

It is logical to suppose that the humans who first entered the Americas and Australasia experienced rates of population growth much greater than usual for hunters and gatherers. They entered regions in which they had no special enemies, they had outrun many of their old enemies, and initially the supplies of food must have been cornucopian.

Addition of a new species to an ecosystem can produce amazing ripple effects throughout the system, and humans, as the first species capable of extensive use of reason and of tools in the New World, Australia, and New Zealand, must have had an effect all out of proportion to their numbers. Humans can swiftly adapt their hunting techniques so as to turn the predictable defensive behavior of a species of animal to their own advantage. For instance, they can provoke the dominant male or males to make a stand, leaving the females and young defenseless to attack from another angle. Humans can quickly learn to stampede herd animals over cliffs and into swamps, can learn to attack when and where animals gather to mate, can learn to attack pregnant and very young animals even more preferentially than the usual predators. Humans can set fires to forest and grasslands and, if they do so often enough, radically change their biotas forever. Humans, even if armed only with the torch and with weapons of stone and fire-hardened wood, are the most dangerous and unrelenting predators in the world.

When humans first entered the Americas and Australasia, they found no shortage of large animals. Mammoths, giant ground sloths, saber-toothed tigers, and other nightmarishly huge creatures dominated in the New World, and vast herds of giant buffalo, native horses, and camels were thundering across American grasslands. In Australia, large monotremes and marsupials reigned, including kangaroos one-third larger than any living today, and the *Thylacoleo carnifex,* a meat-eater that looked rather like a chipmunk, except that it had fangs and claws and was more than two meters long, not counting the tail. No such mammalian monsters greeted the Maori on the beach, but the largest moas were twice as tall as a man and outweighed him by more than double. In general, one can say that the Americas were as rich in large animals as the Old World. Australia was inferior, but not enormously so, and even New Zealand had its giants.[3]

And yet by the time the *marinheiros* appeared on the Maori, Aborigine, and Amerindian horizons, the giants of the Americas and Australasia were gone. There were no mammalian American carnivores to compare in size with the Old World's lions and tigers, and no herbivores to compare with the elephant, rhinoceros, or hippopotamus, as the French naturalist, the comte de Buffon, pointed out disparagingly in the eighteenth century. The tapir, South America's largest quadruped, "exceeds not the size of a calf six months old, or a very small mule."[4] Patriotic Americans can point proudly to their condor, the largest bird extant, but the truth remains that the New World's native biota in historical times has been inferior to that of the Old World in large quadrupeds. Americans, however, can reinflate their egos by pointing with scorn to the biotas of Australia and New Zealand, which are inferior in quadrupeds to even that of America.

In general, the world lost more kinds of large land animals in the millennia around the end of the Pleistocene than at any similarly brief period for many millions of years, and in no areas were the losses as great as in the Americas and Australia. A few thousand years later, this wave of extinctions reached the last large islands to be inhabited by humans, New Zealand and Madagascar, and their losses, in proportion to the sizes of their biotas, were as great or even greater.[5] The fields and forests of these impoverished lands and islands, when the *marinheiros* came, were more open to invading fauna than any other in the world. Had they been as thickly populated with herds of grazers and browsers and packs of carnivores as they had been when the very first humans arrived, or as, for instance, South Africa was when the Dutch settled there in the middle of the seventeenth century, the spread and triumph of European livestock, tame and feral, would have been slow and would have required considerably more human intervention that it did. The triumph of European humans, until recently always dependent on horses, cattle, sheep, and all, would also have been slower, perhaps as slow and perhaps as inconclusive as that of the Europeans in South Africa, where their livestock had to share the veldt with some of the largest and most dangerous animals now extant, and with more livestock parasites and pathogens, living in and on the local wildlife, than in any of the Neo-Europes. Fifty years after the first horses were introduced into South Africa, their total was about 900. A half century after horses were put ashore in the pampa, the total of their numbers swirling across those grasslands was beyond counting.[6]

The times and means of the extinctions of the giants are matters of great significance in the story of how the Neo-Europes became Neo-European. A number of scientists, most especially Paul S. Martin, have put forward a theory to explain the extinctions that has engendered great controversy among paleontologists, archeologists, and other experts, a theory that, if true, throws a strong light on the shadowy prehistory of the Neo-Europes. Martin points to a large body of evidence that there was a coincidence in timing throughout the world between the appearance of human big-game hunters and the demise of the giants, which were the most attractively large meals available. Where humans and giants had dwelled together for many millennia, as in the Old World, the latter had learned to be wary of the biped hunters, and many – not all, but many – of the larger animals survived well into modern times and even to our own day: elephants and lions in Africa, and elephants, tigers, wild horses, and camels in Asia. Where the large animals did not have the benefit of hundreds of thousands of years of adjusting to the human presence, as in the Americas and Australasia, the hunters were able to slaughter them in such quantities as to eliminate most of them completely.[7]

The theory strikes some as outrageous. How could Stone Age hunters eliminate whole species, even genera, of such presumably dangerous animals? However, counter-theories of universal climatic change (longer winters, drier summers, or what have you) seem even less satisfactory: There simply was no such change, not, at least, that affected the several parts of the world in question at the several and different times at which they lost their giants. And why would climatic change kill off large animals and not small ones? Perhaps the small ones needed less to eat, and so survived the poverty times better than the large ones. Perhaps, but the *deus ex climatica* theory has, at present, less evidence to shore it up than the overkill theory. Perhaps deadly parasites and pathogens, previously present only in the Old World, came into the Americas and Australasia with the hunters and the other creatures that arrived at the same time and by the same means. But why would these kill large animals but not small animals? We are back to the hunters as our best means to account for the disappearance of the giants.

The hunters, of course, would not have had to attack the large carnivores to eliminate them, because the carnivores would have died off automatically if their prey, the large herbivores, disappeared. As for the huge plant-eaters, we do have archeological evidence – for instance, mammoth bones and projectile points in contiguity – that humans did kill some of them, and we have very persuasive evidence that humans, utilizing fire, were responsible for elimination of several species of very large creatures soon after 1000 A.D. in Madagascar and New Zealand. The Maori use of fire transformed the eastern half of the South Island from forest to grassland, or, to put it another way, from a landscape in which moas could live to one in which they could not.[8]

The "stupidity" of animals unaccustomed to attack by humans must have been important. To a considerable extent, animals learn how to avoid danger not by individual experience but by means of heredity; generations are required to imprint in the genes data concerning new dangers. The human hunters were much smaller than any creatures the giants had had to fear before; in fact, the humans did not resemble anything the American and Australasian giants had seen before. The huge land animals were about as unequipped to protect themselves against human aggression as whales are in our time. In the first half or so of the nineteenth century, European and Neo-European sea hunters, though they had only wind and muscle to propel their ships and boats, and no weapon more effective than the hand-thrown harpoon, were able to kill off all but a trace few of certain species of whales in the Atlantic and Pacific. These huge, powerful, and intelligent animals were physically capable of defending themselves against the hunters by avoidance or attack, but they simply did not know how to or even that they had to.[9] The great exception, Moby Dick, was not a manifestation of abstract malevolence so much as an outstandingly fast learner.

There is no reason that the stories of whales and whalers and of the giant animals of the Americas and Australasia and the invading hunters should not have been much the same. If the hunters did kill off the the giant land animals, who had no ocean vastnesses in which to lose themselves, then this goes a long way to explain the success of feral Old World livestock in the Neo-Europes in the past few hundred years. It offers an explanation for the mysterious vacant or perhaps we might say vacated econiches in Australia in 1788, into which the invaders quickly moved. For example, before the spread of goats, camels, and other such stock with their flinty mouths and iron bellies, there were no large browsers in Australia feeding heavily on shrubs and bushes. There are now – by the thousands. Goats have spread widely in the outback, and as of the middle of our century, Australia had the largest population of wild camels in the world, 15,000 to 30,000.[10]

Martin's theory also helps explain the history of the fauna of the pampa, where feral European livestock had their most spectacular success. The pampa is one hundred degrees of latitude distant from the Bering Strait, the presumed point of entry for the first humans to come to the Americas, and so we are justified in speculating that the pampa was one of the last areas to be occupied by the hunters and that their disruption of its ecosystem was recent, relative to the rest of the fertile Americas. When the *marinheiros* arrived in the sixteenth century and Old World livestock stiffly made their way ashore, major niches still gaped open in the ecosystem. Hence the astonishing spread of cattle and horses in the following decades. Even sheep, meek and mild, managed to live independently on the pampa – not by the millions, but by the thousands.[11]

The portmanteau biota even provided the pampa with its chief carnivore. The local flesh-eaters should have been adequate to keep the feral herds down, but obviously were not. Perhaps they had not yet recovered from the first wave of humans, those who had come by land from the north. For whatever reason, the herds of Old World livestock rolled over the local flesh-eaters, attaining populations of tens of millions, which would have risen even a bit higher but for the rule that meals will eventually engender eaters. By no later than the middle of the eighteenth century, and in all probability long before that, the most important animal predators on the pampa were Old World dogs, strayed and gone wild, wise in the ways of humans and livestock, and running in packs like their distant ancestors. They subsisted on carrion, feral pigs, and whatever else they could pull down. Compared with lions, leopards, and Eurasian and North American wolves, the dogs were unimpressive, but there were so many of them that the Iberian settlers had to institute annual campaigns to thin out their numbers.[12]

In 1500, the ecosystem of the pampa was broken, worn, incomplete – like a toy that has been played with too roughly by a thoughtless colossus. The Iberians rebuilt it, albeit often unintentionally, using new parts when the old ones were missing or inadequate, and became (though not until the nineteenth century) its dominant organisms.

A contrasting case is that of the North American plains, where the Europeans had to disassemble an existing eco-system before they could have one that accorded with their needs. As late as three centuries after the coming of the whites, these steppes were still dominated by millions of American buffalo, though the immigrant quadrupeds had had as ample an opportunity to take over as in the pampa. Feral cattle were present in southern Texas in large num-bers in the eighteenth and early nineteenth centuries, and when Texas ranchers drove the longhorns north to take advantage of the expanding northeastern urban markets after the American Civil War, the animals did well. But they do not seem to have been able to prosper in the central and northern reaches of the plains on their own. Wild horses spread from Mexico to Canada, but they never ranged the plains in such numbers as on the pampa. The rapidity of their advance was probably more a matter of Amerindian trading and rustling than of the animals' natural tendency to migrate.

Buffalo larger than any we know today roamed North America for many thousands of years before humans came; they died out during the same period as the mammoths, horses, and camels. Our present-day buffalo survived, perhaps because they were faster on their feet, perhaps because they were a shade smarter, perhaps a bit less contemptuous of the threat of the new bipeds, perhaps because they reproduced faster. We do not know why, but their presence in North America in historical times, along with other medium-sized giants such as moose, wapiti, musk ox, and grizzlies, does provoke speculation. Such large animals did not survive in South America or Australasia. Björn Kurtén has pointed to the Eurasian origin of most of the North American survivors among the large quadrupeds, and he suggests that they were able to live on because of long previous conditioning to human hunters.[13] The Europeans had to slaughter these, particularly the buffalo, before they and their livestock and plants could assume their present positions in the biota of the plains.

We cannot prove or disprove Martin's theory here, but only note that it does provide an explanation for much about the Neo-Europes that is otherwise obscure. And it places the Amerindians, Aborigines, and Maori, on the one hand, and the European invaders, on the other, in a fresh and intellectually provocative relationship: not simply as adversaries, with the indigenes passive, the whites active, but as two waves of invaders of the same species, the first acting as the shock troops, clearing the way for the second wave, with its more complicated economies and greater numbers.

So much for the influence on the Neo-Europes of the events of the millennia and epochs prior to the *marinheiros* putting to sea. Let us turn to the last 500 years, where we are on firmer ground.

The members of the portmanteau biota had at least the same advantage as had the first humans and their associated organisms that crossed into the New World from Eurasia: the advantage of moving into virgin territory and, with luck, leaving a lot of enemies behind. Back in the Old World, most particularly in the densely populated areas of civilization, many organisms had taken advantage of contiguity with humans and their plants and animals to become their parasites and pathogens. These freeloaders often were slower to emigrate to the Neo-Europes than were humans and the organisms that humans intentionally brought with them. For example, Europeans brought wheat to North America and created the first of their several wheat belts in the Delaware River valley in the eighteenth century, where the plant thrived in the absence of its enemies. Then its old nemesis, the Hessian fly, unjustly blamed on George III's mercenaries, who supposedly brought it across the Atlantic in their straw bedding, arrived and obliged farmers of that valley to find a new staple. *Mayetiola destructor* – it was named with its economic significance in mind – has also reached New Zealand, but in Australia and the pampa, as of the 1970s, it was still unimportant, if present at all.[14]

Many kinds of livestock pathogens have lagged far behind their usual hosts in transoceanic crossings. Rabies, a disease of cats, bats, and wild rodents in the Old World, apparently did not reach the Americas until the middle of the eighteenth century and has never established itself in Australasia.[15] Rinderpest exploded in western Europe in the eighteenth century, killing multitudes of cattle, and reached southern and eastern Africa in the late nineteenth century, slaughtering literally millions of domesticated and wild ungulates, but it has never gained a permanent foothold in the New World, Australia, or New Zealand.[16] Foot-and-mouth disease, an established scourge in most major livestock producing countries, has appeared a number of times in the Neo-Europes, but it has always been eradicated in North America and Australasia. It has established itself in South America, but that continent was free from the malady for centuries after the first arrival of Old World livestock.[17] In the article "Diseases of Animals" in the fifteenth edition of the *Encyclopaedia Britannica* there is a table entitled "Animal Diseases Usually Confined to Certain Regions of the World." It includes the names of thirteen major infections. Of these, only two are established in the Neo-Europes: contagious pleuropneumonia in Australia and foot-and-mouth disease in southern South America. By quarantine, fumigation, vigilance, and, if necessary, even slaughter of sick or suspect livestock, the Neo-Europeans continue to maintain their advantage vis-à-vis animal diseases over the livestockmen of the central slabs of Pangaea.[18]

The Neo-Europeans' advantage vis-à-vis their own diseases was for years almost as pronounced, though the colonists crossed the waters in greater numbers than their animals and resisted all the previously mentioned techniques to halt the spread of their own pathogens. From the fifteenth century in the Canaries to the middle of the nineteenth century in New Zealand, the European intruders remarked on the healthiness of their new homes, the lack of new diseases to catch, and of old diseases as well. The region around Buenos Aires – its name is its bond – had a good climate, and the Spaniards there lived long and hale in the sixteenth century, even to 90 and 100 years said Juan López de Velasco.[19] A Jesuit, Father Bressani, reported from New France in 1653 that no European associated with the Huron mission had died of natural causes in sixteen years, "while in Europe those years are few when some one does not die in our Colleges, if their inmates are at all numerous."[20] The first Yankees recommended "all cold complections to take Physick in *New England;* for a sup of New-England's aire is better than a whole draught of old *England's* ale." Real estate publicity? Yes, but not entirely phony. In Andover, Massachusetts, the average age at death for the first settlers was 71.8 years, an impressive longevity for that era.[21] In 1790, the governor of New South Wales reported that "a finer and more healthy climate is not to be found in any part of the world." Of 1,030 people who had disembarked with him two years earlier, many with scurvy and half of them convicts from Britain's malnourished lower classes, only seventy-two had died, "and by the surgeon's returns, it appears that twenty-six of those died from disorders of long standing, and which it is more than probable would have carried them off sooner in England."[22] In New Zealand, the pakeha claimed that theirs was the healthiest land in the world, and they cited statistics to prove it. In 1859, the death rate for British infantrymen in the United Kingdom was 16.8 per 1,000, but in New Zealand only 5.3. In 1898, among every 10,000 male babies born alive in New Zealand, 9,033 survived the first year; in New South Wales and Victoria, 8,672; in England, 8,414.[23]

This was a matter of improved diet and a rising standard of living, and it is significant that Old World pathogens were often slower to migrate overseas than Old World peoples, and slower yet to become naturalized. Smallpox virus never established itself permanently in Australasia, and never in the pampa or North America until after the colonial era. There were not enough people to maintain the disease as an endemic infection. Epidemic smallpox provided the Neo-Europeans with horrors every generation or so, at a minimum, but in all probability a higher percentage of them escaped the infection than did Europeans. Malaria plasmodia did not become naturalized in North America until the 1680s, and their date of arrival in southern South

America is uncertain. They never established themselves permanently in Australasia, though the climate in parts of northern Australia is close to ideal for their mosquitoes.[24]

But we must not overemphasize the importance of when a given disease was or was not established in a given colony. The prevalence of pathogens – the density, so to speak, of the disease environment – is more important, and the challenge of infection was less in the Neo-Europes for many years after the Old World peoples arrived than back where they came from. To make an analogy, there are Irishmen in Denver, Colorado, and in Dublin, Ireland; a person can walk ten blocks in Denver without meeting one, but not ten steps in Dublin.

Thousands of Europeans, for whom pestilence ranging from plague to grippe had been a constant presence from birth onward – the source of some troubles and the climax of the others, such as economic depression, famine, and war[25] – had crossed the seams of Pangaea and stolen a march on their microscopic tormentors. There was a price to pay, of course – a minor one, but not to be safely overlooked. Being removed from the Afro-Eurasian biota for as little as one generation made for vulnerability. For example, Neo-Europeans born in the colonies of British North America grew up in a region in which smallpox was an epidemic rather than an endemic disease and often reached young adulthood without exposure to this killer. When aristocrats among them went to Oxford and Cambridge for European polishing, they stood a very good chance of catching "that Loathsome Vile and dangerous disease before they are seasoned to the Air of England in which a great many of our Countrymen and Women have lost their lives." This quite real danger had many effects, and some were not at all self-apparent. For instance, the threat tended to cripple the Anglican church in the colonies, because only a bishop could ordain its ministers, and its only bishops resided in the British Isles. One might well want to serve God as an Anglican clergyman, but the journey to England was long and expensive, and those going there risked getting smallpox for their trouble. The Church of England, already in a position of weakness in the Nonconformist-dominated colonies, limped along, whereas its rivals, who could ordain their ministers on the safe side of the Atlantic, bounded on ahead.[26]

If a generation or two away from those pathogens could create such vulnerability, what would ten thousand years or double or triple that do? The indigenes of the Americas and Australasia were almost defenseless against the onslaught of Old World pathogens that the Europeans brought with them. The Amerindians, Aborigines, and Maori had out-run many of the pathogens that had afflicted their ancestors and had found few in their new homes to greet them. And these avant-garde of humanity were safe on the far sides of the seams of Pangaea when deadly new pathogens developed in the centers of population created by the Old World Neolithic Revolution. Neither Aborigines nor Maori ever built up dense centers like the cities of the Old World, nor did they have large herds of domesticated animals with which to share and hybridize new strains of pathogens. The Amerindians created cities, but much later than in the Middle East, and they had no herds of domesticated animals, except in the Incan region. The Amerindians probably lagged as far behind the Europeans in the cultivation of pathogens as they did in metallurgy.[27]

The indigenes of the Americas and Australasia paid for their salubrious millennia all at once; they were as defense-less as babes against most of the pathogens the Old World peoples carried. Indeed, they may have been even more vulnerable to the imported diseases than babes-in-arms back in the Old World, because those babes were de-scended from generations who had lived with those infec-tions. The latter had been culling out the most vulnerable members of Old World populations for millennia, eliminating them from the gene pool. In contrast, the Old World pathogens had not had a crack at the peoples of the Americas and Australasia, who had been at least as isolated as the Guanches and probably more so. Like the Guanches, they have, and presumably had 500 years ago, the hematological stigmata of peoples who have lived remote from Eurasia and Africa and therefore, from the bulk of humanity for thousands of years: few or no members with B-type blood, and in the case of the Amerindians, percentages of O type running up to total.[28] The Amerindians, Aborigines, and Australasians were true isolates. They had been different from Europeans, Asians, and Africans for thousands of years, and so, perhaps, were the capabilities of their immune systems.

But this is pure speculation, and we have no need of genetics to explain the ease with which the pathogens of exotic diseases spread among the indigenes of the Neo-Europes. Infectious diseases and populations of potential victims are like fires and forests: If there have been no fires for a long time, then when they do start there will be general conflagrations, perhaps even fire storms. Any people on earth when exposed to a virulent strain of smallpox for the first time will suffer infection rates of up to 100 percent, and death rates of one-fourth, one-third, and more, death rates that even modern medicine can reduce only slightly, and that the folk remedies and panic of those who have never known the scourge before will in all likelihood elevate. In 1972, a pilgrim returning from Mecca brought smallpox to Yugoslavia, where it had not been known for forty-two years. Before public health measures stopped its spread, 174 Yugoslavs contracted the disease, and 35 died.[29] If a people of the scientific sophistication of the modern Yugoslavs could do no better than to hold the death rate down to one-fifth of the infected, we should not be surprised to read reports of one-third or one-half of

Sydney Aborigines, Narragansetts, and Araucanians dying when hit by similar pathogens.

The only truly effective way to deal with the major communicable pathogens of the world is directly, thus building – if one survives – immunity against them. This can be done by inoculation with killed or attenuated virus or closely related but mild strains; or one can simply get the disease, preferably while a child and thus more apt to survive than later. The former method characterizes the advanced societies of the last century or so; the latter has characterized most human societies during all of recorded history. Absolute quarantine – perpetual isolation – is a superficially attractive method of dealing with the threat; it may save the individual, but it condemns the group to eventual disaster, because isolation can never be permanent. During the Caste War in Yucatan, which began in the middle of the nineteenth century, some of the Maya, the Cruzob who worshipped the Talking Cross, withdrew from all contact with outsiders. They did so not primarily to avoid smallpox, but their retreat had that effect. In 1915, their leaders opened negotiations with the Mexicans, and immediately acquired smallpox. A virgin-soil epidemic like those of the sixteenth century ensued, reducing the Cruzob from about 8,000 or 10,000 to approximately 5,000.[30] These Amerindians went through the gauntlet of the Old World Neolithic twice.

One of the most important factors in the success of the portmanteau biota is so simple that it is easy to overlook. Its members did not function alone, but as a team. Sometimes they worked against each other, as in the case of farmers and Hessian flies, but more often they helped each other, at least in the long run. Sometimes the mutual support is obvious, as with Europeans importing honeybees to pollinate their crops. Sometimes the connection is obscure: In the Great Plains, the whites and their hirelings killed off almost all the buffalo – encouraging the spread of venereal pathogens, some of which were certainly immigrants. A physician serving the Sioux at Fort Peck toward the end of the last century assessed the tragedy of venereal infections among their women not simply as a result of immorality but as the result of a more general change: "They were chaste till the disappearance of the buffalo."[31]

For a clearer example of the portmanteau biota as a mutual-aid society, let us consider the history of forage grasses, because these weeds (remember, a weed is not necessarily an obnoxious plant, only an opportunistic plant) were vital to the spread of European livestock and therefore to Europeans themselves. There are about 10,000 grass species, but a mere forty account for 99 percent of the sown grass pastures of the world. Few, if any, of the forty are native to the great grasslands outside the Old World. Twenty-four of the forty occur naturally and have apparently grown for a very long time in an area comprising Europe minus northern Scandinavia, plus North Africa and the Middle East. It is an area so small that at one time most of it was within the Roman Empire.[32] Our most important forage grasses are native to the general part of the world where most of our livestock were first tamed, and where they have grazed on these grasses since the first millennia of the Neolithic.

The mutual adaptation of these grasses and grazers extends even further back than the Neolithic. The family Bovidae, which includes cattle, sheep, goats, buffalo, and bison, arose and evolved during the Pliocene and Pleistocene in northern Eurasia. Many members migrated to Africa, a few to North America, but none to South America or Australasia.[33] For thousands of years, Old World grazing animals and certain grasses, plus the other weeds of Eurasia and North Africa, have been adapting to each other. The Old World quadrupeds, when transported to America, Australia, and New Zealand, stripped away the local grasses and forbs, and these, which in most cases had been subjected only to light grazing before, were often slow to recover. In the meantime, the Old World weeds, particularly those from Europe and nearby parts of Asia and Africa, swept in and occupied the bare ground. They were tolerant of open sunlight, bare soil, and close cropping and of being constantly trod upon, and they possessed a number of means of propagation and spread. For instance, often their seeds were equipped with hooks to catch on the hides of passing livestock or were tough enough to survive the trip through their stomachs to be deposited somewhere farther down the path. When the livestock returned for a meal the next season, it was there. When the stockman went out in search of his stock, they were there, too, and healthy.

Félix de Azara observed the process under way in the pampa as gauchos and huge herds of European quadrupeds subjected the local flora to trauma it had never known in the heyday of the guanaco and rhea, replacing the "tall pastures" with the "soft, modern pastures" by means of *pata y diente,* hoof and tooth.[34] Thomas Budd, writing in seventeenth-century Pennsylvania, saw it, too: "If we sprinkle but a little English hay-seed on the Land without plowing, and then feed Sheep on it, in a little time it will so encrease, that it will cover the land with English grass."[35] In New South Wales, the settlers cut down trees so fast, exposing the native grasses to the burning sun, and the livestock cropped the indigenous grasses and forbs so fast that kangaroo grass disappeared from around Sydney within a few decades after the coming of the whites. Where the land lay bare, European plants, artificially sown and self-sown, spread aggressively.[36] In New Zealand, European weeds seem to have leaped ahead of the white frontier. William Colenso, the naturalist, came upon one specimen of burdock – one only – in a dense and seldom-entered part of the Seventy-Mile Bush in 1882, and "gazed on it with astonishment, much like Robinson Crusoe on seeing the print of a European foot in the sand!" He did not destroy it and did not return until the following spring, by which time feral cattle had got into the area and carried the plant's sticky burrs all over, with the result that there were hundreds of burdock plants "four feet high, thick, bushy and strong, insomuch that a few plants together offered quite an obstacle to the traveller that way."[37]

The co-evolution of Old World weeds and Old World grazers gave to the former a special advantage after the two spread in the Neo-Europes, and added on top of that was the advantage these plants had of having evolved along with the development of Old World agriculture. The plow, an Old World invention, is a disruptive, even violent, instrument, as Smohalla, an Amerindian prophet of the Columbia River valley knew: "You ask me to plow the ground. Shall I take a knife and tear my mother's bosom?"[38] The Old World weeds began adapting to survive and follow after the plow with its first invention in Mesopotamia 6,000 years ago,[39] and to disguise themselves, both in the seed and in the ear, as wheat, flax, and other Old World crops. When European farmers swept into the Neo-Europes, their weeds swept along with them.

The Great Plains region of North America is the most mysterious exception to the success story of Old World weeds in the Neo-Europes, as it is to the success story of Old World feral quadrupeds in the Neo-Europes. The native plants of this grassland had withstood the grazing pressure of scores of millions of buffalo, a species of Eurasian provenance, for hundreds of their generations, and there the buffalo lived on into post-*marinheiro* time. They formed a tight partnership with the native grasses and forbs, each sustaining and perpetuating the other and fending off the entry of any great number of exotic plants and animals. The European livestock and grasses, though they had won victory after victory together in the temperate zones since the first millennia of the Neolithic Revolution, were stalled there. The climate was in large areas too hot in the summer, too cold in the winter, and too dry in general for many of the European plants, and the buffalo and their floral partners had the heavy advantage of incumbency. The invaders made little progress until the dominant creature of their biota arrived in force, with rifle. After the United States Civil War, bands of Old World riflemen entered the plains and destroyed the buffalo, thus removing a vital element in the native biota. With the buffalo went the ability of the plains Amerindians to live independently and hold out against the new order. Old World ranchers and farmers, cattle and sheep swept forward onto the plains. Some Sioux women, their way of life broken like a clay pot, succumbed to prostitution. The venereal bacteria moved opportunistically, sharply reducing the Sioux birth rate, and thereby making the land safer for aliens from abroad. Whites, blacks, cattle, pigs, horses, wheat and its weeds thrived, and around the houses, barns, and water troughs, Old World mice, rats, grasses, and forbs did so, too.

It might profit us to look at the cooperation of the members of the portmanteau biota from another angle. There is little or nothing intrinsically superior about Old World organisms compared with those of the Neo-Europes. "Superior," in truth, is a term that has no meaning in this context, except as one organism fits into a given ecosystem and another does not. Old World organisms are almost always "superior" when the competition takes place in their home environment. Hence the tiny number of Neo-European weeds, varmints, and pathogens naturalized in the Old World, and the success of the portmanteau biota wherever colonial environments have been Europeanized.

What does "Europeanized" mean in this context? It refers to a condition of continual disruption: of plowed fields, razed forests, overgrazed pastures, and burned prairies, of deserted villages and expanding cities, of humans, animals, plants, and microlife that have evolved separately suddenly coming into intimate contact. It refers to an ephemeralized world in which weed species of all phyla prosper and the other life forms are to be found in large numbers only in accidental enclaves or special parks. A few organisms native to the Neo-Europes were already in the weed category when the Europeans arrived, because every biota has life forms adapted to take advantage of the bad fortune of others, and these forms have even expanded geographically since the coming of the *marinheiros*. In New Zealand, indigenous plants that the imported livestock do not find palatable have greatly increased in the ravaged upland pastures.[40] This case, however, is one of the exceptions to the rule, the rule being that weeds, in the broadest sense of the word, are more characteristic of the biotas of lands anciently affected by the Old World Neolithic than any others.

We need a specific example: In primeval Australia, the weeds called dandelions might have languished in small numbers or even died out, as the weeds the Norse brought to Vinland must have done. We shall never know, because that Australia has not existed for two hundred years. When dandelions spread, they did so, in a manner of speaking, in another land, one containing and transformed by European humans and their plants, bacteria, sheep, goats, pigs, and horses. In that Australia, dandelions have a more secure future than kangaroos.

A richer example might be Old World house sparrows and starlings in North America, as compared with the indigenous passenger pigeons. In the early nineteenth century, there were none of the first two anywhere in North America (or in any of the other Neo-Europes), and billions of the third. The sparrow and starling in question are creatures of urban and rural Europe, not wild Europe, creatures of the edges of woods and isolated copses, of cultivated fields and grazed meadows; they prosper on the food in garbage and trash and the seedy droppings of large animals. They are birds well adapted to the Old World humanized environment – even to the point of not appealing to the human palate. Passenger pigeons are extinct; they were creatures of heavy woods who lived largely on mast. As the European frontiersman advanced, with torch and ax and livestock, North America became more and more suitable for sparrows and starlings, and less and less so for passenger pigeons, which apparently could not sustain reproduction in the scattered flocks to which the Europeanized landscape reduced them, and for which the Neo-Europeans did acquire a taste – much as their livestock did for the native grasses, tender and unaccustomed to reproducing under such stress. Therefore, scores of millions of sparrows and starlings live in North America, as in all the Neo-Europes, and no passenger pigeons whatsoever.[41]

The success of the portmanteau biota and of its dominant member, the European human, was a team effort by organisms that had evolved in conflict and cooperation over a long time. The period of that co-evolution most significant for the success overseas of this biota with sails and wheels occurred during and after the Old World Neolithic, a multispecies revolution whose aftershocks still rock the biosphere.

12

⚜

Conclusion

INTERLINK'D FOOD-YIELDING LANDS!

Land of coal and iron! land of gold! land of cotton, sugar, rice!

Land of wheat, beef, pork! land of wood and hemp! land of the apple and the grape!

Land of the pastoral plains, the grass-fields of the world! land of those sweet-air'd interminable plateaus!

Land of the herd, the garden, the healthy house of adobie!
                    —Walt Whitman, "Starting from Paumanok"

IN THE LAST CHAPTER I made use of a metaphor to describe the roles of the first arrivals in the Americas and Australasia, the indigenes, and of the second to arrive, the Europeans and Africans. I suggested that the Amerindians, Aborigines, and Maori were shock troops – marines – seizing beachheads and clearing the way for the second wave. They chiefly came on foot: the Amerindians entirely so, in all probability; the Aborigines on foot, with a few spells of paddling between Indonesian islands; the Maori only by seacraft. It might be helpful to elaborate on the metaphor (metaphor, please, not theorem), dividing the second wave into a pair of successive waves. We might think of the earlier of the pair to arrive in the Neo-Europes (consisting of those who came chiefly in the age of sail) as the army, landing with its heavy equipment, extensive support units, and greater numbers to take over from the marines. The members of this army came with weapons, fought many battles, and spent much or all of their lives under stern discipline. It is well known that the first Afro-Americans were slaves, but it is not so widely realized that half to two-thirds of the whites to migrate to North America before the American Revolution were indentured servants who had contracted away their freedom for up to seven years in return for passage to the New World. Until 1830, the majority of migrants to Australia were convicts, which leaves New Zealand alone to be founded by free laborers.[1]

The next great batch of Old World peoples, almost all of them Europeans, to come to the Neo-Europes crossed the oceans chiefly by steamship. I think of them collectively as the civilian wave, because they harvested the benefits of the prior invasions, rather than launching invasions themselves. They came without weapons and without much in the way of institutional organization above the kinship level. They came, with very few exceptions, as free and independent individuals.

They came in the greatest numbers: Over 50 million crossed the oceans to the Neo-Europes between 1820 and 1930.[2]

These 50 million came because they were pushed from behind – the population of Europe was growing, but the supply of cultivable land was not – and because in the middle of the nineteenth century the application of steam power to oceanic travel made the passage overseas safer and cheaper than ever before. But there was also the matter of the pull, of the conviction held by these people that their lot would be better in the alien lands beyond the seams of Pangaea than at home.

In the middle of the eighteenth century, white Australia and New Zealand were still in the future, but it was obvious that Europeans, their agriculture, and their plants and animals were doing very well in North America. The strongest possible proof of colonial success was the extraordinarily high rate of natural increase of Old World peoples in North America. Early in the 1750s, Benjamin Franklin proudly recorded that there were about a million Britons in North America, although a mere 80,000 had immigrated from Europe. At the end of the century, Thomas Malthus, seeking evidence of how fast humans might increase under optimal conditions, looked to the northern colonies of British North America, where the two great checks, "misery and vice," did not seem to be operating. In New Jersey, for instance, "the proportion of births to deaths on an average of seven years ending in 1743, was as 300 to 100. In France and England, taking the highest proportion, it is 117 to 100."[3] In the southern colonies from Virginia to Georgia, intermediate between the cool salubrity of New England and the middle colonies and the hot, wet insalubrity of the West Indies, the statistics were not as encouraging, but all in all British North America was a dazzling success.

The Iberian pampa was not a failure at the end of the eighteenth century, but no one could call it much of a success. The population was small and growing very slowly. In 1790, Alejandro Malaspina, an Italian navigator sailing for Spain, exasperated by the paradox of a society somehow managing to stagnate in the midst of prodigal natural wealth, blamed the people for their plight: They were without morality or discipline.[4] If they were, it was because the pampa was still largely untamed. The city of Buenos Aires, although a century older than Philadelphia, was closer to the frontier than the capital of Pennsylvania was. The vast numbers of cattle and horses on the pampa had sustained the hostile Amerindians and tempted many of the local subjects of the kings of Spain and Portugal to retrogress to a life of hunting and gathering on horseback. The gaucho was more like an Australian bushranger than an Australian shepherd. The gift of the European herds, ironically, discouraged the growth of European families and civilization. The overweening success of the livestock and forage plants of the portmanteau biota had stymied its human component. In addition, the policy of imperial Spain over many decades had been such as to subordinate the pampa to other parts of the empire and leave it an economic, social and intellectual backwater, reinforcing its biotic oddity.[5] But it was clear to Malaspina, and to anyone with half an eye, that there was no necessity for European society on the pampa to be retarded forever. Millions of thriving European animals and plants indicated that this was a land destined to become at least as European as North America.

The success of European ecological imperialism in the Americas was so great that Europeans began to take for granted that similar triumphs would follow wherever the climate and disease environment were not outright hostile. Captain Cook, after a short stay in New Zealand, predicted a bright future for European colonists there. When Joseph Banks, one of the scientists who sailed with him, was asked by a Parliamentary committee for his opinion of Australia as a site for a colony, he answered that settlers in New South Wales "would necessarily increase." As for what good they might do the mother country, why, they would be a market for manufactured goods; and Australia, larger than all of Europe, was certain to "furnish Matter of advantageous Return."[6] Necessarily? This was arrogance! Matter of advantageous return? What would that be? He was, of course, perfectly right in his simpleminded optimism.

The migrants from Europe, who were to validate the prophecies of Cook and Banks and the like, were, omitting such ephemera as gold rushes, drawn to the lands overseas in accordance with three factors. The lands had to have temperate climates; the migrants wanted to go where they could be more comfortably European in life style than at home, not less. Second, to attract Europeans in great numbers, a country had to produce or show a clear potentiality for producing commodities in demand back home in Europe – beef, wheat, wool, hides, coffee – and its resident population had to be too small to supply that demand. And so it was that so many Europeans in the nineteenth century poured into cornucopian North America, into Australasia, and into southern Brazil, particularly São Paulo, where coffee plantations were springing up, and also into the cool agricultural and pastoral provinces farther south.[7] They poured in multitudes onto the pampa of Rio Grande do Sul, Uruguay, and Argentina, bleaching out whatever Amerindian and African traces that might have existed. Mountainous Chile – "perhaps the worst constructed and worst located nation on this planet," said Ezequiel Martínez Estrada, "it is like a plant that sprouts between two stones" – produced few things in quantity or cheaply that Europe wanted, and in 1907 only 5 percent of her people were foreign-born, as compared with more than 25 percent on the pampa.[8]

The other factor was personal and visceral. The peasants of nineteenth century Europe may or may not have pined after political and religious freedoms, but they certainly yearned after freedom from hunger. Famine and fear of famine had been constants in the lives of their ancestors, time out of mind. Most food shortages in Europe of the ancien régime were local, but no less deadly for that, because the distribution systems were poor. As for general shortages, France, agriculturally the richest nation in Europe, had sixteen in the eighteenth century. Hunger and periodic starvation were a part of life, and poor people even resorted to infanticide to maintain some sort of balance between food supply and population.[9] In the rough-and-ready fairy tales of the peasantry, the triumphant hero receives as his reward not necessarily the hand of the princess or even heaps of gold, but invariably very large quantities of good food. In one tale, the climactic wedding feast features roast pigs scampering about with forks sticking in their sides for the convenience of protein-hungry guests.[10]

For Europe's peasantry, the image of the lands beyond the oceans shimmered like steam rising from an ox spitted and roasting over hot embers. In North America, famine was unknown except in the first years of settlement or in times of war or extraordinary natural disaster.[11] During Europe's potato famine in the middle of the nineteenth century, while a million Irish died of starvation and disease, Irish laborers on the pampa could earn ten or twelve shillings per day, along with all the meat they could eat.[12] Samuel Butler, who herded sheep in New Zealand's South Island in the 1860s, painted a paradisiacal picture of colonial life. After a year or two, he said, addressing himself to the potential settler,

You will have cows, and plenty of butter and milk and eggs; you will have pigs, and, if you choose it, bees, plenty of vegetables, and, in fact, may live upon the fat of the land, with very little trouble, and almost as little expense.[13]

An immigrant would need to bring some capital with him and to conjure up a run of good luck to reach that plateau of bliss in only a year or two, but tens of millions of Europeans crossed the seams of Pangaea with such prospects in mind. Anthony Trollope, in Australia in the 1870s, reduced the whole matter of what lay behind the migration to Australasia to one sentence: "The labouring man, let his labour be what it may, eats meat three times a day in the colonies, and very generally goes without it altogether at home."[14]

Said meat was not roasted wapiti or kangaroo, but mutton, pork, and beef. Once ashore in the Neo-Europes, many migrants were at first discomforted to find themselves, in both the Northern Hemisphere and Southern Hemisphere, on a diet of non-European foods – raccoon, opossum, sweet and white potatoes, and, very often, maize – but in time, in all these locations, they were able to return to a diet based on Old World staples. In North America, the Old World pioneers had a two-century love affair with maize, but even there, wheaten bread has finally replaced cornbread. The change was predictable: Nearly every animal and plant and food source that Crèvecoeur mentioned in a positive way in his classic *Letters from an American Farmer* (1782) was of European origin, with the passenger pigeon as the outstanding exception.

And so the Europeans came between the 1840s and World War I, the greatest wave of humanity ever to cross oceans and probably the greatest that ever will cross oceans. This Caucasian tsunami began with the starving Irish and the ambitious Germans and with the British, who never reached peaks of emigration as high as some other nationalities, but who have an inextinguishable yearning to leave home. The Scandinavians joined the exodus next, and then, toward the end of the century, the southern and eastern European peasantry. Italians, Poles, Spaniards, Portuguese, Hungarians, Greeks, Serbs, Czechs, Slovaks,

Ashkenazic Jews – for the first time in possession of knowledge of the opportunities overseas and, via railroad and steamship, of the means to leave a life of ancient poverty behind – poured through the ports of Europe and across the seams of Pangaea to lands as unfamiliar to their grandparents as Cathay. Russia, which sent 5 million to Siberia between the 1880s and World War I, sent another 4 million to the United States.[15] It was as if these millions realized that a window of opportunity was open and that it would not stay open forever.

Of these 50 million, the United States received two-thirds and kept a higher proportion of them than the other recipients, from which many returned to Europe or migrated elsewhere, often to the United States. The influx changed the United States forever, providing it with the farmers to fill in its north-central frontier and with the labor required for its burgeoning industrial revolution. The immigrants, especially the "new immigrants" from southern and eastern Europe, changed its big east-coast cities forever. To this day, many of the descendants of the "old immigrants" from northwest Europe find New York and Pittsburgh and Chicago, where lasagne and kielbasa are readily available, to be exotic, almost alien. Argentina received fewer immigrants than the United States, about 6 million between 1857 and 1930, and a great many of them left to go elsewhere, but immigration affected Argentina even more powerfully. Just before World War I, 30 percent of the Argentine population was foreign-born, as against about half that in the United States.[16] The immigrants transformed the pampa. The Irish and Basques led the way in sheep raising; wool became the nation's most important export in the 1880s. Italian sharecroppers plowed pasture and made it into wheat fields, and by the end of the century their new homeland was one of the world's greatest sources of surplus grain.[17] Brazil took in 5.5 million immigrants between 1851 and 1960 and kept about 2.5 million, most of whom settled in the southern nub of the country from Rio de Janeiro just north of the Tropic of Capricorn to Uruguay. And Uruguay, despite its small size, received over half a million Europeans, confirming its European qualities.[18] Between 1815 and 1914, 4 million Europeans migrated to Canada, very few of them French, and although great numbers moved on, those who remained were enough to anglicize the nation; thus, from the middle of the nineteenth century, the descendants of the founders of New France have been a fretful minority in their own land.[19] The migration of hundreds of thousands to Australasia, most of them from the British Isles, between the middle of the nineteenth century and World War I confirmed the antipodean Neo-Europes as Neo-Britains. New Zealand has remained so, by and large. But since World War II, Australia has received more immigrants in proportion to its population size than any other nation except Israel, and now lasagne and kielbasa are almost as easy to find in Sydney as in New York City.[20]

The impact of the migration of Europeans across the seams of Pangaea to the Neo-Europes was not limited to those lands. Europe's population, already soaring – indeed, its growth was the push behind the European exodus – continued to grow as it was relieved of the weight of the departing millions; and these, once overseas, provided Europe's industries with new markets, new sources of raw materials, and new prosperity, helping to maintain its population increases. Between 1840 and 1930, the population of Europe grew from 194 million to 463 million, double the rate of increase in the rest of the world. In the Neo-Europes, the numbers of people bounded upward at rates previously unknown, or at least unrecorded. Between 1750 and 1930, the total population for the Neo-Europes increased by almost fourteen times over, whereas that of the rest of the world increased by only two and one-half times.[21] Because of the explosion in population in Europe and the Neo-Europes, the number of Caucasians increased over five times between 1750 and 1930, as compared with a 2.3 increase for Asians. Africans and Afro-Americans increased by less than two times, in spite of an enormous increase in blacks in the United States from 1 million in 1800 to 12 million in 1930.[22] In the last fifty years, the prior surge in the Caucasian division of humanity ahead of the others has been largely canceled by their tardy but immense increases, but that surge remains one of the very greatest aberrations in the demographic history of the species. The 30 million square kilometers of land gained by the whites as both a cause and effect of their population surge remain in their control, a situation this minority considers permanent.

In the nineteenth century, the Neo-European populations soared not only because of immigration but also because their resident populations were enjoying the highest rates of natural increase these countries would ever achieve. Death rates were hearteningly low, and food plentiful and good by Old World standards, and the Neo-Europeans were gratefully fruitful and they multiplied. In North America in the eighteenth and early nineteenth centuries, the fertility of the Neo-Europeans was among the highest ever recorded anywhere, as high as fifty to fifty-seven births per thousand inhabitants per year.[23] In Australia in the 1860s, the birth rate was around forty per thousand, and in Argentina, where immigrants were beginning to pour onto the pampa for the first time in large numbers, about forty-six per thousand.[24] In Australia, 1860–2, the number of deaths per thousand was 18.6, births 42.6, for a natural increase of twenty-four humans per thousand per year, as compared with 13.8 in England and Wales, where the population was considered to be growing rapidly.[25] The pakeha birth rate and natural-increase rate in New Zealand were similarly high until well into the 1870s.[26]

These Neo-European populations had in these years what we would consider abnormally large numbers of young adults, which helps explain the high birth and low death rates, but not completely. They also had populations, with the exception of North America, in which men sharply outnumbered women, an imbalance that often increases the death rate and certainly lowers the birth rate. No, the superiority of human existence in the Neo-Europes – for the newcomers – is the most important factor in their natural increase.

If those rates had been maintained, the Neo-Europes could not have remained underpopulated for many generations. Darwin, a man with a better sense of humor than those who admire but do not read his works realize, calculated that if the population of the United States continued to expand at the velocity that had brought it to 30 million in 1860, then it would "in 657 years cover the whole terraqueous globe so thickly, that four men would have to stand on each square yard of surface."[27] The joke strikes us, a century later, as hollow. If the Neo-Europeans fill up their lands and eat all their own food, who shall feed the world? Fortunately, the nineteenth-century rates of natural increase soon fell off as the immigrant population pyramid evolved toward a normal distribution of ages and the young adults grew older and started dying, and as birth rates declined as rising standards of living and urbanization convinced Neo-Europeans that very few children would die before growing up, and that large families were the enemy and not the ally of prosperity. The death rates of the Neo-Europes are among the lowest in the world, but so are their birth rates. The Neo-European rates of natural increase are low, and a great deal of the food that the Neo-Europes produce is available for export.

The Neo-Europes collectively and singly are important, more important than their sizes and populations and even wealth indicate. They are enormously productive agriculturally, and with the world's population thrusting toward 5 billion and beyond, they are vital to the survival of many hundreds of millions. The reasons for this productivity include the undeniable virtuosity of their farmers and agricultural scientists and, in addition, several fortuitous circumstances that require explanation. The Neo-Europes all include large areas of very high photosynthetic potential, areas in which the amount of solar energy, the sunlight, available for the transformation of water and inorganic matter into food is very high. The quantity of light in the tropics is, of course, enormous, but less than one might think, because of the cloudiness and haziness of the wet tropics and the unvarying length of the day year-round. There are no long, long summer days in the tropics. These factors, added to such matters as tropical pests, diseases, and the scarcity of fertile soil, render the torrid zone of lower agricultural potential than the temperate zones. Also, most of the plants best able to utilize the intense light of the tropics, plants like sugar-cane and pineapple, contain very little protein, without which malnutrition is inevitable. As for the agricultural potential of the rest of the world, the polar areas are, for obvious reasons, useless, and the zone between 50° S latitude and the Antarctic Circle is almost entirely water. On the other hand, the zone between 50° N and the Arctic Circle includes more land than water, land with a high photosynthetic potential because of its very long and often bright summer days. Alaska and Finland can produce vegetables of huge size: strawberries as large as plums, for example. However, the growing season there is so short that many of the world's important food plants do not have sufficient time to grow leaves large enough to utilize the abundant light efficiently.

Taking all in all, the zones of the earth's surface richest in photosynthetic potential lie between the tropics and fifty degrees latitude north and south. There most of the food plants that do best in an eight-month growing season thrive. Within these zones the areas with rich soils that receive the greatest abundance of sunlight and, as well, the amounts of water than our staple crops require – the most important agricultural land in the world, in other words – are the central United States, California, southern Australia, New Zealand, and a wedge of Europe consisting of the southwestern half of France and the northwestern half of Iberia. All of these, with the exception of the European wedge, are within the Neo-Europes; and a lot of the rest of the Neo-European land, such as the pampa or Saskatchewan, is nearly as rich photosynthetically, and is as productive in fact, if not in theory.[28]

As was stated in the Prologue, the total value of all agricultural exports in the world in 1982 was $210 billion. Of this, the United States, Canada, Argentina, Uruguay, Australia, and New Zealand accounted for $64 billion, or a little over 30 percent. They account for even more of the world's most important export crop: wheat. In 1982, $18 billion worth of wheat passed over national boundaries, of which the Neo-Europes exported about $13 billion worth.[29] The Neo-Europes' share of world grain exports – in fact, North America's share alone – is greater than the Middle East's share of petroleum exports.[30]

An extraordinarily, perhaps frighteningly, large number of humans elsewhere in the world depend on the Neo-Europes for much of their food, and it appears that more and more will as world population increases. The trend is not a new one: Accelerating urbanization, industrialization, and population growth obliged Great Britain to give up hopes of autarchy nearly a century and a half ago, and in 1846 Britain repealed the Corn Law, lifting all duties on foreign grains. At the beginning of the next century, its farmers were producing only enough wheat to feed Britain for eight weeks annually; in both world wars, submarine blockade, constricting its access to the Neo-Europes, almost starved Britain into defeat. In the nineteenth century, a great deal of Britain's imported grain came from tsarist Russia, but many of the same demographic and economic factors that forced Britain to accept dependence on others for food have since had their effect on communist Russia, and in the 1970s the USSR began to buy enormous quantities of grain from the Neo-Europes, and continues to do so. Increasingly, the Third World also turns to the Neo-Europes for food.[31] Often in defiance of ideology and perhaps of good sense, more and more members of our species are becoming dependent on parts of the world far away where pale strangers grow food for sale. A very great many people are hostage to the possible effects of weather, pests, diseases, economic and political vagaries, and war in the Neo-Europes.

The responsibilities of the Neo-Europeans require unprecedented ecological and diplomatic sophistication: statesmanship in farm and embassy, plus greatness of spirit. One wonders if their comprehension of our world is equal to the challenge posed by the current state of our species and of the biosphere. It is an understanding formed by their own experience of one to four centuries of plenty, a unique episode in recorded history. I do not claim that this plenty has been evenly distributed: The poor are poor in the Neo-Europes, and Langston Hughes's nagging question "What happens to a dream deferred?" still nags, but I do insist that the people of the Neo-Europes almost universally believe that great material affluence can and should be attained by everyone, particularly in matters of diet. In Christ's Palestine, the multiplication of the loaves and fishes was a miracle; in the Neo-Europes it is expected.

The Americas and Australasia have provided windfall advantages to humanity twice, once in the Paleolithic and again in the last half millennium. The profits from the first entry into these lesser divisions of Pangaea were largely used up in the first few thousand years of the Holocene.

CONCLUSION

Today we are drawing on the advantages accruing from second entry, but widespread erosion, diminishing fertility, and the swift growth in the numbers of those dependent on the productivity of Neo-European soils remind us that the profits are finite. We are in need of a flowering of ingenuity equal to that of the Neolithic or, lacking that, of wisdom.

Appendix

What was the "smallpox" in New South Wales in 1789?

THE DISEASE THAT struck the Australian Aborigines in 1789 was undoubtedly new to them, as evidenced by its impact upon them, and it seems unlikely that it had often raged in their continent before. But was it smallpox? Smallpox is a disease that combines virulence and extreme communicability and has no dormant state in humans or any other species – it can only rage, it cannot lurk. Even the virus living in the scabs from the pustules of its victims soon dies; there is nothing like a spore state. So the British must have brought it with them. But they could not have done so – not according to the record and what we know of the disease. There were no active cases of smallpox on board the First Fleet on the high seas, nor in the French ships that were cruising in the waters of New South Wales in 1789. In fact, the written record does not indicate any ship with the disease on board at or near New South Wales in 1788 or 1789. Ordinarily, such evidence, being purely negative, would not be worth much, but smallpox is such a frightful disease, and the Europeans in and around New South Wales at that time were so conscious of what devastation it could wreak, that it would be very odd, indeed, if one or more of them had it and no one thought to mention it in a letter, diary, or report.[1]

None of the white settlers caught the disease, which is not surprising, because most likely they had all been immunized to this "childhood disease" back in Europe. But a number of white children had been born in Sydney, and none of these caught it either, despite the presence of Aborigines with active cases in the settlement. The only non-Aborigine who caught the disease in Sydney in 1789 was a seaman belonging to a visiting ship. He was – and this may be significant – an Amerindian from North America. He died of it.[2]

Perhaps the disease was smallpox, but introduced by Malay seamen, visiting far northern Australia. Perhaps, but what a coincidence that they should bring smallpox just in time for it to meet the British on the beach, so to speak. Perhaps it was not smallpox, but chicken pox, a pustular disease with a dormant stage. Chicken pox is considered a minor disease today, but severe cases often lead to dangerous pneumonic infection and even to death.[3] Among a people like the Aborigines who had never been exposed to it or related viral infections before, it might have been more severe than in epidemiologically experienced populations.

But chicken pox is about as communicable as smallpox. Why did none of the white children, individually about as immunologically inexperienced as the Aborigines, catch it? Perhaps the sick Aborigines were quarantined. Maybe the white children were still young enough to be shielded by antibodies passed on to them from their mothers' bloodstreams and through their mothers' milk. Or maybe they were simply lucky, which would confound all analysis (especially if sophisticated). Or perhaps the native Australians, who had been in isolation for thousands of years, lacked any and all immunological defenses to some infection so minor among the Europeans that the settlers never noticed it in themselves. If so, then we would have to take another look at "smallpox" wherever it appeared for the first time.

Notes

Chapter 1. Prologue

1 The statistics for this brief discussion come from *The New Rand McNally College World Atlas* (Chicago: Rand McNally, 1983), *The World Almanac and Book of Facts, 1984* (New York: Newspaper Enterprise Association, 1983), *The Americana Encyclopedia* (Danbury, Conn.: Grolier, 1983), and T. Lynn Smith, *Brazil; People and Institutions* (Baton Rouge: Louisiana Press, 1972), 70.

2 *Food and Agricultural Organization of the United Nations Trade Yearbook, 1982* (Rome: Food and Agricultural Organization of the United Nations, 1983), XXXVI, 42–4, 52–8, 112–14, 118–20, 237–8; *The Statesman's Year-book, 1983–84* (London: Macmillan, 1983), xviii; Lester R. Brown, "Putting Food on the World's Table, a Crisis of Many Dimensions," *Environment* 26 (May 1984):19.

3 *The World Almanac and Book of Facts, 1984* (New York: Newspaper Enterprise Association, 1983), 156.

4 For purposes of this book, I shall define North America as that part of the continent north of Mexico.

5 Colin McEvedy and Richard Jones, *Atlas of World Population History*

(Harmondsworth: Penguin Books, 1978), 285, 287, 313–14, 327; Robert Southey, *History of Brazil* (New York: Greenwood Press, 1969), III, 866.
6 Huw R. Jones, *A Population Geography* (New York: Harper & Row, 1981), 254.
7 American buffalo are really bison (buffalo are ox-like animals that live in Asia and Africa), but pedantically accurate terminology in this context would only lead to confusion.
8 Joseph M. Powell, *Environmental Management in Australia, 1788–1914* (Oxford University Press, 1976), 13–14.

Chapter 2. *Pangaea revisited, the Neolithic reconsidered*

1 Robert S. Dietz and John C. Holden, "The Breakup of Pangaea," *Continents Adrift and Continents Aground* (San Francisco: Freeman, 1976), 126–7.
2 John F. Dewey, "Plate Tectonics," *Continents Adrift and Continents Aground,* 34–5.
3 Björn Kurtén, "Continental Drift and Evolution," *Continents Adrift and Continents Aground,* 176, 178; Charles Elton, *The Ecology of Invasions by Animals and Plants* (Great Britain: English Language Book Society, 1966), 33–49.
4 E. C. Pielou, *Biogeography* (New York: Wiley, 1979), 28–31, 49–57.
5 Peter Kalm, *Travels into North America,* trans. John R. Forster (Barre, Mass.: The Imprint Society, 1972), 24.
6 Wilfred T. Neill, *The Geography of Life* (New York: Columbia University Press, 1969), 98, 104.
7 Brace C. Loring, *The Stages of Human Evolution,* 2nd ed. (Englewood Cliffs, N.J.: Prentice-Hall, 1979), 54, 59, 61, 68.
8 Loring, *Stages of Human Evolution,* 76–7; Bernard G. Campbell, *Humankind Emerging* (Boston: Little, Brown, 1976), 248; David Pilbeam, "The Descent of Hominoids and Hominids, *Scientific American* 250 (March 1984):93–96.
9 Loring, *Stages of Human Evolution,* 78.
10 Campbell, *Humankind Emerging,* 383–4; Loring, *Stages of Human Evolution,* 95.
11 A. G. Thorne, "The Arrival and Adaptation of Australian Aborigines," *Ecological Biogeography of Australia,* ed. Allen Keast (The Hague: Dr. W. Junk, 1981), 178–9; D. Merrilees, "Man the Destroyer: Late Quaternary Changes in the Australian Marsupial Fauna," *Journal of the Royal Society of Western Australia* 51 (Part 1 1968):1–24;

D. Mulvaney, "The Prehistory of the Australian Aborigine," *Avenues of Antiquity, Readings from the Scientific American,* ed. Brian M. Fagan (San Francisco: Freeman, 1976), 84; Geoffrey Blainey, *Triumph of the Nomads, A History of Aboriginal Australia* (Woodstock, N.Y.: Overlook Press, 1976), 6, 16, 51–66.

12 Paul S. Martin, "The Discovery of America," *Science* 179 (9 March 1973):969; James E. Mosimann and Paul S. Martin, "Simulating Overkill by Paleoindians," *American Scientist* 63 (May–June 1975):304; Paul S. Martin and H. E. Wright, eds., *Pleistocene Extinctions, the Search for a Cause* (New Haven: Yale University Press, 1967), *passim.*

13 François Bordes, *The Old Stone Age* (New York: McGraw-Hill, 1968), 218.

14 *Encyclopaedia Britannica,* 11th ed. (Cambridge University Press, 1911), II, 348–51; XIX, 372; Gordon V. Childe, *Man Makes Himself* (London: Watts & Co., 1956), *passim.*

15 Hereafter I shall refer to the indigenes of Australia simply as Aborigines, never using the word for other peoples.

16 Juliet Clutton-Brock, *Domesticated Animals from Early Times* (Austin: University of Texas Press, 1981), 66–8.

17 Clara Sue Kidwell, "Science and Ethnoscience: Native American World Views as a Factor in the Development of Native Technologies," *Environmental History, Critical Issues in Comparative Perspective,* ed. Kendall E. Bailes (Lanham, Md.: University Press of America, 1985), 277–87; Lynn White, Jr., "The Historical Roots of Our Ecologic Crisis," *Science* 155 (10 March 1967):1202–7.

18 Mark Nathan Cohen, *The Food Crisis in Prehistory, Overpopulation and the Origins of Agriculture* (New Haven: Yale University Press, 1977), 86–9, 279–84.

19 Clutton-Brock, *Domesticated Animals from Early Times,* 34.

20 Jack R. Harlan, "The Plants and Animals that Nourish Man," *Scientific American* 235 (September 1976):94–5.

21 Samuel Noah Kramer, *Mythologies of the Ancient World* (Chicago: Quadrangle, 1961), 96–100.

22 Job 39:19–25; *The New English Bible with Apocrypha* (Cambridge University Press, 1971), 607; Sophocles, *The Oedipus Cycle,* trans. Dudley Fitts and Robert Fitzgerald (New York: Harcourt Brace & World, 1949), 199.

23 Job 1:2–3, *New English Bible,* 560.

24 Erik P. Eckholm, *The Picture of Health, Environmental Sources of Disease* (New York: Norton, 1977), 195; Paul Fordham, *The Geography of African Affairs* (Baltimore: Penguin Books, 1965), 26, 30.

25 *The Travels of Marco Polo,* trans. Ronald Latham (Harmondsworth: Penguin Books, 1958), 100.
26 Edward Hyams, *Soil and Civilization* (New York: Harper & Row, 1976), 230–72.
27 *Geoffrey Chaucer. A Bantam Dual-Language Book. Canterbury Tales, Tales of Canterbury,* eds. Kent Hieatt and Constance Hieatt (New York: Bantam Books, 1964), 384–5.
28 Robert McNab, ed., *Historical Records of New Zealand* (Wellington: John McKay, government printer, 1908), I, 14–15.
29 Frederick J. Simoons, "The Geographical Hypothesis and Lactose Malabsorption, A Weighing of the Evidence," *American Journal of Digestive Diseases* 23 (November 1978):964; see also Gebhard Flatz, "Lactose Nutrition and Natural Selection," *Lancet* 2 (14 July 1973):76–7.
30 Julius Caesar, *Caesar's Gallic War,* trans. F. P. Long (Oxford: Clarendon Press, 1911), 15.
31 Genesis 22:17; Job 1:2–3, *New English Bible,* 22, 560.
32 D. B. Grigg, *The Agricultural Systems of the World, An Evolutionary Approach* (Cambridge University Press, 1974), 50–1.
33 Edgar Anderson, *Plants, Man and Life* (Berkeley: University of California Press, 1967), 161–3; James M. Renfrew, *Palaeoethnobotany, The Prehistoric Food Plants of the Near East and Europe* (New York: Columbia University Press, 1973), 85, 96, 164–89; Michael Zohary, *Plants of the Bible* (Cambridge: Cambridge University Press, 1982), 92.
34 Proverbs 24:30–4, *New English Bible,* 778.
35 Samuel Noah Kramer, *The Sumerians, Their History, Culture and Character* (University of Chicago Press, 1963), 105.
36 1 Samuel 5–6; *New English Bible,* 307–8.
37 Frederick Dunn, "Epidemiological Factors: Health and Disease in Hunter-Gatherers," *Man the Hunter,* eds. Richard B. Lee and Irven De Vore (Chicago: Aldine, 1968), 223, 225; Francis L. Black, "Infectious Diseases in Primitive Societies," *Science* 187 (14 February 1975):515–18.
38 William H. McNeill, *Plagues and Peoples* (Garden City, N.Y.: Anchor/Doubleday, 1976), 40–53.
39 T. A. Cockburn, "Where Did Our Infectious Diseases Come From?" *Health and Disease in Tribal Societies, CIBA Foundation Symposium 49 (New Series)* (London: Elsevier, 1977), 103–12.
40 Exodus 30:11–12, *New English Bible,* 95.
41 Deuteronomy 7:15, *New English Bible,* 205.
42 McNeill, *Plagues and Peoples,* 69–71; Henry F. Dobyns, *Their Number Become Thinned, Native American Population Dynamics in*

Eastern North America (Knoxville: University of Tennessee Press, 1983), 9, 11.

43 James B. Pritchard, ed., *Ancient Near Eastern Texts Relating to the Old Testament* (Princeton University Press, 1969), 394–6.

44 Carol Laderman, "Malaria and Progress: Some Historical and Ecological Considerations," *Social Science and Medicine* 9 (November–December 1975):587–94.

45 Paul Ashbee, *The Ancient British, a Social-Archaeological Narrative* (Norwich: Geo Abstracts, University of East Anglia, 1978), 70; Richard Elphick, *Kraal and Castle, Khoikhoi and the Founding of White South Africa* (New Haven: Yale University Press, 1977), 11.

46 *Bede's Ecclesiastical History of the English People,* eds. Bertram Colgrave and R. A. B. Mynors (Oxford: Clarendon Press, 1969), 311–12; J. F. D. Shrewsbury, "The Yellow Plague," *Journal of the History of Medicine and Allied Sciences* 4 (Winter 1949):5–47; Charles Creighton, *A History of Epidemics in Britain* (Cambridge University Press, 1891), I, 4–8; Elphick, *Kraal,* 231–2.

47 A. E. Mourant, Ada C. Kopeć, and Kazimiera Domaniewska-Sobczak, *The Distribution of the Human Blood Groups and Other Polymorphisms* (Oxford University Press, 1976), maps 1, 2, 3.

48 A. P. Okladnikov, "The Ancient Population of Siberia and Its Culture," *The Peoples of Siberia,* eds. M. G. Levin and L. P. Potapov (University of Chicago Press, 1956), 29.

49 *Goode's World Atlas,* 12th ed. (Chicago: Rand McNally, 1964), 11–13; James R. Gibson, *Feeding the Russian Fur Trade, Provisionment of the Okhotsk Seaboard and the Kamchatka Penninsula, 1639–1856* (Madison: University of Wisconsin Press, 1969), xvii-xviii.

50 A. P. Okladnikov, *Yakutia Before Its Incorporation into the Russian State* (Montreal: McGill–Queen's University Press, 1970), 444.

51 Terence Armstrong, George Rogers, and Graham Rowley, *The Circumpolar Arctic, A Political and Economic Geography of the Arctic and Sub-Arctic* (London: Methuen, 1978), 24.

52 "Introduction," *Peoples of Siberia,* 1.

53 Peter Simon Pallas, *A Naturalist in Russia, Letters from Peter Simon Pallas to Thomas Pennant,* ed. Carol Urness (Minneapolis: University of Minnesota Press, 1967), 60, 64, 86, 87.

54 L. P. Potapov, "The Altays," *Peoples of Siberia,* 311; William Tooke, *View of the Russian Empire* (New York: Arno Press and *New York Times,* 1970), III, 271–2.

55 Élisée Reclus, *The Earth and Its Inhabitants, Asia, I, Asiatic Russia* (New York: D. Appleton & Co., 1884), 357, 360, 396.

56 S. M. Shirokogoroff, *Social Organization of the Northern Tungus* (Shanghai: The Commercial Press, 1933), 208.

57 Shirokogoroff, *Social Organization of Northern Tungus*, 208; W. G. Sumner, ed., "The Yakuts," *Journal of the Anthropological Institute of Great Britain and Ireland* 31 (1901):75, 79–80, 96; Waldemar Jochelson, "The Yukaghir and Yukaghirized Tungus," *Memoirs of the American Museum of Natural History* 13 (1926):27, 62–8; Waldemar Jochelson, "The Yakut," *Anthropology Papers of the American Museum of Natural History* 30 (1934):132; Waldemar Bogoras, "The Chukchi of Northeastern Siberia," *American Anthropologist* 3 (January–March 1901): 102–4; Stepan Petrovich Krasheninnikov, *Explorations of Kamchatka, 1735–1741*, trans. E. A. P. Crownhart-Vaughan (Portland: Oregon Historical Society, 1972), 272; Reclus, *Earth and Inhabitants, Asia*, I, *Asiatic Russia*, 341; Kai Donner, *Among the Samoyed in Siberia* (New Haven: Human Relations File, 1954), 86.

58 Gibson, *Feeding Russian Fur Trade*, 196; Tooke, *View of the Russian Empire*, I, 547, 591, 594; II, 86–9; August Hirsch, *Handbook of Geographical and Historical Pathology* (London: New Sydenham Society, 1883), I, 133; Bogoras, "Chukchi," *American Anthropologist* 3 (January–March 1901):91; Sumner, "Yakuts," *Journal of the Anthropological Institute of Great Britain and Ireland* 31 (1901):104–5; Jean-Baptiste Barthélemy de Lesseps, *Travels in Kamtschatka* (New York: Arno Press and *New York Times*, 1970), I, 94, 128–9, 199; II, 83–4; Waldemar Jochelson, "Material Culture and Social Organization of the Koryak," *Memoirs of the American Museum of Natural History* 10, Pt. 2 (1905–8):418; Jochelson, "Yukaghir," *Memoirs of the American Museum of Natural History* 13 (1926):26–7; Peter Simon Pallas, *Reise durch verschiedene Provinzen des Russischen Reichs* (Graz: Akademische Druck- u. Verlagsanstalt, 1967), III, 50.

59 Jochelson, "Yukaghir," *Memoirs of the American Museum of Natural History* 13 (1926):27; M. V. Stepanova, I. S. Gurvich, and V. V. Khramova, "The Yukahirs," *Peoples of Siberia*, 788–9.

60 Frank Lorimer, *The Population of the Soviet Union, History, and Prospects* (Geneva: League of Nations, 1946), 11, 26, 27; Donald W. Treadgold, *The Great Siberian Migration* (Princeton University Press, 1957), 32, 34; Robert R. Kuczynski, *The Balance of Births and Deaths*, II, *Eastern and Southern Europe* (Washington D.C.: The Brookings Institution, 1931), 101.

61 *The Cambridge Encyclopedia of Russia and the Soviet Union*, eds. Archie Brown, John Fennell, Michael Kaser, and H. T. Willetts (Cambridge University Press, 1982), 70–1.

62 Donner, *Among the Samoyed*, 138.

Chapter 3. The Norse and the Crusaders

1 George C. Vaillant, *Aztecs of Mexico: Origin, Rise and Fall of the Aztec Nation* (Harmondsworth: Penguin Books, 1965), 160.

2 David Day, *The Doomsday Book of Animals* (New York: Viking Press, 1981), 223–4.

3 It is worth noting here that another group of sailors, those of the Indian Ocean, had crossed an undersea ridge before the Norse and were doing so in numbers annually, riding the monsoon winds back and forth across the Carlsberg Ridge that extends southeast from Arabia under the waters that divide the ports of the Middle East and India from those of East Africa. This, too, is a Pangaean seam, but it is of minor importance compared with the Mid-Atlantic Ridge biogeographically, because it divides continents that have connections elsewhere.

4 G. J. Marcus, *The Conquest of the North Atlantic* (Oxford University Press, 1981), 63–70.

5 Marcus, *Conquest*, 67, 71–8; Bruce E. Gelsinger, *Icelandic Enterprise, Commerce and Economy in the Middle Ages* (Columbus: University of South Carolina Press, 1981), 239, n. 26.

6 Marcus, *Conquest*, 83–4; Gelsinger, *Icelandic Enterprise*, 47; C. N. Parkinson, ed., *The Trade Winds: A Study of British Overseas Trade during the French Wars, 1793–1815* (London: Allen & Unwin, 1948), 87.

7 Richard F. Tomasson, *Iceland, the First New Society* (Minneapolis: University of Minnesota Press, 1980), 60–2; Marcus, *Conquest*, 64; Finn Gad, *The History of Greenland*, trans. Ernst Dupont (London: C. Hurst Co., 1970), I, 53, 84.

8 *The Vinland Sagas*, eds. and trans. Magnus Magnusson and Hermann Palsson (Baltimore: Penguin Books, 1965), 65–7, 71, 99.

9 *Vinland Sagas*, 55.

10 Frederick J. Simoons, "The Geographical Hypothesis and Lactase Malabsorption," *American Journal of Digestive Diseases* 23 (November 1978):964–5.

11 *Vinland Sagas*, 65.

12 Samuel Eliot Morison, *The European Discovery of America. The Northern Voyages, A.D. 500–1600* (Oxford University Press, 1971), 49.

13 *Vinland Sagas*, 61.

14 *Vinland Sagas*, 65, 94; Marcus, *Conquest*, 64; Samuel Eliot Morison, *Admiral of the Ocean Sea, A Life of Christopher Columbus* (Boston: Little, Brown, 1942), 395, 397; Tomasson, *Iceland*, 58; *The Australian Encyclopedia* (Sydney: The Grolier Society of Australia, 1979), III, 25, 26.

15 Marcus, *Conquest*, 91–2, 99; Gelsinger, *Icelandic Enterprise*, 93.

16 *Vinland Sagas*, 66, 99, 100, 102.

17 Tomasson, *Iceland*, 63; P. Kubler, *Geschichte der Pocken und der Impfung* (Berlin: Verlag von August Hirschwald, 1901), 45; August Hirsch, *Handbook of Geographical and Historical Pathology* (London: New Sydenham Society, 1883), I, 135, 145; George S. MacKenzie, *Travels in the Island of Iceland During the Summer of the Year MDCCCX* (Edinburgh: Archibald Constable & Co., 1811), 409–10. Almost any infectious disease from the continents could cause havoc. Six hundred Icelanders died of measles in an epidemic in 1797. When that disease struck the people of the Faroes in 1846 after a respite of seventy-five years, 6,100 of 7,864 at risk fell ill: MacKenzie, *Travels in the Island of Iceland*, 410; Abraham M. Lilienfeld, *Foundations of Epidemiology* (Oxford University Press, 1976), 24. The vulnerability of the North Atlantic Norse extends into our own time. Measles, which keeps fading away in Iceland, has been introduced from Europe and America at least eleven times in the twentieth century, igniting epidemics each time (because of modern nutrition and medical care, they are no longer deadly): Andrew Cliff and Peter Haggett, "Island Epidemics," *Scientific American* 250 (May 1984):143.
18 Ronald G. Popperwell, *Norway* (London: Ernest Benn, 1972), 94–5; Tomasson, *Iceland*, 63.
19 Marcus, *Conquest*, 89, 99, 121, 155.
20 Sigurdur Thorarinsson, *The 1000 Years Struggle Against Ice and Fire* (Reykjavik: Bokautgafa Menningarsjods, 1956), 24–5.
21 Marcus, *Conquest*, 90; Gelsinger, *Icelandic Enterprise*, 173.
22 Gelsinger, *Icelandic Enterprise*, 6; Thorarinsson, *1000 Years*, 13, 15–16, 18; Marcus, *Conquest*, 97–8, 156.
23 *Vinland Sagas*, 22.
24 Gelsinger, *Icelandic Enterprise*, 173; Marcus, *Conquest*, 159–60, 163.
25 *Vinland Sagas*, 60.
26 Marcus, *Conquest*, 78, 95–6, 106–7, 108–16; Gelsinger, *Icelandic Enterprise*, 52–8.
27 Marcus, *Conquest*, 50–4.
28 Marcus, *Conquest*, 103.
29 *Vinland Sagas*, 87, 97.
30 E. G. R. Taylor, *The Haven-Finding Art* (New York: Abelard-Schuman, 1957), 94; Joseph Needham, *Science and Civilisation in China*, IV, *Physics and Physical Technology*, Part III, *Civil Engineering and Nautics* (Cambridge University Press, 1971), 698.
31 R. W. Southern, *The Making of the Middle Ages* (London: Hutchinson's Library, 1953), 51; G. C. Coulton, ed., *A Medieval Garner, Human Documents from the Four Centuries Preceding the Reformation*, 10–16; *Vinland Sagas*, 71.

32 Robinson Jeffers, "The Eye," *Robinson Jeffers, Selected Poems* (New York: Random House, 1963), 85.
33 Marcus, *Conquest,* 64; Joshua Prawer, *The World of the Crusaders* (New York: Quadrangle Books, 1972), 73.
34 Prawer, *World,* 73.
35 Edward Peters, ed., *The First Crusade, the Chronicles of Fulcher of Chartres and Other Source Materials* (Philadelphia: University of Pennsylvania, 1971), 25.
36 *Chronicles of the Crusades* (London: Henry G. Bohn, 1848), 89.
37 Hans E. Mayer, *The Crusades,* trans. John Gillingham (Oxford University Press, 1972), 137–9.
38 Joshua Prawer, *The Latin Kingdom of Jerusalem, European Colonialism in the Middle Ages* (London: Weidenfeld and Nicolson, 1972), 82; Prawer, *World,* 73–4; Jean Richard, *The Latin Kingdom of Jerusalem,* trans. Janet Shirley (Amsterdam: North Holland, 1979), A, 131; Mayer, *Crusades,* 177.
39 William, archbishop of Tyre, *A History of Deeds Done Beyond the Sea,* trans. Emily A. Babcock and A. C. Krey (New York: Columbia University Press, 1943), I, 507, n. 508.
40 Mayer, *Crusades,* 150, 153, 161.
41 James A. Brundage, ed., *The Crusades, A Documentary Study* (Milwaukee: Marquette University Press, 1962), 75.
42 Jacques de Vitry, *History of the Crusades, A.D. 1180* (London: Palestine Pilgrims Society, 1896), 67.
43 Vitry, *History of the Crusades,* 64–5.
44 Prawer, *The Latin Kingdom of Jerusalem,* 506–8.
45 Friedrich Prinzing, *Epidemics Resulting from Wars* (Oxford: Clarendon Press, 1916), 13.
46 *Chronicles of Crusades,* 432.
47 *Chronicles of Crusades,* 55.
48 Darrett B. Rutman and Anita H. Rutman, "Of Agues and Fevers: Malaria in the Early Chesapeake," *William and Mary Quarterly,* 3rd series 33 (January 1976):43.
49 Mayer, *Crusades,* 150, 177.
50 L. W. Hackett, *Malaria in Europe, an Ecological Study* (Oxford University Press, 1937), 7; Carol Laderman, "Malaria and Progress: Some Historical and Ecological Considerations," *Social Science and Medicine* 9 (November–December 1975):589, 590–02; Milton J. Friedman and William Trager, "The Biochemistry of Resistance to Malaria," *Scientific American* 244 (March 1981):154, 159; "Prevention of Malaria in Travelers, 1982," *United States Public Health Service, Morbidity and Mortality Weekly Report, Supplement* 31 (16 April

1982):10, 15; Israel J. Kligler, *The Epidemiology and Control of Malaria in Palestine* (University of Chicago Press, 1930), 105; Thomas C. Jones, "Malaria," *Textbook of Medicine*, eds. Paul B. Beeson and Walsh McDermott (Philadelphia: Saunders, 1975), 475.

51 T. A. Archer, ed., *The Crusade of Richard I, 1189–92* (London: David Nutt, 1900), 84–5, 88–9, 92, 115, 117, 132, 194, 199, 205, 243, 245, 247, 281, 305, 312–14, 318–19, 322; Ambroise, *The Crusade of Richard the Lion-Heart*, trans. Merton Jerome Hubert (New York: Columbia University Press, 1941), 196, 198, 201, 203, 207, 219, 446; Kligler, *Epidemiology and Control of Malaria in Palestine*, 2, 111.

52 Archibald Wavell, *Allenby, a Study in Greatness* (London: George P. Harrap & Co., 1940), 195, 156.

53 Kligler, *Epidemiology and Control of Malaria in Palestine*, 87; *History of the Great War Based on Official Documents. Medical Services, General History*, W. G. MacPherson, ed. (London: His Majesty's Stationery Office, 1924), III, 483.

54 Steven Runciman, *A History of the Crusades*, II, *The Kingdom of Jerusalem* (Cambridge University Press, 1955), 323–4; Mayer, *Crusades*, 159.

55 Carol Laderman, "Malaria and Progress," *Social Science and Medicine* 9 (November–December 1975), 588; H. M. Giles et al., "Malaria, Anaemia and Pregnancy," *Annals of Tropical Medicine and Parasitology* 63 (1969):245–63.

56 Mayer, *Crusades*, 274–5.

57 Needham, *Science and Civilisation in China*, IV, *Physics and Physical Technology*, Part III, *Civil Engineering and Nautics*, 698.

58 Noel Deere, *The History of Sugar* (London: Chapman & Hall, 1949), I, 73–258; Charles Verlinden, *The Beginnings of Modern Colonization, Eleven Essays with an Introduction*, trans. Yvonne Freccero (Ithaca: Cornell University Press, 1970), 18–24, 29, 47.

59 Marcus, *Conquest*, 67.

60 *Vinland Sagas*, 90.

Chapter 4. The Fortunate Isles

1 John Mercer, *The Canary Islands, Their Prehistory, Conquest and Survival* (London: Rex Collings, 1980), 155–63, 198, 217; Raymond Mauny, *Les Navigations Médiévales sur les Côtes Sahariennes Antérieures à la Découverte Portugaise (1434)* (Lisbon: Centro de Estudos Históricos Ultramarinos, 1960), 44–8, 92–6.

2 Mercer, *Canary Islands*, 2–13; W. B. Turrill, *Pioneer Plant Geography, The Phytogeographical Researches of Sir Joseph Dalton Hooker* (The

Hague: Nijhoff, 1953), 2–4, 206, 211; Sherwin Carlquist, *Island Biology* (New York: Columbia University Press, 1974), 180.

3 Pierre Bontier and Jean Le Verrier, *The Canarian, or, Book of the Conquest and Conversion of the Canarians,* trans. Richard H. Major (London: Hakluyt Society, 1872), 92.

4 T. Bentley Duncan, *Atlantic Islands: Madeira, the Azores and the Cape Verdes in Seventeenth Century Navigation* (University of Chicago Press, 1972), 12; Charles Verlinden, *The Beginnings of Modern Colonization, Eleven Essays with an Introduction,* trans. Yvonne Freccero (Ithaca: Cornell University Press, 1970), 220.

5 A. H. de Oliveira Marques, *History of Portugal, I, From Lusitania to Empire* (New York: Columbia University Press, 1972), 158; Duncan, *Atlantic Islands,* 12–16; Joel Serrão, ed., *Dicionário de História de Portugal* (Lisbon: Iniciativas Editoriais, 1971), I, 20, 797.

6 Sidney M. Greenfield, "Madeira and the Beginnings of New World Sugar Cane Cultivation and Plantation Slavery: A Study in Institution Building," *Comparative Perspectives on Slavery in New World Plantation Societies,* eds. Vera Rubin and Arthur Tuden, *Annals of the New York Academy of Sciences* 292 (1977):537.

7 Duncan, *Atlantic Islands,* 26.

8 David A. Bannerman and W. Mary Bannerman, *Birds of the Atlantic Islands* (Edinburgh: Oliver & Boyd, 1966), II, xxxv–xxxvii; Greenfield, "Madeira," *Comparative Perspectives on Slavery,* 537–9.

9 Gomes Eannes de Azurara, *The Chronicle of the Discovery and Conquest of Guinea,* trans. Charles R. Beazley and Edgar Prestage (New York: Burt Franklin, n.d.), II, 245–6; *Voyages of Cadamosto,* trans. G. R. Crone (London: Hakluyt Society, 1937), n. 7; Samuel Purchas, ed., *Hakluytus Posthumus, or Purchas His Pilgrimes* (Glasgow: James MacLehose & Sons, 1906), XIX, 197; Edward Arber, ed., *Travels and Works of Captain John Smith* (New York: Burt Franklin, n.d.), II, 471; Juan de Abreu de Galindo, *Historia de la Conquista de las Siete Islas de Canaria,* ed. Alejandro Cioranescu (Santa Cruz de Tenerife: Goya Ediciones, 1955), 60; Frank Fenner, "The Rabbit Plague," *Scientific American* 190 (February 1954):30–5.

10 *Voyages of Cadamosto,* 9; Azurara, *Chronicle,* II, xcix.

11 Bannerman, *Birds,* II, xxi; Azurara, *Chronicle,* II, 246–7; *Voyages of Cadamosto,* 4, 7, 9–10.

12 Marques, *History of Portugal,* I, 153; Verlinden, *Beginnings,* 210, 212; *Voyages of Cadamosto,* 10; Azurara, *Chronicle,* II, 247–8; Maria de Lourdes Esteves dos Santos de Ferraz, "A Ilha da Madeira na Época Quatrocentista," *Studia, Centro de Estudos Históricos Ultramarinos,* Lisbon, 9 (1962):179, 188–90.

13 Greenfield, "Madeira," *Comparative Perspectives on Slavery*, 545, 547; Vitorino Magalhaes Godinho, *Os Descobrimentos e a Economia Mundial* (Lisbon: Editora Arcádia, 1965), II, 430; see also Virginia Rau and Jorge de Macedo, *O Açúcar da Madeira Nos Fins do Século XV, Problemas de Produção e Comercio* (Lisbon: Junta-Geral do Distrito Autónomo do Funchal, 1962).

14 Serrão, *Dicionário de História de Portugal*, II, 879.

15 Duncan, *Atlantic Islands*, 11.

16 Duncan, *Atlantic Islands*, 25.

17 Robin Bryans, *Madeira, Pearl of the Atlantic* (London: Robert Hale, 1959), 30.

18 Bentley, *Atlantic Islands*, 29.

19 Greenfield, "Madeira," *Comparative Perspectives on Slavery*, 541.

20 Maria de Lourdes Esteves dos Santos de Ferraz, "A Ilha da Madeira," *Studia* 9 (1962):169; Serrão, *Dicionário de História de Portugal*, II, 879.

21 Francisco Sevillano Colom, "Los Viajes Medievales desde Mallorca a Canarias," *Anuario de Estudios Atlánticos* 18 (1972):41; Godinho, *Descobrimentos*, II, 521; Serrão, *Dicionário de História de Portugal*, 879.

22 Ferdinand Columbus, *The Life of the Admiral Christopher Columbus by His Son Ferdinand*, trans. Benjamin Keen (New Brunswick: Rutgers University Press, 1959), 60; Godinho, *Descobrimentos*, II, 520–1, 581.

23 Sherwin Carlquist, *Island Ecology* (New York: Columbia University Press, 1974), 180–1; Mercer, *Canary Islands*, 4, 7, 18.

24 Ilse Schwidetzky, "The Prehispanic Population of the Canary Islands," *Biogeography and Ecology in the Canary Islands*, ed. G. Kunkel (The Hague: Dr. W. Junk, 1976), 20; Mercer, *Canary Islands*, 17–18, 59, 64–5, 112.

25 Mercer, *Canary Islands*, 59–60, 64; Schwidetzky, "Prehispanic Population," *Biogeography and Ecology in the Canary Islands*, 23; Ilse Schwidetzky, *La Población Prehispánica de las Islas Canarias* (Santa Cruz de Tenerife: Publicaciones del Museo Arqueológico, 1963), 127–9.

26 Mercer, *Canary Islands*, 10; Leonard Huxley, *Life and Letters of Sir Joseph Dalton Hooker* (London: John Murray, 1918), II, 232; David Bramwell, "The Endemic Flora of the Canary Islands; Distribution, Relationships and Phytogeography," *Biogeography and Ecology in the Canary Islands*, 207.

27 Mercer, *Canary Islands*, 115–19.

28 Godinho, *Descobrimentos*, 520.

29 Mercer, *Canary Islands*, 160–8, 177–8; Bontier and Le Verrier, *Canarian*, 123, 131. For more complete documentation of the French invasion, with the originals plus modern Spanish translations, see Jean

de Bethencourt, *Le Canarien, Crónicas Francesas de la Conquista de Canarias*, trans. Elias Serra and Alejandro Cioranescu (La Laguna de Tenerife: Fontes Canarium, 1959–64), 3 vols.

30 Greenfield, "Madeira," *Comparative Perspectives on Slavery*, 543.

31 Azurara, *Chronicle*, 238; Bontier and Le Verrier, *Canarian*, 128; Abreu de Galindo, *Historia de Conquista*, 145–6.

32 Mercer, *Canary Islands*, 188–93; Abreu de Galindo, *Historia de Conquista*, 145.

33 Mercer, *Canary Islands*, 195–6.

34 Mercer, *Canary Islands*, 198–203; Alonso de Espinosa, *The Guanches of Tenerife*, trans. Clements Markham (London: Hakluyt Society, 1907), 93.

35 Mercer, *Canary Islands*, 207–9.

36 Juan de Abreu de Galindo, *The History of the Discovery of the Canary Islands*, trans. George Glas (London: R. & J. Dodsley, 1764), 82.

37 Bontier and Le Verrier, *Canarian*, 135, 149; Espinosa, *Guanches*, 102; Azurara, *Chronicle*, 209.

38 Mercer, *Canary Islands*, 66–7.

39 Azurara, *Chronicles*, 238.

40 Gonzalo Fernández de Oviedo y Valdés, *Historia General y Natural de las Indias* (Madrid: Ediciones Atlas, 1959), I, 24.

41 Mercer, *Canary Islands*, 65–6, 201; Espinosa, *Guanches*, 89.

42 Mercer, *Canary Islands*, 148–59; Bontier and Le Verrier, *Canarian*, 137.

43 Abreu de Galindo, *Historia de Conquista*, 169.

44 Azurara, *Chronicles*, 240; Espinosa, *Guanches*, 83.

45 Abreu de Galindo, *Historia de Conquista*, 93; Mercer, *Canary Islands*, 178.

46 Abreu de Galindo, *Historia de Conquista*, 80; Mercer, *Canary Islands*, 182–3.

47 Espinosa, *Guanches*, x, 45–73; Abreu de Galindo, *Historia de Conquista*, 41, 301–13.

48 Espinosa, *Guanches*, 89, 96–7, 103.

49 Espinosa, *Guanches*, 106–7.

50 Espinosa, *Guanches*, 92; Abreu de Galindo, *Historia de Conquista*, 183.

51 Charles S. Elton, *The Ecology of Invasions by Animals and Plants* (London: Methuen, 1958), Ch. IV; Alfred W. Crosby, *Epidemic and Peace, 1918* (Westport, Conn.: Greenwood Press, 1976), 235–6.

52 Abreu de Galindo, *Historia de Conquista*, 161.

53 Abreu de Galindo, *Historia de Conquista*, 154–5, 169; Leonardo Torriani, *Descripción e Historia del Reino de las Islas Canarias*, trans.

and ed. Alejandro Cioranescu (Santa Cruz de Tenerife: Goya Ediciones, 1978), 115.

54 Bontier and Le Verrier, *Canarian*, 92.

55 Torriani, *Descripción*, 116; Abreu de Galindo, *Historia de Conquista*, 169.

56 Espinosa, *Guanches*, 104–8; José de Viera y Clavijo, *Noticias de la Historia General de las Islas Canarias* (Santa Cruz de Tenerife: Goya Ediciones, 1951), II, 108.

57 Espinosa, *Guanches*, 108.

58 *Diccionario de la Lengua Española* (Madrid: Real Academia Española, 1970), 886, 1016; Elias Zerolo, *Diccionario Enciclopédico de la Lengua Castellana* (Paris: Casa Editorial Garnier Hermonos, n.d.), II, 324; Juan Bosch Millares, "Enfermedades y Terapéutica de los Aborígines," *Anales de la Clínica Médica del Hospital de San Martín* (Las Palmas, Canary Islands) 1 (1945):172–3; Dr. Francisco Guerra, personal communication.

59 Alfred W. Crosby, "Virgin Soil Epidemics as a Factor in the Aboriginal Depopulation in America," *The William and Mary Quarterly*, 3rd series 33 (April 1976):289–99. For a recent example, see Robert J. Wolfe, "Alaska's Great Sickness, 1900: An Epidemic of Measles and Influenza in a Virgin Soil Population," *Proceedings of the American Philosophical Society* 126 (8 April 1982):92–121.

60 Torriani, *Descripción*, 46; Richard Hakluyt, ed., *Voyages* (London: Everyman's Library, 1907), IV, 26.

61 Abreu de Galindo, *Historia de Conquista*, 60.

62 Thomas D. Seeley, "How Honeybees Find a Home," *Scientific American* 247 (October 1982):158; Espinosa, *Guanches*, 61, 63; Abreu de Galindo, *Historia de Conquista*, 83, 262, 312; Felipe Fernández-Armesto, *The Canary Islands After the Conquest, The Making of a Colonial Society in the Early Sixteenth Century* (Oxford: Clarendon Press, 1982), 86.

63 Fernández-Armesto, *Canary Islands*, 70; Abreu de Galindo, *Historia de Conquista*, 239.

64 Hakluyt, *Voyages*, IV, 25–6; Fernández-Armesto, *Canary Islands*, 74; James J. Parsons, "Human Influences on the Pine and Laurel Forests of the Canary Islands," *Geographical Review*, 71 (July 1981):260–4.

65 Ferdinand Columbus, *Columbus by His Son*, 143; Mercer, *Canary Islands*, 219; Bontier and Le Verrier, *Canarian*, 135; Fernández-Armesto, *Canary Islands*, 219; Parsons, "Human Influences," *Geographical Review* 71 (July 1981):259–60.

66 Gunther Kunkel, "Notes on the Introduced Elements in the Canary

Islands Flora," *Biogeography and Ecology in the Canary Islands,* 250, 256–7, 259, 264–5.

67 Fernández de Oviedo y Valdés, *Historia General,* I, 24; Girolamo Benzoni, *History of the New World,* trans. and ed. W. H. Smyth (London: Hakluyt Society, 1857), 260; Espinosa, *Guanches,* 120; Fernández-Armesto, *Canary Islands,* 6.

68 Fernández-Armesto, *Canary Islands,* 39–40; Mercer, *Canary Islands,* 215, 230.

69 Mercer, *Canary Islands,* 213; Viera y Clavijo, *Noticias,* II, 394; Rafael Torres Campos, *Carácter de la Conquista y Colonización de las Islas Canarias* (Madrid: Imprenta y Litografia del Deposito de la Guerra, 1901), 71; Analola Borges, "La Región Canaria en los Orígenes Americanos," *Anuario de Estudios Atlanticos* 18 (1972):237–8.

70 Mercer, *Canary Islands,* 222–32; *Oeuvres de Christophe Columb,* trans. and ed. Alexandre Cioranescu (No place: Editions Gallimard, 1961), 241; Fernández-Armesto, *Canary Islands,* 20, 40, 127–9, 174.

71 Fernández-Armesto, *Canary Islands,* 11; Abreu de Galindo, *Historia de Conquista,* 298; Espinosa, *Guanches,* 34; Viera y Clavijo, *Noticias,* II, 156, 290, 348, 496–7, 511, 538; Alfred W. Crosby, *The Columbian Exchange, Biological and Cultural Consequences of 1492* (Westport, Conn.: Greenwood Press, 1972), 122–64.

72 Abreu de Galindo, *Historia de Conquista,* 387; Benzoni, *History of New World,* l, 260.

73 Mercer, *Canary Islands,* 27–41, 241–58; Espinosa, *Guanches,* xviii; Fernández-Armesto, *Canary Islands,* 5.

74 Fernández-Armesto, *Canary Islands,* 13, 15, 21, 31, 33, 35–7, 41.

75 Alexander de Humboldt and Aimé Bopland, *Personal Narrative of Travels to the Equinoctial Region of the New Continent* (London: Longman, Hurat, Rees, Orme & Brown, 1818), I, 293.

76 Viera y Clavijo, *Noticias,* 394.

77 Viera y Clavijo, *Noticias, passim.*

Chapter 5. Winds

1 Two of their better-known books on the subject are, respectively, *The Discovery of the Sea* (Berkeley: University of California Press, 1981) and *Admiral of the Ocean Sea, A Life of Christopher Columbus* (Boston: Little, Brown, 1942).

2 Joseph Needham, *Science and Civilisation in China,* IV, *Physics and Physical Technology,* Part III, *Civil Engineering and Nautics* (Cambridge University Press, 1971), 487–91, 518, 524, 562–3, 567, 594–9.

3 Samuel Eliot Morison, *Admiral of the Ocean Sea, A Life of Christopher Columbus* (Boston: Little, Brown, 1942), 183–96; Carlo M. Cipolla, *Guns, Sails and Empires: Technological Innovation and the Early Phases of European Expansion, 1400–1700* (New York: Pantheon Books, 1965), 75–6.
4 J. H. Parry, *The Discovery of the Sea* (Berkeley: University of California Press, 1981).
5 Aristotle, *Meteorologica,* trans. H. D. P. Lee (Cambridge: Harvard University Press, 1952), 179–81; *The Geography of Strabo,* trans. Horace L. Jones (London: Heinemann, 1917), VIII, 367–71.
6 Morison, *Admiral,* 230.
7 J. C. Beaglehole, *The Life of Captain James Cook* (Stanford University Press, 1974), 107–8.
8 Pierre Chaunu, *European Expansion in the Later Middle Ages,* trans. Katherine Bertram (Amsterdam: North Holland, 1979), 106.
9 *The Voyage of John Huyghen van Linschoten to the East Indies* (New York: Burt Franklin, n.d.), II, 264.
10 Raymond Mauny, *Les Navigations Médiévales sur les Côtes Saharien-nes Antérieures à la Découverte Portugaise (1434)* (Lisbon: Centro de Estudos Históricos Ultramarinos, 1960), 16–17.
11 Parry, *Discovery,* 101-2.
12 Joseph de Acosta, *The Natural and Moral History of the Indies,* trans. Edward Grimstone (New York: Burt Franklin, n.d.), I, 116.
13 Willy Rudloff, *World Climates: with Tables of Climatic Data and Practical Suggestions* (Stuttgart: Wissenschaftliche Verlagsgesellschaft, 1981), 15; Parry, *Discovery,* 119; Glenn T. Trewartha, *An Introduction to Climate* (New York: McGraw-Hill, 1968), 107–8; "Monsoons," *Encyclopaedia Britannica, Macropaedia* (Chicago: Encyclopaedia Britannica, Inc., 1982), XII, 392.
14 *The Four Voyages of Christopher Columbus,* trans. J. M. Cohen (Baltimore: Penguin Books, 1969), 207.
15 Baily W. Diffie and George D. Winius, *Foundations of the Portuguese Empire, 1415–1580* (Minneapolis: University of Minnesota Press, 1977), 147.
16 Parry, *Discovery,* 124–6; Chaunu, *European Expansion,* 130.
17 Eric Axelson, *Congo To Cape, Early Portuguese Explorers* (London: Faber & Faber, 1973), 100–1, 107–10, 114.
18 Charles M. Andrews, *The Colonial Period of American History* (New Haven: Yale University Press, 1934), I, 98; J. Franklin Jameson, ed., *Narratives of New Netherland, 1609–1664* (New York: Scribner, 1909), 75.

19 Acosta, *Natural and Moral History*, I, 114; Samuel Purchas, ed., *Hakluytus Posthumus, or Purchas His Pilgrimes* (Glasgow: James MacLehose & Sons, 1905–7), XIV, 433.
20 Ferdinand Columbus, *The Life of the Admiral Christopher Columbus by his Son Ferdinand*, trans. Benjamin Keen (New Brunswick: Rutgers University Press, 1959), 51; G. R. Crone, *The Discovery of America* (New York: Weybright & Talley, 1969), 90.
21 Purchas, *Pilgrimes*, XIX, 261.
22 Vincent Jones, *Sail the Indian Sea* (London: Gordon & Cromonesi, 1978), 40–7; G. R. Crone, *The Discovery of the East* (New York: St. Martin's Press, 1972), 28–9; Charles Ley, ed., *Portuguese Voyages, 1498–1663* (London: Dent, 1947), 4–7.
23 Samuel Eliot Morison, *Portuguese Voyages to America in the 15th Century* (Cambridge: Harvard University Press, 1940), 95–7.
24 *The Travels of Marco Polo*, trans. Ronald Latham (Harmondsworth: Penguin Books, 1958), 300.
25 David Day, *The Doomsday Book of Animals* (New York: Viking Press, 1981), 19–21.
26 C. R. Boxer, *The Portuguese Seaborne Empire, 1415–1825* (London: Hutchinson & Co., 1969), 44.
27 Jones, *Sail the Indian Sea*, 59–68; João de Barros, *Da Asia*, I, (Lisbon: Livraria San Carlos, 1973), 318.
28 Jones, *Sail the Indian Sea*, 68–73; Barros, *Da Asia*, I, 319.
29 *Travels of Polo*, 248.
30 R. G. Barry and R. J. Chorley, *Atmosphere, Weather and Climate* (London: Methuen & Co., 1968), 157–8; Trewartha, *Introduction to Climate*, 89, 92, 102–8.
31 Crone, *Discovery of the East*, 36.
32 Jones, *Sail the Indian Sea*, 106–7.
33 Crone, *Discovery of the East*, 38; Jones, *Sail the Indian Sea*, 107; Chaunu, *European Expansion*, 132.
34 Samuel Eliot Morison, *The European Discovery of America, The Southern Voyages, A.D. 1492–1616* (Oxford University Press, 1974), 356–7; Charles E. Nowell, ed., *Magellan's Voyage Around the World, Three Contemporary Accounts* (Evanston: Northwestern University Press, 1962), 91–4.
35 Morison, *Southern Voyages*, 359–97.
36 Morison, *Southern Voyages*, 405.
37 Morison, *Southern Voyages*, 406, 440.
38 Nowell, *Magellan's Voyage*, 122–3.
39 Nowell, *Magellan's Voyage*, 123–4.
40 Nowell, *Magellan's Voyage*, 172.

41 Morison, *Southern Voyages,* 444–5; Nowell, *Magellan's Voyage,* 199.
42 Nowell, *Magellan's Voyage,* 10; Morison, *Southern Voyages,* 441, 451.
43 Morison, *Southern Voyages,* 406; Nowell, *Magellan's Voyage,* 255–6.
44 Norwell, *Magellan's Voyage,* 259; Morison, *Southern Voyages,* 460–2.
45 Morison, *Southern Voyages,* 467, 469.
46 Morison, *Southern Voyages,* 507–10, 531.
47 Carl Ortwin Sauer, *The Early Spanish Main* (Berkeley: University of California Press, 1969), 216.
48 Morison, *Southern Voyages,* 545–55.
49 William L. Schurz, *The Manila Galleon* (New York: Dutton, 1939), 19, 22, 32, 47, 219, 220–1.
50 J. E. Heeres, *The Part Borne by the Dutch in the Discovery of Australia, 1606–1765* (London: Luzac & Co., 1899), xiii-xiv.
51 Francesco Carletti, *Razonamientos de Mi Viaje Alrededor del Mundo (1594–1606),* trans. Francisco Perujo (México: Instituto de Investigaciones Bibliográficas, Universidad Nacional Autónoma de México, 1983), 109.
52 Alfred W. Crosby, *The Columbian Exchange, Biological and Cultural Consequences of 1492* (Westport, Conn.: Greenwood Press, 1972), passim.
53 Purchas, *Pilgrimes,* I, 251.

Chapter 6. Within reach, beyond grasp

1 John Huyghen Linschoten, *The Voyage of John Huyghen Linschoten to the East Indies* (New York: Burt Franklin, n.d.), I, 235–40.
2 K. W. Goonewardena, "A New Netherlands in Ceylon," *Ceylon Journal of Historical and Social Studies* 2 (July 1959):203–41; Charles Boxer, *Women in Iberian Expansion Overseas, 1415–1812* (Oxford University Press, 1975), *passim;* Jean Gelman Taylor, *The Social World of Batavia, European and Eurasian in Dutch Asia* (Madison: University of Wisconsin Press, 1983), *passim.*
3 Richard Hakluyt, ed., *Voyages* (London: Everyman's Library, 1907), IV, 98.
4 John W. Blake, ed. and trans., *Europeans in West Africa, 1450–1560* (London: Hakluyt Society, 1912), I, 163–4.
5 William Bosman, *A New and Accurate Description of the Coast of Guinea* (London: Frank Cass, 1967), 236–8; Robin Law, *The Horse in West African History* (Oxford University Press, 1980), 44–5, 76–82; *Voyages of Cadamosto,* trans. G. R. Crone (London: Hakluyt Society, 1937), 30, 33.
6 *Voyages of Cadamosto,* 143, see also pages 96, 123, 125, 141.

7 Philip D. Curtin, "Epidemiology and the Slave Trade," *Political Science Quarterly* 83 (June 1968):202–3.
8 Roger Tennant, *Joseph Conrad, a Biography* (New York: Atheneum, 1981), 76.
9 C. R. Boxer, *Four Centuries of Portuguese Expansion, 1415–1825* (Johannesburg: Witwatersrand University Press, 1965), 27; original on page 266 of the first volume of João de Barros, *Da Asia* (Lisbon: Livravia San Carlos, 1973).
10 Philip D. Curtin, *The Image of Africa, British Ideas and Action, 1780–1850* (Madison: University of Wisconsin Press, 1964), 60, 88–9, 91, 94–5.
11 Curtin, *Image of Africa*, 89; Donald L. Wiedner, *A History of Africa South of the Sahara* (New York: Vintage Books, 1964), 75–8; Tom W. Shick, "A Quantitative Analysis of Liberian Colonization from 1820 to 1843 with Special Reference to Mortality," *Journal of African History* 12 (No. 1, 1971):45–59.
12 Joseph de Acosta, *The Natural and Moral History of the Indies,* trans. Edward Grimstone (New York: Burt Franklin, n.d.), I, 233.
13 Alfred W. Crosby, *The Columbian Exchange, Biological and Cultural Consequences of 1492* (Westport, Conn.: Greenwood Press, 1972), 64–121.
14 Francisco Guerra, "The Influence of Disease on Race, Logistics and Colonization in the Antilles," *Journal of Tropical Medicine and Hygiene* 69 (February 1966):23–35.
15 Curtin, "Epidemiology," *Political Science Quarterly,* 83 (June 1968):202–3.
16 John Prebble, *The Darien Disaster, A Scots Colony in the New World, 1698–1700* (New York: Holt, Rinehart & Winston, 1968), *passim;* Herbert I. Priestly, *France Overseas Through the Old Regime* (New York: Appleton-Century, 1939), 104–6; Jean Chaia, "Échec d'une tentative de colonisation de la Guyane au XVIIIe Siècle,"*Biologie Médicale* 47 (Avril 1958):i-lxxxiii.
17 Kenneth F. Kiple, *The Caribbean Slave: A Biological History* (Cambridge University Press, 1984), *passim.*
18 G. C. Bolton, *A Thousand Miles Away, A History of North Queensland to 1920* (Sydney: Australian National University Press, 1970), vii, 76, 149, 249, 251; Raphael Cilento, *Triumph in the Tropics, a Historical Sketch of Queensland* (Brisbane: Smith & Paterson, 1959), 289, 291, 293, 421, 437; Bruce R. Davidson, *The Northern Myth, a Study of the Physical and Economic Limits to Agricultural and Pastoral Development in Tropical Australia* (Melbourne University Press, 1966), 112–46.
19 William Bradford, *Of Plymouth Plantation,* ed. Samuel Eliot

Morison (New York: Knopf, 1963), 28. The British attitude toward the tropics is nicely set forth in Karen Ordahl Kupperman's "Fear of Hot Climates in the Anglo-American Colonial Experience," *William and Mary Quarterly*, 3rd series, 41 (April 1984):213–40.
20 Genesis, 22:17–18, *New English Bible*, 22.
21 Walter Raleigh, *The Discovery of Guiana*, in *Voyages and Travels Ancient and Modern* (New York: Collier & Son, 1910), 389.

Chapter 7. Weeds

1 The statistics for this brief discussion come from *The New Rand McNally College World Atlas* (Chicago: Rand McNally, 1983), *The World Almanac and Book of Facts* (New York: Newspaper Enterprise Association, 1983), *The Americana Encyclopedia* (Danbury: Grolier, 1983), XXI, and T. Lynn Smith, *Brazil, People and Institutions* (Baton Rouge: Louisiana University Press, 1972), 70.
2 J. D. Hooker, "Note on the Replacement of Species in the Colonies and Elsewhere," *The Natural History Review* (1864):125.
3 Jack R. Harlan, *Crops and Man* (Madison: American Society of Agronomy, Crop Science Society of America, 1975), 86, 89.
4 Herbert G. Baker, *Plants and Civilization* (Belmont, Calif.: Wadsworth Publishing, 1966), 15-18.
5 Harlan, *Crops*, 91; Noel Vietmeyer, "The Revival of the Amaranth," *Ceres*, 15 (September–October 1982):43–6.
6 Harlan, *Crops*, 101.
7 Gonzalo Fernández de Oviedo, *Natural History of the West Indies*, trans. Sterling A. Stoudemire (Chapel Hill: University of North Carolina Press, 1959), 10, 97, 98.
8 Alfred W. Crosby, *The Columbian Exchange, Biological and Cultural Consequences of 1492* (Westport, Conn.: Greenwood Press, 1972), 66–7; Charles Darwin, *The Voyage of the Beagle* (Garden City, N.Y.: Doubleday, 1962), 120.
9 Bartolomé de las Casas, *Apologética Historia Sumaria* (México: Universidad Nacional Autónoma de México, Instituto de Investigaciones Históricas, 1967), I, 81–2.
10 Elinor G. K. Melville, "Environmental Degradation Caused by Overgrazing of Sheep in 16th Century Mexico," unpublished manuscript.
11 Alonso de Molina, *Aqui Comiença vn Vocabulario enla Lengua Castellana y Mexicana* (México: Juan Pablos, 1555), 238.
12 Jerzy Rzedowski, *Vegetación de México* (México: Editorial Limusa, 1978), 69–70.

13 G. W. Hendry, "The Adobe Brick as a Historical Source," *Agricultral History* 5 (July 1931):125.
14 Andrew H. Clark, "The Impact of Exotic Invasion on the Remaining New World Mid-Latitude Grasslands," *Man's Role in Changing the Face of the Earth,* ed. William L. Thomas, Jr. (University of Chicago Press, 1956), II, 748–51; Joseph B. Davy, "Stock Ranges of Northwestern California," United States Bureau of Plant Industry, Bulletin No. 12 (1902), 38, 40–2.
15 Michael Zohary, *Plants of the Bible* (Cambridge University Press, 1982), 93; Hendry, "Adobe Brick," *Agricultural History* 5 (1931):125.
16 Donald Jackson and Mary Lee Spense, eds., *The Expeditions of John Charles Frémont,* I, *Travels from 1838 to 1844* (Urbana: University of Illinois Press, 1970), 649.
17 Clark, "Impact of Exotic Invasion," *Man's Role,* II, 750; R. W. Allard, "Genetic Systems Associated with Colonizing Ability in Predominantly Self-Pollinated Species," *The Genetics of Colonizing Species,* eds. H. G. Baker and G. Ledyard Stebbins (New York: Academic Press, 1965), 50; M. W. Talbot, H. H. Biswell, and A. L. Hormay, "Fluctuations in the Annual Vegetation of California," *Ecology* 20 (July 1939):396–7; W. W. Robbins, "Alien Plants Growing without Cultivation in California," *California Agricultural Experiment Station, Bulletin No. 637* (July 1940), 6–7; L. T. Burcham, "Cattle and Range Forage in California: 1770–1880," *Agricultural History* 35 (July 1961):140–9.
18 *Obras de Bernabé Cobo* (Madrid: Ediciones Atlas, 1956), I, 414; Garcilaso de la Vega, *Royal Commentaries of the Incas and General History of Peru,* trans. Harold V. Livermore (Austin: University of Texas Press, 1966), I, 601–2; Abundio Sagastegui Alva, *Manual de las Malezas de la Costa Norperuana* (Trujillo, Peru: Talleres Gráficos de la Universidad Nacional de Trujillo, 1973), 229, 231, 234, 236.
19 John Fitzherbert, *Booke of Husbandry* (London: John Awdely, 1562), f. xiii verso, xiiii recto.
20 *Henry V,* act V, sc. II; *I Henry IV,* act II, sc. III; *King Lear,* act IV, sc. IV.
21 John Josselyn, *An Account of Two Voyages to New England Made During the Years 1638, 1663* (Boston: William Veazie, 1865), 137–41; Edward Tuckerman, ed. "New-England's Rarities Discovered," *Transactions and Collections of the American Antiquarian Society* 4 (1860):216–19. It would be very easy to supply the scientific names for most of these plants and others soon to be mentioned, but I have not done so for fear of giving an air of exactitude to what must be, no matter how freely I resort to Latin and Greek, an imprecise account.
22 Edmund Berkeley and Dorothy S. Berkeley, eds., *The Reverend*

John Clayton, a Parson with a Scientific Mind. His Writings and Other Related Papers (Charlottesville: University Press of Virginia, 1965), 24; Josselyn, *Account*, 138. Henry Wadsworth Longfellow learned of this Algonkin name for this plant, which he wove into Hiawatha's dream of the coming of the whites: "Wheresoe'er they tread, beneath them/ Springs a flower unknown among us,/Springs the White-man's Foot in blossom." *The Poems of Longfellow* (New York: Modern Library, 1944), 259.

23 U. P. Hedrick, *A History of Horticulture in America to 1860* (Oxford University Press, 1950), 19, 119, 121–2; Peter Kalm, *Travels into North America* (Barre, Mass.: The Imprint Society, 1972), 70–1, 398; Robert Beverley, *The History and Present State of Virginia* (Chapel Hill: University of North Carolina Press, 1947), 181, 314–15; Michel-Guillaume St. Jean de Crèvecoeur, *Journey into Northern Pennsylvania and the State of New York*, trans. Clarissa S. Bostelmann (Ann Arbor: University of Michigan Press, 1964), 198; Mark Catesby, *The Natural History of Carolina, Florida, and the Bahama Islands* (London: 1731-43), I, x; II, xx; John Lawson, *A New Voyage to Carolina* (London: 1709; Readex Microprint, 1966), 109–10; Joseph Ewan and Nesta Ewan, eds., *John Banister and His History of Virginia, 1678–1692* (Urbana: University of Illinois Press, 1970), 355–6, 367.

24 Robert W. Schery, "The Migration of a Plant," *Natural History* 74 (December 1965):44.

25 Kalm, *Travels*, 174, 264; Carl O. Sauer, "The Settlement of the Humid East," *Climate and Man, Yearbook of Agriculture* (Washington, D.C.: United States Department of Agriculture, 1941), 159–60.

26 Schery, "Migration of a Plant," *Natural History* 74 (December 1965):41–4.

27 Lyman Carrier and Katherine S. Bort, "The History of Kentucky Bluegrass and White Clover in the United States," *Journal of the American Society of Agronomy* 8 (1916):256–66.

28 Schery, "Migration of a Plant," *Natural History* 74 (December 1965):41–9.

29 Douglas H. Campbell, "Exotic Vegetation of the Pacific Regions," *Proceedings of the Fifth Pacific Science Congress, Canada, 1933, Pacific Science Association* (University of Toronto Press, 1934), I, 785.

30 Lewis D. de Schweinitz, "Remarks on the Plants of Europe Which Have Become Naturalized in a More or Less Degree in the United States," *Annals Lyceum of Natural History of New York* 3 (1832): 148–55.

31 Gonzalo Fernández de Oviedo y Valdés, *Historia General y Natural de las Indias* (Madrid: Ediciones Atlas, 1959), II, 356.

32 Félix de Azara, *Descripción e Historia del Paraguay y del Río de la Plata* (Madrid: Imprenta de Sanchiz, 1847), I, 56–8.
33 Charles Darwin, *The Voyage of the Beagle* (Garden City, N.Y.: Doubleday, 1962), 119–20; Oscar Schmieder, "Alteration of the Argentine Pampa in the Colonial Period," University of California Publications in Geography, II, No. 10 (27 September 1927), 310; Mariano B. Berro, *La Agricultura Colonial* (Montevideo: Colección de Clásicos Uruguayos, v. 148, 1975), 138–40.
34 W. H. Hudson, *Far Away and Long Ago, A History of My Early Life* (New York: Dutton, 1945), 64, 68–9, 71–2, 148; U. P. Hedrick, ed., *Sturtevant's Edible Plants of the World* (New York: Dover, 1973), 535; Alexander Martin, *Weeds* (New York: Golden Press, n.d.), 148; Berro, *Agricultura*, 140–1.
35 Francis Bond Head, *Journeys Across the Pampas and Among the Andes*, ed. Harvey Gardiner (Carbondale: Southern Illinois Press, 1967), 3–4; Darwin, *Voyage*, 119.
36 Carlos Berg, "Enumeración de las Plantas Europeas que se Hallen como Silvestres en las Provincias de Buenos Aires y en Patagonia," *Anales de La Sociedad Científica Argentina* 3 (April 1877): 183–206.
37 Schmieder, "Alteration," University of California Publications in Geography, II, No. 10 (1927), 310.
38 W. H. Hudson, *The Naturalist in La Plata* (New York: Dutton, 1922), 2.
39 Commonweath of Australia, *Historical Records of Australia,* Series I, *Governors' Dispatches to and From England* (The Library Committee of the Commonwealth Parliament, 1914–25), IV, 234–41.
40 Joseph Dalton Hooker, *The Botany of the Antarctic Voyage of H.M. Discovery Ships Erebus and Terror in the Years 1839–1843* (London: Lovell Reeve, 1860), I, pt. 3, cvi–cix.
41 *Historical Records of Australia,* Series III, X, 367.
42 Henry W. Haygarth, *Recollections of Bush Life in Australia,* (London: John Murray, 1848), 131; see also *Historical Records of Australia* Series III, X, 367.
43 Hooker, *Botany of Antarctic Voyage,* I, pt. 3, cvi–cix.
44 A. Grenfell Price, *The Western Invasions of the Pacific and Its Continents* (Oxford: Clarendon Press, 1963), 194.
45 Alex. G. Hamilton, "On the Effect Which Settlement in Australia Has Produced upon Indigenous Vegetation," *Journal and Proceedings of the Royal Society of New South Wales* 26 (1892):234.
46 Hamilton, "Effect Which Settlement in Australia Has Produced," *Journal and Proceedings of the Royal Society of New South Wales* 26

(1892):185, 209–14; Thomas Perry, *Australia's First Frontier, the Spread of Settlement in New South Wales, 1788–1829* (Melbourne University Press, 1963), 13, 27; R. M. Moore, "Effects of the Sheep Industry on Australian Vegetation," *The Simple Fleece: Studies in the Australian Wool Industry*, ed. Alan Barnard (Melbourne University Press and Australian National University, 1962), 170-1, 174, 182; Joseph M. Powell, *Environmental Management in Australia, 1788-1914* (Oxford University Press, 1976), 17–18, 31–2.

47 Edward Salisbury, *Weeds and Aliens* (London: Collins, 1961), 87.

48 Walter C. Muenscher, *Weeds* (New York: Macmillan, 1955), 23.

49 "Weeds," *Australian Encyclopedia*, IV, 275–6.

50 Angel Lulio Cabrera, *Manual de la Flora de Los Alrededores de Buenos Aires* (Buenos Aires: Editorial Acme, 1953), *passim;* Arturo E. Ragonese, *Vegetación y Ganadería en la República Argentina* (Buenos Aires: Colección Científica del I.N.T.A., 1967), 28, 30.

51 Hooker, *Botany of Antarctic Voyage*, I, pt. 3, cvi–cix.

52 Carlos Berg, "Enumeración de las Plantas Europeas," *Anales de la Sociedad Científica Argentina* 3 (April 1877):184-204; Thomas Nuttall, *The Genera of North American Plants* (New York: Hafner, 1971; facsimile 1818 ed.), 2 vols., *passim;* John Torrey and Asa Gray, *A Flora of North America* (New York: Hafner, 1969; facsimile 1838–43 ed.), 2 vols., *passim.*

53 Francis Darwin, ed., *The Life and Letters of Charles Darwin* (London: John Murray, 1887), II, 391; Jane Gray, ed. *Letters of Asa Gray* (Boston: Houghton Mifflin, 1894), II, 492.

54 For background, see Janet Browne, *The Secular Ark, Studies in the History of Biogeography* (New Haven: Yale University Press, 1983).

55 W. B. Turrill, *Pioneer Plant Geography. The Phytogeographical Researches of Sir Joseph Dalton Hooker* (The Hague: Nijhoff, 1953), 183.

56 E. W. Claypole, "On the Migration of Plants from Europe to America, with an Attempt to Explain Certain Phenomena Connected Therewith," Montreal Horticultural Society and Fruit Growers' Association, Annual Report, No. 3 (1877–8), 79–81; Hooker, *Botany of Antarctic Voyage*, I, pt. 3, cv.

57 Asa Gray, "The Pertinacity and Predominance of Weeds," *Scientific Papers of Asa Gray* (Boston: Houghton Mifflin, 1889), 237–8.

58 Claypole, "On the Migration of Plants," *Montreal Horticultural Society*, No. 3 (1877–8), 79.

59 Hooker, *Botany of Antarctic Voyage*, I, Pt. 3, cv.

60 Salisbury, *Weeds*, 22; Hugo Iltis, "The Story of Wild Garlic,"

Scientific Monthly 67 (February 1949):124; Talbot, Biswell, and Hormay, "Fluctuations in Annual Vegetation of Califonia," *Ecology* 20 (July 1939):397.
61 Salisbury, *Weeds,* 97, 188.
62 Henry N. Ridley, *The Dispersal of Plants Throughout the World* (U.K.: L. Reeve & Co., 1930), 364; Peter Cunningham, *Two Years in New South Wales* (London: Henry Colburn, 1828), I, 200.
63 Salisbury, *Weeds,* 147–8.
64 Otto Solbrig, "The Population Biology of Dandelions," *American Scientist* 59 (November–December 1971):686–7.
65 G. S. Dunbar, "Henry Clay on Kentucky Bluegrass, 1838," *Agricultural History* 51 (July 1977):522.
66 Salisbury, *Weeds,* 220–2; M. Grieve, *A Modern Herbal* (New York: Dover, 1971), II, 640–2; Leroy G. Holm et al., eds., *The World's Worst Weeds, Distribution and Biology* (Honolulu: University Press of Hawaii, 1977), 314–19.
67 John C. Kricher, "Needs of Weeds," *Natural History* 89 (December 1980):144; Robert F. Betz and Marion H. Cole, "The Peacock Prairie – A Study of a Virgin Illinois Mesic Black-Soil Prairie Forty Years after Initial Study," *Transactions of the Illinois State Academy of Science* 62 (March 1969):44–53.

Chapter 8. Animals

1 Ward H. Goodenough, "The Evolution of Pastoralism and Indo-European Origins," *Indo-European and Indo-European Origins* (Philadelphia: University of Pennsylvania Press, 1970), 255, 258–9.
2 Alfred W. Crosby, *The Columbian Exchange, Biological and Cultural Consequences of 1492* (Westport, Conn.: Greenwood Press, 1972), 65; Edgars Dunsdorfs, *The Australian Wheat-Growing Industry, 1788–1948* (Melbourne: The University Press, 1956), 15–16, 34–5, 47.
3 Watkin Tench, *Sydney's First Four Years* (Sydney: Angus & Robertson, 1961), 48–9.
4 Anthony Leeds and Andrew P. Vayda, eds., *Man, Culture and Animals, the Role of Animals in Human Ecological Adjustments* (Washington, D.C.: Association for the Advancement of Science, 1965), 233.
5 Victor M. Patiño, *Plantas Cultivadas y Animales Domésticos en América Equinoctial, V, Animales Domésticos Introducidos* (Cali: Imprenta Departmental, 1970), 308.
6 Mark Catesby, *The Natural History of Carolina, Florida and the Bahama Islands* (London: 1731–43), II, xx.

7 Thomas Morton, "New English Canaan," *Tracts and Other Papers Relating Principally to the Origin, Settlement, and Progress of the Colonies in North America,* ed. Peter Force (New York: Peter Smith, n.d.), II, 61.

8 E. M. Pullar, "The Wild (Feral) Pigs of Australia: Their Origin, Distribution and Economic Importance," *Memoirs of the National Museum of Victoria* No. 18 (18 May 1953):8–9.

9 Pullar, "Wild (Feral) Pigs," *Memoirs of the National Museum of Victoria* No. 18 (18 May 1953):16–18; Crosby, *Columbian Exchange,* 75–9; "Cerdo," *Gran Enciclopedia Argentina* (Buenos Aires: Ediar, 1956), II, 267; W. H. Hudson, *Far Away and Long Ago, a History of My Early Life* (New York: Dutton, 1945), 170-2; Joseph Sánchez Labrador, *Paraguay Cathólico. Los Indios: Pampas, Peulches, Patagones,* ed. Guillermo Fúrlong Cárdiff (Buenos Aires: Viau y Zona, Editores, 1936), 168.

10 Peter Martyr D'Anghera, *De Orbo Novo,* trans. F. A. MacNutt (New York: Putnam, 1912), I, 180; Bartolomé de las Casas, *Apologética Historia Sumario,* ed. Edmundo O'Gorman (México: Universidad Nacional Autónoma de México, Instituto de Investigaciones Históricas, 1967), I, 30; Antonio de Herrera, *The General History of the Vast Continents and Islands of America,* trans. John Stevens (London: Wood & Woodward, 1740), II, 157.

11 Bartolomé de las Casas, *Historia de las Indias,* ed. Agustín Millares Carlo (México: Fondo de Cultura Económica, 1951), I, 351; Patiño, *Plantas,* V, 312.

12 Crosby, *Columbian Exchange,* 79; Marc Lescarbot, *The History of New France,* trans. W. L. Grant (Toronto: Champlain Society, 1907), I, xi–xii.

13 Robert Beverley, *The History and Present State of Virginia* (Chapel Hill: University of Carolina Press, 1947), 153, 318.

14 Crosby, *Columbian Exchange,* 78; Pullar, "Wild (Feral) Pigs," *Memoirs of the National Museum of Victoria* No. 18 (18 May 1953):10–11; Tracy I. Storer, "Economic Effects of Introducing Alien Animals into California," *Proceedings of the Fifth Pacific Science Conference, Canada* 1 (1933):779.

15 Henry W. Haygarth, *Recollections of Bush Life in Australia* (London: John Murray, 1848), 148.

16 Harry F. Recher, Daniel Lunney, and Irina Dunn, eds., *A Natural Legacy: Ecology in Australia* (Rushcutter's Bay, N.S.W.: Pergamon Press, 1979), 136; Eric C. Rolls, *They All Ran Wild, the Story of Pests on the Land in Australia* (Sydney: Angus & Robertson, 1969), 338.

17 Pullar, "Wild (Feral) Pigs," *Memoirs of the National Museum of Victoria* No. 18 (18 May 1953):13–15.

18 Hudson, *Far Away*, 170, 172. Today's pigs are no different from yesterday's in their ability to go wild. In 1983, an estimated 5,000 wild pigs were roaming the Cape Kennedy Space Center in Florida, descendants of tame swine owned by local residents whose land the National Aeronautics and Space Administration bought in the 1960s to expand the base. "Space Center's Problem Pigs a Taste Treat at Florida Jail," *New York Times*, 12 September 1983, p. A20.

19 John E. Rouse, *The Criollo, Spanish Cattle in the Americas* (Norman: University of Oklahoma Press, 1977), 21, 24, 33, 44–6, 50, 52–3, 64–5.

20 Crosby, *Columbian Exchange*, 88.

21 Juan Agustín de Morfí, *Viaje de Indios y Diario Nuevo México* (México: Bibliófilos Mexicanos, 1935), 165.

22 Rollie E. Poppino, *Brazil, the Land and People*, 2nd ed. (Oxford University Press, 1973), 71, 109, 233.

23 Crosby, *Columbian Exchange*, 91; Horacio C. E. Gilberti, *Historia Económica de la Ganadería Argentina* (Buenos Aires: Solar/Hachette, 1974), 20–5; Paolo Blanco Acevedo, *El Gobierno Colonial en el Uruguay y los Orígines de la Nacionalidad* (Montevideo: 1936), II, 7, 15.

24 Esteban Campal, ed., *Azara y su Legado al Uruguay* (Montevideo: Ediciones de la Banda Oriental, 1969), 176; see also Thomas Falkner, *A Description of Patagonia* (Chicago: Armann & Armann, 1935), 38.

25 Hudson, *Far Away*, 288.

26 Martin Dobrizhoffer, *An Account of the Abipones, an Equestrial People* (London: John Murray, 1822), I, 219; Crosby, *Columbian Exchange*, 88.

27 Rouse, *Criollo*, 92; Ray Allen Billington, *Westward Expansion, a History of the American Frontier* (New York: Macmillan, 1974), 4, 60.

28 John Lawson, *A New Voyage to Carolina* (London: 1709; Readex Microprint, 1966), 4.

29 Lewis C. Gray, *History of Agriculture in the Southern United States to 1860* (Washington, D.C.: Carnegie Institute of Washington, 1933), I, 141.

30 Frank L. Owsley, "The Pattern of Migration and Settlement on the Southern Frontier," *Journal of Southern History* 11 (May 1945):151.

31 Michel Guillaume St. Jean de Crèvecoeur, *Journey into Northern Pennsylvania and the State of New York*, trans. Clarissa S. Bostelmann (Ann Arbor: University of Michigan Press, 1964), 333, 336.

32 *The Reverend John Clayton, A Parson with a Scientific Mind. His Writings and Other Related Papers*, eds. Edmund Berkeley and Dorothy S. Berkeley (Charlottesville: University Press of Virginia, 1965), 88.

33 John White, *Journal of a Voyage to New South Wales* (Sydney: Angus & Robertson, 1962), 142, n. 242, n. 257; Commonwealth of Australia, *Historical Records of Australia,* Series I *Governors' Dispatches to and From England* (The Library Committee of the Commonwealth Parliament, 1914–25), I, 55, 77, 96.

34 *Historical Records of Australia,* Series I, I, 550–1.

35 *Historical Records of Australia,* Series I, I, 310, 461, 603, 608; II, 589; V, 590–2; VI, 641; VIII, 150–1; IX, 715.

36 *Historical Records of Australia,* Series I, IX, 349; X, 91–2, 280, 682; "Cowpastures," *Australian Encyclopedia,* II, 134.

37 Haygarth, *Recollections,* 55.

38 Peter Cunningham, *Two Years in New South Wales* (London: Henry Colburn, 1828), I, 272.

39 "Cattle Industry," *Australian Encyclopedia,* I, 483.

40 T. L. Mitchell, *Three Expeditions into the Interior of Eastern Australia* (London: T. & W. Boone, 1838), II, 306.

41 Haygarth, *Recollections,* 59–61, 65–6.

42 Peter Martyr D'Anghera, *De Orbo Novo,* I, 113; Robert M. Denhardt, *The Horse of the Americas* (Norman: University of Oklahoma Press, 1975), 27–84; Crosby, *Columbian Exchange,* 79–85.

43 Patiño, *Plantas,* V, 137–8.

44 Samuel Purchas, ed., *Hakluytus Posthumus, or Purchas His Pilgrimes* (Glasgow: James MacLehose & Sons, 1905–7), XIV, 500.

45 Morfí, *Viaje,* 334; Frances Perry, ed., *Complete Guide to Plants and Flowers* (New York: Simon & Schuster, 1974), 463; Oscar Sánchez, *Flora del Valle de México* (México: Editorial Herro, S.A., 1969), 186–8; Robert T. Clausen, *Sedum of North America North of the Mexican Plateau* (Ithaca: Cornell University Press, 1975), 554.

46 Denhardt, *Horse,* 92.

47 Denhardt, *Horse,* 92, 126.

48 Frank G. Roe, *The Indian and the Horse* (Norman: University of Oklahoma Press, 1955), 64–65. See also William Bartram, *Travels of William Bartram,* ed. Mark Van Doren (New York: Dover, 1955), 187–8; Fairfax Harrison, *The John's Island Stud (South Carolina), 1750–1788* (Richmond: Old Dominion Press, 1931), 166–71.

49 Peter Kalm, *Travels into North America* (Barre, Mass.: The Imprint Society, 1972), 115, 226, 255, 366; Denhardt, *Horse,* 92; John Josselyn, *An Account of Two Voyages to New England Made During the Years 1638, 1663* (Boston: William Veazie, 1865), 146.

50 Adolph B. Benson, ed., *The America of 1750, Peter Kalm's Travels in North America* (New York: Wilson-Erickson, 1937), II, 737; *Rev.*

John Clayton, 105; Gray, *History of Agriculture,* I, 140; Beverley, *History and Present State of Virginia,* 322.

51 Tom L. McKnight, "The Feral Horse in Anglo-America," *Geographical Review* 49 (October 1959):506, 521; see also Hope Ryden, *America's Last Wild Horses* (New York: Dutton, 1978).

52 Crosby, *Columbian Exchange,* 84–5; Antonio Vázquez de Espinosa, *Compendium and Description of the West Indies,* trans. Charles Upson Clark (Washington, D.C.: Smithsonian Institution, 1942), 675, 694; Blanco Acevedo, *Gobierno Colonial en el Uruguay,* 7, 15.

53 William MacCann, *Two Thousand Mile Ride through the Argentine Provinces* (London: Smith, Elder & Co., 1852), I, 23.

54 Falkner, *Description of Patagonia,* 39.

55 *Historical Records of Australia,* Series I, I, 55.

56 "Horses," *Australian Encyclopedia,* III, 329.

57 "Brumby," *Australian Encyclopedia,* I, 409; A. G. L. Shaw and C. M. H. Clark, eds., *Australian Dictionary of Biography* (Cambridge University Press, 1966), I, 171; Rolls, *They All Ran Wild,* 349.

58 Haygarth, *Recollections,* 61, 74, 77–8, 83; "Vermin," *Walkabout,* 38 (September 1972):4–7; Anthony Trollope, *Australia,* eds. P. D. Edwards and R. B. Joyce (St. Lucia: University of Queensland Press, 1967), 212.

59 Haygarth, *Recollections,* 77, 81; Trollope, *Australia,* 212.

60 Rolls, *They All Ran Wild,* 349–51.

61 *Judges* 14:8; Rémy Chauvin, *Traité de Biologie de l'Abeille* (Paris: Masson et Cie, 1968), I, 38–9.

62 John B. Free, *Bees and Mankind* (London: Allen & Unwin, 1982), 115; Elizabeth B. Pryor, *Honey, Maple Sugar and Other Farm Produced Sweetners in the Colonial Chesapeake* (Accokeek, Md.: The Accokeek Foundation, 1983), *passim;* Patiño, *Plantas,* V, 23–5; *Obras de Bernabé Cobo* (Madrid: Ediciones Atlas, 1956), I, 332–6; Nils E. Nordenskiold, "Modifications on Indian Culture through Inventions and Loans," *Comparative Ethnographic Studies* No. 8 (1930):196–210; Ricardo Piccirilli, Francisco L. Romay, and Leoncio Gianello, eds., *Diccionario Histórico Argentino* (Buenos Aires: Ediciones Históricas Argentinas, n.d.), I, 4; Eva Crane, ed., *Honey, a Comprehensive Survey* (New York: Crane, Russak & Co., 1975), 126–7, 477.

63 Crane, *Honey,* 475; Everett Oertel, "Bicentennial Bees, Early Records of Honey Bees in the Eastern United States," *American Bee Journal* 116 (February 1976):70–1; (March, 1976):114, 128.

64 Crane, *Honey,* 476.

65 Crane, *Honey,* 476; Oertel, "Bicentennial Bees," *American Bee Journal* 116 (May 1976):215; (June 1976):260.

66 Washington Irving, *A Tour on the Prairie,* ed. John F. McDermott (Norman: University of Oklahoma Press, 1956), n. 50.

67 Irving, *Tour,* 52–3.

68 Paul Dudley, "An Account of a Method Lately Found in New-England for Discovering where the Bees Hive in the Woods, in order to get their Honey," *Philosophical Transactions of the Royal Society of London* 31 (1720–1):150; Crèvecoeur, *Journey,* 166. See also *The Portable Thomas Jefferson,* ed. Merril Peterson (New York: Viking Press, 1975), 111; Irving, *Tour,* 50.

69 Crane, *Honey,* 4; "Beekeeping," *Australian Encyclopedia,* I, 275; "Bees," *Australian Encyclopedia,* I, 297; *Historical Records of Australia,* Series I, XI, 386.

70 Cunningham, *Two Years,* I , 320–1; James Backhouse, *A Narrative of a Visit to the Australian Colonies* (London: Hamilton, Adams & Co., 1843), 23; Henry W. Parker, *Van Dieman's Land, Its Rise, Progress and Present State, with Advice to Emigrants* (London: J. Cross, 1834), 193.

71 Crane, *Honey,* 68–70.

72 Trollope, *Australia,* 211.

73 Crane, *Honey,* 116–39.

74 *Obras de Bernabé Cobo,* I, 350–2; Garcilaso de la Vega, *Royal Commentaries of the Incas and General History of Peru,* trans. Harold V. Livermore (Austin: University of Texas Press, 1966), I, 589–90.

75 *Acuerdos del Extinguido Cabildo de Buenos Aires,* Series I (Buenos Aires: Talleres Gráficos de la Penitenciaria Nacional, 1907–34), I, 96; II, 406; III, 374; IV, 76–7; Alexander Gillespie, *Gleanings and Remarks Collected During Many Months of Residence at Buenos Aires* (Leeds: B. Dewirst, 1818), 120.

76 John Smith, *A Map of Virginia with a Description of the Country* (Oxford: Joseph Banks, 1612), 86–7. For the story of poor Bermuda and rats, see *Travels and Works of Captain John Smith,* ed. Edward Arber (New York: Burt Franklin, n.d.), II, 658–9.

77 Marc Lescarbot, *The History of New France* (Toronto: Champlain Society, 1914), III, 226–7.

78 *Historical Records of Australia,* Series I, I, 143–4.

79 Rolls, *They All Ran Wild,* 330.

80 "Mammals, Introduced," *Australian Encyclopedia,* IV, 111.

81 Paul L. Errington, *Muskrat Population* (Ames: Iowa University Press, 1963), 475–81; see also Hans Kampmann, *Der Waschbar* (Hamburg: Verlag Paul Parey, 1975).

82 Albert B. Friedman, ed., *The Penguin Book of Folk Ballads of the English-speaking World* (Harmondsworth: Penguin Books, 1976), 432–4.

Chapter 9. Ills

1 Alfred W. Crosby, "Virgin Soil Epidemics as a Factor in the Aboriginal Depopulation in America," *William and Mary Quarterly*, 3rd series 33 (April 1976):293–4.

2 Donald Joralemon, "New World Depopulation and the Case of Disease," *Journal of Anthropological Research* 38 (Spring 1982):118.

3 This is, of course, a matter of ambiguities and controversies. See Calvin Martin, *Keepers of the Game. Indian–Animal Relationships and the Fur Trade* (Berkeley: University of California Press, 1978), 48; William Denevan, "Introduction," *The Native Population of the Americas in 1492,* ed. William Denevan (Madison: University of Wisconsin Press, 1976), 5; Marshall T. Newman, "Aboriginal New World Epidemiology and Medical Care, and the Impact of Old World Disease Imports," *American Journal of Physical Anthropology* 45 (November 1976):671; Henry F. Dobyns, *Their Number Become Thinned, Native American Population Dynamics in Eastern North America* (Knoxville: University of Tennessee Press, 1983), 34.

4 Ronald M. Berndt and Catherine H. Berndt, *The World of the First Australians* (London: Angus & Robertson, 1964), 18; Peter M. Moodie, *Aboriginal Health* (Canberra: Australian National University Press, 1973), 29; A. A. Abbie, "Physical Changes in Australian Aborigines Consequent Upon European Contact," *Oceania* 31 (December 1960):140.

5 Bartolomé de las Casas, *Historia de las Indias,* ed. Agustín Millares Carlo (México: Fondo de Cultura Economica, 1951), I, 332; *Journals and Other Documents of the Life and Voyages of Christopher Columbus,* trans. Samuel Eliot Morison (New York: Heritage Press, 1963), 68, 93; *The Four Voyages of Christopher Columbus,* trans. J. M. Cohen (Baltimore: Penguin Books, 1969), 151. For slightly different numbers, see Peter Martyr D'Anghera, *De Orbo Novo,* trans. F. A. MacNutt (New York: Putnam, 1912), I, 66; Andrés Bernáldez, *Historia de los Reyes Católicos Don Fernando y Doña Isabel,* in *Crónicas de los Reyes de Castilla desde Don Alfonso el Sabio, Hasta los Católicos Don Fernando y Doña Isabel* (Madrid: M. Rivadeneyra, 1878), III, 660.

6 Bernáldez, *Historia de los Reyes Católicos,* III, 668; *Journals and Other Documents of Columbus,* 226–7.

7 Louis Becke and Walter Jeffery, *Admiral Philip* (London: Fisher & Unwin, 1909), 74–5.

8 Macfarlane Burnet and David O. White, *Natural History of Infectious Disease* (Cambridge University Press, 1972), 100.

9 There are sequels galore to this story. For instance, Jacques Cartier returned to France from his 1534 voyage to Canada with ten Amerindians on board. In seven years all had died of European diseases but one, a young girl. See Bruce G. Trigger, *The Children of Aataentsic, A History of the Huron People to 1660* (Montreal: McGill–Queen's University Press, 1976), I, 200–1.

10 I shall always be referring to the often fatal variola major smallpox. The mild variola minor did not appear until late in the nineteenth century. Donald R. Hopkins, *Princes and Peasants, Smallpox in History* (University of Chicago Press, 1983), 5–6.

11 Michael W. Flinn, *The European Demographic System, 1500–1800* (Baltimore: Johns Hopkins Press, 1981), 62–3; Ann G. Carmichael, "Infection, Hidden Hunger, and History," *Hunger and History, The Impact of Changing Food Production and Consumption Patterns on Society,* eds. Robert I. Rotberg and Theodore K. Rabb (Cambridge University Press, 1985), 57.

12 Alfred W. Crosby, The *Columbian Exchange, Biological and Cultural Consequences of 1492* (Westport, Conn.: Greenwood Press, 1972), 47–58.

13 Harold E. Driver, *Indians of North America* (University of Chicago Press, 1969), map 6; Jane Pyle, "A Reexamination of Aboriginal Population Claims for Argentina," *The Native Population of the Americas in 1492,* ed. William Denevan (Madison: University of Wisconsin Press, 1976), 184–204; Dobyns, *Their Number Become Thinned,* 259.

14 *The Merck Manual,* 12th ed. (Rahway, N.J.: Merck Sharp & Dohme Research Laboratories, 1972), 37–9; Martin Dobrizhoffer, *An Account of the Abipones, an Equestrial People of Paraguay* (London: John Murray, 1822), II, 338.

15 John Duffy, "Smallpox and the Indians in the American Colonies," *Bulletin of the History of Medicine* 25 (July–August 1951):327.

16 William Bradford, *Of Plymouth Plantation,* ed. Samuel Eliot Morison (New York: Knopf, 1952), 271.

17 Trigger, *Children,* II, 588–602.

18 Dobyns, *Their Number Become Thinned,* 15.

19 Crosby, "Virgin Soil Epidemics," *William and Mary Quarterly,* 3rd series 33 (April 1976):290–1.

20 Richard White, *Land Use, Environment, and Social Change. The Shaping of Island County, Washington* (Seattle: University of Washington Press, 1980), 26–7; Robert H. Ruby and John A. Brown, *The Chinook Indians, Traders of the Lower Columbia River* (Norman: University of Oklahoma Press, 1976), 80.

21 Juan López de Velasco, *Geografía y Descripción Universal de las Indias desde el Año de 1571 al de 1574* (Madrid: Establecimiento Tipográfico de Fortanet, 1894), 552.

22 Pedro Lautaro Ferrer, *Historia General de la Medicina en Chile*, I, *Desde 1535 Hasta la Inauguración de la Universidad de Chile en 1843* (Santiago de Chile: Talca, de J. Martín Garrido C., 1904), 254–5; José Luis Molinari, *Historia de la Medicina Argentina* (Buenos Aires: Imprenta López, 1937), 98; Dauril Alden and Joseph C. Miller, "Unwanted Cargoes," unpublished manuscript, University of Washington, Seattle.

23 Roberto H. Marfany, *El Indio en la Colonización de Buenos Aires* (Buenos Aires: Talleres Gráficos de la Penitenciaría Nacional de Buenos Aires, 1940), 24; Molinari, *Historia de la Medicina Argentina*, 98–9; Pedro Leon Luque, "La Medicina en la Epoca Hispanica," *Historia General de la Medicina Argentina* (Córdoba: Dirección General de Publicaciones, 1976), 50–1; Eliseo Cantón, *Historia de la Medicina en el Río de la Plata* (Madrid: Imp. G. Hernández y Galo Saez, 1928), I, 369–74; Alden and Miller, "Unwanted Cargoes."

24 Rafael Schiaffino, *Historia de la Medicina en el Uruguay* (Montevideo: Imprenta Nacional, 1927–52), I, 416–17, 419; Dobrizhoffer, *Abipones*, 240.

25 Thomas Falkner, *A Description of Patagonia*, (Chicago: Armann & Armann, 1935), 98, 102–3, 117; *Handbook of South American Indians*, ed. Julian H. Steward (Washington D. C.: United States Government Printing Office, 1946–59), VI, 309–10; see also Guillermo Fúrlong, *Entre las Pampas de Buenos Aires* (Buenos Aires: Talleres Gráficos "San Pablo," 1938), 59.

26 Cantón, *Historia de la Medicina*, I, 373–4.

27 Commonwealth of Australia, *Historical Records of Australia*, Series I, *Governors' Dispatches to and From England* (The Library Committee of the Commonwealth Parliament, 1914–25), I, 63, 144.

28 *Historical Records of Australia*, Series I, I, 159; J. H. L. Cumpston, *The History of Small-pox in Australia, 1788–1900* (Commonwealth of Australia, Quarantine Service, publication no. 3, 1914), 164.

29 John Hunter, *An Historical Journal at Sydney and at Sea* (Sydney: Angus & Robertson, 1968), 93.

30 Cumpston, *History of Small-pox in Australia*, 3, 7, 147–8, 160; Peter M. Moodie, *Aboriginal Health* (Canberra: Australian National University Press, 1973), 156–7; Edward M. Curr, *The Australian Race* (Melbourne: John Ferres, 1886), I, 213–14.

31 Curr, *Australian Race*, I, 214, 226–7.

32 Henry Reynolds, *Aborigines and Settlers, the Australian Experience,*

1788–1939 (North Melbourne: Cassell Australia, 1972), 72; Cumpston, *History of Small-pox in Australia,* 147–8, 154; George Angas, *Savage Life and Scenes in Australia and New Zealand* (London: Smith Elder & Co., 1847), II, 226; see also W. C. Wentworth, *A Statistical Account of the British Settlements in Australia* (London: Geo. B. Whittaker, 1824), 311.

33 Quoted in abbreviated form from Alice Marriott and Carol Rachlin, *American Indian Mythology* (New York: New American Library, 1968), 174–5.

34 *Winthrop Papers, 1631–1637* (Boston: Massachusetts Historical Society, 1943), III, 167.

35 Moodie, *Aboriginal Health,* 217–18.

36 Alvar Nuñez Cabeza de Vaca, *Relation of Nuñez Cabeza de Vaca* (United States: Readex Microprint Corp., 1966), 74–5, 80.

37 Daniel Drake, *Malaria in the Interior Valley of North America, a Selection,* ed. Norman D. Levine (Urbana: University of Illinois Press, 1964), *passim.*

38 This is as good a place as any to deal with the old legend of intentional European bacteriological warfare. The colonists certainly would have liked to wage such a war and did talk about giving infected blankets and such to the indigenes, and they may even have done so a few times, but by and large the legend is just that, a legend. Before the development of modern bacteriology at the end of the nineteenth century, diseases did not come in ampules, and there were no refrigerators in which to store the ampules. Disease was, in practical terms, people who were sick – an awkward weapon to aim at anyone. As for infected blankets, they might or might not work. Furthermore, and most important, the intentionally transmitted disease might swing back on the white population. As whites lived longer and longer in the colonies, more and more of them were born there and did *not* go through the full gauntlet of Old World childhood diseases. These people were dedicated to quarantining smallpox, not to spreading it.

39 Jacquetta Hawkes, ed., *Atlas of Ancient Archeology* (New York: McGraw-Hill, 1974), 234.

40 Richard B. Morris, ed., *Encyclopedia of American History* (New York: Harper & Bros., 1953), 442.

41 Jesse D. Jennings, *Prehistory of North America* (New York: McGraw-Hill, 1974), 220–65; Melvin L. Fowler, "A Pre-Columbian Urban Center on the Mississippi," *Scientific American,* 223 (August 1975):93–101; Robert Silverberg, *The Mound Builders* (New York: Ballantine Books, 1974), 3, 16–81.

42 *Narratives of the Career of Hernando de Soto,* trans. Buckingham Smith (New York: Allerton Book Co., 1922), I, 65, 70–1.

43 Garcilaso de la Vega, *The Florida of the Inca,* trans. John Varner and Jeannette Varner (Austin: University of Texas Press, 1962), 315–25.
44 Dobyns, *Their Number Become Thinned,* 294.
45 John R. Swanton, *The Indians of the Southeastern United States* (Smithsonian Institution Bureau of American Ethnology, bulletin 137, 1946), 11–21; Driver, *Indians of North America,* map 6; Alfred Kroeber, *Cultural and Natural Areas of Native North America* (Berkeley: University of California Press, 1963), 88–91; William G. Haag, "A Prehistory of Mississippi," *Journal of Mississippi History* 17 (April 1955):107; Dobyns, *Their Number Become Thinned,* 198.
46 Erhard Rostlund, "The Geographical Range of the Historic Bison in the Southeast," *Annals of the Association of American Geographers* 50 (December 1970):395–407.
47 *Narratives of the Career of De Soto,* I, 66–7; Garcilaso de la Vega, *Florida of the Inca,* 298, 300, 302, 315, 325.
48 *Narratives of the Career of De Soto,* I, 27, 67; II, 14.
49 Charles Creighton, *A History of Epidemics in Britain* (Cambridge University Press, 1891), I, 585–9; Julian S. Corbett, ed., *Papers Relating to the Navy During the Spanish War, 1585–1587* (Navy Records Society, 1898), XI, 26.
50 John R. Swanton, *Indian Tribes of the Lower Mississippi Valley and Adjacent Coast of the Gulf of Mexico* (Smithsonian Institution Bureau of American Ethnology, bulletin no. 43, 1911), 39. See also Dobyns, *Their Number Become Thinned,* 247–90; George R. Milner, "Epidemic Disease in the Postcontact Southeast: A Reappraisal," *Mid-Continent Journal of Archeology* 5 (No. 1, 1980):39–56. The archeologists are beginning to produce physical evidence that supports the hypothesis of fierce epidemics, swift population decline, and radical cultural change in the Gulf region in the sixteenth century. See Caleb Curren, *The Protohistoric Period in Central Alabama* (Camden, Ala.: Alabama Tombigbee Regional Commission, 1984), 54, 240, 242.
51 T. D. Stewart, "A Physical Anthropologist's View of the Peopling of the New World," *Southwest Journal of Anthropology* 16 (Autumn 1960):266–7; Philip H. Manson-Bahr, *Manson's Tropical Diseases* (Baltimore: Williams & Wilkins, 1972), 108–9, 143, 579–82, 633–4. See also Newman, "Aboriginal New World Epidemiology," *American Journal of Physical Anthropology* 45 (November 1976):669.
52 Crosby, *Columbian Exchange,* 122–64.
53 Crosby, *Columbian Exchange,* 209; J. R. Audy, "Medical Ecology in Relation to Geography," *British Journal of Clinical Practice* 12 (February 1958):109–10.

Chapter 10. New Zealand

1 Graeme R. Stevens, *New Zealand Adrift, the Theory of Continental Drift in a New Zealand Setting* (Wellington: A. H. & A. W. Reed, 1980), 240.

2 Gordon R. Williams, ed., *The Natural History of New Zealand, an Ecological Survey* (Wellington: A. H. & A. W. Reed, 1973), 4; Joseph Banks, *The Endeavour Journal of Joseph Banks, 1768–1771*, ed. J. C. Beaglehole (Sydney: Augus & Robertson, 1962), II, 8,

3 Stevens, *New Zealand*, 249–54. For a careful appraisal of New Zealand's vertebrates, see P. C. Bull and A. H. Whitaker, "The Amphibians, Reptiles, Birds and Mammals," *Biogeography and Ecology of New Zealand*, ed. G. Kuschel (The Hague: Dr. W. Junk, 1975), 231–76.

4 How the Amerindian sweet potato became a Polynesian staple is a fascinating and controversial matter; see D. E. Yen, *The Sweet Potato and Oceania* (Honolulu: Bernice P. Bishop Museum bulletin no. 236, 1974).

5 J. C. Beaglehole's *The Discovery of New Zealand* (Oxford University Press, 1961) is a fine little book on this period.

6 W. J. Wendelken, "Forests," *New Zealand Atlas*, ed. Ian Wards (Wellington: A. R. Shearer, 1976), 98; Janet M. Davidson, "The Polynesian Foundation," *Oxford History of New Zealand*, eds. W. H. Oliver with B. R. Williams (Oxford University Press, 1981), 7.

7 Peter Buck, *The Coming of the Maori* (Wellington: Whitcombe & Tombs, 1950), 19, 64, 103; W. Colenso, "Notes Chiefly Historical on the Ancient Dog of the New Zealanders," *Transactions and Proceedings of the New Zealand Institute* 10 (1877):150. Hereafter I shall refer to this journal as *TPNZI*.

8 D. Ian Pool, *The Maori Population of New Zealand, 1769–1971* (University of Auckland Press, 1977), 49–51.

9 Richard A. Cruise, *Journal of Ten Months' Residence in New Zealand* (Christchurch: Capper Press, 1974), 37.

10 *The Journals of Captain James Cook on His Voyages of Discovery*, I, *The Voyage of the Endeavour, 1768–1771*, ed. J. C. Beaglehole (Cambridge: Hakluyt Society, 1955), 276–78.

11 Robert McNab, *Murihiku* (Wellington: Whitcombe & Tombs, 1909), 92–100, 208; *Historical Records of New Zealand*, ed. Robert McNab (Wellington: John MacKay, 1908–14), I, 459; Kenneth B. Cumberland, "A Land Despoiled: New Zealand about 1838," *New Zealand Geographer*, 6 (April 1950):14.

12 *Irish University Press, British Parliamentary Papers . . . Colonies, New Zealand,* II, 100, 615. Hereafter the title of this source will be abbreviated to *BPPCNZ*.

13 Harrison M. Wright, *New Zealand, 1769–1840. Early Years of Western Contact* (Cambridge: Harvard University Press, 1959), 27–8.

14 Wright, *New Zealand*, 44.

15 Herman Melville, *Omoo, a Narrative of Adventures in the South Seas* (Evanston: Northwestern University Press, 1968), 10, 71.

16 *Historical Records of New Zealand,* I, 553; Georg Forster, *Florulae Insularum Australium Prodromus* (Gottingae: Joann. Christian Dieterich, 1786), 7; Elmer D. Merrill, *The Botany of Cook's Voyages* (Waltham, Mass.: Chronica Botanica Co., 1954), 227; T. Kirk, "Notes on Introduced Grasses in the Province of Auckland," *TPNZI* 4 (1871): 295.

17 John Savage, *Savage's Account of New Zealand in 1805 together with the Schemes of 1771 and 1824 for Commerce and Colonization* (Wellington: L. T. Watkins, 1939), 63.

18 Cruise, *Ten Months,* 315–16.

19 W. R. B. Oliver, "Presidential Address: Changes in the Flora and Fauna of New Zealand," *TPNZI,* 82 (February 1955):829.

20 Wright, *New Zealand,* 67–8.

21 Wright, *New Zealand,* 65; *An Encyclopedia of New Zealand,* ed. A. H. McLintock (Wellington: R. E. Owen, 1966), II, 390; K. A. Wodzicki, *Introduced Mammals of New Zealand, An Ecological and Economic Survey* (Wellington: Department of Scientific and Industrial Research, 1950), 227–8.

22 A. E. Mourant, Ada C. Kopeć and Kazimiera Domaniewska-Sobczak, *The Distribution of the Human Blood Groups and Other Polymorphisms* (Oxford University Press, 1976), 105, map 2; R. T. Simmons, "Blood Group Genes in Polynesians and Comparisons with Other Pacific Peoples," *Oceania* 32 (March 1962):198–9, 209; J. R. H. Andrews, "The Parasitology of the Maori in Pre-Columbian Times," *New Zealand Medical Journal* 84 (28 July 1976):62–4; P. Houghton, "Prehistoric New Zealanders," *New Zealand Medical Journal* 87 (22 March 1978):213, 215; *Journals of Cook,* I, 278; Banks, *Endeavour Journal,* I, 443–4; II, 21–2.

23 Buck, *Coming of Maori,* 404–9; C. Servant, *Customs and Habits of the New Zealanders, 1838–42,* trans. J. Glasgow (Wellington: A. H. & A. W. Reed, 1973), 41.

24 Buck, *Coming of Maori,* 365, 369–70; Banks, *Endeavour Journal,* I, 461; II, 13–14; Wright, *New Zealand,* 73–4.

25 Arthur S. Thomson, *The Story of New Zealand: Past and Present–Savage and Civilized* (London: John Murray, 1859), II, 286–7, 334, 336–7.

26 René Dubos and Jean Dubos, *The White Plague: Tuberculosis, Man and Society* (Boston: Little, Brown, 1952), 8–10.

27 J. C. Beaglehole, *The Life of Captain James Cook,* (Stanford University Press, 1974), 269; L. K. Gluckman, *Medical History of New Zealand Prior to 1860* (Christchurch: Whitcoulls, 1976), 26; James Watt, "Medical Aspects and Consequences of Cook's Voyages," in *Captain James Cook and His Times,* ed. Robin Fisher and Hugh Johnston (Vancouver: Douglas & McIntyre, 1979), 141, 152, 156.

28 At that time, science did not differentiate between syphilis and gonorrhea and was inclined to think of all venereal infections in the singular.

29 Gluckman, *Medical History,* 191–5; *Historical Records of New Zealand,* II, 204.

30 Peter Buck, "Medicine amongst the Maoris in Ancient and Modern Times," thesis for doctorate of medicine, New Zealand, Alexander Turnbull Library, Wellington, New Zealand, 82–3; W. H. Goldie, "Maori Medical Lore," *TPNZI* 37 (1904):84; Gluckman, *Medical History,* 167–8.

31 Robert C. Schmitt, "The Okuu – Hawaii's Epidemic," *Hawaii Medical Journal,* 29 (May-June 1970):359–64.

32 Savage, *Account of New Zealand,* 87.

33 Thomson, *Story of New Zealand,* I, 305–8.

34 *The Letters and Journals of Samuel Marsden,* ed. John R. Elder (Dunedin: Coulls Somerville Wilkie, 1932), 67; J. L. Nicholas, *Narrative of a Voyage to New Zealand* (Auckland: Wilson & Horton, n.d.), I, 84–5.

35 William Yate, *An Account of New Zealand* (Shannon: Irish University Press, 1970), 103.

36 Raymond Firth, *Economics of the New Zealand Maori* (Wellington: R. E. Owen, 1959), 443.

37 Cruise, *Ten Months,* 20.

38 *Encyclopedia of New Zealand,* I, 111–12; Wright, *New Zealand,* 97–9.

39 D. U. Urlich, "The Introduction and Diffusion of Firearms in New Zealand, 1800–1840," *Journal of the Polynesian Society* 79 (December 1970):399–409.

40 Charles Darwin, *Voyage of the Beagle* (Garden City; N.Y.: Doubleday, 1962), 426.

41 J. S. Polack, *New Zealand: Being a Narrative of Travels and Adventures* (London: R. Bentley, 1838), I, 290–2.

42 Polack, *New Zealand*, I, 313.

43 *Letters and Journals of Marsden*, 230; Polack, *New Zealand*, I, 315; *The Early Journals of Henry Williams*, ed. Lawrence M. Rogers (Christchurch: Pegasus Press, 1961), 342.

44 Nicholas, *Narrative*, II, 249; Darwin, *Voyage*, 423; *BPPCNZ*, II, pt. 2, 64.

45 Yate, *Account*, 75.

46 Richard Sharell, *New Zealand Insects and their Story* (Auckland: Collins, 1971), 176; William Charles Cotton, *A Manual for New Zealand Bee Keepers* (Wellington: R. Stokes, 1848), 7, 8, 51–2; *Encyclopedia of New Zealand*, I, 186; W. T. Travers, "On Changes Effected in the Natural Features of a New Country by the Introduction of Civilized Races," *TPNZI* 2 (1869):312.

47 *Letters and Journals of Marsden*, 383

48 Nicholas, *Narrative*, I, 121, 257; II, 396; *Letters and Journals of Marsden*, 63–70, 76, 239, 246; *The Missionary Register* (August 1820): 326–7, 499–500; *Marsden's Lieutenants*, ed. John R. Elder (Dunedin: Otago University Council, 1934), 167; John B. Marsden, *Memoirs of the Life and Labours of Samuel Marsden* (London: Religious Tract Society, 1858), 153–4, 157; H. T. Purchas, *A History of the English Church in New Zealand* (Christchurch: Simpson & Williams, 1914), 36–7; Gluckman, *Medical History*, 209; Cruise, *Ten Months*, 20; Wright, *New Zealand*, 97–8.

49 Thomson, *Story of New Zealand*, I, 212.

50 Thomson, *Story of New Zealand*, I, 213; Pool, *Maori Population*, 119.

51 Augustus Earle, *Narrative of a Residence in New Zealand*, ed. E. H. McCormick (Oxford University Press, 1966), 121–2; *Early Journals of Williams*, 87–9, 92; Pool, *Maori Population*, 126; Joel Polack, *Manners and Customs of the New Zealanders* (Christchurch: Capper Press, 1976), II, 98.

52 *Historical Records of New Zealand*, I, 555; Cruise, *Ten Months*, 284.

53 Earle, *Narrative*, 178.

54 *Duperry's Visit to New Zealand in 1824*, ed. Andrew Sharp (Wellington: Alexander Turnbull Library, 1971), 55.

55 *BPPCNZ*, I, pt. 1, 19, 22.

56 *Historical Records of New Zealand*, I, 555.

57 Darwin, *The Voyage of the Beagle*, (Garden City, N.Y.: Doubleday, 1962), 434; Judith Binney, "Papahurihia: Some Thoughts on Interpretation," *Journal of the Polynesian Society*, 75 (September 1966):321–2.

58 *Letters and Journals of Marsden*, 441.

59 Ormond Wilson, "Papahurihia, First Maori Prophet," *Journal of the Polynesian Society*, 74 (December 1965):473–83; J. M. R. Owens, "New Zealand before Annexation," *The Oxford History of New Zealand*, 38–9.

60 Darwin, *Voyage*, 424–5.

61 Michael D. Jackson, "Literacy, Communication and Social Change," *Conflict and Compromise, Essays on the Maori since Colonisation*, ed. I. H. Kawharu (Wellington: A. H. & A. W. Reed, 1975), 33; *Encyclopedia of New Zealand*, II, 869–70.

62 Jackson, "Literacy," *Conflict and Compromise*, 33, 37; Yate, *Account*, 239–40.

63 Judith Binney, "Christianity and the Maori to 1840–a Comment," *New Zealand Journal of History* 3 (October 1969):158–9.

64 Marsden, *Memoirs of Samuel Marsden*, 130.

65 Wright, *New Zealand*, 174–5; Ernst Dieffenbach, *Travels in New Zealand* (Christchurch: Capper Press, 1974), II, 19; Edward Markham, *New Zealand, or the Recollection of It* (Wellington: R. E. Owen, 1963), 55.

66 J. Watkins, "Journal of 1840–44," typescript, Alexander Turnbull Library, Wellington, New Zealand.

67 T. Lindsay Buick, *The Treaty of Waitangi* (Wellington: S. & W. MacKay, 1914), 29.

68 *Historical Records of New Zealand*, II, 609–11.

69 Alan Ward, *A Show of Justice: Racial Amalgamation in Nineteenth Century New Zealand* (University of Toronto Press, 1973), 27.

70 Keith Sinclair, *A History of New Zealand* (Oxford University Press, 1961), 36–40; Buick, *Treaty*, 24–6.

71 *BPPCNZ*, II, 124.

72 *BPPCNZ*, I, 336; II, 7, 124; III, 78–9.

73 *BPPCNZ*, I, pt. 1, 119; pt. 2, 183; II, pt. 2, 106, 186; III, 27.

74 *BPPCNZ*, III, 27–8.

75 Buick, *Treaty*, 104–14.

76 Buick, *Treaty*, 118–20.

77 Buick, *Treaty*, 135FF.

78 E. Jerningham Wakefield, *Adventure in New Zealand*, ed. and abridged by Joan Stevens (Christchurch: Whitcombe & Tombs, 1955), 86–7.

79 Harold Miller, *Race Conflict in New Zealand, 1814–1865* (Auckland: Blackwood & Janet Paul, 1966), 220.

80 Dieffenbach, *Travels*, I, 393.

81 William Colenso, "Memorandum of an Excursion Made in the

Northern Island of New Zealand," *The Tasmanian Journal* 2 (1846): 280.

82 Joseph Dalton Hooker, *The Botany of the Antarctic Voyage of H. M. Discovery Ships Erebus and Terror in the Years 1839–1843* (London: Lovell Reeve, 1860), II, 320–2.

83 *Encyclopedia of New Zealand*, II, 213.

84 P. R. Stevens, "The Age of the Great Sheep Runs," *Land and Society in New Zealand, Essays in Historical Geography*, ed. R. F. Watters (Wellington: A. H. & A. W. Reed, 1965), 56–7.

85 Ferdinand von Hockstetter, *New Zealand, Its Physical Geography, Geology and Natural History*, trans. Edward Sauter (Stuttgart: J. G. Cotta, 1867), 162, 284.

86 Muriel F. Loyd Prichard, *An Economic History of New Zealand* (Auckland: Collins, 1970), 78.

87 Wodzicki, *Introduced Mammals*, 151; Robert V. Fulton, *Medical Practice in Otago and Southland in the Early Days* (Dunedin: Otago *Daily Times* and *Witness* newspapers, 1922), 13; Lady (Mary Anne) Barker, *Station Life in New Zealand* (Avondale, Auckland: Golden Press, 1973), 183–4.

88 J. D. Hooker, "Note on the Replacement of Species in the Colonies and Elsewhere," *The Natural History Review* (1864):124.

89 W. T. L. Travers, "Remarks on a Comparison of the General Features of the Provinces of Nelson and Marlborough with that of Canterbury," *TPNZI* 1, pt. III (1868):21.

90 Barker, *Station Life*, 83.

91 Pool, *Maori Population*, 234–5.

92 Thomson, *Story of New Zealand*, I, 212.

93 *New Zealand Gazette and Britannia's Spectator*, 21 November 1840; Thomson, *Story of New Zealand*, I, 212; Ralph W. Kuykendall, *The Hawaiian Kingdom, 1778–1854* (Honolulu: University of Hawaii Press, 1938), 412–13; August Hirsch, *Handbook of Geographical and Historical Pathology* (London: New Sydenham Society, 1883), I, 134; *The Journal of Ensign Best, 1837–1843*, ed. Nancy M. Taylor (Wellington: R. E. Owen, 1966), 258; Richard A. Greer, "Oahu's Ordeal – the Smallpox Epidemic of 1853," *Hawaii Historical Review* 1 (July 1965): 221–42.

94 Thomson, *Story of New Zealand*, I, 214–16.

95 N. L. Edson, "Mortality from Tuberculosis in the Maori Race," *New Zealand Medical Journal* 42 (February 1943):102, 105.

96 F. D. Fenton, *Observations on the State of the Aboriginal Inhabitants of New Zealand* (Auckland: W. C. Wilson, for the New Zealand government, 1859), 21, 29.

97 Thomson, *Story of New Zealand*, II, 285.

98 Pool, *Maori Population*, 234–6.
99 Wright, *New Zealand,* 165; David Hall, *The Golden Echo* (Auckland: Collins, 1971), 143.
100 *BPPCNZ*, VI, 195.
101 Thomson, *Story of New Zealand,* II, 293–4.
102 Ann Parsonson, "The Pursuit of Mana," *Oxford History of New Zealand,* 153.
103 Firth, *Economics,* 449.
104 *BPPCNZ*, VI, 167.
105 *BPPCNZ*, XIII, 127.
106 Miller, *Race Conflict,* 44.
107 I. H. Kawharu, "Introduction," *Conflict and Compromise, Essays on the Maori since Colonisation,* 43; Keith Sinclair, *The Origins of the Maori Wars* (Wellington: New Zealand University Press, 1957), 5.
108 Sinclair, *History of New Zealand,* 99–100.
109 Miller, *Race Conflict,* 54; Edgar Holt, *The Strangest War. The Story of the Maori Wars, 1860–1872* (London: Putnam, 1962), 168–9.
110 James Cowan, *The New Zealand Wars* (Wellington: R. E. Owen, 1956), II, 10.
111 Pool, *Maori Population*, 237; Prichard, *Economic History,* 97, 108, 408; Sinclair, *History of New Zealand,* 91.
112 Dieffenbach, *Travels,* II, 45, 185; J. D. Hooker, "Note on the Replacement of Species in the Colonies and Elsewhere," *Natural History Review* (1864):126–7; Darwin, *Voyage,* 434; J. M. R. Owens, "Missionary Medicine and Maori Health: the Record of the Wesleyan Mission to New Zealand before 1840," *Journal of the Polynesian Society* 81 (December 1972):429–30; Wodzicki, *Introduced Mammals,* 89; W. T. L. Travers, "Notes on the New Zealand Flesh-Fly," *TPNZI* 3 (1870):119; T. Kirk, "The Displacement of Species in New Zealand," *TPNZI* 28 (1895):5–6; Samuel Butler, *A First Year in Canterbury Settlement,* eds. A. C. Brassington and P. B. Maling (Auckland: Blackwood & Janet Paul, 1964), 50.
113 Charles Darwin, *The Origin of Species* (New York: Mentor, 1958), 332.
114 W. T. L. Travers, "On the Changes Effected in the Natural Features of a New Country by the Introduction of Civilized Races," *TPNZI* II (1869):312–13.
115 Pool, *Maori Population*, 237; *New Zealand Official Yearbook 1983* (Wellington: Department of Statistics, 1983), 85.
116 *New Zealand Official Yearbook 1983,* 81, 420, 423, 432, 436.

In preparing this chapter I should also have consulted Peter Adams,

Fatal Necessity. British Intervention in New Zealand, 1830–1847 (Auckland: Auckland University Press, 1977), which I did not find until too late, an inexplicable oversight on my part.

Chapter 11. Explanations

1 Adam Smith, *An Inquiry into the Nature and Cause of the Wealth of Nations* (Oxford: Clarendon Press, 1976), II, 577.

2 James Mooney, *The Ghost-Dance Religion and the Sioux Outbreak of 1890,* ed. Anthony F. C. Wallace (Chicago: University of Chicago Press, 1965), 28

3 Paul S. Martin, "Prehistoric Overkill: The Global Model," *Quaternary Extinctions, A Prehistoric Revolution,* eds. Paul S. Martin and Richard G. Klein (Tucson: University of Arizona Press, 1984), 360–3, 370–3; Peter Murry, "Extinctions Downunder: A Bestiary of Extinct Australian Late Pleistocene Monotremes and Marsupials," *Quaternary Extinctions,* 600–25; Michael M. Trotter and Beverley McCulloch, "Moas, Men, and Middens," *Quaternary Extinctions,* 708–9.

4 *Was America a Mistake? An Eighteenth Century Controversy,* eds. Henry Steele Commager and Elmo Giordanetti (Columbia: University of South Carolina Press, 1967), 53.

5 Martin, "Prehistoric Overkill," *Quaternary Extinctions,* 358.

6 Daphne Child, *Saga of the South African Horse* (Cape Town: Howard Timmins, 1967), 5, 10, 14–15, 192–3; Michiel W. Henning, *Animal Diseases in South Africa* (South Africa: Central News Agency, 1956), 718–20, 785–91.

7 Martin, "Prehistoric Overkill," *Quaternary Extinctions,* 358.

8 Robert E. Dewar, "Extinctions in Madagascar, the Loss of Subfossil Fauna," *Quaternary Extinctions,* 574–93; Atholl Anderson, "The Extinction of Moa in Southern New Zealand," *Quaternary Extinctions,* 728–40.

9 George Perkins Marsh, *Man and Nature* (Cambridge: Harvard University Press, 1965), 99–100; Michael Graham, "Harvest of the Seas," *Man's Role in Changing the Face of the Earth,* ed. William L. Thomas, Jr. (University of Chicago Press, 1956), II, 491–2.

10 M. D. Fox and D. Adamson, "The Ecology of Invasions," *A Natural Legacy, Ecology in Australia,* eds. Harry F. Recher, Daniel Lunney, and Irina Dunn (Rushcutter's Bay, N.S.W.: Pergamon Press, 1979), 136; 142–3; Archibald Grenfell Price, *Island Continent, Aspects of the Historical Geography of Australia and Its Territories* (Sydney: Angus & Robertson, 1972), 106.

11 Herbert Gibson, *The History and Present State of the Sheep-Breeding*

Industry in the Argentine Republic (Buenos Aires: Ravenscroft & Mills, 1893), 10, 12–13.

12 Alexander Gillespie, *Gleanings and Remarks Collected During Many Months of Residence at Buenos Aires* (Leeds: B. Demirst, 1818), 120, 136; Joseph Sánchez Labrador, *Paraguay Cathólico. Los Indios: Pampas, Peulches, Patagones,* ed. Guillermo Fúrlong Cárdiff (Buenos Aires: Viau y Zona, Editores, 1936), 168–9, 204; Richard Walter, *Anson's Voyage Round the World in the Years 1740–44* (New York: Dover, 1974), 63; Rafael Schiaffino, *Historia de la Medicina en el Uruguay* (Montevideo: Imprenta Nacional, 1927–52), III, 16–17.

13 Björn Kurtén, *The Age of Mammals* (London: Weidenfeld & Nicolson, 1971), 221.

14 O. W. Richards and R. G. Davies, *Imms' General Textbook of Entomology* (London: Chapman & Hall, 1977), II, 995; Percy W. Bidwell and John I. Falconer, *History of Agriculture in the Northern United States, 1620–1860* (Washington, D.C.: Carnegie Institution of Washington, 1925), 93, 95–6; E. L. Jones, "Creative Disruptions in American Agriculture, 1620–1830," *Agricultural History* 48 (October 1974), 523.

15 *The Merck Veterinary Manual* (Rahway, N.J.: Merck & Co., 1973), 232; Folke Henschen, *The History and Geography of Disease,* trans. Joan Tate (New York: Delacorte Press, 1966), 41; Charles Darwin, *The Voyage of the Beagle* (Garden City, N.Y.: Doubleday, 1962), 354–5; Hilary Koprowski, "Rabies," *Textbook of Medicine,* 14th ed., eds. Paul B. Beeson and Walsh McDermott (Philadelphia: Saunders, 1971), 701.

16 J. F. Smithcors, *Evolution of the Veterinary Art, a Narrative Account to 1850* (Kansas City: Veterinary Medicine Publishing Co., 1957), 232–5; *Merck Veterinary Manual,* 263; Helge Kjekshus, *Ecology, Control and Economic Development in East African History: the Case of Tanganyika* (London: Heinemann, 1977), 126–32.

17 United States Department of Agriculture, *Animal Diseases, Yearbook of Agriculture, 1956* (Washington, D.C.: United States Government Printing Office, 1956), 186; Manuel A. Machado, *Aftosa, a Historical Survey of Foot-and-Mouth Disease and Inter-American Relations* (Albany: State University of New York Press, 1969), xi, xiii, 3, 15–16, 110.

18 *Encyclopaedia Britannica, Macropaedia* (Chicago: Encyclopaedia Britannica, 1982), V, 879.

19 Juan López de Velasco, *Geografía y Descripción Universal de las Indias desde el Año de 1571 al de 1574* (Madrid: Establecimiento Tipográfico de Fortanet, 1894), 281.

20 *The Jesuit Relations and Allied Documents,* ed. Reuben Gold Thwaites (Cleveland: Burrows Brothers, 1896–1901), XXXVIII, 225.
21 *The Founding of Massachusetts, Historians and Documents,* ed. Edmund S. Morgan (Indianapolis: Bobbs-Merrill, 1964), 144–45; Bernard Bailyn et al., *The Great Republic* (Boston: Little, Brown, 1977), 88.
22 *Commonwealth of Australia, Historical Records of Australia,* Series I, *Governors' Dispatches to and From England* (The Library Committee of the Commonwealth Parliament, 1914–25), I, 144.
23 Arthur S. Thomson, *The Story of New Zealand: Past and Present – Savage and Civilized* (London: John Murray, 1859), II, 321; C. E. Adams, "A Comparison of the General Mortality in New Zealand, in Victoria and New South Wales, and in England," *Transactions and Proceedings of the New Zealand Institute* 31 (1898):661.
24 John Duffy, *Epidemics in Colonial America* (Baton Rouge: Louisiana State University Press, 1953), 21–2, 104, 108; St. Julien R. Childs, *Malaria and Colonization in the Carolina Low Country, 1526–1696* (Baltimore: Johns Hopkins Press, 1940), 146–7, 202.
25 Michael W. Flinn, *The European Demographic System, 1500–1800* (Baltimore: Johns Hopkins Press, 1981), 47.
26 "Speeches of Students at the College of William and Mary Delivered May 1, 1699," *William and Mary Quarterly,* Series II, 10 (October 1930):326; Daniel J. Boorstin, *The Americans, the Colonial Experience* (New York: Random House, 1958), 126.
27 T. D. Stewart, "A Physical Anthropologist's View of the Peopling of the New World," *Southwest Journal of Anthropology,* 16 (Autumn 1960):257–79; Aidan Cockburn, *The Evolution and Eradication of Infectious Diseases of Man* (Baltimore: Johns Hopkins Press, 1963), 20–103; Frank Fenner, "The Effects of Changing Social Organization on the Infectious Diseases of Man," *The Impact of Civilisation on the Biology of Man,* ed. S. V. Boyden (Canberra: Australian National University Press, 1970), 48–76.
28 A. E. Mourant, Ada C. Kopeć, and Kazimiera Domaniewska-Sobczak, *The Distribution of Human Blood Groups and Other Polymorphisms* (Oxford University Press, 1976), map 2, map 16; John Mercer, *The Canary Islanders, Their Prehistory, Conquest and Survival* (London: Rex Collings, 1980), 57.
29 Donald R. Hopkins, *Princes and Peasants, Smallpox in History* (University of Chicago Press, 1983), 98.
30 Nelson Reed, *The Caste War of Yucatan* (Stanford University Press, 1964), 250–1; Victoria Bricker, *The Indian Christ, the Indian King* (Austin: University of Texas Press, 1981), 117.

31 A. B. Holder, "Gynecic Notes Taken Among the American Indians," *American Journal of Obstetrics*, 25 (June 1892):55.

32 W. Hartley and R. J. Williams, "Centres of Distribution of Cultivated Pasture Grasses and Their Significance for Plant Introduction," *Proceedings of the Seventh International Grassland Congress, Palmerston North, New Zealand* (Wellington: 1956), 190–2.

33 Edwin H. Colbert, *Evolution of Vertebrates*, 3rd ed. (New York: Wiley, 1980), 416, 419.

34 Oscar Schmieder, "Alteration of the Argentine Pampa in the Colonial Period," University of California Publications in Geography, II, No. 10 (27 September 1927), 309–10.

35 Thomas Budd, *Good Order Established in Pennsilvania and New-Jersey* (Ann Arbor: University Microfilms, 1966), 10.

36 Joseph M. Powell, *Environmental Management in Australia, 1788–1914* (Oxford University Press, 1976), 17–18; Peter Cunningham, *Two Years in New South Wales* (London: Henry Colburn, 1828), I, 194–200; II, 176; Thomas M. Perry, *Australia's First Frontier, the Spread of Settlement in New South Wales, 1788–1829* (Melbourne University Press, 1963), 13.

37 W. Colenso, "A Brief List of Some British Plants (Weeds) Lately Noticed," *Transactions and Proceedings of the New Zealand Institute* 18 (1885):289–90.

38 James Mooney, "The Ghost Dance Religion and the Sioux Outbreak of 1890," *Annual Report of the Bureau of Ethnology to the Smithsonian Institution, 1892–93*, XIV, pt. 2, 72.

39 D. B. Grigg, *The Agricultural Systems of the World, An Evolutionary Approach* (Cambridge University Press, 1974), 50.

40 L. Cockayne, *New Zealand Plants and Their Story* (Wellington: R. E. Owen, 1967), 197.

41 Frank M. Chapman, "The European Starling as an American Citizen," *Natural History* 89 (April 1980):60–5; J. O. Skinner, "The House Sparrow," *Annual Report of the Smithsonian Institution for 1904*, 423–8; A. W. Schorger, *The Passenger Pigeon, Its Natural History and Extinction* (Madison: University of Wisconsin Press, 1955), 212–15.

Chapter 12. Conclusion

1 David W. Galenson, *White Servitude in Colonial America, an Economic Analysis* (Cambridge University Press, 1981), 17; *Australian Encyclopedia*, III, 376.

2 Huw R. Jones, *A Population Geography* (New York: Harper & Row, 1981), 254.

3 *The Papers of Benjamin Franklin,* IV, *July 1, 1750, through June 30, 1753,* ed. Leonard W. Labaree (New Haven: Yale University Press, 1961), 233; Thomas R. Malthus, *First Essay on Population, 1798* (New York: Sentry Press, 1965), 105–7.

4 Alejandro Malaspina, *Viaje al Río de la Plata en el Siglo XVIII* (Buenos Aires: Sociedad de Historia Argentina, 1938), 296–8.

5 Nicolás Sánchez-Albornoz, *The Population of Latin America, a History,* trans. W. A. R. Richardson (Berkeley: University of California Press, 1974), 114–15, 134–5.

6 *Sources of Australian History,* ed. Clark Manning (Oxford University Press, 1957), 61–3.

7 Sánchez-Albornoz, *Population of Latin America,* 154.

8 Ezequiel Martínez Estrata, *X-Ray of the Pampa,* trans. Alain Swietlicki (Austin: University of Texas Press, 1971), 91; Arthur P. Whitaker, *The United States and the Southern Cone: Argentina, Chile and Uruguay* (Cambridge: Harvard University Press, 1976), 63–4; Arnold J. Bauer, *Chilean Rural Society from the Spanish Conquest to 1930* (Cambridge University Press, 1975), 62, 70–1.

9 Fernand Braudel, *Civilization and Capitalism, 15th–18th Century,* I, *The Structure of Everyday Life, the Limits of the Possible,* trans. Sian Reynolds (New York: Harper & Row, 1981), 73–88; William L. Langer, "Infanticide: An Historical View," *History of Childhood Quarterly* I (Winter 1974):353–65; Michael W. Flinn, *The European Demographic System, 1500–1800* (Baltimore: Johns Hopkins Press, 1981), 42, 46, 49–51, 96.

10 Robert Darnton, "The Meaning of Mother Goose," *New York Review of Books,* 31 (2 February 1984):43.

11 Robert W. Fogel et al., "Secular Changes in American and British Stature and Nutrition," *Hunger and History, The Impact of Changing Food Production and Consumption on Society,* eds. Robert I. Rotberg and Theodore K. Rabb (Cambridge University Press, 1985), 264–6.

12 William MacCann, *Two Thousand Mile Ride through the Argentine Provinces,* (London: Smith, Elder & Co., 1852), I, 99.

13 Samuel Butler, *A First Year in Canterbury Settlement,* ed. A. C. Brassington and P. B. Maling (Auckland: Blackwood & Janet Paul, 1964), 126.

14 Anthony Trollope, *Australia,* eds. P. D. Edwards and R. B. Joyce (St. Lucia: University of Queensland Press, 1967), 284.

15 Donald W. Treadgold, *The Great Siberian Migration,* (Princeton University Press, 1957), 34; Salvatore J. LaGumina and Frank J. Cavaioli, *The Ethnic Dimension in American Society* (Boston: Holbrook Press, 1974), 155.

16 William Woodruff, *Impact of Western Man, A Study of Europe's Role in the World Economy, 1750–1960* (New York: St. Martin's Press, 1967), 80; Sánchez-Albornoz, *Population of Latin America,* 163–4.

17 James R. Scobie, *Argentina, A City and a Nation,* 2nd ed. (Oxford University Press, 1971), 83–4, 118–19, 123.

18 Woodruff, *Impact of Western Man,* 77–78; Sánchez-Albornoz, *Population of Latin America,* 155.

19 Woodruff, *Impact of Western Man,* 69–70.

20 Woodruff, *Impact of Western Man,* 86; *Australian Encyclopedia,* III, 376–9; *New Zealand Encyclopedia,* II, 131–2.

21 The champion reproducers among the Neo-Europeans seem to be the French of Canada, who multiplied themselves eighty times over between 1760 and 1960, without any appreciable immigration and with considerable emigration. Jacques Henripin and Yves Perón, "La Transition Démographique de la Province de Québec," *La Population du Québec: Études Rétrospectives,* ed. Hubert Charbonneau (Montreal: Les Editions du Boréal Express, 1973), 24.

22 Kingsley Davis, "The Migrations of Human Populations," *Scientific American* 231 (September 1974):99.

23 Joseph J. Bogue, *The Population of the United States* (Glencoe, Ill.: Free Press, 1959), 29; Robert V. Wells, *The Population of the British Colonies in America Before 1776* (Princeton University Press, 1975), 263 and *passim;* Henripin and Penón, "La Transition Démographique," *La Population du Québec,* 35–6.

24 Kingsley Davis, "The Place of Latin America in World Demographic History," *The Milbank Memorial Fund Quarterly* 42, pt. 2 (April 1964): 32.

25 W. D. Borrie, *Population Trends and Policies, A Study of Australian and World Demography* (Sydney: Australasian Publishing Co., 1948), 40.

26 Demographic Analysis Section of the Department of Statistics, New Zealand, *The Population of New Zealand, CICRED Series,* 23; Miriam G. Vosburgh, "Population," *New Zealand Atlas,* ed. Ian Wards (Wellington: A. R. Shearer, government printer, 1976), 60–1.

27 Charles Darwin, *The Origin of Species and the Descent of Man* (New York: Modern Library, n.d.), 428.

28 Jen-Hu Chang, "Potential Photosynthesis and Crop Productivity," *Annals of the Association of American Geographers,* 60 (March 1970): 92–101.

29 *Food and Agricultural Organization of the United Nations, Trade Yearbook, 1982* (Rome: Food and Agricultural Organization of the United Nations, 1983), XXXVI, 42–4, 52–8, 112–14, 118–20, 237–8.

30 Lester R. Brown, "Putting Food on the World's Table, a Crisis of Many Dimensions," *Environment,* 26 (May 1984):19.
31 Dan Morgan, *Merchants of Grain* (Harmondsworth: Penguin Books, 1980), 25.

Appendix

1 J. H. L. Cumpston, *The History of Small-pox in Australia, 1788–1900* (Commonwealth of Australia, Quarantine Service, publication no. 3, 1914), 165; Edward M. Curr, *The Australian Race* (Melbourne: John Ferres, 1886), I, 223–6.
2 David Collins, *An Account of the English Colony in New South Wales* (Sydney: A. H. & A. W. Reed, 1975), I, 54.
3 Richard T. Johnson, "Herpes Zoster," *Textbook of Medicine,* eds. Paul B. Beeson and Walsh McDermott (Philadelphia: Saunders, 1975), 684–5.

Index

INDEX